STEVE BISHOP

KUYPER

A PRIMER

cántaro
publications

cantaroinstitute.org

Kuyper: A Primer, Steve Bishop
Published by Cántaro Publications, a publishing imprint of
Cántaro Institute, Jordan Station, ON.

Book design by Paul Aurich

ISBN 978-1-998711-22-2

Printed in the United States of America

Short Contents

Long Contents

Appendix

Timeline

1837 Born 29 October in Maassluis

1841 Moves to Middleburg with his family

1855 Enrols as a student at Leiden University

1863 Minister in DRC at Beesd

1864 Begins correspondence with Groen Van Prinsterer

1867 Minister at Utrecht

1870 Moves to Amsterdam pastor at Hervormde Kerk

1874 Leaves pastorate to be enter politics

1877 Begins *Ons Program*

1879 Forms ARP

1880 VU, Amsterdam opens

1880 –1901 Professor of theology at the VU

1886 Forms the *Doleantie*

1892 His son Wilhem dies

1895 Begins series on common grace

1898 Delivers the Stone Lectures at Princeton

1899 His wife dies

1900 The *South-African Crisis* published

1901 – 05 PM of the Netherlands

1905 – 07 Grand tour of the Mediterranean

1911 Begins work on *Pro Rege*

1918 *To Be Nearer Unto God* published in English

1920 Dies in The Hague

Introduction

ABRAHAM KUYPER IS PERHAPS most famous today for the following quote:

> There is not a square inch in the whole domain of our human existence over which Christ, who is Sovereign over all, does not cry: "Mine!"

He not only said it he lived it. He was a church historian, a church pastor, a church reformer, a newspaper editor, shaped a political party, became a politician, founded a Christian university, founded a newspaper, a journalist, was a professor of theology, and later became prime minister of the Netherlands. He did so with his actions shaped by his Christian faith. It is no wonder that the Dutch journalist Charles Boissevain described Kuyper as "an adversary, who has ten heads and a hundred arms."[1] And yet tragically his name is hardly known among contemporary Christians outside of neo-Calvinist circles.[2] (Although fortunately, this is starting to change.)

---

1. Cited in J. C. Rullman [1876–1936], *Abraham Kuyper een Levensschets* (Kampen: J.H. Kok, 1928), 232. The original reads: "een tegenstander, die tien hoofden en honderd armen bezit."

2. The term neo-Calvinist has been used to describe the movement initiated by Kuyper and Herman Bavinck. The term was original used pejoratively. The first mention of the term applying to the approach of Kuyper and Bavinck *et al* appears to be in an 1887 review of Wilhelm Geesink's *Calvinisten in Holland* by J. Reitsma (George Harinck,

In 1898, B. B. Warfield said of him, "Dr Kuyper is probably the most considerable figure in both political and ecclesiastical Holland."[3]

Kuyper took over the leadership of the Anti-Revolutionaries from Groen Van Prinsterer and eventually became Prime Minister (1901–1905). He founded a Christian university, The Free University, in Amsterdam and was editor of two newspapers.

Kuyper also found time to write over 200 books, over 2000 meditations, and innumerable articles for his newspaper *De Standaard*. His main works include *The Principles of Sacred Theology* (1980), *The Work of the Holy Spirit* (1946), the 1898 Stone Lectures: *Lectures on Calvinism* (1931) and the more recently translated and published *Common Grace* (2013–2010) and *Pro Rege* (2016–2019). In his *Lectures*, he developed the idea of Calvinism as a *Weltanschauung*, a whole "world-and-life-view"; his Calvinism

---

"Herman Bavinck and the Neo-Calvinist Concept of the French Revolution," in, *Neo-Calvinism and French Revolution,* ed. James Eglinton and George Harinck (London: Bloomsbury, 2016), 21 fn 43. Anne Anema (1872–1966), a colleague of Kuyper's at the VU Amsterdam, used the term as a convenient term to describe the movement and the term stuck (Anne Anema, *Calvinisme en rechtswetenschap: een studie* (Amsterdam, 1897), p. xvi.).

The first mention of the term that I have found is by a Mr Rutherford with the title "Calvinism and Neo-Calvinism, or the Divine intention in the Atonement," *The Evangelical Repository*, 1–2 (1855): 106; though, obviously, the term here had nothing to do with Kuyper or Bavinck.

3. B. B. Warfield, "Introductory Note," in Abraham Kuyper *Principles of Sacred Theology* (Grand Rapids, MI: Eerdmans 1968 [1898]), xii.

was not a narrow five points! (Although he did hold to the five points of Calvinism.)

Commenting on this Kuyperian emphasis D. M. Lloyd-Jones, in 1975, wrote:

> The Christian is not only to be concerned about personal salvation. It is his duty to have a complete view of life as taught in the Scriptures...We must have a world view. All of us who have ever read Kuyper, and others, have been teaching this for years.[4]

Abraham Kuyper is a bit like marmite—you love him or hate him. As one Dutch biographer claimed, "Where Kuyper was, there was trouble."[5] There is no doubt that he is a controversial figure. He certainly lived this out in his life and writings. He was inspiring, energetic, strong-willed, hard-working, and a strategic thinker and activist. However, he had his weaknesses. These include:

- His appropriation of cultural stereotypes—particularly in his discussion of African and Asian folk.
- He was a workaholic — this resulted in several nervous breakdowns.
- It appears he did not have many friends, only followers.
- He did not suffer fools gladly, and he thought those who did not agree with him were fools.

- He was something of a hypochondriac — he continually refers to his illnesses in his letters from America to his family.

---

4.   D. M. Lloyd-Jones, "The French Revolution and After," *The Christian and the State in Revolutionary Times,* Westminster Conference Papers (Cambridge: Westminster Conference, 1976),101.

5.   "Waar Kuyper was, kwam ruzie." Cited in Aart Deddens "Editorial" *Sophie (Special Abraham Kuyper)* (February 2021), 2.

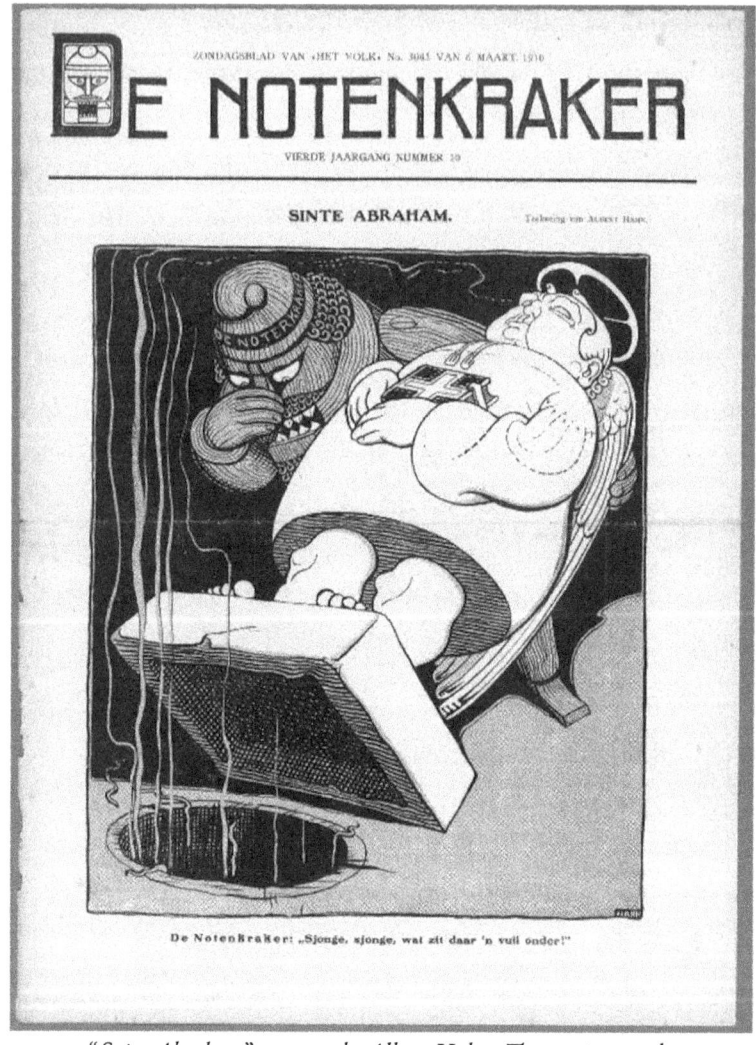

"Saint Abraham" cartoon by Albert Hahn. The caption reads:
"Boy there's some dirt under there!"

- In his writings, he was often polemical, brash, and rhetorical.
- He could be stubborn and dominant, intolerant, and impatient
- He was unable—or unwilling—to mentor and train successors.

I mention these in case anyone should be tempted to idolize the man. Nonetheless, despite these tendencies, he is well worth examining. He was a man with many human failings and yet despite this, he was greatly used by God. In what follows I will focus primarily on his positive attributes. He was a man of vision and sometimes this single-minded vision often clouded his judgement.

The book is in five parts. The first is a brief biography of Kuyper, the second examines some of the key themes in his writings, and the third section looks key theological topics in Kuyper. A fourth section examines how he put these into action and shows that his square inch quote was also more than rhetoric. His ideas certainly had legs! The fifth and final section examines his legacy.

In the past reading Kuyper meant reading him in Dutch, fortunately, this is no longer the case. The Abraham Translation Project have translated several of Kuyper's important works. Thanks, in part, to this initiative, it seems that Kuyper and Kuyper studies are undergoing a resurgence and a rejuvenation. This book is aimed at those who are as yet largely unfamiliar with Kuyper and want to get to "know" him better.

Dates of Kuyper's Major English Publications

1882.01 "Alexander Comrie: (1) His Life and Work in Holland. (2) His Conflict in Holland (3) Lessons from his Career," *The Catholic Presbyterian* 7 (37) (Jan 1882), 20–29; 7 (39) (March 1882), 192–20; and 7 (40) (April 1882), 278–284.

1891.07 "Calvinism and Confessional Revision," *Presbyterian and Reformed Review* 2, no. 7 (1891): 369–399.

1892.05 "Calvinism and Art," In *Christian Thought. Lectures and papers on philosophy, Christian evidence, biblical elucidation*, Ninth Series.

1893.04 "Pantheism's Destruction of Boundaries," *Methodist Review* (July/August): 520-537; (Sept/Oct): 762–778.

1898.12 *Encyclopedia of Sacred Theology: Its Principles*. New York: C. Scribner's Sons.

1899–1900 Meditations translated from those in *De Heraut* in several issues of the *Christian Intelligencer*.

1899.17 "Election and selection," *The Independent* 51 (2638): 1693–1694.

1899.19 *Calvinism: Six Stone Lectures*. Grand Rapids: Eerdmans

1899.20 "The Antithesis Between Symbolism and Revelation": Lecture Delivered Before the Historical Presbyterian Society in Philadelphia, PA. Höveker & Wormser.

1900.12 *The South-African Crisis*. London: Stop the War Committee.

1900.19 *The Work of the Holy Spirit*, trans. Henri DeVries, Funk & Wagnalls, New York.

1904.25 "The Biblical Criticism of the Present Day," *Bibliotheca Sacra* 61, no. 243 (1904): 409–442; , no. 244: 66-688

1906.04 "A Fata Morgana," *Methodist Review* 88(2):185-203; (3):355–378.

1906.05 "The True Genius of Presbyterianism," *The Presbyterian* 76(18):12-14.

1908.08 "The Work of God in our Work," *Homiletic Review* 55(2):136–138.

1908.12 "Use and Abuse of Apologetics," *Bibliotheca Sacra* 52 (258): 374–379.

1916.16 *The Evolution of the Use of the Bible in Europe*. Centennial Pamphlets, No. 2. American Bible Society: New York.

1918.11 *To Be Near unto God*. Grand Rapids: Eerdmans. *His Decrease at Jerusalem on the Passion and Death of Our Lord*. Grand Rapids: Eerdmans.

1929.14 *Keep thy Solemn Feasts. Meditations*. Grand Rapids: Eerdmans

1929.13 *When Thou Sittest in Thine House. Meditations on Home Life*. Wm. B. Eerdmans.

1929.14 *Asleep in Jesus*. Meditations. Grand Rapids: Eerdmans.

1929.15 *In the Shadow of Death. Meditations for the Sick Room and at the Death-Bed*. Grand Rapids: Eerdmans.

1933.05 *Women of the Old Testament: Fifty Meditations*. Grand Rapids: Zondervan.

1934.08 *Women of the New Testament: 30 Devotional Messages for Women's Groups*. Grand Rapids: Zondervan.

1934.09 *The Implications of Public Confession*. Grand Rapids: Zondervan.

1934.10 "Chiliasm or the Doctrine of Premillennialism," freely translated from *E Voto* by Rev G. M. Van Perris. Grand Rapids: Zondervan

1934.11 "The Biblical Doctrine of Election," freely translated from *E Voto* by Rev G. M. Van Perris. Grand Rapids: Zondervan

1935.04 *The Revelation of St. John*. Grand Rapids: Eerdmans.

1935 onwards. Various Devotions published in *Christianity Today*.

1948.03 *The Practice of Godliness*. Wm. B. Eerdmans Publishing.

1950.03 *The Class Struggle*. Grand Rapids: Piet Hein.

1950.04 *Abraham Kuyper on Evolution*. Grand Rapids: Youth and Calvinism Group

1954.02 *Principles of Sacred Theology*. Grand Rapids: Eerdmans. = 1898.12 under a different title.

1977–1986. "A Pamphlet Concerning the Reformation of the Church," *The Standard Bearer*.

1991.01 *The Problem of Poverty*—translated by James W. Skillen. Grand Rapids: Baker.

1993.02 "Sphere Sovereignty". In Wayne A. Kobes, "Sphere Sovereignty and the University: Theological Foundations of Abraham Kuyper's View of the University and its Role in Society," PhD Thesis, Florida State University, 1994.

1993.06 *You Can Do Greater Things Than Christ*. Trans. J. Boer. Introduction by J. Boer. Jos: ICS.

1996.05 "Evolution," *Calvin Theological Journal* 31, no. 1 (1996): 11–50.

1998.03 *Abraham Kuyper: A Centennial Reader*. Edited by James D. Bratt. Grand Rapids: Eerdmans. Contains the following:

> Uniformity: The Curse of Modern Life (1869)
> Confidentially (1873)
> Conservatism and Orthodoxy: False and True Preservation (1870)
> Modernism: A Fata Morgana in the Christian Domain (1871)
> "It Shall Not Be So Among You" (1886)
> Perfectionism (1879)
> Common Grace (1902-4)
> Maranatha (1891)
> Manual Labor (1889)
> Our Instinctive Life (1908)
> Calvinism: Source and Stronghold of Our Constitutional Liberties (1874)
> The South African Crisis (1900)
> The Blurring of the Boundaries (1892)
> Evolution (1899)
> Common Grace in Science (1904)
> Sphere Sovereignty (1880)

1998.04 *The Revelation of St. John*. Translated from the Dutch by John Hendrik De Vries. Grand Rapids, MI: William B. Eerdmans.

2001.07 *Particular Grace: A Defense of God's Sovereignty in Salvation*. Translated by Marvin Kamps. Granville, MI: Free Publishing Association.

2002– onwards. Sections from "When Thou Sittest in Thine House," in the *Standard Bearer*.

2003.02 "Missions According to Scripture," *Calvin Theological Journal* 38, no. 2 (2003): 237–247.

2005.01 J. Vree, and J. Zwaan, *Abraham Kuyper's Commentatio* (1860): The Young Kuyper about Calvin, à Lasco, and the Church: I: Introduction, Annotations, Bibliography, and Indices/II: Commentatio. Leiden: Brill.

2009.02 *Our Worship.* Grand Rapids: Eerdmans.

2010.03 "Kuyper on Islam: A Summary and Translation," *Kuyper Center Review* 1 (2010): 138–150.

2011. *Wisdom & Wonder: Common Grace in Science & Art.* Christian's Library Press

2013.03 *Rooted and Grounded.* Grand Rapids: Christian's Library Press

2013.04 *Common Grace Volume 1.* Grand Rapids: Christian's Library Press

2013.05 *Guidance for Christian Engagement in Government.* Grand Rapids: Christian's Library Press

2014.03 *Scholarship: Two Convocation Addresses.* Grand Rapids: Christian's Library Press

2015 *God's Angels His Ministering Spirits.* Vancouver, BC, Friesen Press.

2015 "The Natural Knowledge of God," trans. Harry Van Dyke. *The Bavinck Review* 6 (2015): 73-112.

2015 "The Worship of the Reformed Church and the Creation of its Service Book," trans. James A. De Jong. *Calvin Theological Journal* 50, no. 1 (2015): 59–90.

2024 "Three Little Foxes", ed. Steve Bishop–online: https://sources.neocalvinism.org/.full_pdfs/kuyper/ThreeLittleFoxes-AbrahamKuyper.pdf.

The following volumes were produced by the Abraham Kuyper Translation Project and published by Lexham Press, Bellingham, WA—full details are available from https://abraham-kuyper.com/

2015 *Our Program: A Christian Political Manifesto.* Edited and Translated by Harry Van Dyke

Common Grace: God's Gift for a fallen World. Edited by Jordan J. Ballor & Stephen J. Grabill. Translated by Nelson D. Kloosterman and Ed M. van der Maas

2015 Volume 1

2019 Volume 2

2020 Volume 3 (edited by J. Daryl Charles & Jordan J. Ballor)

Pro Rege: Living Under Christ's Kingship. Edited by John Kok & Nelson D. Kloosterman. Translated by Albert Gootjes

2016 Volume 1

2017 Volume 2

2019 Volume 3

2016 *On the Church.* Edited by John Halsey Wood Jr. and Andrew M. McGinnis. Translated by Harry Van Dyke, Nelson D. Kloosterman, Todd M. Rester, & Arjen Vreugdenhil.

2018 *On Islam.* Edited by James D. Bratt with Douglas A. Howard. Translated by Jan van Vliet.

2019 *On Education.* Edited by Wendy Naylor. Translated by Harry Van Dyke.

2021 *On Business & Economics.* Edited by Peter S. Heslam. Translated by Harry Van Dyke and Peter S. Heslam.

2022 *On Charity & Justice.* Edited by Matthew J. Tuininga.

PART 1

Biography

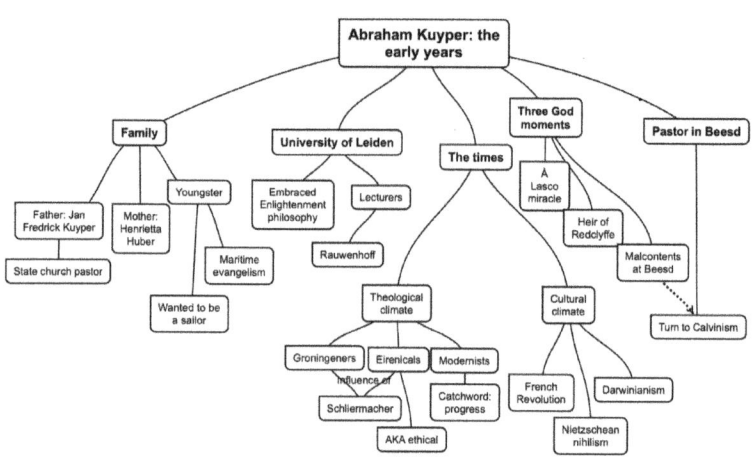

1

Family Background

ABRAHAM KUYPER (1837–1920) was born on Sunday 29 October into a nominally Calvinist family. His father was a pastor in a State Dutch Reformed Church, a somewhat liberal denomination, in Maassilus. Maassilus was a small fishing village in the Netherlands, to the west of Rotterdam and south of The Hague. Jan Frederik Kuyper (1801–1882) had sympathies with the *Afscheiding*, the church that separated from the Dutch State Church in 1837, but he remained faithful to the state church, the *Hervormde Kerk*. Kuyper's mother, Henrietta Huber (1802–1881), was the daughter of a Swiss Army officer. Bram, as he was known, was born during his father's third pastorate on 29 October 1837.

When Kuyper was four the family moved to the city of Middelburg, the capital of the province of Zeeland. There Kuyper thought of being a sailor. He used to go each day to speak to the sailors. He was keen to know all about their activities. Unfortunately, the language of the sailors was rather unsavory. So, Bram took some tracts from his father's study along with cigars. As de Moor-Ringnalda observed:

Armed with these "treasures" he drew to the ships, where the sailors soon gathered around him. They joked, teased him a bit, but Bram remained serious. He sat on a hawser rope on the deck of a ship and said: "Now if you listen carefully to what I read, you will get a cigar as a reward!" Laughing and winking at each other, the "Jantjes" did what the little "boss" had said. ... The laughter and joking ceased and the men listened attentively to what was read to them.

That is how Bram already fought as a small, brave evangelist for the honor of God. — The captain of one of the ships often predicted: "There is a real sailor in that boy. That will be a second Michiel de Ruyter."[1]

Many of Kuyper's writings contained maritime illustrations. At Middelburg, he was home-schooled and had a great love for newspapers and boats at an early age. Commenting on the former

I have read and loved newspapers since I was a young lad. My dear father disapproved of my infatuation—that I was hooked on the daily paper already as a boy of ten or eleven—and finally forbade me to stick my nose in the paper again. But my passion for journalism was so strong then already that whenever I was able to get my hands on a newspaper (though I should not have, because doing so was disobedient), I would sneak it

---

1. A. M.de Moor-Ringnalda, *Een Maassluiser jongen wordt Minister-President Het leven van Dr. Atrakam Kuyper* [A Maassluis boy becomes Prime-Minister] (Nijkerk: C. F. Callentack, 1937), 15–16. Anna Margaritha de Moor-Ringnalda (1906–1999) was a Dutch Christian novelist, she was married to a Reformed minister, Dr. J. C. de Moor.

into the attic and there I would sit as a young boy, on a packing box, reading the *Opregte Haarlemmer*.[2]

No wonder, then, that before I went to university I was already a minipolitician.[3]

His father taught him English, and his mother French. She had been a governess and so qualified to teach.

In 1849 the family moved once more, this time to Leiden. His hopes of becoming a sailor were thus hindered. At Leiden Kuyper studied at the gymnasium until 1855. There he was influenced by his history teacher Robert Fruin (1823–1899). Fruin was a follower of Leopold von Ranke (1795–1886) and later, in 1860, became the professor of Dutch national history at Leiden University.

The sea began to lose its appeal for Kuyper; he said to his father, "I just rolled up my tarpaulins, I want to study theology."[4] So, in 1855 Kuyper enrolled at the University of Leiden, his father's alma mater, originally to study literature and theology.

---

2. The *Opregte Haarlemsche Courant* was an old Dutch newspaper.

3. Abraham Kuyper, *On Charity and Justice*. Abraham Kuyper Collected Works in Public Theology (Bellingham, WA, Lexham Press, 2022), 239.

4. de Moor-Ringnalda, *Een Maassluiser Jongen*, 18.

Kuyper as a student in 1862

2

Student

THE TIME KUYPER WAS born into was one of conflict and shifting sands—liberalism and modernism were challenging orthodoxy. Herman Bavinck (1854–1921) illustrates the cultural shifts in his introduction to the third edition of Groen's *Unbelief & Revolution*:

> Rousseau has yielded way to Darwin, Kant to Hegel, deism to pantheism, rationalism to mysticism, and optimism to pessimism. While man was formerly envisioned as an angel, he is now looked upon as a clever animal.[1]

At the University of Leiden Kuyper embraced this Enlightenment philosophy. After gaining a BA in classical literature he enrolled again to read theology again at Leiden. In 1860 L. W. E. Rauwenhoff (1828–1889), then a young professor, delivered a lecture on the resurrection. He claimed no modern person could believe that the resurrection of a physical body was

---

1. "Voorrede," in *Ongeloof en revolutie. Eene reeks van historische voorlezingen*, 3rd. edn., by G. Groen van Prinsterer (Kampen: J. H. Bos, 1904), v–xiii.

a fact—at the end of his lecture Kuyper and the other students gave him a standing ovation. This is indicative of the state of the theological climate and of the state of Kuyper's heart at the time.

In mid-nineteenth-century Netherlands, there were several competing schools of thought. The most influential were the Groningers, the Eirenicals, and the Modernists.

The Groningers

As the name suggested this theological school was originally associated with the University of Groningen. They held views similar to the German theologian Fredrick Schleiermacher (1868–1934), who had been described as the father of modern liberal theology. The Groningers attempted to bridge the Christian faith and post-Enlightenment thought.[2] They emphasized a heart approach to theology. It was a form of Christian humanism and held to an Arian view of Christology[3] and Pelagian[4]

---

2. Louis Berkhof, *Systematic Theology* (Edinburgh: Banner of Truth,1989), 97.

3. "Arianism is, theologically speaking, the view that the Son is 'God but not true God': Christ is divine, God in an attenuated sense, but of a different nature and essence from God the Father. It derives its name from the Egyptian presbyter Arius of Alexandria, who expressed these views, and who was condemned by the Council of Nicaea (the first Ecumenical Council) in 325." *New Dictionary of Theology: Historical and Systematic* (Second Edition), edited by Martin Davie, Tim Grass, Stephen R Holmes, John McDowell and T A Noble (Leicester: IVP, 2016).

4. Pelagius (c. 354–418) denied that there was original sin and placed a strong emphasis on free will.

anthropology.[5] They repudiated rationalism but rejected the authority of the Scriptures; they disliked the term infallibility but viewed the Scriptures as "faultless." They adopted an anti-intellectual attitude. During Kuyper's childhood, the Groningen school was prevalent in the Dutch State church; their influence was greatest around the 1840s and 50s.

The Eirenicals

Like the Groningers there were traces of the influence of Schleiermacher on the Eirenicals or Ethicals as they were sometimes known. Ethical was used in the sense of existential, it was to be understood in terms of life or ethos. Truth was to be found in experiences. They too were anti-intellectualists. They rejected any notion of the supernatural and placed an emphasis on the personal and the experience of faith. William Masselink provides a good description: "They moved the starting point for religion from Christ to the Christian; from Scripture to experience; and from the objective to the subjective."[6]

The Modernists

The key idea for the modernists was progress. Science and reason would triumph. Rationalism was fundamental for the modernists; verification was the method to be used in finding truth. They rejected the bodily resurrection of Christ. Kuyper

---

5. Louis Praamsma, *Let Christ be King: Reflections on the Life and Times of Abraham Kuyper* (Jordan Station, Ontario: Paideia Press, 1985), 32. Louis Praamsma (1910–1984), a church historian, moved from The Netherlands to Canada in 1910. His doctorate from the Free University was on "Abraham Kuyper as Church Historian."

6. William Masselink, *General Revelation and Common Grace* (Grand Rapids: Eerdmans, 1953), 31.

was originally under the thrall of Modernism while he was studying at Leiden. He later wrote regarding Modernism:

> Tell me, with what else but unproven premises and therefore (from their own viewpoint) cheap dogmas does Modernism start in all its preaching? Its confession can be broadly sketched as follows: "I, a modernist, believe in a God who is the Father of all humankind, and in Jesus, not the Christ, but the rabbi from Nazareth. I believe in a humanity which is by nature good but needs to strive after improvement. I believe that sin is only relative and hence that forgiveness is merely something of human invention. I believe in the hope of a better life and, without judgment, the salvation of every soul."[7]

	Fredrich D. E. Schleiermacher (1768–1834)	Groningen theology	Eirenicals theology/ Irenicals	Modernist theology
Where are we?	While nature is material, it always contains or is shaped by at least a minimum of reason. Likewise, reason is not independent of nature but is embodied.	In a world that needs Christian morals and a cultivation of love.	In a world where truth is primarily a matter of the heart.	In an age where natural science leads to great triumphs.
Who are we?	The individualisation of universal reason Humans, physical beings possessing reason, are the organ of reason, the means by which reason works on nature. Humans are the intersection of reason and nature, and	Humans who can be "educated in" Jesus's example to live a life of love and toleration.	Experiential beings —to have a living existential relationship with Christ.	Rational beings We have a natural power to see the truth of God—we are inwardly self-sufficient, not inherently evil.

7. "Modernism: A Fata Morgana in the Christian Domain," in *Centennial Reader*, 116.

	our minds are shaped by historical processes, not constituted by innate concepts independent of nature. We are created imperfect but capable of self-perfection.			
What is God like?	He is not a postulate of the categorical imperative. The three persons of God are aspects of God. .	A supernatural Reality who intervened in the world from above. .		The author of the entire process — a personal spirit. The divine revealed in humanity. He is not over and against nature.
What's wrong?	Sin—the infinite distance inconsciousness from God. We do not have a God-consciousness. An overemphasis on dogma and doctrine to the detriment of an inner individual experience.	Traditional Christian dogmas and the intellectualism of the modernists.	Rationalism and supernaturalism.	Humanity's animal drives.
What's the remedy?	To incorporate freedom and morality in the totality of individual personality. When our God-consciousness is elevated by the influence of Christ's perfect God-consciousness, we have a corporate feeling of blessedness, that is, the connection of sin and evil is broken.	A progressive movement towards God. An emphasis on the emotional side of life. The need for a crisisless, a kind-hearted theology	Be ruled by conscience. Life needs to rule doctrine.	Continuing human progress. The testimony of reason and conscience purified by the Christian mind The life of God within us so that we can achieve true/ genuine freedom
Christology	Jesus is the most perfect consciousness of God. His death on the cross was an example of God's love.	Arian Docetistic? Jesus as an example to be followed.		
View of the Scriptures	They are important but subordinate to our own individual feelings and instincts about God.	Rejected infallibility but accepted "faultlessness".	The human form of the book is vulnerable to lower and higher criticism. However, as it touches our conscience, it becomes God's living Word.	Importance of Higher Criticism. It has value but not authority Emphasis not on its historical but on its religious content

Characteristics	Consciousness of God lies at the foundation of all religions Individuality.	Christian humanism. Emphasis on the human personality of Christ, practical Christian formation. "No creed but Christ". No doctrine but life."	The Existentialists of their time. Truth is not rational but "ethical", i.e. the deeper area of the personal life The personal experience of faith. A Christianized version of post-Kantian freedom-nature scheme	Using orthodox terms to bolster unorthodox opinions Building a bridge between church tradition and modern thought Reformation finds its fulfilment in idealistic thought
Key proponents		Petrus Hofstede de Groot (1802–1886) Johan Frederik van Oordt (1794–1852) Louis Gerlach Pareau (1800–1866)	Daniel Chantiepie de la Saussaye (1818–1874) Johnnes Hermanus Gunning (1829–1905)	J.H. Scholten (1811–1885) Allard Pierson (1831–1896)
Influences	Daniel Chantiepie Kant—reinterpreted theology in terms of a personalisation philosophy	Daniel Chantiepie Erasmus Hugo Grotius Plato via Philip Willem van Heusde (1778–1839)	Schleiermacher Alexandre Vinet (1797–1847) The Réveil movement	Classic German idealism Hegel Schleiermacher

Kuyper's time was a time of massive cultural change. In addition to the rise of modernism there was the impact of the Industrial Revolution, the French Revolution and Darwinism. Freidrich Nietzsche's death in 1900 also had an impact on Dutch society and culture. The key ideas behind these are summarized in the table on the facing page.

With his switch from studying literature and theology to become a theological candidate, his interest in church history was kindled. His tutor, Matthias de Vries (1820–1892), suggested he enter a competition, organized by the theological faculty at the University of Groningen, and write an essay comparing Calvin's and John à Lasco's (1499–1560) views of the church (*The Commentatio*).[8]

---

8.   Jasper Vree and Johan Zwaan, ed., *Abraham Kuyper's Commentatio (1860): The Young Kuyper about Calvin, a Lasco, and the Church.*

	French Revolution	Nietzsche	Darwinism
Where are we?	In a world ruled by the elite	In an irrational world, that cares nothing for humanity and their values	In a world characterized by chance
Who are we?		People who are led by instincts	We are the products of time, chance and energy/matter and survival instincts
What's wrong?	Christianity—revelation and history The divine right of kings	Reason, Christianity	Nothing
What's the Remedy?	Liberation Equality Brotherhood comes through Revolution Rationalism Individualism Atheism Popular sovereignty Social contract	To accept our own instincts Self-preservation and self-promotion The will to power Let the powerful win A rejection of morality that is based on Christian principles	Survival of the fittest —those creatures beast adapted to the environment will survive
Key proponents	Voltaire, Danton, Robespierre	Nietzsche	Darwin, Huxley, Haeckel

Unfortunately, he could not find any of à Lasco's writings. De Vries suggested he visit his father Abraham de Vries, a Mennonite minister.[9] Kuyper did, but at first, he was unable to help.

Vol. 1: Introduction, Annotations, Bibliography, and Indices. Vol. 2: Commentatio. Brill's Series in Church History, 24 (Leiden: Brill, 2005).

9. Vree and Zwaan, ed., *Abraham Kuyper's Commentatio*, 24.

De Vries suggested that he came back at a later date. Kuyper returned to discover a whole pile of à Lasco books—he saw this as a miracle. It was the start of the crumbling of his modernistic framework.

The work Kuyper did on à Lasco won him the gold medal prize in 1860 and it became his dissertation for his doctorate awarded from Leiden in 1862. The *Commentatio* showed the importance of the church in Kuyper's theology. Several aspects in the *Commentatio* recurred as major themes in Kuyper's work. As Vree and Zwaan note:

> much attention is paid to the church as a free organisa-
> tion, created and led by the Holy Spirit, in which
> members of the congregation having voluntary joined
> play the leading role. They are free to choose their in-
> cumbents, are themselves responsible for the defrayal
> of church life, the diaconate and the mission, and free-
> ly administer church property.[10]

However, completing his *Commentatio* and his dissertation meant overwork which resulted in a breakdown. This was to be the first of several breakdowns that were symptomatic of his (over)work ethic. He often worked late into the night and eventually succumbed to total exhaustion.

For almost a year he was unable to do very little, including reading. As he was recovering, Kuyper took to building model boats. He was also able to read *The Heir of Redclyffe* (1853) a novel by Charlotte M. Yonge (1823–1901). Yonge's book has been a suggestion from his then fiancée, later to be his wife,

---

10. Vree and Zwaan, ed., *Abraham Kuyper's Commentatio*, 2.

Johanna Hendrika Shaay (1842–1899). Yonge was influenced by the English Tractarian movement.

The Tractarian movement, also known as the Oxford Movement, was an Anglo-Catholic, High Church, group within the Church of England. They were based in Oxford and produced numerous tracts, as one might expect from their name. The main driving forces behind it were John Keble, John Henry Newman, and Edward B. Pusey. They desired to see a Catholic Revival in the Church of England. Newman later joined the Roman Catholic Church.

The Heir of Redclyffe struck a note with Kuyper.[11] Of the two main characters, Captain Philip Morville and Sir Guy Morville, Kuyper identified with Philip Morville, who came to see the error of his ways, and thus Kuyper became aware of his own failings and pride. This was another key step towards his conversion. The novel also portrayed the church as a mother. This was a theme that shaped Kuyper's view of the church.

God used these two incidents — the Lascania miracle and the reading *The Heir of Redclyffe* — to prepare him for what would happen at his first pastorate in Beesd. By then, he had married his fiancée (Johanna was 21). It was also in his research on Calvin and à Lasco, that he came to see the Calvin he was reading about was different from the jaundiced view portrayed by his lecturers at Leiden.

---

11. See, for example, Andrew White, "The Heir of Redclyffe: Kuyper's Conversion Via Victorian Fiction," *The Big Picture* 2 (2022), https://kirbylaingcentre.co.uk/the-big-picture/online-magazine/issue-02/the-heir-of-redclyffe-kuypers-conversion-via-victorian-fiction/.

3

Beesd (1863–1867)

FOLLOWING HIS MARRIAGE TO Johanna in 1863, they moved into the manse at Beesd, and so Kuyper began his pastoral ministry in his 26th year. It was a church congregation that comprised mainly of the "Little people" (*Kleine Luyden*) — a small group of unlearned farmers and laborers. He originally thought of this group as "malcontents," as they seemed uninterested in his sermons.

The "malcontents" seemed to Kuyper to be fanatics; they did not like Kuyper's approach. Kuyper tried to ignore them, but as a good pastor, he reluctantly decided to visit them. In doing so he saw people with a hunger and desire for prayer and the Bible. The puritan writings of John Owen, Thomas Manton, John Flavel, and Matthew Henry were the staple diet of this group. It was through this group's testimony and lifestyle that Kuyper began to see the poverty of his own approach. Kuyper, the intellectual, became a man of God. One person in particular impressed and influenced Kuyper, Pietje Baltus (1830–1914). When she heard that Kuyper was going to visit her, she said "That rascal might as well stay away, I don't care for him."[1] However, at that moment a thought flashed through her mind: "But…that Dr. Kuyper yet also carries a soul with it for eternity. One day he will also have to appear before God like all men, and if I now believe that he is not on the right track, may I not care about him?"[2] After Kuyper's visit she knelt down and prayed for him—she did this every day.

Baltus had a great impact on Kuyper. Consequently, he began to read Calvin as if for the first time. Kuyper was always indebted to Balthus, and from then on, he had a heart for the "Kleine Luyden" [the little people].[3] Kuyper always kept a picture of her on his desk.

1. Laat die aap maar wegblijven, ik heb er niets mede op ["I've heard so much already of his superficial doctrine, I won't have any of it."] (Cited in 1937–38. "Some third-hand information about Kuyper's conversion." Letter from P. H. A. van Krieken to H. Colijn (trans. Harry Van Dyke), https://allofliferedeemed.co.uk/kuyper/

2. Cited in de Moor-Ringnalda, *Een Maassluiser Jongen*, 28

3. Jan Hoogland observes: the "term that was used frequently by Abraham Kuyper and, according to him, originates from 'Prins Willem van Oranje' (hence, perhaps, the old-fashioned spelling). However, you won't find these words in that combination anywhere in what has been handed down from Prince Willem. It is a typical rhetorical term, with which Kuyper wants to remind people of the origins of the Dutch nation. According to some, his use of this term even has populist traits (Lodewijk Dros, Trouw, December 18, 2016). It is clear that Kuyper had explicit ideological intentions with this term. He used it to refer to people with few aspirations and ambitions, who worked hard and dutifully took on their responsibilities in the family, the household, and their work. Often, it concerned small shopkeepers, craftsmen, and people in the care profession. These were individuals with vital occupations who provided for themselves through hard work without belonging to the elite." Jan Hoogland, "Kleine Luyden" *Sophie (Special Abraham Kuyper)* (February 2021): 25.

Pietje Baltus (1830–1914)

It was not only the malcontents at Beesd that showed Kuyper the poverty of modernism. His lecturer at Leiden, J. H. Scholten, published a study on John's Gospel in which Scholten changed the views he previously espoused. This showed Kuyper how insecure the foundations of modernism were.

Easter 1867 saw Kuyper preach on the resurrection of Jesus as a physical event. He would no longer applaud the modernist views of Scholten and others. Kuyper was now firmly orthodox in his Reformed views.

From then on, as Rullman observes:

Religion is to him not only a Sunday occupation, but in truth a leaven which must permeate all life. For Kuyper, the deepest ground and cohesion of all things lies in God. God is the central power, which must be acknowledged. The service of God is the one straight line that runs through all his life.[4]

While at Beesd he continued his work on à Lasco. He worked on editing the complete works of à Lasco—it was published in 1865. He also intended to write a biography of him too — but this was shelved when in 1867 he was called to Utrecht. While at Beesd Kuyper's reputation grew and in 1867 he was invited to take up the pastorate in Utrecht, only 30 km north of Beesd.

---

4. J. C. Rullman, *Abraham Kuyper*, 233. The original in Dutch reads: "De godsdienst is hem niet alleen een bezigheid voor den Zondag, maar in waarheid een zuurdeesem die het geheele leven moet doordringen. De diepste grond en samenhang aller dingen ligt voor Kuyper in God. God is de centrale macht, die erkend moet worden. De dienst van God is de ééne rechte lijn die door heel zijn leven loopt."

The church building in Beesd.

The parsonage in Beesd

4

Utrecht (1867–1870)

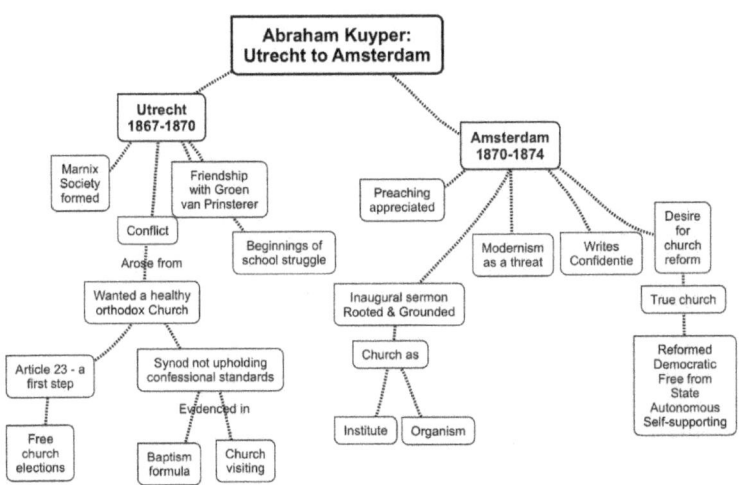

UTRECHT WAS A MEDIEVAL city in the center of the Nether-lands. The State church on Kuyper's arrival boasted approximate-ly 35 000 members. There were 11 ministers — including Kuyper — who preached on rotation and a large consistory administered its affairs. For Kuyper, this move originally "felt like being called to Jerusalem."[1] The feelings did not last long, however.

---

1.   Kuyper, *Charity & Justice*, 241.

Kuyper's interest in church history continued while he was at Utrecht. In 1868 he formed the Marnix Society — an organization whose aim was similar to the English Parker Society — founded to research and publish Dutch Reformation resources.

It seemed wherever Kuyper went he was at the center of conflict. He later reflected:

> Although I was probably a bit overconfident, I then became a kind of guerrilla fighter, hazarding confrontation at my own risk. I was not content to just defend the fortress that was being attacked. I decided to sally forth. Finding an apologetic approach pointless, I decided to attack, lobbing one grenade after another among the opponents.[2]

This arose from Kuyper's desire for a healthy orthodox church and not one that had surrendered to the spirit of the age. Two conflicts arose while he was in Utrecht: the use of the baptism formula and church visiting. These were the beginnings of much-needed church reform.

Synod's desire was for a national church with complete freedom of doctrine. This was evident by the introduction of three permissible baptism formulae. The biblical and traditional baptism in the name of the Father, the Son, and the Holy Spirit was supplemented by two others: "unto faith, hope, and love" and "unto initiation into Christianity." Kuyper and the church at Utrecht complained, but Synod ignored them. The Utrecht consistory under Kuyper's leading, decreed that no baptism would be recognized unless it was administered in the name of the Father, Son, and Holy Spirit.

The State Church Synod was obliged to carry out an annual enquiry into the spiritual and financial health of the church-

---

2. Kuyper, *Charity & Justice*, 242.

es under their jurisdiction. Unfortunately, they did not take this seriously. Church visits were conducted only once every three years and a questionnaire was issued in the in-between

The Domkerk, Utrecht

years. Kuyper was not impressed. The Utrecht consistory decided to return the questionnaires unanswered.

Kuyper then wrote a brochure (in Dutch): *The Church Inspection in Utrecht in 1868 with an eye to the critical condition of our church in historical perspective.*[3] In it Kuyper questioned the stance of the Synod of the Dutch Reformed Church as they were not upholding the confessional standards. Synod it appears did little to alleviate Kuyper's concerns.

Article 23 became operative in March 1867. Article 23 regarded the right of the congregation to appoint elders and deacons and to call ministers. When church elections took place in 1867 and 1868 the vast majority of congregations voted for orthodox and Reformed men. For Kuyper this was a great victory. However, he was keen to stress that Article 23 was not the complete solution; it was only a stopgap.

In a series of articles in the *De Heraut* newspaper he examined the issue of the "Liberation of the church." For Kuyper this meant liberation from the state and the hierarchy epitomized by the Synod and so becoming a truly and wholly Reformed church. This did not go down well with the liberals in the church. Several of them banded together in an attempt to thwart Kuyper's desires. They formed a quarterly newspaper, *Protestant Protestations*, in which to challenge Kuyper.

It was while at Utrecht that Kuyper met Guillaume Groen van Prinsterer (1801–1876) for the first time. They had previ-

---

3. Abraham Kuyper, *Kerkvisitatie te Utrecht in 1868 met het oog op den kritieken toestand onzer kerk historisch toegelicht* (Utrecht, J.H. van Peursem 1868). (No 1868.05 in Kuiper's Annotated Bibliography).

ously corresponded but had not met. They connected after Kuyper delivered a talk at the public meeting at the cathedral church in May 1869. Kuyper and Groen immediately recognized each other as kindred spirits. Kuyper later wrote:

> It was May 18, 1869. I was in the consistory room of the Domkerk in Utrecht, when I for the first time met the man who by his first look and his first word at once took such a strong hold on me and so profoundly impressed me that from that hour I became his spiritual associate, nay more, his spiritual son.[4]

What united them was that they were both devoted to the school struggle. The struggle for equality for state and private schools. The talk Kuyper gave "An appeal to the nation's conscience"[5] was the opening address for the Association of Christian National Primary Education. This was probably the first time Kuyper spoke in support of the school struggle. A struggle for the existence of schools free from state influence.

In the talk he identifies "five features that constitute the demands of our movement with respect to education." These were piety, historical sense, citizen's self-help, and freedom of conscience.[6] He stresses the need for all parents—irrespective of class or wealth—to be able to provide for their children an education concordant with their beliefs. Again, this shows Kuyper's concern for the "Kleine Luyden."

If I find no suitable school I will teach them myself. The rich are not compelled either; they have the money

---

4. Kuyper, *Charity & Justice*, 243.

5. Reprinted in Kuyper, *On Education*, 317–321.

6. Kuyper, *On Education*, 320.

to provide the kind of education they prefer. And if that financial burden is too heavy for one individual, several can pool their resources and establish a private school. But the common man and the poor man ... these I defend, for these I speak. They are coerced, they are cut to the heart, their conscience is repressed. Or are we to believe that among the poor the life of parents is not as tightly bound up with that of their children? Should the conscience of the parents themselves not feel hurt at the injustice done to the souls of their children? And when that occurs, when the common man and the poor man are compelled (if the philanthropy of others brings no solution) either to deprive his child of an education or to surrender it to a kind of education in which, on his view, the one thing needful is lacking, an education that can form the head but not the heart and therefore militates against his conscience — very well, when that occurs, we want the nation's conscience to render a verdict as to whether it will tolerate this abuse of the lower income groups, this breach of parental rights, this abridgment of freedom of conscience.[7]

In hearing this Groen recognized in Kuyper someone to whom he could pass on his mantle. Kuyper regarded himself as Groen's "spiritual son." As Harry Van Dyke has observed:

The careers of neither Bavinck nor Kuyper, the range of their intellectual output, their reforming zeal in more than one area of life and culture, cannot be understood apart from Groen. It was from him that they learned to

---

7. Kuyper, *On Education*, 320.

see the problem of the spirit of modernity in its widest scope, calling for nothing less than a culture war across the whole spectrum of modern life.[8]

What Groen appreciated about Kuyper was his organizational skills. These were so important in the subsequent development of the Anti-Revolutionary Party (ARP).

In October 1869 Kuyper began writing political articles in the weekly newspaper *De Heraut*. When the editor died in 1871, he took over as the editor in chief. This was the beginning of Kuyper the journalist. Later, in 1872 he became the editor of the daily *Standaard*. He wrote several articles on what became known as the "School struggle." This and the church question became burning issues during Kuyper's time at Amsterdam.

---

8. Harry Van Dyke, "Groen van Prinsterer: Godfather of Bavinck and Kuyper," *Calvin Theological Journal* 47 no. 1 (2012): 72–97.

Guillaume Groen van Prinsterer (1801– 1876)

5

An Aside:
Groen van Prinsterer[1]

ABRAHAM KUYPER AND HERMAN Bavinck were the main instigators of the movement that became known as neo-Calvinism; however, they stood on the shoulders of others. One of these was Guillaume Groen van Prinsterer (1801–1876). Harry Van Dyke describes him as a "godfather" to both Kuyper and Bavinck;[2] and Bratt describes him as "something of a surrogate father to Kuyper."[3] He was visited by several abolitionists from Britain. They had heard of his ideas for social reform, they hoped he would become "Holland's Wilberforce."

Herman Bavinck wrote of him: "Groen's work is significant not only for the past and the present, but also for the future"[4]

---

1. Some of this draws upon my "You Should Know Groen van Prinsterer" Layman's Lounge. Online: https://thelaymenslounge.com/you-should-know-groen-van-prinsterer/

2. Harry Van Dyke, "Groen van Prinsterer: Godfather of Bavinck and Kuyper," 72–97.

3. Bratt, *Abraham Kuyper*, 62.

4. Herman Bavinck in the Foreword to *Unbelief and Revolution*. In *The Bavinck Review* 10 (2019): 75–84.

and D. M. Lloyd Jones: "...a fascinating and most important man. ...He was on all accounts a most remarkable man."[5]

Many of Groen's embryonic ideas were taken up and developed by Kuyper. These included:

- The necessity of Christian education and "the freedom of religion with respect to our children"
- Sphere sovereignty[6]
- The need for a Christian political party
- The impact of modernism on society, and tied to this
- The negative influence of the worldview behind the French Revolution

Groen, an intellectual historian and social commentator, was born into a wealthy aristocratic family. His father, Pieter Jacobus Groen van Prinsterer, a medical doctor, married Adriana Hendrika Caan, the heir to the wealthy Rotterdam merchant family. Like Kuyper and Bavinck after him Groen studied at Leiden University.

Groen the student

At Leiden, he completed two doctoral dissertations, one in the law faculty and the other in the literary faculty. Groen was

---

5. D.M. Lloyd-Jones "The French Revolution and After," *The Christian and the State in Revolutionary Times Westminster Conference Papers* (Cambridge: Westminster Conference, 1976), 94–110.

6. There is some debate over this. George Harinck maintains that it was Kuyper's original idea; Friesen maintains that it goes back to Van Baader. Until recently, the consensus has been that Kuyper was influenced by Groen. It may well be that the notion was commonplace among Reformed European Christians although not as clearly articulated as in Kuyper's work.

no academic slouch and completed both doctorates within a year! At Leiden, he attended the private lectures of Willem Bilderdijk (1756–1831). Bilderdijk was one of the key figures in the Dutch *Réveil,* a pietistic revival that originated geographically in Geneva.[7] Within Bilderdijk's circle were the poet Isaac da Costa (1798–1860) and church historian J. H. Merle d'Aubigné (1794–1872). Although he was not yet a Christian Groen was influenced by these men. He later said of Bilderdijk he "frightened me off unbelief, [rather] than brought me to faith."

Upon graduation in 1823, he was unsure of his next steps. He began work as a barrister in 1824.

Groen the secretary in the King's cabinet

In 1826 the King invited submissions for a general history of the Netherlands. Groen entered. He was one of five authors who received a gold medal for their submissions. Subsequently, he applied for and was appointed to the post of Secretary in the King's Cabinet. It was an administrative post that he held for six years—it was not a position that he enjoyed and, as a result, his health suffered. During this time, he courted and married Elizabeth Maria Magdalena van der Hoop (1807–1879) in 1828. They had no children.

At the time Belgium and the Netherlands were united as one kingdom and Groen spent time in Brussels. During his time there he became acquainted with Merle d'Aubigné, who introduced him to others in the *Réveil* movement.

---

7.   See, for example, Jean D. Decorvet, Tim Grass and Kenneth J. Stewart (ed.), *The Genevan Réveil in International Perspective* (Eugene, OR: Pickwick, 2023).

Groen the Christian

Although brought up in a liberal Christian environment Groen had no personal Christian faith until 1833. He was greatly impressed with the baptism of Isaac da Costa. Additionally, his wife was a Reformed Christian. It was no doubt her prayers and testimony that influenced him. His journey to the Christian faith took several years. It was through his wife that he became increasingly known to those involved in the *Réveil*.

Groen's mother died in 1833 and he became increasingly unwell. He travelled to Switzerland to convalesce and there he once more came under the preaching of Merle d'Aubigné.

Groen the journalist

Groen, like Kuyper after him, knew how important communication was. He published a daily newspaper, *De Nederlander,* from 1850 to 1855 with the intent of reaching the Dutch intellectuals. Later, from 1896, he published a weekly the *Nederlandsche Gedachten* [Dutch Thoughts/Reflections].

This was a resurgence of the paper he produced from 1829 to 1832.

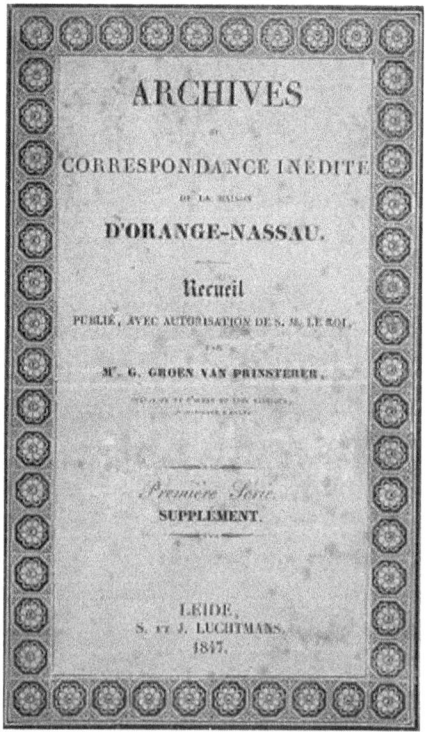

He also recognized the need for a *popular* newspaper to educate and motivate the people, so he invested three thousand guilders as start-up money for Kuyper's *De Standaard* when it was launched in April 1872.

Groen the historian

Groen was fascinated by history; it was not only an academic interest. He agreed with Bilderdik's assertion that "In the past lies the present." In his *Christian Political Action in an Age of Revolution,* he wrote:

> I am enamoured of the past. For sure I am. I do not believe it possible to break with the past. I believe that every notion connected with the future is rooted in the past.

He has been described as the "father of modern Dutch history."[8] He called his approach a "Christian-historical" worldview.[9]

He was appointed to the Palace Archives as an archivist. There he became absorbed in Dutch history and the influence of Christian principles. He published twelve volumes of the *Archives ou Correspondance Inedite de la Maison d'Orange-Nassau.* These established his reputation as a historian.

He also became concerned about the history lessons schoolchildren received. He produced an overview of Dutch history for the use of teachers to help them improve their teaching. This *Handboek der geschiedenis van het Vaderland*

---

8. J. L. Van Essen and H. D. Morton, *Guillaume Groen van Prinsterer: Selected Studies.* (Jordan, Ontario: Wedge Publishing Foundation, 1990), 9.

9. H. Van Dyke, "Groen van Prinsterer: Godfather of Bavinck and Kuyper."

[*Handbook of the History of the Fatherland*] was published in 1841 and was finally completed in 1846. It comprised over 1100 numbered paragraphs. A wealthy benefactor financed a fourth printing of the *Handbook* to enable it to be distributed free to hundreds of Dutch schoolteachers. The book is still in print.

Commenting on Groen's view of history Schutte has this to say:

> To study history, therefore, is for Groen not just a pleasant pastime that can yield many interesting things. It is an essential work for a Christian, who should leave no means unused to learn to know God better. *It stands written! It has come to pass!* That is how Groen loved to summarize his Christian-historical world-view. Notice how Groen's aphorism puts Holy Scripture first, as God's indisputable proclamation of the truth. But God also reveals himself in what comes to pass in history, although on that score human knowledge is limited and imperfect, which is why the book of history will always have to be read while constantly testing it against the written Word. What has happened is not good just because it happened.... The distinctiveness of Groen's position was that he wanted to apply the standards of God's law to the historical process—in which, after all, anti-godly, diabolical forces are active as well.[10]

---

10. Gerrit J. Schutte, *Groen van Prinsterer: His Life and Work*, trans. Harry Van Dyke (Neerlandia, Alberta: Inheritance Publications, 2016).

Groen the politician

He was a member of the Dutch parliament on three occasions and was the leader of the Anti-Revolutionary movement. He was elected to the parliament in 1849, 1855 and 1862. In his early days, he described himself as a "conservative-liberal or liberal-conservative." Later he took a middle position that he described as Christian-Historical. He realized that, as a Christian, he could not align himself with either side. Likewise, he was neither conservative nor progressive.

Groen the school reformer

In 1837 Groen published "Measures Used against the Dissenters judged by Constitutional Law." In it he argued against forcing parents to send their children to schools that did not comport with their worldview was a violation of their God-given right; a God-given right to educate their children in accordance with their religious beliefs. He described the Dutch education system as being un-Christian and anti-Christian.

When his arguments were met with disdain and indifference at best, he realized that more was needed to be done—constitutional reform would be necessary.

In 1860, Groen founded "The Association for Christian National Primary Education." Its purpose was to promote the founding of schools free from state control. He was a vociferous promoter of free schools without government interference and for equal funding for these independent schools.

Groen the Anti-Revolutionary

In the late eighteenth and early nineteenth centuries, revolution was in the air. In addition to the French Revolution in

1789, there were revolutionary outbreaks in Greece, Poland, Austria, Germany, and Hungary. This revolutionary spirit was the backdrop to Groen's book *Unbelief and Revolution*, published in 1847.

Unbelief and Revolution

These fifteen lectures, which were subsequently published, were given to a small group that gathered in Groen's house in the Hague.

In the lectures, he argued that the spirit of the French Revolution of 1789 lives on. His main thesis was that "the cause of the Revolution lies in *unbelief*" (Lecture VIII). However, the term revolution was not only a reference to the French Revolution; it also represented the spiritual and intellectual shift that it brought in. The spirit of secular humanism was damaging the created order for society. Revolution was rooted in a worldview. The birth of modernism took place during this period. The Revolution was as important as the Reformation, but it was the antithesis of the Reformation; it was the Reformation in reverse:

> The Revolution is an all-embracing system for religion, law, and ethics; it is a reversal of ideas (by a rejection of revealed truth) in church, state, and society: Social Revolution.

Its cry of "Fraternity, Liberty and Equality," he thought was important but only if seen through a Christian perspective. The promises of fraternity, liberty and equality resulted in their opposites:

> For justice there came injustice; for freedom, compulsion; for toleration, persecution; for humanity, barbarity; and for morality, dependence.[11]

---

11. Groen van Prinsterer, *Unbelief and Revolution*, Lecture VIII.

Groen drilled down to the starting points and principles of the French Revolution. The first few lectures examined some key factors; these, however important as they were, were not the main reason:

> The principle of this vaunted philosophy was *the sovereignty of Reason*, and the outcome was apostasy from God and materialism. That such an outcome was inevitable once the principle had been accepted is demonstrable from the genealogy of ideas. ... Reason became the touchstone of truth.[12]

Groen the mentor of Kuyper

At first glance, there were many differences between Groen and Kuyper. Kuyper was a theologian by training, a pastor, a polemicist, he was bold and brash, and a populist; Groen was an aristocratic lawyer by training and reserved. Kuyper regarded Calvin as a republican, Groen saw Calvin as a monarchist. However, despite the surface differences, they had much in common. Both were concerned with the school struggle, both realized that the school struggle would involve political involvement, both were at one point newspaper editors, both rejected the notion of popular sovereignty, but more importantly and both had the gospel of the risen Christ as their motivation.

Groen first became aware of Kuyper in 1864 when Kuyper wrote to him requesting help in finding documents relating to the Polish reformer John à Lasco. The two later began to exchange letters. Groen recommended reading for Kuyper—these included works by F. J. Stahl, Edmund Burke, and François Guizot.

---

12. Groen van Prinsterer, *Unbelief and Revolution*, Lecture VIII.

Many of Groen's colleagues and friends were wary of his relationship with Kuyper. However, Groen saw within Kuyper important leadership and organizational skills that he himself lacked. Groen had been described as "a general without an army." In Kuyper, he saw someone who could build and lead an army. Kuyper took Groen's Anti-Revolutionary movement and made it into the first political party in the Netherlands. Kuyper took up Groen's mantle in the setting up of the Anti-Revolutionary Party as the first Dutch national political party.

Groen's death

Groen died on 19 May 1876. Just before his death, he wrote his "Christian historical Testament" in the *Nederlandsche Gedachten*:

> With the publican's prayer: O God, be merciful to me, a sinner.
>
> With the wisdom of the Heidelberg Catechism: my only comfort in life and death.
>
> With the shout of joy: I thank God through Jesus Christ our Lord.
>
> With the battle-cry of the Reformation: Put on the whole armor of God, and the sword of the Spirit, which is the Word of God. *Verbum Dei manet in aeternum*: The Word of God endures forever.
>
> With the motto: Not a statesman! A confessor of the gospel.[13]

He wanted to be remembered not as a statesman but as a confessor of the gospel. He was a statesman because he confessed the gospel. The gospel shaped all he did.

---

13. Cited in Schutte, *Groen van Prinsterer*, 132.

Further reading on Groen

Essen, J. L. van, and Morton, H. Donald 1990. *Guillaume Groenvan Prinsterer: Selected Studies.* Jordan Station, ON: Wedge.

Freeke, Jan 1999, The Life and Work of Groen van Prinsterer, *Banner of Truth*, 430 (July): 17–24.

Kuiper, Roel. *The Antirevolutionary: Life and Works of Groen Van Prinsterer (1801–1876)* Eugene, OR: Pickwick, Publications, 2025.

Schutte, Gerrit J. 2016. *Groen van Prinsterer: His Life and Work.* (Translated by Harry Van Dyke.) Neerlandia, Alberta: Inheritance Publications.

Smitskamp, H. 2017. *Building a Nation on Rock or Sand.* (Translated by Harman Boersema). Ontario: Guardian Books.

Van Dyke, H. 2012. Groen van Prinsterer: godfather of Bavinck and Kuyper. *Calvin Theological Journal* 17(1): 72–97.

Van Dyke, H. 2019. *Challenging the Spirit of Modernity: A Study of Groen van Prinsterer's Unbelief and Revolution* (Studies in Historical and Systematic Theology). Bellingham, WA: Lexham Press.

6

Amsterdam (1870–1874)

SINCE 1867, WHEN FREE church elections were introduced, as a result of Article 23, the Amsterdam church had become an orthodox Reformed body. It was no surprise then that they asked Kuyper to become their minister. Kuyper accepted and took up the role on 12 February 1870. He was the first Calvinist to take up this post; most of the previous ministers had been modernists. The church in Amsterdam had 28 ministers and a membership of 140 000.

His inaugural sermon in Amsterdam was *Rooted and Grounded.*[1] Here, he expounded for the first time his view of the church as an institute and organism. Once more the question of the church was at the forefront of his mind.

He was much appreciated as a preacher in Amsterdam. Many came to hear him preach. His approach was more thematic than expository or exegetical. He most often preached from memory and only wrote down sermons that were delivered for special occasions. Several of his sermons from this

---

1. Abraham Kuyper, *Rooted and Grounded: The Church as Organism and Institution* (Grand Rapids, MI: Christian's Library Press, 2013).

time, at Utrecht, and at Amsterdam were published. He often used examples from everyday life, and above all showed that he was familiar with the needs and concerns of the workers. His preaching was so popular that at four o'clock in the afternoon there was already a queue in front of the church in anticipation for the six o'clock service. Kuyper's preaching was enjoyed as was evident from the packed churches and the overcrowded catechisms.

Kuyper knew so much about many areas of life. His "secret" was, asking and listening. He revealed this secret to a girl who worked in a drapery shop in Amsterdam, where he was buying a silk dress for his wife. He looked at the silk fabrics and showed that he had such an understanding of them that one would think that he was a silk manufacturer. The next day the girl when visiting his house asked Kuyper, how it came about that he already knew so much about silk. The answer he gave:

> Do you want to learn something? Then always try to learn by listening from the people you meet, be they a scholar or a simple worker. When I meet a painter, I ask him to tell me about his paintings. If I speak to a soldier, I ask him about the military conditions. And when I meet a silk manufacturer, I ask his opinion about silk caterpillars and silk culture. Remember this: Talk to each person as much as possible about his own profession and let him do the talking. That's my secret.[2]

Another of his secrets was punctuality and organization. This is how he was so productive. As one Dutch biographer observed:

---

2. Cited in De Moor-Ringnalda, *Een Maassluiser Jongen*, 41–42.

He had a set time for everything and he never deviated from it for a minute. He walked exactly two hours every day. Usually he walked alone and while walking thought about the articles he had to write for *De Standaard* or looked for a good solution to the problems at hand.[3]

His daughter tells of how he worked in his study from nine to twelve-thirty and no one was allowed to disturb him. This was when he was writing his articles for *De Standaard,* the newspaper he founded in 1872.

On his 35th birthday several of his friends gave him the gift a house. De Prins Hendrikkade 183 was a large town house. (It has now been replaced by an office block.)

Modernism for Kuyper was a challenge and a threat to orthodoxy — he knew this first-hand as he had originally been a modernist at Leiden. He described it as a Fata Morgana — an illusion, a mirage. It promised much but failed to deliver. He spent much of his time warning against it.

In 1872 "the mutiny of the seventeen elders" occurred. These elders took a stand against modernist preachers and refused to attend church services if liberal ministers administered the word or the sacrament. Kuyper was asked to be a one-person committee to prepare a response to these elders. Kuyper supported them much to the dismay of the liberal faction. Their action was a response to the problems within the state church.

Kuyper published a proposal to the Special Consistory of the Dutch Reformed Congregation in 1873 that advanced the

---

3.   De Moor-Ringnalda, *Een Maassluiser Jongen,* 43.

idea for separate parishes two for the orthodox, two for the modernists and two for those who had no preference for either modernism or orthodoxy. His idea was that the church properties be distributed evenly between the parishes. It was a pragmatic solution aimed at smoothing conflict between the two factions. Unfortunately, it did not provide the results that Kuyper had hoped. The aim was to promote greater congregational autonomy, which was a step too far for the Synod who despite taking the "question under consideration let the matter drop."[4]

Kuyper's concern for the church was shown in his autobiographical *Confidentie* written to show his own conversion.[5] It was published in 1873. Vanden Berg comments on it: "*Confidentially* stands out as a masterpiece of revealing content. It is a priceless human document. Certainly no one who read *Confidentially*'s spirited pages should possibly be in the dark as to Kuyper's objectives."[6]

In it, Kuyper recounts the miracle of à Lasco, the effects on him in his reading of the *Heir of Redclyffe*, and his confrontation with the malcontents at Beesd. All these events were sent by God to bring about an evangelical conversion and a desire for the church and for church reform. His vision for a true church was one that was:

- Reformed

- Democratic

---

4. Tijze Kuipers, A*braham Kuyper: An Annotated Bibliography 1857-2010*, (Leiden: Brill, 2011), 80.

5. Abraham Kuyper, "Confidentially," in A*braham Kuyper Centennial Reader*, 45–61.

6. Frank Vanden Berg, *Abraham Kuyper* (Eerdmans: Grand Rapids, 1960), 60.

- Free from State influence
- Autonmous and
- Self-supporting

It was a while before Kuyper could see this vision manifested. His ecclesiastical reforms became intertwined with his political and educational work. His vision of "a free church and a free school in a free land" (the heading on the masthead of his *De Standaard* newspaper)—would require political involvement. In the subsequent sections. I will look at the political, ecclesiastical, and educational issues separately.

7

Politics and Perfectionism
(1874–1905)

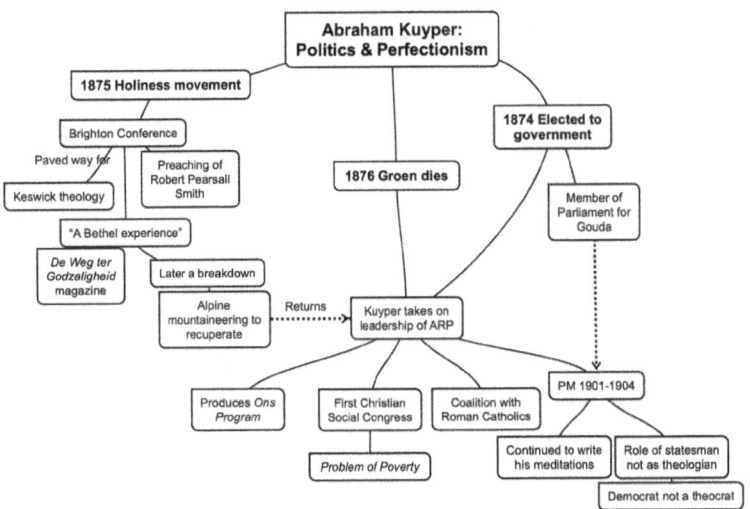

In 1874 Kuyper gave permission for his name to be placed on an election ballot paper — to his surprise, he was elected. It was not the first time he had been put forward for election. Groen had proposed him in 1871 for an election to the Second Chamber.[1]

---

1. The *Tweede Kamer der Staten* [The Second Chamber of the States General] or lower house is the House of Representatives, as opposed to

This time his election meant he had to give up his office as a church minister. He continued to serve as an elder in the Dutch Reformed Congregation of Amsterdam (from 1874 until 1886). In 1874 he moved to The Hague to attend to his political responsibilities.

Initially, he was undecided about taking up the role of a politician. Can one serve God in politics? Even if it meant giving up his post in the Amsterdam church? Was he giving up the pulpit for politics? It was during his time in Amsterdam that several important issues were at the forefront of Kuyper's mind, particularly education and the church. He saw that journalism was one way in which he could motivate Christians, but he also saw that for changes to take place in education and the church it needed a political change. He thus took up his role as a politician. It was during this period that Kuyper was becoming overworked. His workaholism soon caught up with him again.

In the summer of 1875 Kuyper visited England to hear the holiness teaching of Robert Pearsall Smith (1827–1898). The conference was entitled the "Convention for the Promotion of Scriptural Holiness."[2] The Evangelical Alliance invited many from the continent to attend. Kuyper was one of those invited. Those speaking at the event also included E. H. Hopkins, Stevenson A. Blackwood, H. W. Webb-Peploe, and Theodore Monod.[3] These meetings paved the way for the Keswick Con-

---

the First Chamber or the Senate. The Second Chamber is the main legislative body. It is elected by a party-list of proportional representation.

2. David Bundy, "Keswick and the Experience of Evangelical Piety" in *Modern Christian Revivals*, ed., Edith Waldvogel Blumhofer and Randall Herbert Balmer (Illinois: University of Illinois Press, 1993).

3. David D. Bundy 2012. Keswick: *A Bibliographic Introduction to the Higher Life Movements* (Wilmore, Ky.: First Fruits Press, 2012).

POLITICS AND PERFECTIONISM

vention, first organized by Canon Thomas Harford-Battersby, the vicar of St John's Church in Keswick, in the Lake District.[4]

Kuyper was impressed by these meetings. He compiled a report in the 6 and 7 June 1875 issues of *De Standaard*. Kuyper presented a paper to the third Southern Missionary Festival at 's Heer-Arendskerke on 23 June on the holiness movement in Britain, where he described it as a "Bethel experience."[5]

The Brighton visit had a major effect both on Kuyper and on Pearsall Smith. Pearsall Smith had been counselling a young female alone in his hotel room and put his arm around her. The young lady alleged it was contact of a sexual nature and Pearsall Smith was sent home.[6] Consequently, Pearsall Smith withdrew from his holiness "ministry."

The Dutch group was hosted by Kuyper in August 1875 in his home.[7] They started a magazine *De Weg ter Godzaligheid* (The Road to Godliness) with the aim of spreading the holiness idea of "sanctification by faith." It ran for twelve issues from October 1875 until 1877. Kuyper contributed only one piece to this magazine.[8] In it, he takes to task Gunning's view of a second conversion.

---

4. Charles Price and Ian Randall, *Transforming Keswick: The Keswick Convention Past, Present & Future* (Carlisle: OM Publishing, 2000).

5. This was reported in *Het derde Zuider Zendingsfest*, 7–21 (1875.07).

6. David Bebbington, *Holiness in Nineteenth-Century England* (Carlisle: Paternoster, 2000), 76–77; see also, M. J. D. Roberts, "Evangelism and Scandal in Victorian England: The Case of the Pearsall Smiths," *History* (2010): 437–457.

7. Bundy "Keswick and the Experience of Evangelical Piety," 130.

8. Kuyper, "Aan Ds. J.H. Gunning," *De Weg ter Godzaligheid* 1 (3): 33–38.

Kuyper soon after the visit had a breakdown. This was attributed to overwork. At the time he suffered from insomnia and was taking the sedative chloral hydrate which was popular at the time. In an interview, Kuyper said, "More than a year, from March 1876 to May 1877, when I was unable even to do something, I could no longer write a postcard and could read no more than two consecutive pages."[9]

It is not clear why Kuyper found the Brighton meetings so enthralling. The holiness approach was theologically far from his Reformed theology. He later wrote a series of 18 articles *against* perfectionist doctrine.

> Our judgement would in all likelihood have been different from the very beginning had we been as familiar with the history of Perfectionism, the theological articulation of Perfectionism, and the historical polemics against Perfectionism as we are now.[10]

To recover from his breakdown Kuyper convalesced in southern Europe not by resting but by Alpine climbing. He commented:

> "When I have completed a difficult climb, I am as happy as a schoolboy." Another time he admitted, "Walking among the large crowd of people moving through the streets of London and climbing high mountains are the only things that can calm my nerves. In London, amidst the hustle and bustle, I feel like a forgotten man. But in the mountains, I have a desire to climb higher and higher

---

9. J. de Brujin, *Abraham Kuyper: A Pictorial Biography* (Grand Rapids, MI: Eerdmans, 2014) 115.

10. Kuyper, "Perfectionism," in *Abraham Kuyper: A Centennial Reader*, 161.

until the moment comes when one cannot go any further. Then I come to the recognition that God did not create the world primarily for us humans to enjoy, but so that He could delight in the works of His hands."[11]

In May 1877 he returned to the Netherlands, recovered. It was while he was recuperating that Kuyper's mentor Groen van Prinsterer died. On Kuyper's return, the Anti-Revolutionary members inevitably looked to him to lead them.

Kuyper had already been working on some principles for the Anti-Revolutionary Party some of which Groen van Prinsterer had seen and had agreed with. Although Groen felt that a general program was *unnecessary* and *dangerous*.[12] These were originally published in *De Standaard* and eventually became *Ons Program* [Our Program].[13] Like many of Kuyper's books, the chapters for *Ons Program* began life as a series of articles in *De Heraut* and *De Standaard*.[14] Its aim was "to

---

11. Cited in de Moor-Ringnalda, *Een Maassluiser Jongen*, 50.

12. Cited in P. J. Hoedemaker, *The Politics of Antithesis: The Antirevolutionary Government of Abraham Kuyper 1901–1905* (Aalten: Panocrator Press, 2021), 8.

13. Abraham Kuyper, *Our Program: A Christian Political Manifesto Abraham Kuyper Collected Works in Public Theology*, ed. and trans. Harry Van Dyke (Bellingham, WA: Lexham Press, 2015).

14. These were published in *De Standaard* from April 17 to February 179. The book was published in 1879. An abridged edition was published in 1880. The English version was originally published as *Guidance For Christian Engagement In Government* in 2013 by Christian's Library Press—it republished in 2015 as *Our Program* by Lexham Press as part of the Abraham Kuyper Collected Works in Public Theology. Sections of it were translated and published in James W. Skilen and McCarthy, Rockne M., ed., *Political Order and the Plural Structure of Society* (Atlanta: Scholars Press, 1991)

serve antirevolutionaries as a guide for promotional activities and to prepare them for the formal establishment of an Anti-Revolutionary Party."[15]

Kuyper was also involved with the issue of poverty and what became termed "the social question." He gave the opening speech at the First Christian Social Congress in November 1891 addressing these issues.[16]

With Kuyper's election in 1874 he left church ministry for a wider ministry. He did not leave his faith at the Chamber's door; Kuyper's faith was integral to his political views, intentions, and practice. He served in the Dutch parliament for two periods 1874–1875 as a member of Parliament for Gouda and 1894–1901. He was Prime Minister from 1901–1904.

Prelude to power

In the election of 1897, the Right gained 45 seats and the Left 55. The 45 seats on the Right saw Kuyper's party the ARP have 17 seats, the Catholics 22, 5 for the Free Anti-Revolutionaries and 1 for the Christian Historical Party.[17] This meant that Kuyper as the ARP's leader was elected to the Second Chamber.[18]

---

15. Kuyper, *Our Program.*

16. This has been published in Kuyper, *On Business and Economics,* 2021, 173–229. It was also published as *The Problem of Poverty.*

17. The Christelijk Historische Partij, was a Dutch conservative Reformed political party, which was formed in 1903 with the merger of the Free Anti Revolutionary Party and the Christian Historical Voters' League. Both parties were formed as a result of a rejection of Kuyper's ARP political views.

18. In this section I am indebted to McKendree Langley's excellent *The Practice of Political Spirituality Episodes from the Public Career of Abraham Kuyper, 1879–1918* (Jordan Station, Ont: Wedge Press, 1984).

N. G. Pierson (1839–1909), a moderate Union Liberal, became the new Prime Minister. Kuyper noticed that there was a conflict between popular and royal sovereignty, and he tried to get the government to clarify their position.

Kuyper was keen to support the government's social reform agenda. However, he was not a supporter of the principles on which they advocated social reform. For example, the ownership of private property was supported by the government and by Kuyper. However, for Kuyper and his party, it was based on the principle of stewardship; for the government, it was based on reason and evolutionary development.

Kuyper took every opportunity he could to point out the difference in principles and foundations between the Christians and Humanistic motives for government: "The Christian principle which is the source of my convictions, my confession, and even my politics. I will maintain even as a democrat."[19]

Despite the different starting points, however, Kuyper maintained that cooperation was still possible. Kuyper's faith did not stop him from being practical. He knew that the ARP could not command a parliamentary majority. For the ARP to be in power meant then a coalition with other parties, but this did not mean losing their commitment to Calvinistic principles. He could see that a political coalition between the Roman Catholics was a possibility.

This raises the question of how Calvinists and Roman Catholics can work together. Would it mean a compromise in faith? Kuyper knew that the theology of Roman Catholicism

---

19. Cited in Langley, *The Practice of Political Spirituality*, 67.

and Calvinism was irreconcilable; however, they could work together for common political aims.

In the 1901 election the coalition between the ARP and the Catholic party was in the majority—the ARP had 24 seats, the Free Anti-Revolutionaries 7, the Roman Catholics 25, and the Christian Historical Party 2. The Left had 42 seats. Thus, Queen Wilhelmina appointed Kuyper as the new Prime Minister.

Kuyper as PM

In 1901 at the age of 64, Kuyper became Prime Minister and Minister of Internal Affairs. He was given a leave of absence from his post at the VU.[20] He also halted writing editorials for *De Staandard,* the newspaper he edited. He did, however, continue to write his meditations.

In the Queen's annual speech, written by Kuyper, she outlined what her government planned to do. She noted that the cabinet policy would be based on "Christian foundations of society."[21]

Even though he was enmeshed in politics, Kuyper still wrote for and was concerned for the church and for Christians. Typically, in 1900 he described three threats to church and society (three small foxes)—these were intellectualism, mysticism, and pragmatism. He identified these with three characteristics of being human: thinking (the head), feeling (the heart), and willing (the hand). The book was published in 1901, the year Kuyper took up the premiership.

Langley notes:

---

20. On the formation of the VU, Amsterdam see the next chapter. Kuyper was the professor of theology.

21. Cited in Langley, *The Practice of Political Spirituality,* 73.

At the beginning of December, the Prime Minister issued a note of clarification to Parliament. This note was a helpful articulation of the cabinet's Christian position then under attack by the opposition.

In this written document, Kuyper affirmed that there are two types of Christian principles: (1) theological principles in a more exclusive sense that deal with the doctrine of salvation and (2), political principles related to Christian norms for public affairs. This second type of Christian principle, affirming the necessary religious basis for public conduct, would be the concern of the Prime Minister and his cabinet. While the Christian political and social principles were related to theological concepts, they had a special place in the common grace aspect of life. The Prime Minister pointed out that while it was true that there were many self-confessed Christians even in secular parties, the controversy surrounding Christian political principles concerned the validity or irrelevance of God's Law and His normative authority for public life. In the Prime Minister's view, divine revelation has a definite bearing on state policy. He also expressed appreciation for the Christian Democratic parties which, unlike the class parties of the parliamentary Right and Left, embraced members from both the higher and lower classes.[22]

There was concern from the non-confessional parties about Kuyper's Christian faith and the impact upon the government's

---

22. Langley, *The Practice of Political Spirituality*, 74–75.

policies. Kuyper continually stressed that he spoke as a statesman not as a theologian. The opposition parties also tried to drive a wedge between the Calvinist ARP and the Roman Catholic party. Kuyper acknowledged that they were far apart theologically, and they had different views regarding the role of reason and faith. However, this was no different than the opposition parties who also had disagreements between themselves and that among humanistic rationalists there were many different definitions of reason! Ecclesiastical differences did not impact their political discussions.

For Kuyper, the basis for the gospel's implications for political life was not based on Left or Right but in the antithesis.[23] Kuyper was partisan, he was a Calvinist, but this meant he could have mutual respect for other perspectives, and that could result in a pluralist framework which could result in co-operation. He continually stressed that he was a Christian Democrat and not a theocrat. He wanted to work for public justice for both the upper and lower classes. Since his time in Beesd his heart was for the "Kleine Luyden."

Kuyper's program of political change included: educational reform; restraining immoral influences on society such as drunkenness, public indecency, pornography, and gambling; and dealing with the rapid change brought about by the industrial revolution.

Unfortunately, a few external factors prevented Kuyper from fulfilling his own political program. In 1903 the rail workers' strike threatened to become a general strike. This caused much national disruption. Kuyper admitted that it

---

23. On the antithesis see Part II.

caught the government unprepared. He, however, announced three bills. The first was for the creation of a national railroad brigade that could, if necessary, prevent such future strikes. The second was for the creation of a State Commission to investigate the present grievances of the railway workers. The third was for an investigation into possible criminal acts committed by the strikers.

The purpose of these acts was to protect the rights of all social groups, which for Kuyper was the main aim of government. Kuyper also underlined his belief in the importance and legitimacy of labor unions.

The passing of these acts meant that a general strike failed. Throughout Kuyper had emphasized that the conflict was not just about politics but stemmed from a clash of religious worldviews.

> Mr. Chairman, after listening to the twenty-five speakers who preceded me, I want to make a few concluding remarks. The recent discussion in this Chamber concerns the nature of law. But a basic difficulty arises when God is eliminated from law since legal certainty also vanishes. I know that many people have tried to find this certainty in the written law. But human codified law is in itself an insufficient basis for law. There must be a higher authority than written law; this is the question that is presently being debated. From the viewpoint of the Koran and the Jews, there is an absolute revelation of law which cannot be applied in new ways. On the other hand, under Christian leadership, law must be sought which is not inflexible, but which

can be applied according to differences in time, place and circumstance. In response to Troelstra and Marx, we Christians say that the standard for law is not found in men, but that the idea of law comes from God. But because man is created in God's image, he too, has an idea of the highest law that is universally valid as determined by God's control over the world. It has been asked why we also oppose the Liberals when the Socialists have caused the present danger. My response is that neither Anti-Revolutionaries nor Catholics will limit their struggle to merely opposing Social Democrats because in doing so they would lose their own distinctive principles. The great antithesis between Liberals and what they term "clericals" is that the Liberals ignore God's revelation. We derive revelation not only from the Holy Scriptures but also from nature and reason while recognizing that the defects of nature and reason must have the necessary corrective of Special Revelation.[24]

In his premiership Kuyper did manage to pass legislation that meant Christian schools could receive government subsidies (see chapter 9). The VU was granted the same status as their public universities — see the next section (chapter 24). He also prepared the way for legislation for the protection of women and young people in industry.

---

24. Cited in Langley, *The Practice of Political Spirituality*, 100.

8

Church Reformer (1883–1896)

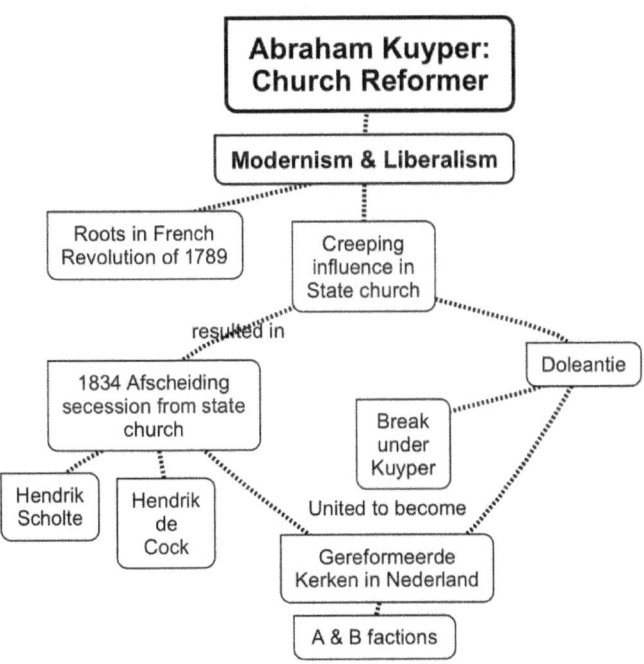

**Abraham Kuyper:
Church Reformer**

Modernism & Liberalism

Roots in French
Revolution of 1789

Creeping
influence in
State church

resulted in

1834 Afscheiding
secession from state
church

Doleantie

Break
under
Kuyper

Hendrik
Scholte

Hendrik
de
Cock

United to become

Gereformeerde
Kerken in Nederland

A & B factions

DUTCH CHURCH NAMES CAN at times be confusing—here is a list in roughly chronological order.[1]

---

1. Sources: C. Pronk, *A Godly Heritage: The Secession of 1834 and Its Impact on Reformed Churches in the Netherlands and North America*

As D. Van Keulen puts it: "The course of the theological rivers and streams in the GKN was not always peaceful."[2]

	Dutch Name	English Name	Founded	Description
NHK	Nederlands Hervormde Kerk	Dutch Reformed Church	1816	King William I imposes new church order 'Het Algemeen Regelement' (General Regulations)— Reformed church becomes NHK
CAGK	Christelijk Afgescheiden Gereformeerde Kerk	Christian Secession Reformed Church	1834	The *Afscheiding* (Secession) The CAGK was internally divided— it was not until the 1850s that one can speak of a properly functioning federation of churches
CGK	Gereformeerde Kerken onder het Kruis the Christelijke Gereformeerde Kerk in Nederland (=)	Reformed Churches under the Cross Christian Reformed Netherlands	1834	

(Grand Rapids, MI: Reformation Heritage Books. 2019); Karl Janssen, "Reformed Churches in the Netherlands: An Historical Overview," *Lux Mundi* 25, no.4 (2016): 89–94.

2. Dirk Van Keulen, "Theological Course of the Reformed Churches in the Netherlands," in *Vicissitudes of Reformed Theology in the Twentieth Century*, edited by George Harinck and Dirk van Keulen (Leiden: Brill, 2024), 88.

GG	Ledeboeriaanse Gemeenten = Gereformeerde Gemeenten onder het Kruis (later, the Gereformeerde Gemeenten)	Ledeboer Congregation Reformed Congregations under the Cross Reformed Congregations	1841	NHK suspend Lambertus Ledeboer (1808–1863) results in GG
NDGK	Nederduits Gereformeerde Kerken	.Nether-German Reformed Churches	1885	*Doleantie*—split under Kuyper
CGKN	Christelijke Gereformeerde Kerken Nederland	Christian Reformed Church in the Netherlands	1869	The merger of the Reformed Church under the Cross and the Separared Christian Congregations
GKN	Gereformeerde Kerken Nederland	The Reformed Churches in the Netherlands	1892	Merger of *Afscheiding* (CGK) secession of 1834 and (NDGK) Doleantie of 1886
GGNNA	Gereformeerde Gemeenten in Nederland en Noord-Amerika	Reformed Congregations in The Netherlands and North America. In North America called: Protestant Church in the Netherlands	1907	Under G.H. Kersten united a number of ".Cross-minded churches" that did not unite with the CAGK but continued as independent churches. They united with the more or less independently organized Ledeborianen
OGG	Oud (Old) Gereformeerde Gemeenten, Netherlands	Old Reformed Congregations	1907	Those that refused to join the GGNNA in 1907. Laurens Boone (1860–1935) unites another group of independent Ledeboeriaanse Gemeenten

	Federatie van Oud Gereformeerde Gemeenten	Federation of Old Reformed Congregations	1912	A group of independent Ledeboeriaanse Gemeenten unite
	Gereformeerde Kerken in Hersteld Verband		1926	Split from GKN —these are a more liberal wing
GKV	Gereformeerde Kerken Vrijgemaakt	Reformed Churches in the Netherlands (Liberated)	1944	Led by Klaas Schilder who was suspended by the GKN (Article 31 controversy)
GGN	Gereformeerde Gemeenten in Nederland	The Reformed Congregations in the Netherlands	1953	Founded when Cornelius Steenblok was dismissed from GG — affiliated with the North American Netherlands Reformed Congregations
PKN	Protestantse Kerk in Nederland .	Protestant Church in the Netherlands .	2004	Merger of GKN and NHK with Dutcuh Evangelical Lutheran Church (ELK)
GG u/tC	Gereformeerde Gemeenten under the Cross, Netherland .			
PKN	Protestantse Kerk in Nederland .	Protestant Church in the Netherlands .		Often referred to as the "Churches Cross" or "Cross —minded" (Kruisgezinden), and the Ledeboerianen (followers of L. G. C. Ledeboer)

NHK	Nederlands Hervormde Kerk	Reformed Church of the Netherlands		
HHK	Hersteld Hervormde Kerk (Restored Reformed Church), Netherlands			

Although Kuyper had resigned from the church pastoral ministry at Amsterdam when he took up politics, he remained an elder. Additionally, he was still concerned with the struggle for church reform. While he was a pastor in Utrecht, he and the Consistory had come into conflict with the church hierarchy over their refusal to respond to a questionnaire rather than be visited. They also refused, as previously mentioned, to recognize any baptism formula other than "in the name of the Father, Son, and Holy Spirit." They were holding out against the modernizing tendencies of the Synod.

Kuyper had become increasingly disillusioned by the creeping modernism and liberalism of the Dutch State Church. Kuyper had written regarding modernism in 1871. He saw one of the roots of modernism in the French Revolution.[3] He wrote: "… the French revolution also at its very core was really an effort of desperation to tear off God's bonds of holy ordination."[4] And:

> …something entirely different also happened in the French revolution. Namely that a totally different world and life perspective, which up to then had been

---

3. He called the French Revolution "de tweede zondeval" "the second fall." Cited in Deddens, "Editorial," *Sophie:* 2.

4. Kuyper, *God's Angels His Ministering Spirits* (Vancouver, BC, Friesen Press), Kindle loc 4425.

promoted only in the books of a few scholars began to assert itself against the Christian perspective of that in real life.[5]

It was an ongoing struggle. In 1834 the group that became known as the *Afscheiding*, which is Dutch for separation, seceded from the main state church the Nederlands Hervormde Kerk (Dutch Reformed Church) (NHK).

This secession was seen by the *Afscheiding* supporters not as a departure from the Reformed Church, but rather as preserving the Reformed Church against the reorganization imposed by the state. It can be seen as part of a revival that swept Europe.[6] The key leaders of the *Afscheiding* were Hendrik P. Scholte (1805–1868) and Hendrik de Cock (1801–1842). There was much persecution of the seceders including imprisonment and fines.

Fifty years later came another secession from the state church, this time led by Kuyper. This was known as The *Doleantie*, which is Dutch for grieving.[7]

For Kuyper and his followers, the *Doleantie* was a matter of the protection of orthodoxy. Not all, however, saw it that way. One, Revd Henstra, regarded the *Doleantie* as largely "a working out of the theories of Dr. Abraham Kuyper in his Tract."[8]

---

5. Kuyper, *God's Angels*, Kindle loc 4885.

6. The *Réveil*, which is French for awakening, started in 1819 in Geneva, Switzerland and rapidly spread around Europe.

7. It stems from Latin and is the same root word as the English doleful.

8. Cited in Theodore Plantinga, 1995. "The Dissenters of 1892," in *Secession, Doleantie and Union: 1834–1892*, ed. Hendrik Bouma (Pella, IO: Inheritance Publications, 1995), 214.

Cornelis Pronk poses a pertinent question: 'Why did Kuyper and his followers not join them [i.e. the Secession churches]?' Pronk suggests that it was because Kuyper

> believed the Secession was premature, "a fruit plucked too soon and sick in its core." This had to do with his view of the church. He did not agree with the Seceders, who considered the state-supported church to be a false and apostate church from which one had to withdraw according to articles 28 and 29 of the Belgic Confession. Rather, Kuyper saw the church as sick. He made a distinction between the hierarchical form of government of the church and the church itself. In his view, the Secession sinfully erred as it cut itself off from the true—albeit sick—church, the "mother of believers."[9]

Three years before the *Doleantie* Kuyper wrote the polemical *Tract of the Reformation of the Church*.[10] It was published to coincide with the 400th anniversary of Luther's birth. Kuyper wrote as a church pastor with a heart for the right functioning of the church. His concern was for a pure church. It was a program for church reformation. In it he argues for the separation of church and state. This text is the basis for a manual for Reformed church government. It paved the way for the *Doleantie* secession from the state church. On this see chapter 23.

In 1892, the *Afscheiding* and the *Doleantie* combined to form the Gereformeerde Kerken Nederland (GKN).

---

9. Cornelis Pronk, *A Godly Heritage: The Secession of 1834 and Its Impact on Reformed Churches in the Netherlands and North America.* Grand Rapids: Reformation Heritage Books, 2019), Kindle loc 7481.

10 In Kuyper, *On the Church.*

Not all agreed with the merger.[11] The main objections against the union were fivefold:

1. The congregations were not consulted.
2. The principles of the Secession and *Doleantie* are so contrary to each other that a union can lead only to conflict and endless confusion.
3. Not all *Doleantie* churches can be accepted as true Reformed churches.
4. The necessary love as a condition for this "marriage" is missing.
5. Leaders of the *Doleantie* churches have taught things about regeneration and baptism that cannot be acknowledged as Reformed.[12]

These objections were discussed at the 1892 synod and the proposal to unite was passed almost unanimously. However, three congregations took the decision to remain as the Christian Reformed Church — eventually other congregations disillusioned with the union rejoined. The church is now known as the Christelijke Gereformeerde Kerken in Nederland (CGKN), the sister churches of the Free Reformed Churches of North America.

Although the *Afscheiding* and the *Doleantie* united, there were still tensions between the two groups, so much so that the designation A and B were used to show which grouping they had previously been aligned with.

---

11. For some of the debates see Cornelis Van Dam, ed., *The Challenges of Church Union: Speeches and Discussions on Reformed Identity and Ecumenicity* (Winnipeg: Premier Publishing, 1993).

12. Pronk, *A Godly Heritage*, kindle loc. 7491.

Eventually, this led some to react against Kuyper's teachings on common grace and presumptive regeneration. These they maintained were at odds with orthodox Reformed doctrine.

In 1905 at Utrecht a session was held to attempt a compromise between the A and B factions, however, it resulted only in an uneasy truce. This truce lasted for three decades but after the Second World War the disagreements re-surfaced, with the result that several, mainly A congregations, separated under the leadership of Klaas Schilder (1890–1952)[13] and Seakle Greijdanus (1871–1948) to form what became known as the Liberated Churches.

---

13. On Schilder see Henry Vander Kam, *Schilder: Preserver of the Faith* (New York: Vantage Press, 1996). On Schilder and the Liberated Church see, R. van Reest, *Schilder's Struggle for the Unity of the Church* (Neerlandia, AB: Inheritance Publications, 1990). Several works by Schilder have been translated in Klaas Schilder, *The Klaas Schilder Reader: The Essential Theological Writings*, ed. G. Harinck, M. De Jong, and R. Mouw (Bellingham, WA: Lexham Press, 2022).

9

Education[1]

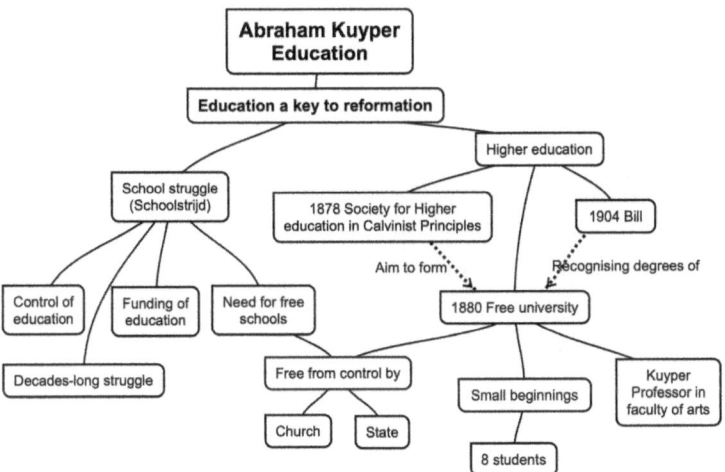

KUYPER WAS AN INSPIRED organizer and a born agitator—
traits that Groen van Prinsterer lacked.[2] Groen recognized this
and stood aside for Kuyper to take the lead. Kuyper took over

---

1. On Kuyper and education see also chapter 25 in Part IV—there is
   inevitably some overlap with this section.

2. A. Th. van Deursen, *The Distinctive Character of the Free University
   in Amsterdam 1880–2005. A Commemorative History* (Grand Rapids:
   Eerdmans, 2018), 3.

from his mentor as the leader of the Ani-Revolutionaries (ARP) and formed it into the first political party in the Netherlands. Kuyper also saw the need for communication and the mobilizing of the people. This he did by taking over editorship of the *De Heraut* and by starting his own daily newspaper, *De Standaard*, for which he was the editor-in-chief. The ARP and the newspapers became the tools for agitation and communication among the Reformed peoples in the Netherlands. Kuyper's aim was to redeem and transform society and to do that he realized education was a key to achieve this and one means of education was newspapers. He took seriously his journalism. In 1910 he established an association of Christian Press. As Snel affirms: "For Dutch journalists around 1900, it was not a question of who the leading journalist of their generation was: that was Kuyper."[3]

As previously mentioned, Kuyper had always had an interest in newspapers. In his speech, delivered during his twenty-fifth anniversary as editor-in-chief of *De Standaard*, the jubilee, Abraham Kuyper, said:

> I have read and loved newspapers since I was a young lad. My dear father disapproved of my infatuation – that I was hooked on the daily paper already as a boy of ten or eleven – and finally forbade me to stick my nose in the paper again. But my passion for journalism was so strong then already that whenever I was able to get my hands on a newspaper (though I should not have,

---

3. "Voor Nederlandse journalisten rond 1900 was het niet de vraag wie de leidende journalist van hun generatie was: dat was Kuyper." Johan Snel, "Kuyper als Journalist" *Sophie (Special Abraham Kuyper)* (February 2021): 4.

because doing so was disobedient), I would sneak it into the attic and there I would sit as a young boy, on a packing box, reading the *Opregte Haarlemmer*.[4]

The school struggle (*Schoolstrijd*), as it became known, was the fight for parents, and not the state, to control the education of their own children. The ARP's policy was that "the government should not be operating schools as a rule but only by way of exception." The motto of the ARP was "Free schools the norm, State schools a supplement." It was a struggle that was to last for decades and one that Kuyper soon realized was to require political change. It was one of the catalysts for Kuyper's venture into politics.

Kuyper became a member of parliament in 1874 when he won the seat in Gouda, he then resigned from his church ministry post. His first political speech in the lower house of Parliament was on the state control of education.[5] This shows the importance Kuyper placed on the school issue and on education.

There he argued regarding the role of education:

Education is a distinct public interest. Education touches on one of the most complicated and intricate questions, one that involves every issue, including the deepest issues that invite humanity's search for knowledge—issues of anthropology and psychology, religion and sociology, pedagogy and morality, in short,

---

4. Kuyper, *On Charity & Justice*, 239. The remarks were made at the celebration of twenty-five-year anniversary as editor-in-chief of *De Standaard*.

5. Ideas for a National Education System Speeches as a Member of Parliament, December 7 and 8, 1874. It was translated and published in Kuyper, *On Education*, 139–163.

issues that encroach on every branch of social life. Now it seems to me that such an element of cultural life has the right in every respect to an absolutely independent organization; always in the sense that education should function in the spirit of what the British call a body corporate.[6]

Several years before becoming a member of parliament, in 1869, he addressed the Society for Christian National Education where he argued for the freedom of Christian parents to control the education of their children.

It was in 1875 that discussions began regarding an explicitly Christian University. For Kuyper Christian education concerned both school and university. He fought for both over several decades.

Unfortunately, in 1876 Kuyper suffered another nervous breakdown—possibly brought upon by over exertion—he once again went abroad to recuperate. In 1877 he returned to the Netherlands and in 1878 The Society for Higher Education in Calvinist Principles was established at Utrecht, with the aim of forming the Free University in Amsterdam.[7]

During the election year of 1879 Kuyper asserted that the Jan Kappeyne Van de Coppello's Liberal government had failed on two counts: equality and education. In terms of equality, they had failed to widen the vote and in terms of the freedom of education they maintained that Christian parents pay dou-

---

6. Kuyper, *On Education*, 142

7. The "free" in the Free University meant that it would be free from state and church involvement, but also free to practice scholarship on the basis of a Christian worldview.

ble to send their children to Christian schools.[8] The ARP's key campaigns focused on the need for the widening of the vote, their opposition to Kappenye's bill, and that the party should be independent of other political groups.

As previously mentioned, one of the main reasons that Kuyper went into politics was the education issue. His concern was for fairness and justice. He wanted freedom for parents to be able to choose the school based on their religious beliefs and for equality between state and non-state funded schools and universities. In a speech in February 1904, he emphasized: "There can only be talk of fairness and justice, when every principled viewpoint is represented not merely in one academic discipline but in all of them with complete equality!"[9]

Kuyper proposed a Higher Education Bill. There were several objections to the Bill, the aim of which was to provide equality between state and non-state funded higher educational institutions.

The bill however was passed on 24 March 1904. It was subsequently rejected by the First Chamber (the Dutch equivalent to the British House of Lord's). Kuyper asked Queen Wilhelmina to dissolve the First Chamber, she did and after the elections the bill was passed by the Chamber. This bill provided the legal basis for the Free University (VU Amsterdam), which was founded in 1880 and meant that the degrees they awarded were officially recognized.

The Free University (VU University Amsterdam)
The Free University had small beginnings. There were eight students in the first year, almost as many as the professors. They

8. Langley, *Political Spirituality*,16–17.

9. Kuyper, *On Education*, 142.

had to hold a Reformed theological position, which was also to shape their lecturing and research.[10]

Kuyper was a professor of theology until 1901, there were two other professors in the theological faculty, F. L. Rutgers (1836–1917) and Philippus Jacobus Hoedemaker (1839–1910). Hoedemaker resigned his post after the *Doleantie*. He disagreed with Kuyper and Lohman over the separation of church and state. He later joined the Dutch Reformed Church (the NHK), the state church. The three other lecturers were J. Wolter (1849–1817), a classicist, D. P. D. Fabius (1851–1931), a legal scholar, and F. W. J. Dilloo (1841–1892).

In 1881 Kuyper also became a professor in the faculty of arts. He lectured on linguistics, literature, and aesthetics. He lectured on the Dutch language and literature from 1883–1901.

Kuyper also taught homiletics, the art of preaching. Vanden Berg explains part of the process the students had to go through. It is worth quoting him at some length:

> To Kuyper the sermon was something alive, a power; it was vital, living preaching of the Word, the cardinal means to deepen and to enrich the life of the church. Through the years he impressed on the aspiring clergymen that preaching is to lay the full Word of God before the soul of the church. He imbued them with that conviction of his. That thought received his full emphasis. This followed naturally from his exalted conception of the gospel ministry and of preaching. The sermon must possess unity. The preacher must himself be stirred

---

10. Kuyper, *On Education*, 92.

without guiltily surrendering to sentimentality. There must be close spiritual rapport between him and his listeners. These were Kuyper's general principles of preaching.

Then, too, there were the inevitable practice sessions. A nightmarish feeling crept over the seminarian who saw his "turn" coming up within a short time. On a certain day Kuyper would give the young man a Scripture text and tell him to come to the Kuyper residence at two o'clock on a Sunday afternoon about a week or ten days later to submit his quite detailed sermon outline. At that hour the aspiring theologian called, was ushered into Kuyper's study, and handed the professor his outline. Kuyper would read it with complete concentration for perhaps ten minutes, then hand it back with his criticism, which was in nine cases out of ten everything except flattering. The student now returned to his lodgings in a more or less dejected state of mind to revise his outline, reckoning, of course, with the professorial comments, and complete his sermon. And he had to memorize his discourse. Under no circumstances would Kuyper permit him to read it. He must also deliver it as if he were facing an actual congregation.

On a Saturday afternoon about three weeks later came the practice session. When the seminarians were in a lighter mood and talked among themselves, they called those sessions "preaching for Bram." In not so jocular moments, they had a more realistic name for them — "the homiletic torture chamber." The student "preached his sermon." Two fellow seminarians, appointed in advance, gave their oral estimate of the effort. Then Kuyper gave the closing criticism, which, for the "preacher" of the day, was rarely encouraging and sometimes almost merciless.

The reason Kuyper demanded such a high standard in student sermons was his exalted conception of the ministry and of preaching. He wanted the sermon to be not a cold, intellectual discussion but a living ministry of the Word, a bearer of the Gospel, of the power of God unto salvation to him who believes. The students took Kuyper's severe criticisms to heart and did not think of protesting against such a method. From a professor of ordinary format they perhaps would not have "taken" such treatment. From Kuyper they did. Why? Because, although it brought them now and then a discouraging hour, they felt in their hearts that he was right. They realized in their own minds that it must be as he wanted it to be.[11]

It was not until 1883 that the Free University purchased its first building, Keizersgracht 162—it was opened in 1885. Previously, they had used rooms in an attic of a missionary church ran by the Free Church of Scotland of Amsterdam.

The school struggle (*Schoolstrijd*)

The school struggle was a decades-long fight for parents to educate their children as they saw fit in schools that promoted the same worldview as their parents.

The constitution of 1806 needed public schools to teach "Christian and social virtues." However, all this meant was that a form of deism was promoted. The Bible was eventually removed from the classrooms as it was thought to be offensive to

---

11. Vanden Berg, *Abraham Kuyper*, 105–106.

Jews, Muslims, and secularists. The 1834 secession churches wanted the Bible to be central to schooling.

Several schools were founded but were closed down by government authorities. This was one of the reasons for many emigrating to North America in the 1840s. In 1848 things eased by 1850 there were 13 Christian schools. Running the schools proved too expensive in terms of time and money.

The struggle came to a head when successive governments seemed to be doing what they could to dissuade the setting up of private schools, including Christian schools. J. R. Thornbeke's government's Freedom of Education Act in 1848 meant that private schools had to meet the standards of state schools, but without any state funding. The motivation behind these changes was to promote civic morality in the hope it would solidify national unity.

Groen was opposed to these changes, in 1869, at a meeting of the Association of Christian National School Education Kuyper gave the opening address. Kuyper took up Groen's mantle and became heavily involved in the school struggle.

1878 was a key year. The liberal Kappeyne Van de Coppello's government proposed a bill that would improve schools and school buildings, however, there was no money for private Christian schools—they were being priced out of existence. Kuyper was involved in the organization of a People's petition to oppose the bill. It was organized through *De Standaard* and in conjunction with the Roman Catholic Herman Schaepman (1844–1903)—Jellema notes that within five days 305 000 Calvinists and 164 000 Catholics had signed it. It was presented to King Willem III.[12] However, the king signed the bill anyway—there was nothing he could do about it constitutionally.

The petition marked the birth of a new movement. A movement to establish for free Christian schools the same rights as public school. It showed that Calvinist and Catholics had common cause and could therefore work together in politics. Kuyper, Lohman, and Schaepman came together in a coalition. The coalition between the Roman Catholics and the Calvinists enabled them to win the majority of seats in the Second Chamber.

In 1888 the Catholic–Calvinist coalition won 52 of the 100 seats and the ARP Baron Aeneas Mackay (1838–1909) was named prime minister. The MacKay government lasted from 1888 to 1891. Several measures were passed that provided subsidies for schools. It was not enough for Kuyper. Kuyper became increasingly unhappy with Lohman and MacKay—they were too conservative, and Lohman was too liberal for Kuyper, Kuyper thought he was too much of the "*Réveil* rather than a true Calvinist."[13] Eventually, Lohman left the ARP and formed his own party, the Free Anti-Revolutionary Party in 1898; it later became the Christian Historical Union.[14] The break came over the suffrage question—Kuyper wanted to extend it, Lohman and the right wing of the ARP did not.

---

12. Dirk W. Jellema, "Abraham Kuyper's Attack on Liberalism," *The Review of Politics* 19, no. 4 (1957), 475.

13. Jellema, "Abraham Kuyper's Attack on Liberalism," 477.

14. This was formed with the merger of the Free Anti-Revolutionary Party and the Christian Historical Voters' League.

In 1901 the Coalition won again this time with 58 out of the 100 seats. Kuyper became prime minister (from 1901 to 1905).

10

North America and
The Stone Lectures

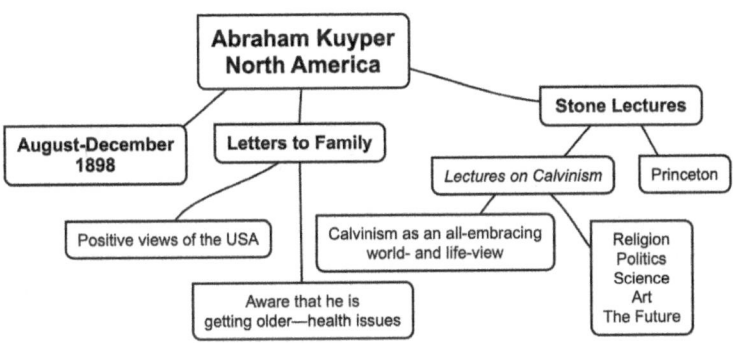

KUYPER HAD GREAT REGARD for North America. He visited America in 1898 to deliver the Stone lectures and receive an honorary doctorate from Princeton. Peter Heslam[1] has looked in detail at the background of the lectures and his visit.

Kuyper left for America on 11 August and sailed from Liverpool on 20 August on the RMS Lucania; he arrived in New York City on 27 August.

---

1. Peter Heslam, *Creating a Christian Worldview* (Carlisle: Paternoster, 1998).

During his time in the States, he visited Boston, Detroit, Grand Rapids, Chicago, Pella, Des Moines, Niagara Falls, New Brunswick, Baltimore, Washington, DC, Hartford as well as Princeton and New York. He left the States on 10 December and arrived back in the Netherlands on 30 December stopping off at Boulogne, London, Paris, and Brussels.

Kuyper wrote to his family during his time away—these letters have been translated and published in *Kuyper in America*.[2] There we have Kuyper's thoughts and feelings during that four-month stay. The letters provide valuable insight into his views of America and into his own thoughts and feelings. He experienced the loneliness that arose from the separation from his family. Several of the letters start with how upset he feels at the lack of letters from them: "That was quite a disappointment this week not to hear anything from home"[3] and "I still have not received a word from home whilst in America."[4]

Many times Kuyper writes positively about the United States, although he does not seem enamored of most of the food! We are also given glimpses into the state of his health. He continually reminds his family that he is getting older—he turned 61 during the trip—and that his health is not what it used to be; we have numerous mentions of his dental problems, his diarrhoea (he is that open!) and how he is coping (or not) with the unusual September heatwave.

---

2. Abraham Kuyper, *Kuyper in America* (Sioux Center: Dordt Press, 2013).

3. Kuyper, *Kuyper in America*, 19, letter 5.

4. Kuyper, *Kuyper in America*, 22, letter 6.

He delivered his Stone Lectures in English, and these were later published as *Lectures on Calvinism*. They have been published in numerous editions. For many, this was the first introduction to Kuyper. The individual lectures were on a wide range of topics and focused on Calvinism as a life system or a worldview rather than a tight theological system. The topics he covered—each taking up one lecture—were: Religion, Politics, Science, Art, and The Future. Some of the topics may seem surprising, but they were chosen to show how Calvinism was an all-embracing worldview—they were examples of his square inch approach. Calvinism was not to be restricted to theological issues, as important as they are, but was to shape, inform and develop all areas of life. Some of these ideas will be examined in parts 2 and 3.

11

The Mediterranean Tour

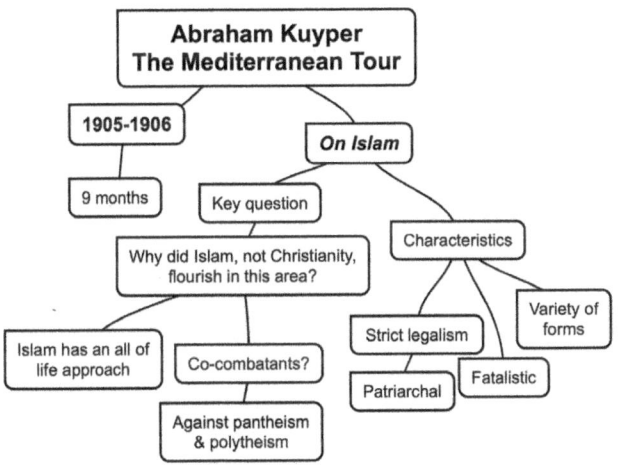

KUYPER WAS DEFEATED IN the 1905 election and had to make way for a more liberal government. The socialists in the coalition group were unhappy with Kuyper's dealings with the railroad strike of 1903. Both the liberals and the socialists campaigned against "Abraham the Terrible."[1] To overcome

---

1. Dirk Jellema, "Abraham Kuyper's Attack on Liberalism," 478.

the sense of defeat, he took time out to travel around the Mediterranean Sea.

Kuyper's had become well known abroad. So much so that everywhere he visited, he was well received and enjoyed almost universal appreciation. He recorded his thoughts during his travels in articles that later became a book; parts of which have been translated and published in *On Islam*.[2]

The journey took him almost nine months. The area was the birthplace of European civilization and was an interface between East and West, and between Asia and Europe. In the book published after his travels he discusses a wide range of issues including Asia's rising nationalism, the issues surrounding Zionism and the mystery of Islam. The only time he broke his tour was to return to the Netherlands in 1906 to deliver a speech on the 150th anniversary of the poet Willem Bilderdijk (1756–1831).

On Islam is partly autobiography, partly travel diaries, partly sociological observations, partly cultural anthropology, and partly political musings. What is most remarkable is the descriptions and observations of this mainly Muslim area. It provides insight into early twentieth-century Islam. This is a complex landscape, not only religiously but also geographically, culturally, and politically.

Kuyper was seeking in his travels to explore the enigma that was Islam. One crucial question he examines is why has Islam flourished but Christianity faded in this area? Kuyper saw much of value in Islam:

> ...it is seriously mistaken to imagine for even a moment that the spiritual patrons of Buddhism, Confucianism, and Shintoism are men without knowledge,

---

2. Originally published in Dutch as *Om de oude wereldzee* [Around the Ancient World Sea] in 1907.

Kuyper in 1905.

insight, and willpower. Their learning may be different,
but their critical faculties are no smaller than ours.[3]

In particular, he seems to appreciate its all-of-life approach and
the commitment it endears among its followers. As he puts it:

---

3. Abraham Kuyper, *On Islam*, ed. James D. Bratt with Douglas A.
    Howard, trans. Jan van Vliet (Washington, WA: Lexham Press, 2018), Ch 1.

> Muslims do not have separate social, religious, and po-
> litical spheres; rather, all of life is bound together in one
> Qur'anic sphere, and this life relies on personal love for
> a living tradition.[4]

At times he seems optimistic about collaboration: "we cannot exclude the possibility that [Moslems] will ultimately join us in the battle against pantheism and polytheism." However, he notes that "it is enough to observe that the strict legalistic and regulated character of Islamic ritual leads to little more than a shallow deism." He also identifies with some followers, such as the Sufi, a yearning for mysticism: "This inner movement in the life of the soul arose from three factors: world-aversive asceticism, mystical inwardness, and pantheism's thought-system."[5]

He notes the patriarchal and sometimes oppressive nature of Islam towards women: "In Islam the female is merely incidental. She is no more than a footnote to the male and, ideally, is denied any independent existence."[6]

However, he finds that the Christianity of the area has succumbed to cultural and Islamic pressures. This is particularly true in the treatment of women, for example:

> Even in a Christian church I found women considered
> just as inferior as in a mosque. The imitation goes so far
> as the use of prayer rugs in the church the same as you
> would find in a mosque. The spiritual maturity of the
> Christian folk of Asia Minor is minimal.

---

4   Kuyper, *On Islam*, Ch 1.

5. Kuyper, *On Islam*, Ch 2.

6. Kuyper, *On Islam*, Ch 2..

...the position of the woman in Christian families follows the Turkish manner and remains downtrodden. They have been unable to maintain the much higher Christian perception of women. Even in Christian families the husband eats alone at the table and is served by his wife who sits down with the remaining female staff and the children only when her husband is finished.[7]

The Islamic world that Kuyper travelled in displayed a great variety of forms — there is not one such monolithic religion that is Islam. He identifies a number of different "differentiated sects": "one finds—besides the Sunnis—Shiites, Ismailis, Nosairis, Ansaris, Mutawilés, Druze, and Yazidis or Satan worshipers."[8]

In essence, he identifies two apparently contradictory tenets of Islam, their "fatalism and their obligation to promote the faith by the sword." Interestingly he notes that "At the moment Muslims are still in a state of political despondency, so courtesy and kindness can soften their mood considerably."

---

7. Kuyper, *On Islam,* ch 2.
8. Kuyper, *On Islam,* ch 4.

12

His Final Years

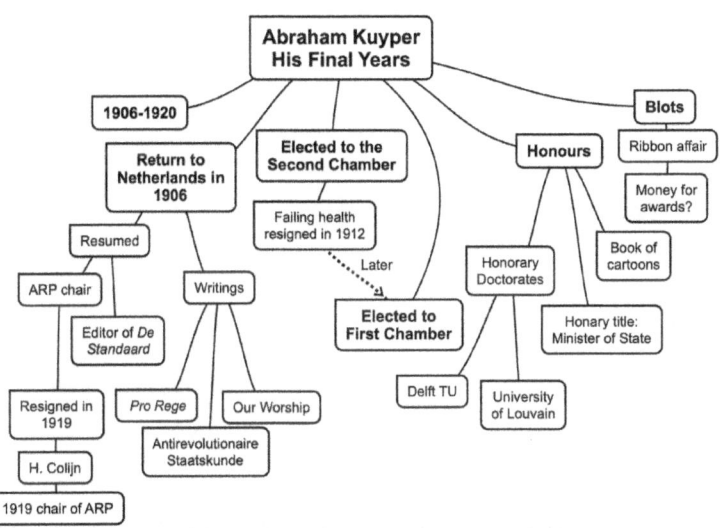

KUYPER RETURNED TO THE Netherlands in 1906 after his Mediterranean tour. He still held political ambitions. However, when the Liberal government of De Meeter fell Kuyper's desire to form the next government was frustrated when Theodorus [Theo] Heemskerk (1852– 1932) of the ARP was asked to form the new government. Heemskerk was PM from 1908 to 1913. This caused some animosity between Kuyper and Heemskerk.

Kuyper felt he should have been PM. Kuyper, however, continued to be active in politics.

A few months later—because of a vacancy—Kuyper was elected in the Ommen district to the Second Chamber; he was not, however, offered a place in Heemskerk's cabinet. His failing health and hearing meant that in 1912 Kuyper had reluctantly to resign his seat for Ommen. It seemed his political career was over. However, in July 1913 South Holland Province elected him to the First Chamber.

During this time Kuyper got the know Hendrikus "Hendrik" Colijn (1869–1944). He suggested that the ARP nominate Colijn for a seat in the Second Chamber. Colijn was successfully elected by the Sneek district. Colijn eventually went on to become the leader of the ARP and editor of *De Standaard.*

In 1907, Kuyper once again took over from Herman Bavinck as the chair of the ARP.[1] He also resumed the editorship of *De Heraut.* Throughout this time as the premier he continued to write his meditations but now also began again writing the editorials. He also concentrated on writing *Pro Rege;* this took him from 1911 to 1918 when it was first published in Dutch.

He also published during this time *Onze Eeredienst*[2]—it began as a series of articles in 1897 and was finally published in 1911. This book developed Kuyper's ideas of liturgy and worship within the institutional church. It shows, contrary to what some have suggested, Kuyper's continued interest in the

1. Bavinck took over from Kuyper as chair of the ARP in 1905.
2. Translated as *Our Worship*, ed. Harry Boonstra (Grand Rapids: Eerdmans, 2009.02)

Albert Hahn's "Abraham de Geweldige" cartoon

institutional church. It was one of the last major works Kuyper produced.

In 1908 he was awarded the honorary title of Minister of State bestowed on Queen Wilhelmina's birthday and was awarded an honorary doctorate by Delft Technological University. He received another honorary doctorate in

1909 from the Catholic University of Louvain, Belgium. In 1913 he was made a commander in the Order of the Netherlands Lion, the oldest and highest civilian order of chivalry in the Netherlands.

1909 saw a book of cartoons on Kuyper another was published several years later that contained Albert Hahn's iconic cartoon "Abraham the Great."

He completed his final book, *Antirevolutionaire Staatskunde*[3] in 1917. This was the second volume, the first of which appeared in 1916. The first volume dealt with the principles and the second dealt with the practical application.

In 1916, the 2000th issue of *De Heraut* was published. As mentioned before Kuyper wrote over 2000 meditations for it. These were obviously important to Kuyper as he continued to write these even when he was prime minister. He wrote many of them on Sunday mornings often instead of going to a church service.[4] Many of these were first published in English in 1918 as the book *Draw Near Unto God*.

By 1913, there were signs of impending war. The Netherlands was neutral when war broke out. Kuyper sided with the Germans in WWI. It was more an anti-British rather than a pro-German stance; he opposed the British ever since the Anglo–Boer War (1888–1902).

By 1915 many were becoming uncomfortable with Kuyper's dogmatic leadership of the ARP. This prompted Herman Bavinck and four others to write *Leader and Leadership in*

---

3. In English the title was Anti-Revolutionary Political Theory. It had the subtitle With a Further Explanation of Our Program.

4. On Kuyper's (lack of) church attendance see http://stevebishop.blog spot.com/2024/12/kuypers-lack-of-sunday-church.html.

the Anti-Revolutionary Party.[5] This called for a restructuring of the party to reduce the party's dependence on Kuyper.

During his twilight years, he still continued to be involved with the ARP. He did not resign his position as party leader until 1919. In 1909 he delivered an address on the 400th anniversary of the birth of Calvin at the ARP's 17th national convention. The opening speech was "Wij, Calvinisten" [We, Calvinists]. He stressed that the antithesis was the bedrock of the coalition between Protestants and Roman Catholics. He also stressed the importance of Calvin for the ARP:[6] "For those others, Calvin is a fossil from history, but for us his spirit is still alive."[7]

The ribbon affair (*Lintjes Affair*) was something of a blot on Kuyper's reputation. In 1903 Kuyper awarded an Amsterdam businessman, Rudolph Lehman, the officer's cross of the Order of Orange-Nassau. Later that year Lehman gave 11 000 gilders to the ARP. Kuyper was accused of granting the decoration in return for money. In 1909 when it came to light the opposition attempted to make political capital of this. Kuyper acknowledged that he had not acted with discretion, and he regretted it. It was, however, blown up out of all proportions. It did, however, tarnish somewhat Kuyper's name. It shows that all make mistakes and are prone to errors of judgment. Kuyper later said: "Even though sackcloth disgraces not the man, I may have sinned against the standards of due caution and wise policy."[8]

---

5.   The five were Anne Anema, Herman Bavinck, Pieter Arie Diepenhorst, Theodorus Heemskerk, and Simon de Vries.

6.   This was also the occasion of the 400th anniversary of the birth of Calvin.

7.   Kuyper, "Wij, Calvisten."

8.   Jan de Bruin, *Het Boetekleed Ontsiert de Man Niet: Abraham Kuijper en de Lintjesaffaire* (1909–1910) (Uitgeverij Prometheus, 2005).

Kuyper's health continued to deteriorate, but it was not until 1912 that he finally left the Second Chamber. This was also the year of the 40th anniversary of *De Standaard*. In 1913, he was once again elected to the First Chamber where he remained until his death. During this time, he lived in the Kanaalstraat, now named Dr Kuyperstraat, in The Hague.

Kuyper continued to give talks and speeches, including those to the ARP (1913, 1917, 1918), to the Confederation of Reformed Young Men (1913), and to the Eudokia Institute in Rotterdam (1915). Several of his works were also published including in 1918 *To Be Nearer Unto God* translated by J. H. De Vries.

He also published a number of works including *In The Woman's Position of Honour* (1914), compiled from articles concerning women's emancipation and suffrage originally published in *De Standaard*.

Two of Kuyper's daughters wrote (in Dutch) of their father's "sunset" years—from New Year's Eve 1917 onwards.[9] In January 1917 he suffered from influenza and bronchitis which led to "lung fever." This sickness took a great toll on him, and he never fully recovered to full health.

His close friends Jan Woltjer (1849–1917) and F. L. Rutgers (1836–1917), professors at the VU Amsterdam both died in 1917, this too had a detrimental effect on Kuyper's health.

---

9. H. S. S. Kuyper and J. H. Kuyper, *De levensavond van Dr. A. Kuyper* (Kampen: J.H. Kok, 1921). See the summary and review in Henry Beets, "The Calvinism of Dr. A. Kuyper—Two Publications of Loving Tribute to Dr. A. Kuyper. [Parts 1–4]," *Banner* 56 (February 1921): 69, 100–101; (March 1921): 164–165; (April 1921), 229.

In 1919 he gave up the ARP party chair. Colijn was elected chair in his place. He continued, however, to edit and write for *De Standaard* and *De Heraut*. He then handed over his editorial duties for *De Standaard* later that year to a committee comprising Colijn, A. W. F. Idenburg, A. Anema, J. Schouten, J. A. de Wilde, and A. Zijlstra. In 1922 Colijn took up the editorship. Kuyper still had his seat in the First Chamber; he held that up until 21 September 1920 when he finally tended his letter of resignation.

On Sunday 1 February 1920 he suffered a stroke while taking a walk. Beets summarizes Kuyper's daughters' reminiscences:

> But slowly on there was a hearty submission to God's
> will, bringing peace to his mind, and a quiet desire that
> the Lord might take him away (p. 93). He became as a
> weaned child (p. 100).[10]

His poor health meant that he became bed-ridden. Above his bed was a painting depicting the crucifixion, which he bought when he was a student. He died in the Hague on 8 November 1920 surrounded by his family and his friend A. W. F. Idenburg (1861–1935), a previous governor of the Dutch East indies.[11]

He was buried in the cemetery Oud Eik en Duinen. His funeral was a national and public event.[12] It was estimated that

---

10. Henry Beets, "The Calvinism of Dr. A. Kuyper".

11. On Idenburg, see P. Holtrop, "The Governor a Missionary? Dutch Colonial Rule and Christianization during Idenburg's Term of Office as Governor of Indonesiaw (1909–16)," *Studies in Church History. Subsidia*, 13 (2000): 142–156. doi:10.1017/S0143045900002830.

12. A short video clip of it is available on YouTube. https://www.youtube.com/watch?v=kC5_TZMuKUM and https://www.youtube.com/watch?v=nn5auO1Iy-s (date of access 3 February 2024).

there were 20–30 000 people who lined the streets at his funeral and approximately 10 000 people in the churchyard, such was the respect the Dutch had for him. His legacy lives on.

13

Kuyper's Children

MOST BIOGRAPHIES OF KUYPER provide little material on Kuyper's family and his family life. Vanden Berg notes:

> Kuyper's domestic life was a happy one. The spirit of Christ pervaded the home, Mrs. Kuyper was an understanding wife and devoted mother. With her husband, she trained their children well. She was a capable household manager, a warm-hearted, gracious hostess, a cultured lady who spoke the modern languages especially English) fluently. She stood beside and with Kuyper as an inestimable blessing in his life and work. Five sons and three daughters were born to the Kuypers. Of the sons, one died in 1892 at the age of nine years.
>
> Except at luncheon and at dinner, Kuyper had few hours he could give to his family in close companionship. On festive occasions, however, he laid all else aside to spend the evening in the family circle. Dinner, especially, was the time of joyous family life, even when guests were present, as they frequently were.

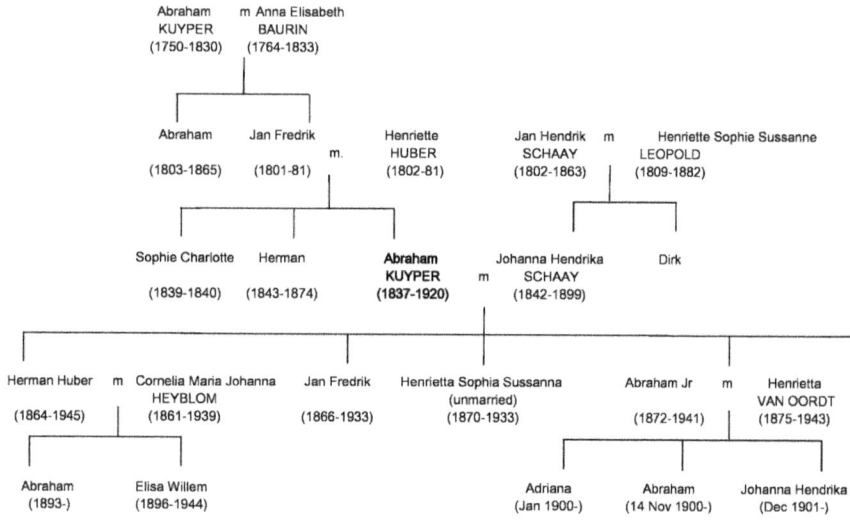

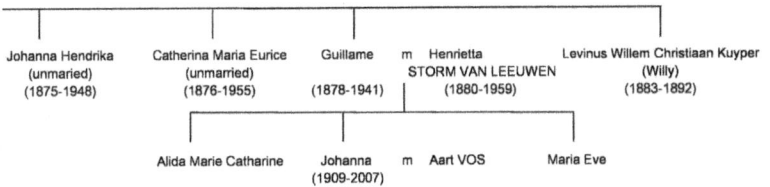

Johanna Hendrika (unmaried) (1875-1948)

Catherina Maria Eurice (unmarried) (1876-1955)

Guillame (1878-1941)

m   Henrietta STORM VAN LEEUWEN (1880-1959)

Levinus Willem Christiaan Kuyper (Willy) (1883-1892)

Alida Marie Catharine

Johanna (1909-2007)

m   Aart VOS

Maria Eve

Kuyper's seventieth birthday photograph

Sitting from left to right: Henriëtte S. S. Kuyper, C. M. J. Kuyper-Heyblom (wife of H. H. Kuyper), C. M. E. (Cato) Kuyper. Standing from left to right: J. H. (Jo) Kuyper, Abraham Kuyper (son of H. H. Kuyper), Adriana Kuyper (daughter of A. Kuyper Jr.), Guillaume Kuyper, Abraham Kuyper, Willem Kuyper (son of H. H. Kuyper), H. H. Kuyper, Abraham Kuyper Jr., and his wife, the writer H. Kuyper-van Oordt.

And in the Kuyper household, the family altar was still held in honor.

With his wife and children in the family living room, Kuyper was all life and joy. At luncheon and dinner, too. Whoever saw him at such times received the impression that he was a man not plagued by cares and difficulties. Seeing him so, one did not surmise what a tremendous load he was carrying. He bore that load not downstairs but up in his study.[1]

---

1. Vanden Berg, *Abraham Kuyper*, 178–179.

He had five sons and three daughters. None of Kuyper's daughters married. Perhaps no one was able to live up to their father's expectations?

Although Kuyper had a high view of the family, practice did not often marry theory. Two of his daughters Henriette and Johanna, in *De levensavond van Dr. A. Kuyper* [The Last Days of Dr A. Kuyper], wrote: "From my earliest childhood I had to learn that my Father belonged primarily to his vocation for the Dutch people, and secondarily to his family."[2]

Herman Huber [H. H.] Kuyper (1864–1945)

Herman, Abraham Kuyper's eldest son, was born in Beesd on 22 July 1864. He studied theology at the VU in 1863 and was later appointed professor of theology at the VU in 1899. He taught the ecclesiastical history of Holland and the encyclopedia of theology. When F. L. Rutgers retired, he also taught church polity.

He wrote *De post-acta of nahandelingen van de Nationale Synode von Dordrecht in 1618 en 1619 gehouden* (Amsterdam: Höveker & Wormser, 1899).

He was evacuated from Arnhem in 1945 and died at Groningen in 1945.

He wrote several articles in *De Heraut* that were perceived to be "Nazi friendly."[3] He thought, in the spirit of

---

2. H. S. S. Kuyper and J. H. Kuyper, *De levensavond van Dr. A. Kuyper* (Kampen: J.H. Kok, 1921), 7. The original reads: "Van mijn vroegste jeugd heb ik moeten leeren, dat mijn Vader in de eerste plaats aanzijn levensroeping voor Neerlands volk en eerst in de tweede plaats aan zijn gezin toebehoorde."

3. Ron Gleason, *Herman Bavinck: Pastor, Churchman, Statesman, and Theologian* (Presbyterian & Reformed, 2010), 333.

Herman Huber Kuyper (1864–1945)

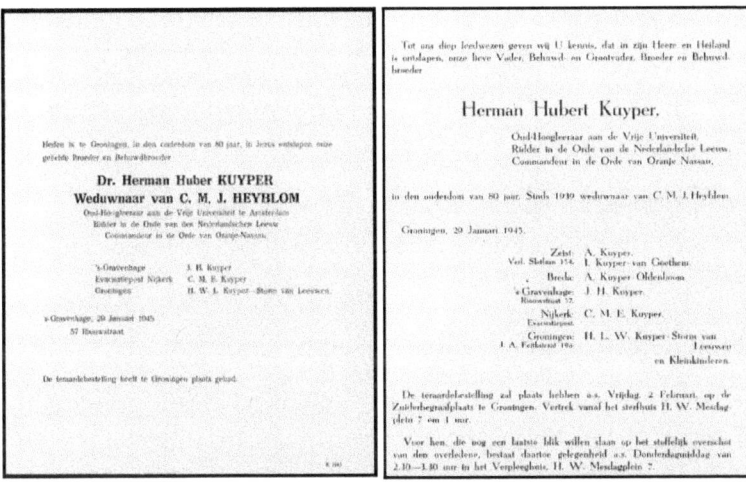

Documents concerning the death of H.H. Kuyper

Romans 13, that the German occupation forces represented the legitimate government.

His son Elisha William joined the Waffen SS as a journalist he went to the Eastern front and was killed in January 1944.

Johan Frederik Hendrik Kuyper (1866–1933)

Fredrick moved to Michigan and attended Hope College. He became a dentist and practised dentistry in Badung and Padang in the East Indies. While in Bandung during 1912 he became enthralled with theosophy, much to his father's disgust. Abraham Kuyper wrote to Idenburg that "Theosophy poisoned" young Kuyper. Abraham Kuyper attacked theosophy in many letters to his friend, A. W. F. Idenburg who was in the Indies, and at a party public meeting.[4] De Tollenaree writes:

---

4. See, Herman A.O. de Tollenaere, "The Politics Of Divine Wisdom: Theosophy and labour, national, and women's movements in Indonesia and South Asia 1875–1947" (PhD Diss, Katholieke Universiteit

Kuyper wrote 'It is so horrible how, also in this country, the civilized élite abjure Christianity and wallow in Theosophy'. The Indies worried him still more. Idenburg wrote to Kuyper: 'This theosophy progresses terribly here. I really consider it as still more dangerous (in our times) than Islam.' 'So, this will be the future religion of our poor Indies.'[5]

From Grooyer and van Reest:

Kuyper was always unique in giving corrections, even with respect to his own children. One of his sons attended a high school at Zetten. He had a deep desire to go to America and there develop his career. He had already intimated his desire several times, but without success, for Papa apparently wanted his son first to complete his study at home.

Frits, the son, would repeatedly talk to his fellow students about wanting so badly to go to the far west and become an American. They convinced him to write one more friendly but insistent letter to his father with the request for permission to go to America. Frits did. In his letter he reminded his father that he did not have the same gifts as his father did and that he would probably end up being a village preacher somewhere in the Netherlands and that people later would disparagingly say,

---

Nijmegen, 1996); and J. de Bruijn and G. Puchinger, ed., *Briefwisseling Kuyper-Idenburg* (Franeker, Wever, 1985).

5.   De Tollenaere, "The Politics Of Divine Wisdom," 111.

"Isn't he the son of that famous Kuyper? Well, he sure did not accomplish much!"

Frits and his friends with excitement awaited the answer from Amsterdam. Now Zetten did not have a post office, but a few days after Frits had sent his letter, a notice arrived from the Hemmen post office that a package had arrived for him from Amsterdam. He and his friends marched to Hemmen with hearts full of expectation, for whenever a package arrived for a student, that was a real event for both him and his roommates. The package was opened in Frits' room, but they looked in vain for a letter from father. Instead, there were two other items. The first was a large, sweet anise bread so popular with the Dutch; the second, a winter vest. These were two objects that said a lot more than even the longest letter could possibly have said. The bread was to keep Frits sweet; the vest served to tell him "First do one more winter in the Netherlands." It would take Frits a long time before he again broached the subject with his father.[6]

Henriëtte Sophia Suzanna Kuyper (1870–1933)

"Jetta" or "Harry", the eldest daughter of Abraham Kuyper, was born when Kuyper was minister of the Reformed church in Amsterdam.[7] She was the author of several travel books. She was partly raised in Nice, France and spoke fluent French and was

6. A.C. De Gooyer and Rudolf Van Reest, *Kuyper de Geweldige....van Dichtbij,* trans. and ed. Jan H. Boer and Frances A. Boer-Prins (Baarn, the Netherlands: Bosch & Keunin). *Abraham Kuyper – A Close-Up: A Treasury of the Personal and Pious Kuyper,* 2017.

7. She was affectionately known as Jetta by her family and Harry by her friends.

The three Kuyper sisters

proficient in several other languages including English. In addition to attending school in France, she attended a Swiss finishing school. She was raised with a great love for the Dutch language.

Aart Deddens has this to say of her:

> She lived at least seven lives: Head of the household since her mother died in 1899; her father's secretary; writer, global traveler, caregiver, public speaker, organizer of the women's wing of the antirevolutionary social pillar.[8]

After the death of her mother in 1899 she took on the running of the Kuyper household and assisted her father in his work. During this time, she translated several works into Dutch including a biography of the poet and hymn-writer Frances Ridley Havergal (1900) and *A Lily of France* by Caroline Atwater Mason (1902).

---

8. Aart Deddens "Hoe is het om een beroemde vader te hebben?" *Sophie* (trans. Jan Boer)

She visited Russia in 1903 and received a high Russian decoration of honor. In 1905 she travelled to America, and this visit opened her eyes to the role of women in society. There she gave lectures and spoke at meetings. For her time, she was an emancipated woman and a proto-feminist.

In 1908, she visited Italy and wrote "Letters from Italy" which was later published as a book, and in 1912 she travelled to Flanders.

Henriëtte S.S. Kuyperm (1870–1933)

She also had the opportunity to visit and write about England (*Vacantie in Engeland* [Holidays in England] 1911) and Hungary (*Hongarije in oorlogstijd* [Hungary in Wartime] 1918). She was appointed a member of the Society of Dutch Literature in 1913.

During World War I she nursed and worked in the emergency hospital in the Hague, and as a housekeeper for the Dutch ambulance service in Hungary (December 1915–June 1916). She wrote about her experiences in Hungary in a book *Hongarije in oorlogstijd. In en om de Nederlandsche Ambulance te Boedapest (benevens een uitstapje naar Weenen)*, (Baarn, 1918) [Hungary in Wartime. In and Around the Dutch Ambulance in Budapest (with an Excursion to Vienna)]

While in Hungary she became friends with the Hungarian neo-Calvinist Jenő Sebestyén.[9] At Sebestyén's request she wrote the Foreword for a Hungarian translation of her father's *Lectures on Calvinism*:

Preface by Henriette Kuyper

When in the winter of 1915, as a member of the Dutch hospital mission, I first came to Hungary, it was a great joy for me to discover that my father's lectures on Calvinism had been translated into Hungarian.

Now, during my second stay in Hungary, it brings me even greater joy to hear that my father's masterpiece is now appearing in its second edition in the Hungarian language. This is proof to me that these six lectures, which speak of the privilege of Calvinism and its call-

---

9. On Jenő Sebestyén, see, Steve Bishop, "Jenő Sebestyén: the Hungarian Kuyper," *Findings* 6 (March 2024): 30–36.

ing in the rapidly advancing modern times, have found resonance in the hearts of the Hungarian people. This resonance that is not only an echo of Hungary's glorious past, when Calvinism thrived as a distinct Hungarian Calvinism in nearly Calvinist Hungary but also a prophecy of what Calvinism could mean for Hungary again. Therefore, I am pleased to fulfill the request of Professor Dr. Jenő Sebestyén, who asked me to write a few introductory words for the second Hungarian edition of my father's work.

God granted my father to the Dutch people to rescue them from the deadly embrace of rationalism.

When my father found eternal rest on November 8, 1920, this work was completed. And there is no country in the world where Calvinistic principles, with their significance for all aspects of human life, flourish as splendidly as in the Netherlands. And this rich flourishing is nowhere rooted as deeply, growing as nobly, reaching towards the heavens, drawn with such firm lines, and painted with such clear colors as in my father's six lectures on Calvinism. And if Calvinism is the most beautiful flower of Dutch intellectual life, and these lectures are the most beautiful blossoms of Dutch Calvinism, then the flower we now offer to Hungarian readers is a Dutch flower.

The heart of the Netherlands now turns mercifully towards Hungary and readily assists this country in its great need. However, the best and most lasting help that the Netherlands can give to Hungary is what this book contains. For the pages of this book speak directly to the soul of Hungary, and this soul can remain great and strong even if the people are poor and the country has been devastated. Just like the Netherlands is a small country, its strength and depth come from its powerful and profound soul, drawing its power from the pure and elevated sphere of Calvinism. For individuals as well as nations, ultimately, it is not money, earthly possessions, or material factors that determine the fate and future of people and countries, but the dominating factor of spiritual life, as stated by our Savior: "Seek first the Kingdom of God and His righteousness, and all these things will be added to you."

My prayer is that the resounding message of this book, like the blast of a powerful trumpet, may awaken the soul of Hungary to a higher, richer, and true Calvinistic life!

I believe in the resurrection of Hungary, for I believe in the renewal of the Hungarian soul!

Budapest, October 1921[10]

Before the war, she had hoped to start a Christian women's magazine. After the war, she became involved with the Reformed Youth movement and became their president. She became involved in several cultural and social activities.

She also became an advisor to the government on women's issues and spoke on the subject at the First International Labor Conference in Washington. She wrote many articles, including

---

10. H. S. S. Kuyper Preface to *A Kálvinizmus Lényege. Irta Dr. Kuyper Ábrahám, Hollandia egykori miniszterelnöke.* [The Essence of Calvinism. Written by Dr. Abraham Kuyper, former Prime Minister of the Netherlands.] (Budapest: Holland-Magyar Kálvinista Könyvtar. I, 1922).

those for the *Antirevolutionarioe Staatkunde* and *De Standaard*. In *De Standaard*, she wrote a regular column.

After her father's death she with her sister Johanna compiled material for a memorial book on him.[11] She was an Honorary president of the Association of Girls' Clubs Based on Reformed Principles and a board member of several organizations, including:

- the Society for Peace and the League of Nations;
- Central Commission for Film Censorship;
- Commission of the Juliana van Stolberg Christian School for Girls in The Hague;
- Supervisory Committee for the Dutch–Hungarian Orphanage for Girls;
- Christian Schools for Girls (for the Javanese nobility in Batavia, East Indies.

She died from pneumonia in Switzerland in 1933 and is buried in The Hague.

She was also the author of:

- *Calvinism and the Women's Question.* London: Sovereign Grace Union, 1930.
- Papers read to the S.G.U. Touring Party, at The Hague, Holland, 1929.

And in Dutch:

- *De Pilgrimfathers in Nederland*, 1608–1620 Kampen, J.H. Kok, 1920.

---

11. H. S. S. Kuyper and J. H. Kuyper (Harry and Tokki), *Herinneringen van de Oude Garde aan de Persoon en Levensarbeid van Dr. A. Kuyper* [Memories of Abraham Kuyper's supporters] (Amsterdam: W. ten Have, 1922).

- *On Abraham Kuyper* (with J. H. Kuyper):
- *De Levensavond van Dr. A. Kuyper.* Kampen: J.H. Kok, 1921
- *Herinneringen van de oude garde aan den persoon en den levensarbeid van Dr. A. Kuyper.* Amsterdam, W. ten Have, 1922

Johanna Hendrika Kuyper (1875–1948)

Little is known about Johanna (she was sometimes called Jo). She was a nurse in a Reformed missionary hospital, Petronella Hospital, founded by Dr. J. G. Scheurer in Yogyakarta, Indonesia.

In 1916 she went with her older sister Henriëtte to Hungary as the head of nursing in Budapest. She also worked with her to compile a memorial book on her father *De Levensavond Van Dr A. Kuyper.*

Catharina Maria Eunice Kuyper (1876–1955)

Catharina (also known as Too) became a nurse; she later became director of nursing at the Vrije Universiteit (1927–1932). She wrote a short piece on her father "Abraham Kuyper: His Early Life and Conversion."[12]

In an obituary[13] Dr. D. Langendijk writes:

---

12. Catherine M. E. Kuyper, "Abraham Kuyper: His Early Life and Conversion," in Steve Bishop and John Kok (ed.) *On Kuyper* (Sioux Center: Dordt Press, 2013), 27–32.
13. Overlijdensbericht en knipsel over het overlijden van C.M.E. Kuyper, 1955, inv.nr. 471 // Catharina Maria Eunice Kuyper, 1944-1955 Archief van Abraham Kuyper, Vrije Universiteit Amsterdam. https://sources.neocalvinism.org/archive/?id_item=2193

Born in Nice, it was as if she had inherited something of the French spirit. She was different from her sisters, the least serious in her father's stately home. She had

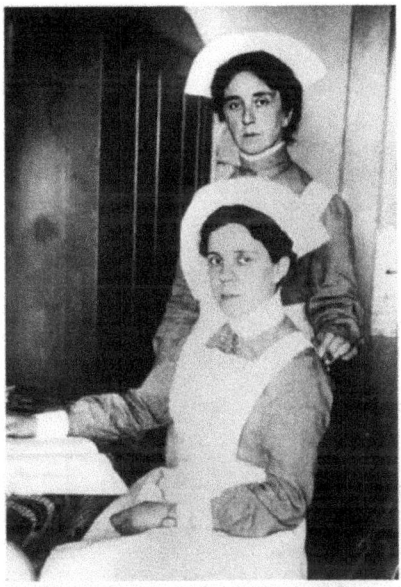

Afb. 2 Henriëtte en Johanna Kuyper als lid van de Nederlandse ambulance.
(Collectie: HDC/Protestants Erfgoed, Vrije Universiteit Amsterdam.)

Details of her death and a list of her living relatives.

sunshine in her life, the favorite of the old Kuyper, who sometimes worried about her, especially when she spent some time in the Dutch East Indies in the palace of the governor-general Idenburg. How many fathers do not, without reason, worry about their children when

129

they are out of sight, and their character does not entirely correspond to theirs!

Dr. Kuyper did not need to worry; things were going well with Cato. As far as I know, she even participated in missionary work in Djokja. During his ministry, Dr. Kuyper had her around him daily; she was his secretary. Later, she went to Hungary, where she did much good work. She served as the director of the hospice of the Free University, and her departure was written about in the Student Almanac of 1955.

One project that wasn't mentioned in the obituary was her involvement in the Children's Kitchens in Budapest in the early 1920s.[14] The aftermath of World War I brought a significant economic crisis in Hungary with droughts, devaluation of the Hungarian currency. Catherina (she was also known as Katalin in Hungary) was involved in raising funds to help. As Aalders reports:

> In the spring of 1922, Catharina Kuyper provided an extensive report on the winter of 1921–1922 in De Standaard. The number of kitchens had expanded to sixteen, allowing 1250 children to have a warm midday meal daily. Now, there was no variation; every eligible child received a warm meal every day. Additionally, each child received two rolls to take home for the evening meal. The children looked somewhat healthier than the previous year.[15]

---

14. Maarten J. Aalders, *Nederlandse en Hongaarse protestanten gedurende het interbellum*, (Amersfoot: Vuurbaak, 2021).

15. Maarten J. Aalders, *Nederlandse en Hongaarse*, 206.

Maarten Alders[16] also points out that she was a founder of the Julianna School in Budapest in 1926, and that she was also honored with a painting and a bust by two renowned artists

Catharina Maria Eunice Kuyper (1876–1955)

---

16. Maarten J. Aalders, "Magyar tisztelgés a Kuyper Ábrahám legfiatalabblánya előtt," in *Erőtlenség Által*. Hitvallók és mártírok. Száműzöttek, menekültek, befogadók, maradók, ed. János M Hermán (Nagyvárad 2018).

LEFT: *the painter Oszkár Glatz (1872–1958) and the sculptor László Hűvős (1883–1972). The text reads: The sculptor László Hűvős modelled the statue of Katalin Kuyper, daughter of the great pro-Hungarian Dutch Prime Minister.*

RIGHT: *Unsigned portrait of C.M.E.'Katalin' Kuyper, by Oszkár Glatz (1872–1958), painted ca. 1926.*

Abraham Kuyper Jr (1872–1941)

Abraham Kuyper Jr was a Reformed Church pastor in Makkum (1899–1906), Vlissingen (1906–1910) and Rotterdam (1910–1939). He married Miss H. Van Oort in March 1899.

He wrote his doctoral dissertation on Johannes Maccovius[17] (Leyden: D. Donner, 1899), a Polish reformed theologian.

Van Asselt, writes:

> in 1899, Abraham Kuyper, Jr., produced a doctoral dissertation on Maccovius, discussing the biographical details of Maccovius's life in the first part, while devoting the second part to Maccovius's methodology. In the third part of his dissertation, Kuyper offered a historical description of some of the Franeker polemics thato

---

17. Abraham Kuyper, Jr., *Johannes Maccovius: Academisch proefschrif* (Leiden: D. Donner, 1899).

Abraham Kuyper Jr (1872–1941)

occurred between Maccovius and Sibrandus Lubbertus
(professor, 1585–1625), and between Maccovius and
William Ames (professor, 1622–33). According to
Kuyper, Maccovius's problems at Franeker with Lubbertus and Ames grew out of theological and philosophical
differences: Lubbertus's infralapsarism vs. Maccovius's su-
pralapsarism, and Ames's Ramism vs. Maccovius's Aristo-
telianism. Moreover, Maccovius's Bohemian way of life
clearly fell short of Ames's standards, who, according to
Keith Sprunger, was a "Puritan of the rigidest sort."

Kuyper called d Maccovius "the pioneer of Reformed scholasticism in the Netherlands" and argued in favor of a kind of Maccovius "renaissance" in neo-Calvinist circles. He saw Maccovius as "a herald announcing the times to come," that is, the theology developed by his father, whom he saw as the "regenerator of Calvinism and the father of a reborn Calvinism according to the awareness of this century."[18]

Guillaume Kuyper (1878–1941)

Guillaume was named after Guillaume Groen Van Prinsterer. He married Henrietta van Leeuwen Storm (1880–1933). They had three daughters. Guillaume became a major in the Dutch army (1902–1932) and then became mayor of Stedum (1932–1941).

Guillaume's second daughter was named Johanna (1909–2007) (aka Johtje), she married Aart Vos. Together Johtje and her husband hid up to 14 Jews at one time in their home during the Nazi occupation of the Netherlands. They were interviewed in the Rescuers: Portraits of Moral Courage in the Holocaust, by Gay Block and Malka Drucker (Holmes & Meier, 1992).[19] There she wrote:

My father was a career army officer, and my mother was the most wonderful woman I've ever met in my life. She was highly intelligent and had a terrifc sense of humour. She translated fifty-two books for English,

---

18. Willem J Van Asselt, "The Theologian's Tool Kit: Johannes Maccovius (1588–1644) and the Development Of Reformed Theological Distinctions," *Westminster Theological Journal* 68(1) (2006): 23–40.

19. Gay Block and Malka Drucker, *Rescuers: Portraits of Moral Courage in the Holocaust*, (Holmes & Meier, 1992).

French, and German into Dutch. She had to do it secretly using my father's name, because women weren't permitted that kind of recognition then. So my father, who was brilliant at mathematics but couldn't speak a word in any other language, got the credit for all her work.

Guillaume Kuyper (1878–1941)

Wilhelm Kuyper (1883–1892)

Willy died aged 9. According to Praamsma, he was named after Levinus Wilhelminus Keuchenius, an Anti-Revolutionary minister and a close friend of Kuyper's.

14

Bibliographical Details

ONE OF KUYPER'S BIOGRAPHERS, Frank Vanden Berg, in the sixties, wrote:

> Dr. Kuyper wrote almost exclusively in Dutch. Only a few of the books have been translated into English but these are important and valuable. And virtually everything that has been written about Kuyper is also in Dutch.

Fortunately, that is not the case today. We have been reasonably served with Kuyper biographies, ranging from the hagiographic (e.g., Vanden Berg 1960, a translation from Dutch) and under-critical (Praamsma (1985) — another translation) to the over-critical (e.g., Koch's (2006)—this by a Catholic writer has yet to be translated into English), and even one for children (in Dutch) by Anne M. de Moor-Ringnalda (1937). Bratt (2013) steers a middle course. The first book-length biography written in English was by James McGoldrick (2000): *God's Renaissance Man*. This drew largely upon Vanden Berg (1960) and Praamsma (1985) and focuses primarily on Kuyper's theological views. Bratt's perspective is wider and is the most authoritative biography published thus far.

Johan Snel's 2020 Dutch biography looks at Kuyper "alpinist, traveller, speaker, scientist, activist, journalist and statesman."[1] Kuyper apparently used this description of himself in a short autobiography written in French.

The best book on Kuyper's political approach is McKendree Langley's *The Practice of Spirituality*.

Tjitze Kuyper's has produced a mammoth work citing and annotating all of Kuyper's writings from 1857–2010. This book is indispensable for any serious Kuyper scholar. It is now available online at The Neo-Calvinism Research Institute (https://sources.neocalvinism.org/kuyper/)

De Bruin's book, *Abraham Kuyper: A Pictorial Biography*, weighing in at over 1.1 kg, is lavish and beautifully produced. On each page there is at least one photograph with detailed supporting text. This is much more than an illustrated companion or supplement to Bratt's 2013 biography. De Bruijn fills in and highlights some of the details that Bratt was unable to include. Bratt is weak on Kuyper's family, but de Bruijn has a stronger emphasis on them. Several family portraits are included in de Bruijn's book.

Mention must also be made of two excellent introductions by two North Americans, one Canadian the other from the USA: Mike Wagenman *Engaging the World with Abraham Kuyper* (Bellingham, WA: Lexham Press, 2019) and Richard Mouw *Abraham Kuyper: A Short and Personal Introduction* (Grand Rapids: Eerdmans, 2011). Wagenman takes snippets from Kuyper's career and examines several key themes that

---

1. Johan Snel, De Zeven *Levens van Abraham Kuyper: Portret van een Ongrijpbaar Staatsman* (Uitgeverij Prometheus, 2020). This has not yet been translated into English.

Kuyper develops: identity, education, politics—what is helpful about Wagenman's book is that it also looks at how Kuyperian perspectives can apply to today. The one weakness is that the book does not consider Kuyper's common grace.

Richard Mouw has provided—as the subtitle indicates—a personal introduction.

The centenary of Kuyper's death was in 2022 Several books were published to commemorate this including

J.R. Joustra and R.J Joustra (ed.) *Calvinism for a Secular Age* (Downers Grove: InterVarsity Press, 2023). This is a re-reading of each of the lectures, looking at what Kuyper said, what Kuyperians have done, and how we should respond.

Another, but much briefer, introduction to Kuyper's Lectures is Jesse Sumpter's *A Short Introduction to Abraham Kuyper's* Lectures on Calvinism (Francis Drake Press, 2020).

On neo-Calvinism more broadly, we have N. Gray Sutanto and Cory Brock—both Bavinck scholars—*Neo-Calvinism.* This is a good introduction to the theology behind neo-Calvinism and that of Bavinck and Kuyper.

In 2013, I edited with John Kok a collection of essays on Kuyper:

Bishop, S. and Kok, J.H., (ed.) 2013. *On Kuyper: A collection of readings on the life, work & legacy of Abraham Kuyper*. Dordt College Press.

In it I have a bibliography of over 300 works dealing with Kuyper.

Since 2014, I have had published annual reviews of what I have termed Kuyperania. These cover the vast majority of works on and about Kuyper written each year. They can be accessed online through the *Koers* journal web archive—or a web search for "Kuyperania."

Bishop, S., 2014. Kuyperania in recent years. *Koers*, 79(1)

Bishop, S., 2015. More kuyperania. *Koers*, 80(3): 1–6.

Bishop, S., 2016. Kuyperania in 2015. *Koers*, 81(1)

Bishop, S., 2017. Kuyperania in 2016. *Koers*, 82(1):1–16.

Bishop, S., 2018. Kuyperania in 2017. *Koers*, 83(1): 1–18.

Bishop, S., 2019. Kuyperania in 2018. *Koers*, 84(1): 1–11.

Bishop, S., 2020. Kuyperania in 2019. *Koers*, 85(1)

Bishop, S., 2021. Kuyperania in 2020. *Koers* 86(1)

Bishop, S., 2023. Kuyperania in 2022. *Koers* 88(1)

Bishop, S., 2025. Kuyperania in 2021 and 2023: An overview of English language works on Kuyper. *Koers* 90 (1)

Study questions

1. "Kuyper was a man of vision and often this single-minded vision clouded his judgement." Would you agree? Why?
2. Describe the difference between the *Afscheiding* and the *Doleantie*.
3. Why did Kuyper not join the *Afscheiding*?
4. Kuyper's time was also a time of massive cultural change—what were the changes and how did they influence Kuyper.
5. What were the key factors in Kuyper's conversion?
6. What were the lessons Kuyper learned from Groen van Prinsterer?
7. Kuyper wanted "a free church and a free school in a free land." What did he understand by this phrase?

8. Why did Kuyper give up church ministry for politics? Was he right to do so?

9. Why did Kuyper the Calvinist seek a political coalition with the Roman Catholics?

9. Was Kuyper right to stop his church attendance to write some of his meditations?

10. To what extent was Kuyper a man of his time and to what extent was he ahead of his time?

11. Why were Kuyper's *Lectures on Calvinism* so influential?

12. Why did Kuyper side with the Germans in World War I?

13. What were some of the controversies and criticisms surrounding Kuyper's life and work?

14. What lessons can be drawn from Kuyper's life?

15. How did Kuyper's ideas and contributions compare to those of other prominent thinkers and leaders of his time?

16. If you were Kuyper, what would you do differently? Why?

Further Reading

Primary Sources

Kuyper, Abraham. "Confidentially," in *Abraham Kuyper: A Centennial Reader*. James D. Bratt (ed). (Michigan: William B. Eerdmans Publishing Company, 1998).

Secondary Sources

Bratt, James. *Abraham Kuyper: Modern Calvinist, Christian Democrat* (Grand Rapids, MI: Eerdmans, 2013).

Kuyper, Catherine M. E. "Abraham Kuyper: His Early Life and Conversion," in Steve Bishop and John Kok (ed.) *On*

Kuyper A Collection of Readings on the Life, Work & Legacy of Abraham Kuyper (Sioux Center: Dordt Press, 2013), 27–32.

Langley, McKendree. *The Practice of Political Spirituality Episodes from the Public Career of Abraham Kuyper, 1879–1918.* (Jordan Station, Ont: Wedge Press, 1984).

McGoldrick, James E. *God's Renaissance Man: Abraham Kuyper* (Darlington: Evangelical Press, 2000).

Praamsma, L. *Let Christ Be King: Reflections on the Life and Times of Abraham Kuyper* (Jordan Station, Ontario: Paideia Press, 1985).

Vanden Berg, Frank. *Abraham Kuyper: A Biography* (St Catherines, ON: Paideia Press, 1978).

A Summary in 12 theses

1. Abraham Kuyper's life and works had an enduring influence on both Christianity and on Dutch history and culture.

2. Abraham Kuyper was a multifaceted figure, known for his contributions to politics, church reform, theology, journalism, and education.

3. Kuyper founded the VU, Amsterdam and served as Prime Minister of the Netherlands, demonstrating his commitment to Christian education and political leadership.

4. His extensive writings, including over 200 books and numerous articles, covered a wide range of topics such as theology, journalism, politics, and culture.

5. Kuyper's emphasis on Calvinism as a comprehensive worldview, beyond just the five points of Calvinism, influenced his approach to life and society.

6. He advocated for a holistic Christian perspective that encompassed all aspects of life, not only personal salvation.

7. Kuyper's vision for the church included elements such as being Reformed, democratic, free from state influence, autonomous, and self-supporting.

8. His work on ecclesiastical reforms intertwined with his political and educational endeavors, reflecting his vision of a free university and school, free from state and church control.

9. Kuyper's publication "Confidentially" highlighted his evangelical conversion and desire for church reform, emphasizing the importance of a true church.

10. He developed the idea of common grace, which was met with some criticism for supposedly deviating from orthodox Reformed doctrine.

11. Kuyper's legacy continues to influence Dutch society and beyond, his ideas on common grace, sphere sovereignty, and worldview are still relevant today.

12. Despite controversies surrounding his teachings, Kuyper's impact on theology, politics, and education is significant.

PART 2

Key Themes

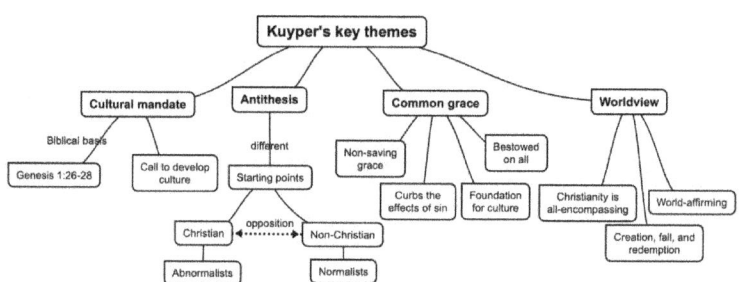

In Brief

If God is sovereign, then his lordship must extend over all of life, and it cannot be restricted to the walls of the church or within the Christian orbit. The non-Christian world has not been handed over to Satan, nor surrendered to fallen humanity, nor consigned to fate. God's sovereignty is great and all-dominating in the life of that unbaptized world as well. Therefore Christ's church on earth and God's child cannot simply retreat from this life. If the believer's God is at work in this world, then in this world the believer's hand must take hold of the plow, and the name of the Lord must be glorified in that activity as well.[1]

KUYPER FIRMLY BELIEVED IN the sovereignty of God as the starting point and ultimate foundation for everything. If we acknowledge that God is in control, then it becomes clear that cultural development is crucial. Simply retreating from God's world is not a valid option.

Kuyper's vision revolves around the idea of God's good creation, which unfortunately became tainted by sin. However, he

---

1.   A. Kuyper, *Common Grace* (Volume 1: The Historical Section): God's Gifts for a Fallen World (Abraham Kuyper Collected Works in Public Theology) (Bellingham, MA: Lexham Press, 2016), xxxvii –xxxviii.

emphasized that through the redemptive work of Christ, this creation can be renewed. As Christians, we have a significant role to play as agents of reconciliation and renewal. This goes beyond just personal transformation; it also encompasses the transformation of structures and institutions.

1. The cultural mandate

This mandate finds its roots in the verses of Genesis 1:26-–28 and Genesis 2:15. It speaks to the call for humanity to subdue, rule, till, and keep the earth. This mandate compels us to develop culture and unlock the full potential of God's magnificent creation. It means expressing the kingdom of Christ in every area of life, leaving no aspect untouched. This implies that while creation is inherently good, it also requires our active participation in its development. As the saying goes, the Bible "begins in a garden and ends in a city,"[2] highlighting the continuous growth and progress of God's creation.

2. The antithesis

The term antithesis means opposition. In the nineteenth century, Hegel used this term, however, in Kuyperian thought it took on a different meaning. It marked a difference between those who held to a Christian starting point and those who did not—the difference lay in their worldview. There is a clear contrast by those who start with the knowledge of God and those who do not.

2. The earliest use of this phrase I have found is by 'P.' in F. N. Peloubet and M. A. Peloubet, *Select Notes on the International Sabbath School Lessons for 1879* (Boston: Ira Bradley & Co., 1878), 242. See also Albert M. Wolters, *Creation Regained: Biblical Basis for a Reformational Worldview.* (Downers Grove: InterVarsity Press, 1985), 41.

Louis Raemaekers's cartoon criticizes Kuyper's use of the antithesis as a form of dominance or suppression over opponents.

For Kuyper, the antithesis means that there are two kinds of people: the regenerate and the unregenerate. Consequently, there are two kinds of "science" (i.e., scholarship) each with different starting points. He uses the terms *abnormalist* and *normalist* to illustrate this key distinction. The conflict is not between faith and science but between opposing scientific systems, each grounded in its own faith.[3] The difference arises from how one understands sin and the depth of its impact.

3. Common grace

Common grace is non-saving grace bestowed on all: Christians and non-Christians. For Kuyper common grace is rooted in the "the sovereignty of God."[4] Kuyper thinks that embracing the doctrine of common grace helps the believer engage rather than retreat from the world. Common grace provides the foundation for meaningful involvement with the world, preventing spiritual and ecclesiastical isolation and thereby enabling believers to exercise stewardship.

Common grace curbs the effects of sin and restrains the deeds of fallen humanity. It upholds the ordinances of creation and provides the basis for Christian cultural involvement; common grace provides the foundation for culture. Common grace reminds us that the creation ordinances of dominion and stewardship over creation, given in the cultural mandate before the fall, are not abolished after the fall. This means withdrawing from culture is not an option for Christians. We are called to be active participants in shaping, enriching, and transforming the world around us.

---

3.   A. Kuyper, *Lectures on Calvinism* (Grand Rapids, MI: Eerdmans, 1931), 133.

4.   *Common Grace* Volume 1, 5.

4. Sphere sovereignty

For Kuyper, things are subject to the sovereignty of God. This conviction led Kuyper, to develop what he described as "sphere sovereignty." Sphere sovereignty maintains that God alone is sovereign. He has established specific laws and norms for different areas of society such as the family, the church, and society. Within their own sphere, these institutions are thus sovereign under God's laws and norms for that aspect of life. No one institution should dominate or dictate to another and there is no hierarchy among them. For example, the state should not dictate how the family brings up a child or a school should not be run as a business.

5. Christianity as a worldview (creation, fall, and redemption)

When Kuyper first introduced Christians to the notion of worldview in his 1888 *Lectures on Calvinism* it was a fresh, innovative, and radical notion. Kuyper first identified the Christian worldview in terms of the narrative embedded within creation, fall, and redemption. Kuyper showed that Christianity is an all-encompassing worldview.

Each of these themes will be examined in more detail in the next few sections.

15

Cultural Mandate

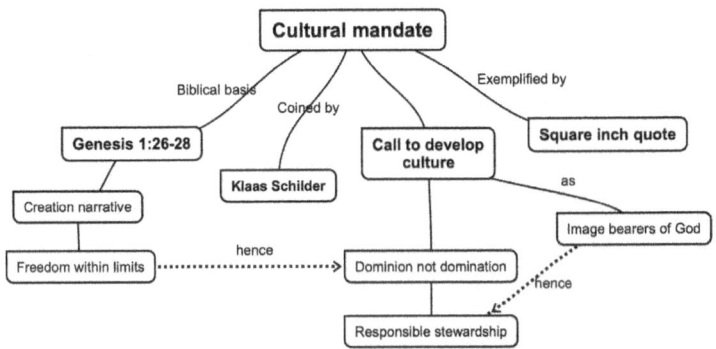

Central to the Kuyperian tradition is Christ's cosmic lordship over all things, which results in an emphasis on the cultural mandate—the call to develop culture to God's glory (Gen 1:26–26; Gen 2:15). These themes are summarized in a famous quote from Kuyper: "There is not a square inch in the whole domain of our human existence over which Christ, who is sovereign Lord of all, does not cry: 'Mine!'"

J. Richard Middleton[1]

1. J. Richard Middleton, "Reflections of a Kuyperian Wesleyan," https://jrichardmiddleton.com/2019/06/12/reflections-of-a-kuyperi

Introduction

AN AMISH BOY AND his mother travelled in their horse-drawn buggy to a shopping mall for the very first time. They were amazed by almost everything they saw, but especially by two silver doors that moved apart and back together. The boy asked, "What is this, Mother?" This was the first time the mother had seen a lift. She responded, "Jedediah, Son, I have never seen anything like this in my life. I don't know what it is."

While they were watching, an old man in a wheelchair rolled up to the doors and pressed a button. The doors opened, and the man rolled between them into a small room. The doors closed, and the boy and his mother heard a strange noise. They watched a small set of lights with numbers on them light up in sequence, stop, and then come back down again. The door opened up again, and a handsome 26-year-old man stepped out. The mother said to her son, "Quickly, go get your father."

The moral of that story is that if we don't understand culture, we can make mistakes! Christians have often had a mixed reaction to culture, but culture is part of God's good creation. We are called to develop and shape culture—this idea has been described as a "cultural mandate."

The term cultural mandate was first coined by Klaas Schilder (1890–1952),[2] Kuyper's square inch quote, cited above, is

---

an-wesleyan/ (This was published as the foreword, in Portuguese, to the book Cosmovisão Cristã: Reflexões éticas contemporâneas a partir da Teologia Arminio-Wesleyana, ed. Vinicius Couto (Sao Paulo: Reflexao Editoria).

2. Klaas Schilder, *Christ and Culture* (Hamilton, ON: Lucerna, CRTS Publications, 2016). See also, N. H. Gootjes, "Schilder on Christ and

an embodiment of the cultural mandate given in Genesis 1:26–28 and Genesis 2:15. This subduing, ruling, tilling, and keeping is a mandate for the development of culture, for the unfolding of the potentialities within the God-given good creation. It is about expressing the kingdom of Christ in all areas of life; no areas are exempt. This implies that although the creation is good, it needs to be developed and opened up. As others have stated, the garden is to be developed into a city. As Kuyper notes: "the glory of Eden pales before the glory of the New Jerusalem." For this to occur there must be development, Kuyper again: "the highest idea of that glory, was not a paradise but the city with its foundations and precious stones and gates of pearl."[3]

Interestingly, Kuyper does not make much use of the term culture. In his *Lectures on Calvinism* (1931 [1899]) he mentions people as "highly cultured" (44) and the "cultured classes" (45) and "cultured circles" (188) and other than in agriculture and horticulture the term culture is not otherwise mentioned. Nevertheless, the phrase "cultural mandate" became useful shorthand for the view that characterizes a Kuyperian perspective.

Kuyper took seriously the ideas behind the cultural mandate, to open up and develop the creation. This opening up and development of the creation includes the family, mission, socio-political ideas, and scholarship. In his meditation on "In the beginning" from his collection of meditations on home life, he observes:

Culture," in *Always Obedient: Essay on the Teachings of Dr. Klaas Schilder*, ed. J. Geertsema (Philipsburg: P&R Publishing,1995), 35–64

3. Abraham Kuyper, *When Thou Sittest in Thine House: Meditations on Home Life* (Eugene, OR: Wipf & Stock, 2009), 76–77.

"In the beginning," narrates not merely, that the first world was not, but only afterward came into being, because God created it, but also implies, that God has made a beginning, and thereby has appointed in all His creation the distinction between the beginning of a matter and its further course.[4]

Kuyper's colleague Herman Bavinck observes: "Obedience to God and dominion over the earth, cult (cultus) and culture (cultuur) go together."[5]

However, the cultural mandate has been misused and misunderstood. Some theologians have attempted to deny that Christianity has anything to do with culture and cultural development. They maintain that this "cultural mandate" is not applicable to today—it was aimed only at Adam and was pre-fall, Adam failed to fulfil it, but Jesus, the second Adam did fulfil it and that means we do not have to embrace it.[6] However, the cultural mandate to develop and fill the earth has not been rescinded after the fall into sin. Therefore, cultural withdrawal is not an option for Christians. (Even to withdraw from culture is to take a cultural position.)

For others, it has become associated with the exploitation of the earth, and they have objected to what they perceive as its anthropocentric focus.

---

4. Kuyper, *When Thou Sittest in Thine House*, 1.

5. Herman Bavinck, *Guidebook for Instruction in the Christian Religion*, ed. and trans. Gregory Parker Jr. and Cam Causing (Peabody, MA: Hendrikson Academic, 2022).

6. For example, David VanDrunen, see, for example his *Living in God's Two Kingdoms: A Biblical Vision for Christianity and Culture* (Crossway, 2010).

Dominion or domination?[7]

Many have placed the blame for the environmental crisis on Christianity because implicit within the cultural mandate as it appears to condone a human-centerd (anthropocentric) attitude and the notion that no item in the physical creation has any purpose save the use to which humans can put it and hence being able to dispense with and dispose of nature as we see fit:

> [The Bible] in its insistence upon dominion and subjugation of nature, encourages the most exploitative and destructive instincts in man … Here can be found the sanction and injunction to conquer nature …. [8]

Bizarrely, Ann Coulter, a right-wing American media personality asserts: "GOD gave us the earth. We have dominion over the plants, the animals, the trees. God said, "Earth is yours. Take it. Rape it. It's yours." [9] Likewise, the radical eco-feminist Andree Collard suggests that, "Genesis presents the view that God created everything and gave it to man to dominate." [10]

The two words translated as subdue (*kabas*) and rule (*radah*) seem to bear out this sort of interpretation: *Kabas* is elsewhere translated as rape (Esther 7:8), Westermann has trans-

---

7. Some of this section draws upon Steve Bishop, "Green Theology and Deep Ecology: New Age or New Creation," *Themelios* 16, no. 3, (1991): 8–14.

8. Ian McHarg, *Design with Nature* (New York: Natural History Press, 1989), 26.

9. Ann H. Coulter, *If Democrats Had Any Brains, They'd Be Republicans* (Crown Forum, 2007).

10. A. Collard, *Rape of the Wild* (The Women's Press, 1989), 17.

lated *radah* as "to tread out the wine press,"[11] and von Rad as "trample."[12] However, a word's meaning is not found in its derivation (cf greenhouse—a greenhouse is neither green nor a house!), or history (cf nice; it originally "meant" ignorant!) but in its context. The meaning of words is context dependent.

Context of the cultural mandate

The context of the cultural mandate is the creation of humanity; the emphasis is on being the image bearers of God. Subduing and ruling are then to be done as God's representatives: he is our role model.

James Barr suggests that humanity's role is "less exploitation and more leadership";[13] this, however, is only satisfactory if we see leadership as servanthood, as exemplified by Jesus the Shepherd-King.[14]

Context of the creation narrative

Widening the context, slightly more places the subduing and ruling within the Hebrew record of creation. One thing is immediately obvious: creation is not merely for humanity. The world exists for the glory of God: creation is not anthropocentric (nor biocentric) it is theocentric. All things exist and have their meaning in God.

---

11. Claus Westermann, *Genesis* 1–11 (London: SPCK, 1974), 142–157.

12. G. Von Rad, *Genesis* (London: SCM, 1972), 60f.

13. James Barr, "Man and Nature—The Ecological Controversy in the Old Testament," *Bulletin of the John Rylands* Library 55 (1972): 9–32.

14. Walter Houston, "'And Let Them Have Dominion …' Biblical Views of Man in Relation to the Environmental Crisis," *Studia Biblical* (1978): 161–184.

The earth is not humanity's to do with it as we see fit. It is God's creation, and as God's delegates we are to take care of it on his behalf; humanity is accountable to God for its treatment of the earth (cf Pss 115:6; 8: 4–6).

Context of the cultural milieu

Another important context is culture. Whatever the meaning the concept of dominion conjured up in the time of writing, it could only have restricted meaning (cf Job 38: 33; 41:9); at the time there was no potential for world destruction. Most likely the original readers would have understood dominion in terms of animal husbandry and the cultivation of the ground.

Dominion cannot, therefore, mean domination; it is to be done as image bearers of God gently and caringly unfolding and developing the potential locked in God's creation. It is to be done with freedom but within limits. God follows on from the cultural mandate with an implicit restriction: humans are not to kill for food (Gen 1:29–30). The law also contains restrictions on human use of the earth. Leviticus, for example, provides restraints on the human use of the non-human creation:[15]

- The eating of blood is forbidden/ prohibited (Lv17:12)
  Fields are not to be reaped to the edges (Lv 19:9)
- Vineyards are not to be stripped bare (Lv 19:10)
- No cross breeding of animals (Lv 19:19)
- The fruit from fruit trees is not to be eaten in the first four years of planting (Lv 19:23–25)
- In the seventh year, the land is to be completely rested (Lv 25: 4–5)

---

15. See, for example, F. W. Welbourn, "Man's Dominion," *Theology* 78 (1975): 561–568.

Likewise in Deuteronomy:

- Eating of some animal foods is forbidden (Deut 14:3–21)
- Animals that die "of themselves" are not to be eaten (Deut 14:21)
- The fruit trees of an enemy are not to be cut down (Deut 20:19)
- Straying animals should be returned to their owner (Deut 22:1–2)
- A neighbors' fallen ox or donkey should be helped (Deut 22:4)
- An ox and donkey should not plough together (Deut 22:10)

Within the garden are certain natural resources (2:11): gold, aromatic resin, onyx. Why are these mentioned if they are not to be developed? (Cf Job 28) The cultural mandate provides a good description of the God-given purpose of humanity opening up and disclosing the potentialities within the good creation as the image bearers of God. Kuyper may not have used the term, but it does provide a good short-hand term for Kuyper's approach.

The cultural mandate and Kuyper's square inch approach are the basis for cultural participation. It is not, however, an excuse for Christian nationalism, imperialism, or domination. Neither is it a proposal for a theocracy, as Kuyper affirms: "... we do not desire a theocracy; rather we oppose it with all or might."[16]

Kuyper's sphere sovereignty mitigates against such an approach—as we shall see in a subsequent chapter.

---

16. Abraham Kuyper, *Our Program: A Christian Political Manifesto.* (Abraham Kuyper Collected Works in Public Theology), ed. and trans. Harry Van Dyke (Bellingham, WA: Lexham Press, 2015), 35.

Study Questions

1. Some have suggested that a better term for the "cultural mandate" would be "creational mandate"— would you agree? Why?
2. Kuyper did not use the term cultural mandate—why has it become so associated with him?
3. Why have some argued that the cultural mandate is not applicable today?
4. Is cultural development essential?
5. How does Kuyper's belief in the sovereignty of God shape his vision for cultural development?

R.H. Niebuhr's *Christ and Culture**

Niebuhr in a neat typology identified five ways in which the relationship between Christianity and culture have been approached.

Christ against culture	Christ of culture	Christ above culture	Christ and culture in paradox	Christ transforms culture
Tertullian	Gnostics	Aquinas	Luther	Calvin
Leo Tolstoy	Abelard		Kierkegaard	Augustine
Monasticism	Ritschl		David	F. D.
Mennonites	Protestant		VanDrunen	Maurice
Anabaptists	Liberalism			

The two main extremes are the Christ of culture and the Christ against culture positions.

In the **Christ against culture** position, he includes Tertullian, Leo Tolstoy, monasticism, and the Mennonites. This is a separation-from-the-world mentality, a rejection of culture. Basically, it asserts that culture is bad—it has been totally corrupted by sin.

Christ above culture—culture is good but needs to be supplemented by grace.

Christ and culture in paradox—this is the typical Lutheran Two Kingdom approach. More recently, this view has been espoused by David VanDrunen.

Christ transforms culture—this position asserts that culture is good but has been distorted through sin. Culture needs to be transformed in the name of Christ.

---

* R. H. Niebuhr, *Christ and Culture* (New York: Harper & Row, 1951).

16

The Antithesis

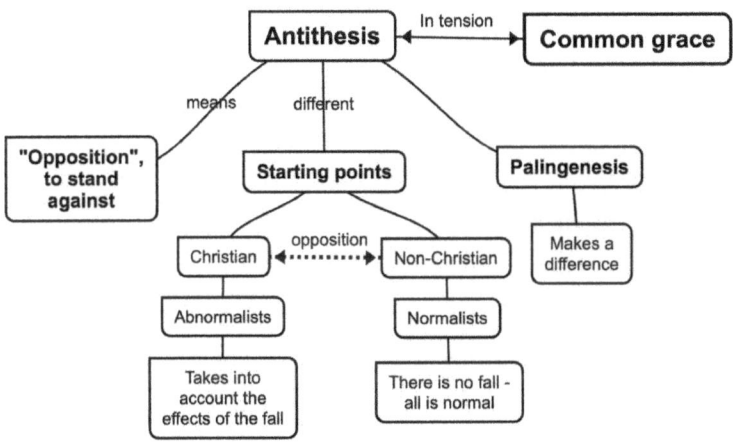

Introduction

SOME HAVE MAINTAINED THAT in advocating and developing the theory of common grace, Kuyper denies the antithesis. On the other hand, Tangelder describes Kuyper as the theologian of the antithesis.[1] I would argue that Tangelder is more correct than the objectors.

---

1. Johan D. Tangelder, "Abraham Kuyper (1837–1920)—The Antithesis Theologian," *Christian Renewal* 3, no. 8, (5th November 1984).

The term antithesis means "opposition" or "to stand against"; two things or principles are set over and against each other. Kant was one of the first to use the term in a philosophical setting.[2] In the nineteenth century, G. F. W. Hegel (1770–1831) utilized the term to describe a dialectical process. However, in Kuyperian thought it took on a different connotation. It refers to the opposition between the kingdom of God and the kingdom of darkness.

It marked a difference between those who held to a Christian starting point and those who did not; the difference was in worldview. There is a noetic antithesis between those who start with the knowledge of God and those who do not.

The antithesis, however, is not an us versus them mentality—a Christian versus non-Christian or elect versus reprobate. The antithesis runs through us all—Christians included! Christian philosopher Herman Dooyeweerd sums this up well:

> the antithesis cuts right through the christian life itself. ... The antithesis is therefore not a dividing line between christian and nonchristian groups. It is the relenting battle between two spiritual principles that cut through the nation and through all mankind. It has no respect for the secure patterns and lifestyles built by Christians.[3]

We are all sinners and are fallen creatures, the fall affects us all. It does not mean that there is no wisdom and insights that are

---

2. Henry Stob, "Observations on the Concept of the Antithesis," in *Perspectives on the Christian Reformed Church: Studies in its History, Theology, and Ecumenicity*, ed. P. De Keir and R. R. De Ridder (Grand Rapids: Baker Book House, 1983), 241.

3. Herman Dooyeweerd, *Roots of Western Culture* (Toronto: Wedge,1979), 3.

to be gleaned from those who are not working from a Christian perspective. Dooyeweerd again helps explain this in discussing Kuyper's antithesis he writes:

> ... the antithesis does not draw a line of personal classification but a line of division according to fundamental principles in the world a line of division which passes transversely through the existence of every Christian personality.[4]

Therefore, it is important that the antithesis and common grace are held together in tension.

Al Wolters makes an important point, echoing Dooyeweerd:

> Since this is an opposition between regimes not realms, it runs through every department of human life and culture, including philosophy and the academic enterprise as a whole, and through the heart of every believer as he or she struggles to live a life of undivided allegiance to God.[5]

The antithesis is the result of humanity's fall into sin. It affects all of creation. It is not, however, dualistic—it is not a separation of life into sacred and secular. As stressed above it is found in all of life not just what has been termed "secular." The antithesis runs through all of life. A diagram "borrowed" from Wolter's book *Creation Regained* may help:[6]

---

4. Herman Dooyeweerd, *The New Critique of Theoretical Thought* (Philadelphia: The Presbyterian and Reformed Publishing Company, 1953) 1, 521.

5. Albert M. Wolters, *Creation Regained: Biblical Basis for a Reformational Worldview.* (Downers Grove: InterVarsity Press, 1985), 167.

6. Wolters, *Creation Regained*, 66–68.

Church
Family
Medicine
Education
Politics
Law
Art
Architecture
Media
Business
Journalism
Thought
Emotion
Animals
Plants
Rocks

If we imagine that this box represents creation in all its variety.

There are at least two ways we can show the antithesis—the opposition between the kingdom of God and the kingdom of the world/ Satan. The first is to draw the line *horizontally* separating the church from the rest of creation—this is a form of sacred/ secular dualism. That is not the antithesis Kuyper had in mind. On the other hand, we could draw the line *vertically*—this is what Kuyper means by the antithesis. It cuts across all of creation, including the human heart.

Different starting points

The antithesis is one reason Kuyper advocates the establishment of specific Christian institutions. A Christian political party or a Christian school will have different starting-points from a party or school based on, for example, naturalistic lines. The foundations will be different and so the out-workings will also be different. Commitment to Christ cannot be

Church	Church
Family	Family
Medicine	Medicine
Education	Education
Politics	Politics
Law	Law
Art	Art
Architecture	Architecture
Media	Media
Business	Business
Journalism	Journalism
Thought	Thought
Emotion	Emotion
Animals	Animals
Plants	Plants
Rocks	Rocks

accommodated or harmonized with naturalism or any other non-Christian philosophy. There is a cosmic battle between light and darkness, between the kingdom of God and the dominion of Satan. There is a marked contrast between belief and unbelief. This notion of antithesis is integral to the idea of rival worldviews. Rivalry is not the only relation between different worldviews: cooperation, emulation and mutual correction will also take place. It should also be appreciated that Kuyper would grant the same freedom to establish distinct schools, political parties, or labor unions to those who adopt rival worldviews in a country. This is in fact what happened in the Netherlands, a process known as *verzuiling* (pillarization).

Three key issues
The antithesis holds three key but interlinked issues.

Palingenesis makes a difference

By the term *palingenesis*, Kuyper means regeneration or the new birth. Kuyper maintains that conversion impacts our thoughts, wills, and actions. We live, see hear, and think differently. Of course, new birth is not instantaneous, but conversion changes us. Kuyper uses the illustration of a tree and a branch grafted onto the tree. In conversion we are grafted into Christ. The old, grafted branch remains for a while but eventually the sap of the main tree takes over and produces the change.

> It is not a better and tenderer growth in one tree producing a richer fruit, while the other tree thrives less prosperously, and consequently bears poorer fruit; but it is a difference in kind. However luxuriantly and abundantly the ungrateful tree may leaf and blossom it will never bear the fruit which grows on the grafted tree. However backward the grafted tree may be at first in its growth, the blossom which unfolds on its branches is fruit blossom.[7]

There is no neutrality

There are no neutral facts — all things are viewed through the eyes of faith. This is closely linked to the notion of worldview. Facts are colored by the worldview of the observer there is no such thing as a brute fact. Facts are embedded in values. Facts are not isolated things. As Remkes Kooistra (1917–2005) writes:

---

7. Abraham Kuyper, *Principles of Sacred Theology*, trans. J. Hendrick De Vries (Grand Rapids, MI: Eerdmans, 1968 [1898]), 152.

Nowhere are there any loose facts, that is, unrelated facts, as there are loose grains on the ground after harvest. A fact is always related to the law, whether the fact is a thing, a relation or an evaluation and from its relation to the law it derives its value at all times.[8]

Every position is based on assumptions about reality. These assumptions cannot be proven. Philosopher of mathematics Paul Ernest has this to say:

Mathematical truth ultimately depends on an irreducible set of assumptions, which are adopted without demonstration. But to qualify as true knowledge, the assumptions require a warrant for their assertion. There is no valid warrant for mathematical knowledge other than demonstration or proof. Therefore the assumptions are beliefs, not knowledge, and remain open to doubt.[9]

Two kinds of people, two kinds of science
As mentioned above Kuyper maintains that regeneration, the new birth, or as he terms it *palingenesis* "breaks humanity in two, and repeals the unity of human consciousness."[10] This leads to two kinds of people which in turn leads to two kinds of science.

We speak none too emphatically, therefore, when we speak of two kinds of people. Both are humans, but

8. Remkes Kooinstra, *Facts and Values: A Christian Approach to Sociology* (St. Catherines, ON: The Association for Reformed Scientific Studies, 1963), 52.

9. Paul Ernest, *The Philosophy of Mathematics Education* (Falmer, Basingstoke, 1991), 14.

10. Kuyper, *Principles of Scared Theology*, 152.

one is inwardly different from the other, and consequently feels a different content rising from his consciousness; thus they face the cosmos from different
points of view, and are impelled by different impulses.
And the fact that there are two kinds of people occasions of necessity the fact of two kinds of human life
and consciousness of life, and of two kinds of science,
for which reason the idea of the unity of science, taken
in its absolute sense, implies the denial of the fact of
palingenesis, and therefore from principle leads to the
rejection of the Christian religion.[11]

There is thus an antithesis, an opposition, arising from palingenesis. Christians and non-Christians view the world
very differently. For Kuyper then the antithesis also means
that there are two kinds of people (regenerate and unregenerate) and thus two kinds of "science" (i.e., scholarship[12])
with different starting points.

Abnormalists and normalists
Kuyper uses the terms abnormalist and normalist to describe this
antithesis or conflict. The conflict is not between faith and science but between opposing scientific systems, each based on their
own faith.[13] The difference stems from the view one has of sin and
how radical was the fall into sin was. Kuyper was an abnormalist:

> ... if the cosmos in its present condition is *abnormal*,
> then a *disturbance* has taken place in the past, and only

---

11. Kuyper, *Principles of Scared Theology*, 154.
12. The Dutch for science (*wetenschap*) is much broader than the natural
    sciences. It can be taken to mean any academic discipline.
13. Kuyper, *Lectures on Calvinism*, 131.

a *regenerating* power can warrant it the final attainment of its goal.[14]

Abnormal or normal then refers to the state of creation and to the extent of the fall. The normalist denies the noetic effects of sin. Thus, if the creation is viewed as normal, then reason may have a higher place than for the abnormalist. For Kuyper, "reason is incomplete with respect to convincing others."[15] Hence the rather low value he placed on apologetics.[16] The issue is to know to what extent the fall has affected reason and the rest of creation. For Kuyper, there was an "abyss" between the two kinds of people and the two kinds of science that couldn't be crossed without God's revelation; this leaves reason helpless. Any attempt at unifying the two "systems" denies the power and reality of rebirth (palingenesis).

Kuyper begins the section on "Two kinds of science" in his *Principles of Sacred Theology* by affirming the unity of the cosmos and the unity of truth. There is one truth and so one science. What does he then mean by two kinds of science?

He clarifies:

What we mean is, that both parts of humanity, that which has been wrought upon by palingenesis and that which lacks it, feels the impulse to investigate the object, and, by doing this in a scientific way, to obtain a systemization of that which exists.... But however

---

14. Kuyper, *Lectures on Calvinism*, 132.

15. Owen Anderson, *Reason and Worldviews: Warfield, Kuyper, Van Til and Plantinga on the Clarity of General Revelation and Function of Apologetics* (Toronto: University Press of America, 2008), 49.

16. On Kuyper's view of apologetics see, Michael Wagenman and Steve Bishop "Abraham Kuyper on Apologetics," *Tydskrif Vir Christelike Wetenskap | Journal for Christian Scholarship* 57, no 1&2 (2021): 1-18.

much they may be doing the same thing formally, their activities run in opposite directions, because they have different starting points; and because of the difference in their nature they apply themselves differently to this work, and view things in a different way.[17]

In other words, they have a different worldview, and these worldviews affect how they approach the creation. Someone who sees the world in full color will see the same things but in a different way to someone who sees only in black and white. They make the same measurements with a thermometer and see the same blood spatter traces but will not see the same color of blood.

To change the metaphor, each person is building a different house because they are building from different architectural plans. The two different kinds of people erect two different kinds of buildings, each they maintain is a "complete building of science."

Some concerns regarding the antithesis

There have been some concerns regarding the antithesis. In what follows I will address some of them. It should be noted that some do contain an element of truth and as such should be taken as warnings against making the antithesis absolute.

It is not a biblical term

This is partly true—the term does however appear in 1 Tim 6:20. The Trinity is not a biblical term—but that does not mean we do not accept the Trinity! Prooftexts are not proofs.

---

17. Kuyper, *Principles of Scared Theology*, 155.

However, if texts are needed then the following show evidence for the antithesis, the conflict between God and Satan throughout the scriptures:

Genesis 3:15
Matthew 6:24
Matthew 7:13–14
John 15:18
1 John 2:15
1 John 3:13

As Dooyeweerd, in an uncharacteristically polemical fashion puts it like this: the "antithesis is not a human invention, but is a great blessing from God. He keeps His fallen creatures from perishing. To deny this is to deny Christ and His work in the world."[18]

It can lead to Niebuhr's Christ against culture position

If the antithesis is not accompanied by common grace, then this may well be the case. The antithesis, although is not God's no to culture or the world. Common grace alone may lead to a Christ of culture position and the antithesis alone may lead to a Christ against nature position. This is why it is important that common grace and antithesis are never alone—they go together and form a "Christ transforms culture" position.

It can lead to isolationism

Linked to the above accusation is the notion that setting up separate Christian institutions could lead to isolationism and/ or exclusivism. Again, there may be some truth in this, but

---

18. Dooyeweerd, *The New Critique*, 1:521.

again such an approach or attitude needs to be mitigated by common grace. Sphere sovereignty also prevents exclusivism[19]—it provides space for all worldviews to set up separate institutions.

It is not applicable today

Peter Heslam writes:

> [Kuyper's] application of the notion of the antithesis, which was relevant to the situation in the Netherlands, was not fitted to the American scene, where Christian and Enlightenment traditions co-existed without open conflict.[20]

This may well be the case in the United States—however, four brief observations are in order. First, it seems to be increasingly not the case, we have seen in the US extreme polarisation of positions and a lack of tolerance for opposing views. Second, such co-existence may be the result of an accommodation by Christians to Enlightenment traditions. Third, it still does not mean that separate Christian institutions, such as Citizens for Public Justice are not needed today. Fourth, the antithesis between the kingdom of dark and the kingdom of light is not a geographical or time-sensitive phenomenon.

Let Kuyper have the last word:

> Independent of what any Statesman may opine or any group of people may affirm, there exists such an Antithesis, which forms the fundamental opposition of

---

19. See chapter 18 below.

20. Peter Heslam, "Architects of Intellectual Thought: Abraham Kuyper and Benjamin Warfield," *Themelios* 24, no. 2 (1999): 13.

our lives. It operates in every sphere and in every sensation of the heart, in every tissue of our thinking, in our antipathies and sympathies, in our entire world and life view, and in the whole of our conception of the personal, familiar, social and political existence.

It exists in our science and in our art, in our jurisprudence and in our pedagogy. It has permeated into everything and in everything it is finding expression in two directions.[21]

---

21. Abraham Kuyper, *Wij, Calvinisten* (Kampen: J.H. Kok, N.V., 1909), 15–18.

Study Questions

1. How does the concept of antithesis differ in Kuyperian thought compared with its use by Hegel?
2. What does Kuyper understand by their being two kinds of science and two kinds of people?
3. What is meant by the term *palingenesis*? How does it relate to the antithesis?
4. Does a stress on the antithesis inevitably leads to Niehbuhr's Christ against culture position?

17

Common Grace

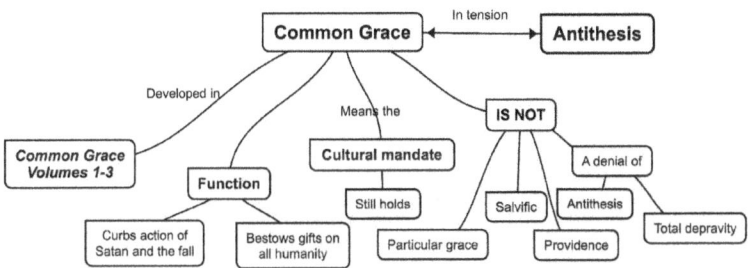

Introduction

"Why does the world turn out to be better than expected and the church worse than expected?" This was a question posed by Kuyper. His answer was common grace.[1] It was the reason why he could call Plato, Aristotle, Kant, and Darwin "stars of the first order ... geniuses of the highest caliber, people

---

1. Abraham Kuyper, *Common Grace. God's Gift for a Fallen World. The Doctrinal Section*. Volume 2. (Abraham Kuyper Collected Works in Public Theology) trans. Nelson D. Kloosterman and Ed M. van der Maas; ed. Jordan J. Ballor and J. Daryl Charles (Bellingham, WA: Lexham Press. 2019), 10, 19, 29, 30.

who expressed very profound ideas, even when they were not professing Christians."[2]

Common grace was a central theme of Kuyper's approach. So much so that he has been described as "the theologian of common grace."[3] James Bratt describes Kuyper's common grace as the "hinge of Kuyper's constructive theology."[4] Louis Berkhof claims that "up to the present Kuyper and Bavinck did more than anyone else for the development of the doctrine of common grace."[5] However, common grace is a controversial subject and is often viewed with suspicion if not loathing by those who do not embrace it. It has even split a denomination.[6] For this reason as well as outlining Kuyper's view of common grace some of the main objections to it will be briefly examined.

Kuyper's common grace

Kuyper wrote a series of articles on common grace over a six-year period for the Dutch newspaper *De Heraut*. They were

2. Abraham Kuyper, *Common Grace. God's Gift for a Fallen World. The Practical Section.* Volume 3. (Abraham Kuyper Collected Works in Public Theology) trans. Nelson D. Kloosterman and Ed M. van der Maas; ed. Jordan J. Ballor and J. Daryl Charles (Bellingham, WA: Lexham Press, 2020), 535.

3. H. R. Van Til, The Calvinistic Concept of Culture (Nutley, NJ: Presbyterian and Reformed Publishing, 1972), 117–136.

4. James Bratt, *Abraham Kuyper: A Centennial Reader* (Grand Rapids: Eerdmans, 1998), viii.

5 Louis Berkhof, *Systematic Theology* (Edinburgh: Banner of Truth, 1958), 434.

6. In 1924, the Protestant Reformed Church in America (PRCA) rejected Kuyper's common grace and so split from the Christian Reformed Church in North America.

completed in 1901 and were then published in book form as *De gemeene gratie* in 1902.13, 1903.13 and 1905.08.[7] Fortunately, a major translation project promoted by the Abraham Kuyper Translation Project to translate these works into English completed its task in 2022.

Kuyper begins his foreword to the first volume with this provocative statement:

> The Reformed paradigm has suffered no damage greater than its deficient development of the doctrine of common grace.[8]

For Kuyper common grace provides the foundation for engagement with the world, thus avoiding spiritual and ecclesiastical isolation and helping believers exercise stewardship. It was common only in the sense that it is universal, as it applies to believers and unbelievers alike.

In his *Principles of Sacred Theology* Kuyper writes of common grace:

> that act of God by which negatively He curbs the operations of Satan, death, and sin, and by which positively He creates an intermediate state for this cosmos, as well as for our human race, which is and continues to be deeply and radically sinful, but in which sin cannot work out its end.[9]

Kuyper distinguished between particular grace—sometimes called saving grace—and common grace. Particular grace abol-

---

7. The numbered dates are those given in Kuipers' 2011 *Abraham Kuyper: Annotated Bibliography.*

8   Kuyper, *Common Grace*, Volume 1, xxxv.

9. Kuyper, *Principles of Scared Theology*, 279.

ishes and undoes the consequences of sin completely for the saved; common grace does not cause conversion but extends to the whole of humankind. There is a close relationship between the two and separation must be opposed:

> ... common grace is only an emanation of particular grace, and that all its fruit flows into particular grace, provided we understand that particular grace itself is not in the least exhausted in the salvation of the elect, but finds its ultimate goal in the glorification of the Son of love, and through this, in the extolling of the virtues of our God.[10]

> Common grace stands in direct contrast to particular grace. Particular grace is personal and is geared to the personal; common grace by contrast always follows the rule that God "makes his sun rise on the evil and on the good, and sends rain on the just and on the unjust" [Matt. 5:45].[11]

> Common grace is the foundation upon which the building of particular grace is erected, and it is particular grace that preserves individual elements of common grace among Israel from eroding.[12]

He uses the illustration of two branches of a tree that are intertwined — but have a common origin.[13] The root system is

---

10. Kuyper, *Common Grace*, Volume 1, 267.

11. Kuyper, *Common Grace*, Volume 1, 321.

12. Kuyper, *Common Grace*, Volume 1, 593.

13. Kuyper, *Common Grace*, Volume 2, 733.

Christ, the first-born of all creation. Kuyper's position on special and common grace is Christological; he writes: "there is (...) no doubt whatever that common grace and special grace come most intimately connected from their origin, and this connection lies in Christ."[14] Particular grace, he asserts, assumes common grace. In *Common Grace* 1 he writes of the interrelationship of particular and common grace:

> the glory of common grace would never have sparkled in its springtime if particular grace had not brought it fully into bloom.[15]

> ...particular grace always presupposes common grace, and the presence of common grace is the necessary pre-condition for any functioning of particular grace. Without common grace any functioning of particular grace would be unthinkable.[16]

and:

> no matter how we look at the data, particular grace presupposes common grace. Without the latter, the former cannot do its work.[17]

> ...particular grace is treated too much in isolation while neglecting its foundation in "common grace" and its ultimate goal: the salvation of the world that

---

14. Kuyper, *Common Grace*, Volume 2, 734.

15. Kuyper, *Common Grace*, Volume 1, 261.

16. Kuyper, *Common Grace*, Volume 1, 505.

17. Kuyper, *Common Grace*, Volume 1, 265.

was created, maintained, and never abandoned by God.[18]

Common grace means that the creation ordinances of dominion and stewardship over nature, given in the cultural mandate before the fall, are not abolished after the fall. As Kuyper affirms:

> thanks to common grace, the foundational creation ordinance that was given before the fall—the mandate that man would achieve mastery over all of the created order—also will be realized after the fall.[19]

Common grace has a twofold effect: on the one hand, it curbs the effects of sin and restrains the deeds of fallen humanity; on the other hand, it upholds the ordinances of creation and provides the basis for Christian cultural involvement, it provides a foundation for culture. The cultural mandate to develop and fill the earth has not been rescinded after the fall into sin. Therefore, as previously stressed, cultural withdrawal is not an option for Christians.

As Kuyper puts it:

> In summary, one can say that common grace produces three kinds of fruit for the kingdom of glory. First, we find such fruit in the development of our human race and of the gifts God embedded within this human race (the honor and glory of the nations). Second, we find such fruit in the development of character and personality among the individual elect (their works that fol-

---

18. Kuyper, *Common Grace*, Volume 1, 377.

19. Kuyper, *Common Grace*, Volume 2, 717.

low them). And third, we find such fruit in the continued existence of this world so that it could be renewed (the new vine in the kingdom of the Father).[20]

It is also important to state what common grace does not imply. It is not saving grace.

> God has let the wonder of common grace operate among all peoples and in all nations, even where this had no direct connection with the salvation of the elect.[21]

It is not ecclesiastical:

> Common grace has operated for ages in China and India without there being any church of Christ in those countries. We still enjoy the fruits that have come from common grace in Greece and Rome in the days when even the name of Christ's church had never yet been mentioned.[22]

For Kuyper common grace is, as previously mentioned, "deduced directly from the sovereignty of God" and is the "root and conviction for all Reformed people."[23]

Common grace is not a denial of total depravity or of limited atonement—Kuyper was an advocate of both.[24] It does not blur the distinction (antithesis) between the regenerate and the

---

20. Kuyper, *Common Grace*, Volume 1, 587.

21. Kuyper, *Common Grace*, Volume 1, 302

22. Kuyper, *Common Grace*, Volume 1, 310–302.

23. Kuyper, *Common Grace*, Volume 1, xxxvii.

24. On the latter see Abraham Kuyper, *Particular Grace: A Defense of God's Sovereignty in Salvation* (Grandville: Reformed Free Publishing Association, 2001).

unregenerate, between the kingdom of light and the kingdom of darkness, or between the church and the world. It does not mean that all things are permissible.

Common grace and providence

Many who dislike common grace maintain that providence is a better term. Kuyper makes a distinction between the two. Providence flows from God's decrees and common grace is determined by God's providential plan.[25] Both operate outside of saving grace; however, as Kuyper rightly points out, belief in providence outside of saving faith is closer to deism than Christianity. He thus laments that among believers there is not a "clear discerning insight into the essence of the doctrine of providence." The ideas seem to be more pagan than biblical. He warns:

> We must seriously guard against the danger of adopting pagan notions and then mixing them with the content of revelation.[26]

He goes on:

> The task before us is precisely the opposite to analyse the content of Scripture as clearly as possible in constructing doctrine, and through this analytical process to exclude all that is unchristian and foreign.[27]

Providence is not a determination of what will happen, but rather the execution of what has already been decreed. It is the

---

25. Kuyper, *Common Grace*, Volume 1, Ch. 3.

26. Kuyper, *Common Grace*, Volume 1, 417.

27. Kuyper, *Common Grace*, Volume 1, 417.

maintenance and governance of all things, not a pagan notion of seeing ahead (*pro vide*). A proper understanding of the providence of God is

> …the confession that the counsel and decrees of God are all-embracing, that the eternal counsel of God encompasses all things, and that nothing can be named or imagined — regardless of how large or small — that is not included in and does not proceed from the decrees of God.[28]

He warns against two extremes associated with wrong notions of providence. A deistic framework where creation and providence take up two separate identities, so that we become independent of God. If creation has an independent existence it leads to atheism via Pelagianism[29] and deism.[30] On the other hand, if the distinction between them is dissolved it leads to pantheism.[31] Our independent existence becomes an illusion. This is false mysticism. God is absorbed into the being of the world. A biblical perspec-

---

28. Kuyper, *Common Grace*, Volume 1, 420.

29. "The label 'Pelagian' is often loosely invoked to damn any doctrine felt to threaten the primacy of grace, faith and spiritual regeneration over human ability, good works and moral endeavour." Martin Davie, Tim Grass, Stephen R Holmes, John McDowell, and T A Noble, ed., *New Dictionary of Theology: Historical and Systematic* (Second Edition), (Leicester: IVP, 2016).

30. Deism is the notion that God exists but stands part from his creation and is no longer involved in it.

31. "Specifically, pantheism's metaphysic, its view of reality, affirms two things: the unity of all reality and the divineness of that unity." Davie, *et al. New Dictionary of Theology*.

tive holds to the truth of an independent existence of things outside the being of God and that this independent existence is possible only because it rests in the will and power of God.

Providence, Kuyper is very clear, is not to be seen as a continuing creation. Creation causes things to "come into existence outside of God" whereas providence entails existing things to exist and develop. Providence, therefore, is not a supplemental creation. The corollary of this is that miracles are not to be viewed as a second creation.

Providence depends on common grace, without common grace, "no providential ordination if God would be manifest at all." However, common grace "is encompassed entirely by God's providential order and hence arises from it."

Objections to Kuyper's common grace[32]

Several objections have been made against Kuyper's common grace. The most serious accusation is that common grace is a heresy and a denial of all that was achieved at the Reformation. I will return to this below. Other objections will be dealt with in turn. But as will be seen most, if not all, of the accusations may be valid against some deviations from Kuyper's common grace but cannot be applied to Kuyper's version. It is Kuyper's version that I will defend here.

---

32. See Steve Bishop, "Abraham Kuyper and Some Critics," *Journal for Christian Scholarship/ Tydskrif vir Christelike Wetenskap* 58, no. 3 &4 (2023) for a further discussion on common grace detractors.

1. It is a denial of the antithesis

However, Kuyper does not deny the antithesis. In volume 2 of his *Common Grace*, he writes:

> ...In all this nothing else is at work other than the antithesis—which seems irreconcilable—between the eternal in God and the temporal in our human existence.[33]

Kuyper's common grace does not nullify the antithesis — they are both important aspects of Kuyper's thought: common grace and the antithesis should be kept together. In fact, common grace presupposes the antithesis. Common grace explains why given the fall, and the consequent antithesis that non-Christians can produce works of insight and beauty and why the world turns out to be better than expected and the church worse than expected.[34]

In *Wij, Calvinisten* [We Calvinists] (1909)—as mentioned previously—in the twilight years of his life he wrote:

> The antithesis is not the product of fantasy, nor has it been constructed by anyone. It is there. It exists, and it dominates our whole life.[35]

Common grace and the antithesis go hand in hand. In R. H. Niebuhr's proposed fivefold typology of the relationship between Christ and culture (see above), the Kuyperian view is that Christ *transforms* culture. This requires both common grace and the antithesis. If common grace alone is emphasized

---

33. Kuyper, *Common Grace*, Volume 2, Ch49 §3.
34. Kuyper, *Common Grace*, Volume 1, 10, 19, 29, 30.
35. Kuyper, *Wij, Calvinisten*, 15–16.

this can lead to a Christ and culture position. If the antithesis is emphasized and common grace denied, then we have a Christ against culture position.

2. Kuyper does not begin and end with Scripture

One critic of common grace quotes an undisclosed reviewer as saying: "but there are no Scripture references." That seems pretty damming until one realizes it would have been true of the Dutch version — the reason for that is that Kuyper assumed his readers knew their Bible and so didn't need to include the reference alongside the copious Scripture quotations. The editors have added the references in the new English translations. All that critique suggests is that the reviewer may not have read the book he or she is reviewing!

Volume 1 of *Common Grace*, the historical section, begins and ends in Scripture. It is difficult to see how anyone who has only a quick glance at this volume can make such an accusation. Part 1 looks at Genesis 1–6, Noah and Adam, part 2 with temptation to Babel and part 3 with Abraham to the Parousia. For someone who is accused of not beginning with Scripture it seems a strange starting point.

Kuyper's vision for the Free University (VU, Amsterdam) was that it should be one "which takes the Bible as the unconditional basis on which to rear the whole structure of human knowledge in every department of life." [36] It is difficult to rec-

---

36. Cited in P. J. Hoedemaker, *Article 36 of the Belgic Confession Vindicated against Dr. Abraham Kuyper: A Critique of His Series on Church and State in Common Grace* (Aalten: Wordbridge, 2019), xi.

oncile Kuyper's words with this accusation—as we shall see in the discussion of Kuyper's view of Scripture.[37]

3. It is a denial of total depravity

The Protestant Reformed Church in America (PRCA) scholars, such as Henry J. Danhof, Herman Hoeksema (1886–1965), and David Engelsma (1939–)[38] maintain *contra* Kuyper that common grace is a denial of total depravity and particular grace and that it can lead to Arminianism—the theological view that in some way *our* faith, *our* decision to follow God, can save us. This seems to be a strange argument, as Kuyper was an adherent of particular grace and a whole-hearted Calvinist, and not Arminian. At best their argument is only against the misuse of the concept of common grace. What we have in their critique is a conflation of soteriology and providence.

It is clear from even a cursory reading of Kuyper that these accusations are without foundation. William Masselink in his study of *General Revelation and Common Grace* when discussing Kuyper's common grace correctly observes:

> Here [in *Common Grace* volume 1] it is clearly stated that both common as well as special grace presuppose the doctrine of the total depravity of man.[39]

---

37. See Chapter 20 below.

38. See, for example, Henry Danhof and Herman Hoeksema, *Sin and Grace*, trans. Cornelius Hanko (Grandville, MI: Reformed Free Publishing Association, 2003); and David J. Engelsma, *Common Grace Revisited Grace* (Grandville, MI: Reformed Free Publishing Association, 2003).

39. William Masselink, *General Revelation and Common Grace A Defense of the Historic Reformed Faith Over Against the Theology*

4. It advocates the free-offer of the gospel

Irrespective of one's view of the free offer it is not a doctrine that Kuyper endorses. The association with the free offer of the gospel and common grace was made by Stonehouse and Murray in their *The Free Offer of the Gospel*.[40] It did not originate with Kuyper — and as Englesma, a critic of common grace (and the free offer) acknowledges:[41]

> It is widely assumed that the well-meant gospel offer, or free offer, has strong backing in the Dutch Reformed theologian, Abraham Kuyper.... This assumption is false[I]t is not true that Kuyper held the doctrine of the well-meant offer-not even in *De Gemeene Gratie*; on the contrary, he was an avowed foe of the theology of the offer.... Kuyper's common grace had nothing to do with this universal grace.[42]

5. The VU and the state of affairs in The Netherlands are testimony to the flaws in common grace

This is the inverse of the genetic fallacy; perhaps we should term it the teleos fallacy?

Kuyper and his ideas cannot be held responsible for them being carried out wrongly, any more than we cannot discredit

---

and Philosophy of the so-called "Reconstructionist" Movement (Grand Rapids: Eerdmans, 1953), 210.

40. Ned Stonehouse and John Murray, *The Free Offer of the Gospel* (Presbyterian & Reformed,1949).

41. Yet elsewhere he implies that it does.

42. David Engelsma, *Hypercalvinism and the Call of the Gospel* (Granville, MI: Reformed Free Publishing Association 1980), 109–115.

Christianity because of the atrocities carried out during the crusades.

The state of affairs in the Netherlands, however, is the result of secularism rather than common grace.

6. The creation structure objection to common grace

Nathan Brummel, a United Reformed Churches of North America minister, wants to develop a positive view of culture along the lines of Herman Hoeksema and Klaas Schilder without resorting to common grace.[43] He thinks that common grace is not necessary.

He is right that Kuyper, contra Hoeksema and others' accusation, "posits a strong theory of total depravity that necessitates common grace."

Surprisingly, Brummel draws upon the Kuyperian Al Wolters and his discussion of the distinction between structure and direction to imply that the fall did not affect the creation essentially. Therefore, Brummel feels he can replace common grace with "the providentially preserved creation structure." This appears to be a definition shift rather than a refutation of common grace, as the two concepts perform the same role.

Brummel also asserts that Kuyper "seems to deny that man after the Fall still possessed the image of God" and that Kuyper "has ignored the reality of God's providence." Brummel presumably has not read Kuyper's treatment of providence in *Common Grace 2*. There Kuyper examines the links between common grace and God's providence.

---

43 Nathan Clay Brummel, *Dutch Reformed Theologians: Explorations in Prominent Theologians and their Central Ideas* (Self-published, 2018), Ch 11 and 12.

For Kuyper, there is a mutual chance interaction —
"an inseparable link" — between providence and common
grace. Providence depends on common grace, without
common grace, "no providential ordination if God would
be manifest at all." However, common grace "is encompassed entirely by God's providential order and hence arises from it."[44]

7. It lies at the root of the present growing apostasy of the church

In the book *Sin and Grace* Danhof and Hoeksema attempt to
show that Kuyper's views were original to Kuyper and had not
previously been seen in Reformed thought or in the Scriptures.
They also maintained that holding on to common grace would
lead to "worldliness."

> We include a criticism of the position that was taken
> especially by Dr. A. Kuyper on so-called common
> grace, and which many brethren promoted as one of
> the foundations of a sound Reformed life-view.[45]

> We are deeply concerned that Dr Kuyper led us in a
> fundamentally wrong direction when he wrote his *De
> Gemeene Gratie* [Common Grace].[46]

It is difficult to see how one doctrine alone can lead to worldliness and apostasy. An overemphasis on common grace to the
detriment of the antithesis may possibly lead to a rationale for

---

44. Kuyper, *Common Grace*, Volume 2, 453.

45. Danhof and Hoeksema, *Sin and Grace*, preface.

46. Danhof and Hoeksema, *Sin and Grace*, preface.

worldliness. However, for Kuyper, common grace and the antithesis are both needed.

For, the PRCA theologian, David Engelsma, common
grace is a corruption of the gospel of grace. Engelsma (over)
emphasizes the antithesis. However, for Kuyper, the antithesis
and common grace—as noted previously—go hand in hand. If
we ignore the antithesis, it may well lead to the issues that Engelsma points out.

In denying common grace and emphasizing the antithesis,
however, it can lead to a dry, negative, and legalistic approach,
one that stresses fence-building rather than bridge-building.

Perhaps the most serious of the complaints is:

8. It is a heresy and is opposed to Reformation doctrines

If common grace involved a denial of total depravity, if Kuyper
did not begin with the Scriptures, and it was a denial of the
antithesis, then it could be seen as being heretical and opposed
to Reformation doctrines, however, this is not the case.

Engelsma claims that neither Calvin nor the Reformers
held to the concept of common grace. Yet there seems to be
at least some evidence to suggest that they did. Calvin in his
Institutes writes:

> But we ought to consider, that, notwithstanding of the
> corruption of our nature, there is some room for divine
> grace, such grace as, without purifying it, may lay it
> under internal restraint.[47]

This is exactly the point Kuyper was making regarding the restraining power of common grace. Kuyper never claimed orig-

---

47. Calvin, *Institutes*, 2.3 §3:

191

inality in his development of the doctrine of common grace; rather he thought of himself as a copyist of Calvin.[48] Kuyper only aimed at making explicit what was implicit in Calvin. Kuyper maintains he is working in Calvin's line.

Calvin also seems to suggest the following:

> ...in reading profane authors, the admirable light of truth displayed in them should remind us that the human mind, however much fallen and perverted from its original integrity, is still adorned and invested with admirable gifts from its Creator. If we reflect that the Spirit of God is the only fountain of truth, we will be careful, as we would avoid offering insult to him, not to reject or condemn truth wherever it appear.... If the Lord has been pleased to assist us by the work and ministry of the ungodly in physics, dialectics, mathematics, and other similar sciences, let us avail ourselves of it.[49]

This sentiment is echoed by Kuyper under the guise of common grace:

> Common grace extends over our entire human life, in all its manifestations. There is a common grace that manifests itself in order and law; there is a common grace that manifests itself in prosperity and affluence; there is a common grace that becomes visible in the healthy development of strength and heroic courage of a nation; there is a common grace that shines in the development of science and art; there is a common grace that enriches a nation through inventiveness in

---

48. Masselink, *General Revelation and Common Grace*, 187.

49. Calvin, *Institutes*, 2.2.15–16.

enterprise and commerce; there is a common grace that strengthens the domestic and moral life; and finally there is a common grace that protects the religious life against an excessive degeneration.[50]

What is nascent in Calvin regarding common grace—through he doesn't use the term—is more developed in Kuyper.

Masselink writes "Hepp states that the first one must yet appear to prove Kuyper departed from John Calvin."[51] Masselink also notes that "The works of John Calvin already contained the doctrine of common grace, although it was not yet developed."[52]

Herman Kuiper (1889–1963) in his study of Calvin's common grace has shown how Calvin does endorse such an approach.[53] He also includes numerous quotes from Reformers and Calvinists who likewise embrace the Reformation and common grace. These include Peter van Mastricht, Johannes Marck, Wilhelmus à Brakel, Bernhardinus de Moor, Jonathan Edwards, Charles Hodge, A. A. Hodge, Herman Bavinck, and V. Hepp, as well as Kuyper. Rather than being a denial of the Reformation, common grace is in line with Reformation thought. Others that Kuiper's does not mention include are Robert Harris (1581–1658),[54] John Knox (1514–1572),[55] and

---

50. Kuyper, *Common Grace*, Volume 1, 497.

51. Masselink, *General Revelation and Common Grace*, 11.

52 Masselink, *General Revelation and Common Grace* 187.

53. Herman Kuiper, *Calvin on Common Grace* (Goes: Oosterbaan & Le Cointre, 1928).

54. Harris was a member of the Westminster Assembly and a Puritan preacher.

55. Knox founded the Presbyterian Church of Scotland and was one of the leaders in the Scottish Reformation.

Heinrich Bullinger (1504–1575)[56] three key Reformers, who did seem to hold to some notion of common grace. Robert Harris said:

> There are graces of two sorts. First, common graces, which even reprobates may have. Secondly, peculiar, such as accompany salvation, as the Apostle has it, proper to God's own children only. The matter is not whether we have the first sort of graces, for those do not seal up God's special love to a man's soul, but it must be saving grace alone that can do this for us.[57]

John Knox wrote:

> After these common mercies, I say, whereof the reprobate are often partakers, he openeth the treasure of his rich mercies, which are kept in Christ Jesus for his Elect. Such as willingly delight not in blindness may clearly see that the Holy Ghost maketh a plain difference betwixt the graces and mercies which are common to all, and that sovereign mercy which is immutably reserved to the chosen children.[58]

Likewise, Bullinger also seems to support a form of common grace:

> For there is in God a certain (as it were) general grace, whereby he created all mortal men, and by which he

---

56. Bullinger was a Swiss Reformer and collaborator of John Calvin. He was one of the authors of the Helvetic Confession.

57. The Nineteenth Sermon. Matthew. 5:9. Blessed are the peace-makers: for they shall bee called the sonnes of God. In *The Works of Robert Harris* [1635].

58. John Knox, *On Predestination*, 87.

sends rain upon the just and unjust: but this grace doth not justify; for if it did, then should the wicked and unjust be justified. Again, there is that singular grace, whereby he doth, for his only-begotten Christ his sake, adopt us to be his sons: he doth not, I mean, adopt all, but the believers only, whose sins he reckons not, but doth impute to them the righteousness of his only-begotten Son our Saviour. This is that grace which doth alone justify us in very deed.[59]

It is clear then that from the foregoing that Kuyper's common grace is no heresy, and it is in the line of the Reformers and Reformation, Calvin included.

Conclusion

Kuyper thinks that resuscitating the doctrine of common grace will help the believer "take hold of the plow" rather than retreat from the world. Common grace provides the foundation for engagement with the world thus avoiding spiritual and ecclesiastical isolation and thereby helping believers exercise dominion.[60]

For Kuyper common grace was not merely an important doctrine, but also important for our worldview and our praxis:

The further we develop this doctrine of "common grace," the more clearly we shall discover the far-reaching significance of this doctrine, not only for dogmatics, but also for our entire world- and lifeview, and for the praxis of life.[61]

---

59. *Decades*, 3rd Decade, Sermon 9, 1:329–330.

60. Kuyper, *Common Grace*, Volume 1, xiv.

61. Kuyper, *Common Grace*, Volume 1, 420.

Common grace extends over our entire human life, in all its manifestations. There is a common grace that manifests itself in order and law; there is a common grace that manifests itself in prosperity and affluence; there is a common grace that becomes visible in the healthy development of strength and heroic courage of a nation; there is a common grace that shines in the development of science and art; there is a common grace that enriches a nation through inventiveness in enterprise and commerce; there is a common grace that strengthens the domestic and moral life; and finally there is a common grace that protects the religious life against an excessive degeneration.[62]

---

62. Kuyper, *Common Grace*, Volume 1, 497–498.

Study Questions

1. Some have suggested that common grace was developed by Kuyper to further his political ambitions. How would you respond to such a suggestion?
2. How do common grace and the antithesis relate?
3. Does common grace inevitably mean the free-offer of the gospel?
4. Is common grace another term for God's providence?
5. Have providence and common grace been confused?
6. How is common grace the basis for particular grace?
7. "Kuyper's zeal for the kingship of Christ in the world had to lead to an acceleration of the process of the secularization of spiritual values," writes Cornelius Pronk. Would you agree? Why or why not?

18

Sphere Sovereignty

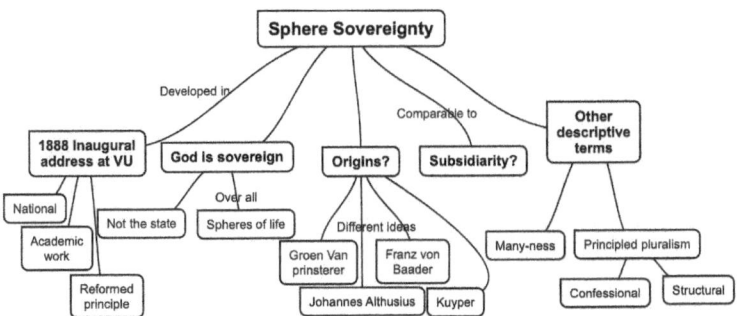

Introduction

ALL THINGS ARE SUBJECT to the sovereignty of God. This conviction led Kuyper, following Groen van Prinsterer, to develop a theory that became known as sphere sovereignty. There are different independent spheres within creation, but God is sovereign over them all. Kuyper developed the notion in part to counter state absolutism—the idea that the state dictates to other areas of life what should and shouldn't be done. Statism maintains that the state makes laws and regulations and is in control of, or sovereign over, many other areas of life.

Consider the question of what role does the state have in raising children. Should the state mandate if a baby should be fed on demand or every few hours? Should the state interfere with the running of household finances? Then what about education? Or business? Or the church? Sphere sovereignty would limit state interference in these other realms, statism would not. Statism starts from the authority of the state. Sphere sovereignty starts from the sovereignty of God rather than the state or any other created thing.

Kuyper's 1888 inaugural address

Although Kuyper's first mention of sphere sovereignty was in 1870 in *De Heraut*.[1] It was in his 1880 inaugural address to the VU that he more fully outlined his position.[2] Kuyper begins his address by identifying three areas: its national significance, its scholarly significance, and its Reformed character.

National significance

In the national arena he identifies a crisis that shaped society — the crisis he has in mind was one of conflict, a conflict over sovereignty: the sovereignty of God or the state. The key question is what or who is sovereign? God, the individual, or the

---

1. George Harinck, "I Look through My Window into Life: Kuyper's Notion of Sphere Sovereignty (1870–1880)," *Journal of Markets & Morality* 23, no. 2 (2020): 265–284.

2. Abraham Kuyper, "Sphere Sovereignty," in *Abraham Kuyper: A Centennial Reader*, ed. James Bratt (Grand Rapids: Eerdmans, 1998). I am using the translation in Bratt's *A Centennial Reader* (A translation by George Kamps is available on the internet: https://reformationaldl.wordpress. com/2019/07/17/sphere-sovereignty-abraham-kuyper/ accessed: 17 Feb 2024.) A newer translation by Harry Van Dyke appears in *On Charity & Justice* (Kuyper, 2022).

state? A Christian cannot answer anything else other than the ultimate sovereign is God. This is Kuyper's starting point. He distances himself from the sovereignty of the state and popular sovereignty. Matthew 28:18 is clear: all authority belongs to God.

He describes sovereignty as "the authority that has the right and the duty to exercise power to break all resistance to its will and to avenge such resistance."

> That perfect and absolute Sovereignty of the sinless Messiah at the same time contains the direct denial and challenge of all absolute Sovereignty on earth in sinful man; because of the division of life into separate spheres, each with its own sovereignty.[3]

He also uses images of cog wheels—"each animated by its own spirit." Human life is not simple nor uniform but "constitutes an infinitely complex organism."[4]

Kuyper does not specify or delineate what he sees as these spheres or cogs; he identifies some—morality, family, social life—but then stresses that we need to

> ...recognise that there are in life as many spheres as there are constellations in the sky and the circumference of each has been drawn on a fixed radius from the center of a unique principle, namely, the apostolic injunction *hekastos en toi idioi tagmati* ["each in its own order": 1 Cor. 15:23]. Just as we speak of a "moral

---

3. *A Centennial Reader*, 467.
4. Here Kuyper is using images that functionalists, such as Émile Durkheim (1858–1917), have used to describe society—this should not be taken to mean that Kuyper was a functionalist!

201

world," a "scientific world," a "business world," the "world of art," so we can more properly speak of a "sphere" of morality, of the family, of social life, each with its own domain. And because each comprises its own domain, each has its own Sovereign within its bounds.[5]

Each of these spheres has its own domain, and within its own domain it is sovereign. Sphere sovereignty maintains that the only sovereign is God. He has established laws or norms for other areas of society such as the family, morality, social life, and so on. Within their own sphere, these areas are thus sovereign under God's laws and norms for that aspect of life. No one institution should dominate or dictate to another, there is no hierarchy of institutions.

An illustration may help:[6]

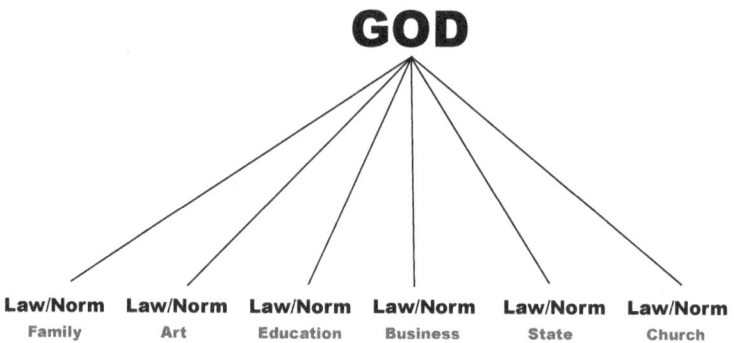

GOD

Law/Norm	Law/Norm	Law/Norm	Law/Norm	Law/Norm	Law/Norm
Family	Art	Education	Business	State	Church

There is a domain of nature, in which the Sovereign exerts power upon matter according to fixed laws. But

---

5. *A Centennial Reader*, 467.

6. Adapted from Alan Storkey, *A Christian Social Perspective* (Leicester: Inter-Varsity Press, 1979), 141.

there is also a domain of the personal, of the house-hold, of science, of social and ecclesiastical life, each of which obeys its own law of life, and each subject to its own chief. There is a domain of thought in which no law may prevail except the law of logic. A domain of conscience where none may exercise sovereign rule except the Holy One. And finally, a domain of faith within whose limits only the individual is Sovereign, and through that faith consecrates himself with his whole being.[7]

It is significant here that Kuyper places the ecclesiastical sphere alongside the other spheres. The church should not control or suffocate the other domains. Likewise, with the state—there is no state sovereignty. Elsewhere Kuyper de-limits the role of the state—it acts almost like a lubricant for the cogs of the other domains, he describes this as the "spe-cial sphere of authority." It is in the engagement of these cogs that results in "the rich, multifaceted multiformity of human life."[8]

The state has several key roles to ensure that the spheres do not encroach on each other. These special roles include:

It must provide for sound mutual interaction among the spheres

To keep them within "just limits"

It must protect the individual from the "tyranny of his own circle"

---

7. *A Centennial Reader*, 467.

8. *A Centennial Reader*, 467–468.

The state must see that "the wheels operate as intended"

It should not shackle freedom but make problems the free movement of life in and for every sphere.[9]

Sphere sovereignty rests on the notion that all sovereignty rests in God. Sovereignty of any kind can then only proceed from him; Christ is the sinless Messiah who has had "absolute and undivided" sovereignty conferred on him — all authority is therefore derived from him. Sphere sovereignty lies in the order of creation, "in the structure of human life."[10]

Kuyper then moves on to discuss scholarship and academic work in relation to sphere sovereignty.

Academic work

Kuyper also maintains that sphere sovereignty should be "the signature of our academic work."[11] It leads to a "sanctified intellectual power, a power to resist whatever superior force would limit freedom in and of our human life."[12]

The key issue here is freedom—will the spheres "florish in freedom or groan under state coercion"?

Sin threatens freedom within each sphere just as strongly as state-power does at the boundary.[13]

Scholarship is a means of defending liberties. Scholarship needs to be sovereign in its own sphere and should not "degenerate

---

9. *A Centennial Reader*, 468.

10. *A Centennial Reader*, 469.

11. *A Centennial Reader*, 472.

12. *A Centennial Reader*, 472.

13 *A Centennial Reader*, 473.

under the guardianship of Church or state."[14] A dishonoring of scholarship is a "sin before God." He goes on to say: "We must resist tooth and nail any imposition upon learning by the church of Christ."[15] The role that the church must play in scholarship is to ensure learning must never be a slave, but "maintain its sovereignty upon its own ground and live by the grace of God."[16] Likewise, for the state, learning is not to be a servant of the state. However, the state should, at the moment, support scholarship because of a sad state of affairs among the public, the wealthy and graduates:

> it would border on the absurd to demand that the state would now suddenly relinquish its hold on the university world. At present the public display too little desire for science; there is too little generosity on the part of the wealthy; and too little energy in the circle of graduates to make such an attempt. For the present the state must continue its support, provided, and this we insist, provided there is a striving in the direction of liberation, and science again grasps "Sphere sovereignty" as its ideal.[17]

Scholarship he stresses should be free—but not free in the sense of "detached from its principle," "that would be the freedom of the fish on dry land, of a flower uprooted from the soil."[18]

---

14. *A Centennial Reader*, 476.

15. *A Centennial Reader*, 477.

16. *A Centennial Reader*, 477.

17. Kamps's translation.

18. *A Centennial Reader*, 486.

He then goes on to discuss what is meant by Christian medicine and Christian logic.[19]

> Do you think that we would confess God's revelation—reformed after its deformation—as the starting point of our efforts and draw upon this source only as the starting point. Of our efforts and draw upon this source only as theologians, scorning it as artists, jurists, and students of letters? Can thou think of a science worthy of the name whose knowledge is divided up into cubbyholes?[20]

He is right when he asserts:

> man [sic] in his antithesis as fallen sinner or self-developing natural creature returns again as the "subject that thinks" or the "object that prompts thought" in every department in every discipline, and with every investigator.[21]

This is the context in which he utters has famous square inch quote.

A Reformed principle

Kuyper is keen to show that sphere sovereignty is a Reformed principle. It places in the foreground a key Calvinistic principle: the sovereignty of God. He alludes to sphere sovereignty being the basis of the "entire Presbyterian church order" and to Calvin's "lesser magistrates" as evidence of this Reformed basis.

---

19. *A Centennial Reader*, 487ff.

20. *A Centennial Reader*, 487.

21. *A Centennial Reader*, 488.

Origins

Gordon Spykman has traced sphere sovereignty back to Calvin and shows through the writing of numerous Calvinists over the years that this approach has been there in embryo.[22] Those Spykman mentions (with copious quotes) include:

- Henry Meeter (1960)
- R. B. Kuiper (1958)
- Geerhadus Vos (1951)
- Louis Berkhof (1949)
- Herman Bavinck (1928)[23] and,
- Groen van Prinsterer.

Spykman maintains that the earliest "theoretical formulation of [it] is traceable to Johannes Althusius (1557–1638), a German churchman and civil official in Eden, whose thinking was shaped in part by Calvin's Geneva."[24] M. R. R. Ossewaarde also supports the idea that sphere sovereignty was in Althusius's thought, for Althusius it was an alternative to

---

22 Gordon Spykman, "Sphere-sovereignty in Calvin and the Calvinist Tradition," in D. E. Holwerda (ed) *Exploring the Heritage of John Calvin* (Grand Rapids: Baker,1976). On Spykman, see, Steve Bishop, "Everything Matters: Gordon Spykman—A Neo-Calvinist Theologian," *Pro Rege* 52, no. 3 (2024): 1–15.

23. Timothy Shaun Price notes that: "Bavinck uses his doctrine of creation to generate a nuanced form of sphere sovereignty. Although he does not always use the language of sphere sovereignty explicitly, he states that there are distinct and diverse spheres that operate in harmony because of an organic ethical unity they share" (Timothy Shaun Price, "Abraham Kuyper and Herman Bavinck on the Subject of Education as seen in Two Public Addresses," *The Bavinck Review* 2 (2011): 59–70.)

24. Spykman, "Sphere-sovereignty," 184.

scholasticism. Althusius called it a "symbiotic association."[25] Although it was Kuyper that brought the idea to prominence and developed it to support his ideas, particularly those regarding education and the relationship between education and the state. Dooyeweerd also traced the origins back to Althusius. However, Glenn Friesen has challenged this and sees its origins in the Christian theosophist Franz von Baader (1765–1841).[26] This has been countered by Roger Henderson.[27] George Harinck maintains that it is Kuyper's own idea.[28]

Although it may or may not have been Kuyper's invention, it was he who developed it into a theory of how societal entities should relate to each other. As the human rights lawyer, Van der Vyver, remarks:

> Within Calvinist circles in The Netherlands, Abraham Kuyper must be single[d] out as the person who expanded the notion of sphere sovereignty beyond the enclave of church-state relations to embrace the relationship between all social institutions.[29]

25. M. R. R. Ossewaarde, "Three Rival Versions of Political Enquiry: Althusius and the Concept of Sphere Sovereignty," *Monist* (2007). Available at: https://ris.utwente.nl/ws/files/6494036/Sphere_Sovereignty_-_the_Monist.pdf.

26. Glenn J. Friesen, "New Research on Groen van Prinsterer and the Idea of Sphere Sovereignty," *Philosophia Reformata* 84, no. 1 (2019): 1–30.

27. Roger Henderson "The Development of the Principle of Distributed Authority, or Sphere Sovereignty," *Philosophia Reformata* 82 (2017): 74–99.

28. George Harinck, "I Look through My Window into Life...," 265–284.

29. J. D. Van der Vyver, "Sphere Sovereignty of Religious Institutions: A Contemporary Calvinistic Theory of Church-State Relations," in

For Kuyper, sphere sovereignty was neither individualism nor corporatism and neither statism nor popular sovereignty. Kuyper describes the limited role of the state (contra statism):

> The state may never become an octopus, which stifles the whole of life. It must occupy its own place, on its own root, among all the other trees of the forest, and thus it has to honor and maintain every form of life which grows independently in its own sacred autonomy.[30]

Social institutions have a unique and divinely appointed role. The state has an active role; it is not a neutral adjudicator in maintaining the boundaries between institutions that need to be constantly evaluated.

In Kuyper's *Lectures on Calvinism* he identifies the threefold task of the state:

- It is to adjudicate cases of conflict between the different spheres
- It is to defend individuals against the abuses of power
- It must coerce citizens to bear personal and financial burdens — i.e., pay taxes![31]

Comparison with subsidiarity

Several have identified points in which sphere sovereignty is similar to the Roman Catholic theory of subsidiarity. There are undoubtedly some parallels and similarities — but there are some differences the main one is that subsidiarity arises

Church Autonomy: A Comparative Study, ed. Gerhard Robbers (Frankfurt am Main: Peter Lang, 2001), Ch 32.

30. Kuyper, *Lectures on Calvinism*, 96.
31. Kuyper, *Lectures on Calvinism*, 97.

out of natural law, whereas sphere sovereignty arises from the sovereignty of God and common grace. For subsidiarity there is a hierarchy of institutions with the church having a higher role, as Ossewaarde explains of subsidiarity:

> The Church functions as the total community (communio) of all Christian life and the state is the total community of all political life.[32]

In contrast, in sphere sovereignty, there is no hierarchy of institutions or spheres. In sphere sovereignty, each sphere is distinct and has its own divinely appointed role.

As Ossewaarde puts it: "The concept of sphere sovereignty is antithetical to the scholastic concept of subsidiarity owing to its radically different metaphysics."[33]

Another term that has been used to describe sphere sovereignty is principled pluralism.

Principled pluralism

Richard Mouw uses the term many-ness to describe Kuyper's pluralism.[34] Another more common term is principled pluralism which is used by Gordon Spykman[35] and James Skillen,[36]

---

32. Ossewaarde, "Three Rival Political Versions."

33. Ossewaarde, "Three Rival Political Versions."

34. Richard Mouw, "Some Reflections on Sphere Sovereignty," in *Religion, Pluralism, and Public Life: Abraham Kuyper's Legacy for the Twenty-first Century*, ed. Luis E. Lugo (Grand Rapids: Eerdmans, 2000).

35. Gordon Spykman, "The Principled Pluralist Position," in *God and Politics: Four Views on the Reformation of Civil Government* (Phillipsburg, NJ: Presbyterian and Reformed Publishing Company, 1989), 78–99.

36. James Skillen, *Recharging the American Experiment: Principled Pluralism for Genuine Civic Community* (Grand Rapids, MI: Baker Books, 1994).

and Christians for Public Justice[37] among others. Spykman defines it thus:

> Principled pluralism holds that all men (sic) live within a network of divinely ordained life-relationships. People do not find meaning and purpose either in their own individuality or as part of some collectivist is whole. Rather, people fulfill their callings within a plurality of communal associations, such as family, school, and state. God ordained each of these spheres of activity as part of the original order. Together they constitute community life.[38]

He goes on to elucidate different forms of pluralism: structural and confessional pluralism. Structural pluralism describes the way God has created different structures that coordinate human interactions — these structures would include the family, marriages church, schools the marketplace and so forth. By confessional pluralism, he refers to the "right of religious groups that make up society to develop their own patterns of in-

---

37. Their website has the following describing principled pluralism:

The Center's philosophy of principled pluralism flows directly from its conviction that governments have not been ordained by God for the purpose of separating believers from unbelievers, giving privilege to Christians and the church, or serving the interests of one nation over others. This is a religious conviction that mandates publicly established religious freedom for all. Governments have the high calling to uphold public justice for all people living within their territories. States are not churches or families; public officials are not national theologians or clergy. States are public-legal communities that exist for the protection and enhancement of the common good. https://cpjustice.org/what-distinguishes-the-center-for-public-justice (Date of access 14 February 2024).

38. Spykman, "The Principled Pluralist Position," 79.

volvement in public life thorough their own associations."[39] He then draws upon sphere sovereignty, which he claims "teaches that each sphere in society has its own independent authority; no one sphere should dominate the role of the others." He adds to the mix another important term, which follows form sphere sovereignty, namely, sphere universality. This is the "cooperative relationship among the various social spheres; they should work together to promote wholesome community life."[40]

Application to the COVID-19 pandemic

Many countries have responded to the coronavirus and the COVID-19 pandemic by restricting citizens' liberties. Typical measures have included:

- A limit on social gatherings, including the closure of church buildings, mosques, and synagogues
- Social distancing—which might be better termed physical distancing (keeping 2 metres apart from others)
- Isolation if one has symptoms
- Restrictions as to when and where to leave the house— for example, only for medicine, food, and one daily exercise walk/run
- Working at home wherever possible
- Reduction in the use of public transport.

These where possible have been made voluntary. This is fully in keeping with the notion of sphere sovereignty. In some cases,

---

39. Spykman, "The Principled Pluralist Position," 79.
40. Spykman, "The Principled Pluralist Position," 80.

these have become to be enforced. This then it could be argued extends the role of the state beyond its own calling and violates the principle of sphere sovereignty. However, if we do not limit our own liberty, it can have severe detrimental effects on others' liberties i.e., hospitalisation, and even death. Does the state then have the right in this case to limit civil liberties? In doing so it is protecting others' liberties. As mentioned above Kuyper outlined three roles for the state including: "each sphere has an obligation to render whatever dues necessary for the maintenance of the overall unity of society as protected by the state."[41]

The state in imposing these measures is within the remit of Kuyper's view of the state, provided, of course, the aim is to protect its citizens from the effects of the virus *and no more.*

Applications

Sphere sovereignty has been applied with great success in several areas. James Skillen describes it as "Kuyper's most distinctive contribution to modern Christianity."[42] Political scientist, David Koyzis concurs: "This crucial motif underpins neo-Calvinist political theory and is perhaps its most distinctive doctrine."[43]

---

41. Kuyper, *Lectures on Calvinism*, 124–125.

42. James Skillen "Why Kuyper now?" in *Religion, Pluralism, and Public Life: Abraham Kuyper's Legacy for the Twenty-First Century*, ed. Luis E. Lugo (Grand Rapids, MI: Eerdmans, 2000), 367.

43. David T. Koyzis, *Political Visions and illusions* (second edn) (Downers Grove: IVP Academic, 2019), 235–236.

Sphere sovereignty has been applied to numerous areas. These include law,[44] responses to poverty,[45] education,[46] philosophy,[47] holistic mission in Asia,[48] and music and the arts.[49] Kim examines the Korean Presbyterian church and argues that the church's failure to follow Reformed theology "regarding social involvement is due to its failure to understand 'sovereignty in the spheres of society'.... Here is the necessity of having a dialogue with A. Kuyper's notion of sphere sovereignty."[50]

---

44. J. D. Van der Vyver, "The Jurisprudential Legacy of Abraham Kuyper and Leo XIII," *Journal of Markets & Morality* 5(1) (2001): 211–249; and Renato Saeger Magalhaes Costa, "A Sphere Sovereignty Theory of the State: Looking Back and Looking Forward," *International and Public Affairs* 3(1) (2019): 13–19. doi: 10.11648/j.ipa.20190301.13.

45. Lawrence J. Belcher, "Poverty and Aid to the Poor: Scripture, Kuyper's Sphere Sovereignty and Entitlement Spending," *Journal of Biblical Integration in Business* (Fall 19) (2016), 73–84.

46. Gordon J. Spykman (coordinator) *Society, State, and Schools: A Case for Structural and Confessional Pluralism* (Grand Rapids: Eerdmans, 1981); Timothy Shaun Price, "Abraham Kuyper and Herman Bavinck on the Subject of Education," 59–70.

47. For example, the work of Herman Dooyeweerd and D. H. Th. Vollenhoven. On Vollenhoven, see Steve Bishop "Why We Should Read Vollenhoven Today," *Ethics in Conversation* 27, no. 5 (2023).

48. Thomas Harvey, "Sphere Sovereignty, Civil Society and the Pursuit of Holistic Transformation in Asia," *Transformation* 33(1) (2016): 50–64. Harvey draws attention to the work of Ng Kam Weng of Malaysia who explores how "the social framework Abraham Kuyper's 'sphere sovereignty' might benefit modern Malaysia."

49. John MacInnis, "Teaching Music in the Reformed/Calvinist Tradition: Sphere Sovereignty and the Arts," *Religions* 8, no. 4 (2017): 51; https://doi.org/10.3390/rel8040051.

50. Luther Jeong Ok Kim, A. *Kuyper's View of Sphere Sovereignty and the Korean Church*. (Atlanta, GA: Covenant Innovation Pub, 2017), 3.

Some objections/issues with sphere sovereignty

McIlroy in his comparison of subsidiarity and sphere sovereignty highlights some problems he sees with sphere sovereignty.[51]

These are:

1. Which spheres are sovereign? Is it natural or socially constructed spheres?

2. Kuyper's definition of the state — or perhaps more properly his lack of definition of the state.

3. The role of the state to other spheres. Following Irving Hexham he identifies a division within Kuyperians between the absolutists and the moderates.

These are not sphere sovereignty defeaters — they merely illustrate the need for clarification and for more work to be done.

Others have asserted that sphere sovereignty has been used to justify apartheid.[52] A theory does not stand or fall on the extremes it has been ostensibly used to support. As previously mentioned, Christianity is not flawed because of the crusades!

However, on the other hand others have used it to support lenient and supportive approaches to immigration and those of other faiths.[53]

---

51. David McIlroy, "Subsidiarity and Sphere Sovereignty: Christian Reflections on the Size, Shape and Scope of Government," *Journal of Church and State* 45 (2003): 739–763.

52. For a discussion on apartheid see Part 5 Chapter 30—this volume.

53. For example, Matthew Kaemingk, *Christian Hospitality and Muslim Immigration in an Age of Fear* (Grand Rapids, MI: Eerdmans. 2018).

Conclusion

Kuyper's sphere sovereignty as he has developed it provides a way out of the impasse between collectivist and individualist models of society. It provides a Christian rationale for pluralism — both confessional and structural. It mitigates Christian imperialism. It has been applied with great success in a range of areas.

It provides a basis for how societal entities should relate to each other, with no one part of society, such as the state or the church being supreme or sovereign over all. Each societal institution or entity has its own key role to play, and no institution should encroach over another.

Study Questions

1. How does sphere sovereignty relate to the role of the church in society?
2. Compare and contrast sphere sovereignty and subsidiarity.
3. How many spheres does Kuyper suggest are part of sphere sovereignty?
4. What role does the state play in sphere sovereignty?

19

Christianity as a Worldview

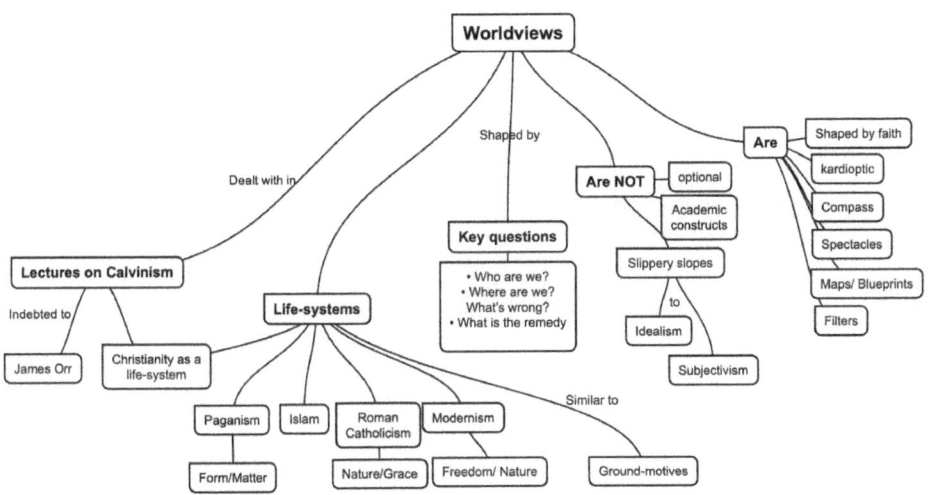

Introduction

"The notion of 'worldviews' is central to Kuyper's thinking," writes Owen Anderson.[1] Peter Heslam comments that Kuyper and worldview are "virtually inseparable."[2] As the description of Kuyper in the Abraham Kuyper Translation Project puts it:

1. Anderson, *Reason and Worldviews*, 36.
2. Heslam, "Architects of Intellectual Thought," 15.

Kuyper's emphasis on worldview formation has had a transforming influence upon evangelicalism, both through the diaspora of the Dutch Reformed churches.[3]

Kuyper's first and fullest development of the notion of worldview was in his 1888 Stone Lectures, *Lectures on Calvinism* — although elements of it had been present in some of his earlier works. It was at the time a fresh, innovative, and radical notion.[4] His development of the notion of worldview was in part due to the Scottish theologian James Orr (1844–1913). Orr in his Kerr lectures (1890–1891), published as *The Christian View of God and the World*,[5] first brought the German term *Weltanschauung* translated as worldview into the Christian arena. Orr developed the idea that he first saw in Kant.[6]

---

3. *Religion and Liberty* 9, no. 1 (Jan & Feb, 1999): 3. Online: https://www.acton.org/pub/religion-liberty/volume-9-number-1/abrham kuyper.

4. Kuyper, *Lectures on Calvinism*, 11.

5. James Orr, *The Christian View of God and the World* (Kerr Lectures for 1890–91) (Edinburgh: Andrew Elliot, 1893).

6. On the history and development of worldview see David Naugle, *Worldview: The History of a Concept* (Grand Rapids: Eerdmans, 2002). This is what Orr has to say:

> A reader of the higher class of works in German theology especially those which deal with the philosophy of religion—cannot fail to be struck with the constant recurrence of a word for which he finds it difficult to get a precise equivalent in English. It is the word "Weltanschauung," sometimes interchanged with another compound of the same signification, "Weltansicht." Both words mean literally "view of the world," but whereas the phrase in English is limited by associations which connect it predominatingly with physical nature, in German the word is not thus limited, but has almost the force of a technical term, denoting the widest view

Orr suggested the idea of Christianity as a life system. This was taken up and developed by Kuyper. Kuyper espoused the notion of Calvinism as a coherent system, a life-system. Kuyper's debt to Orr was shown in a footnote in Kuyper's *Lectures.*

Kuyper identified the Christian worldview in terms of the narrative embedded within creation, fall, and redemption. As Christian philosopher Herman Dooyeweerd puts it:

> [Kuyper] lifted Calvinism, the most radically biblical movement within the Protestant Reformation, out of the narrow sphere of dogmatic theology where it had languished during centuries of inner decline. He raised it to the level of an all-encompassing worldview.[7]

Kuyper often preferred the term "world-and-life view" or "life-system," to the shorter "worldview." The longer form stresses that it is both theoretical and practical—worldview shapes how we think and behave. The shorter form is the term that has been most popularized. This may be one of the reasons for the misuse of the term as a theoretical rather than a pre-theoretical term (see below).

---

which the mind can take of things in the effort to grasp them together as a whole from the standpoint of some particular philosophy or theology. To speak, therefore, of a "Christian view of the world" implies that Christianity also has its highest point of view, and its view of life connected therewith, and that this, when developed, constitutes an ordered whole. (Orr, *The Christian View of God and the World* p. 3)

7. Herman Dooyeweerd, "Kuyper's Philosophy of Science," in *On Kuyper: A Collection of Readings on the Life, Work & Legacy of Abraham Kuyper*, ed. Steve Bishop and John Kok (Sioux Center: Dordt College Press, 2013), 153–178.

Kuyper begins his discussion in his *Lectures on Calvinism* by stating that "Two life systems are wrestling with one another, in mortal combat."[8] These are Modernism (the capital is Kuyper's) and Christianity. He sees Calvinism as "the only decisive, lawful, and consistent defence for Protestant nations against encroaching, and overwhelming Modernism." This is the key theme of all his lectures at Princeton. Therefore, he sees Calvinism as a life-system, not an add-on. Thus, he devotes a lecture each to Religion, Politics, Science, Art, and the Future. He wants to show that as a life-system Calvinism is all-embracing and all-encompassing.

What does Kuyper mean by Calvinism? He identifies several meanings that have been associated with the term. A sectarian, a confessional (as in a subscription to the "dogma of fore-ordination"), a denominational (as in Whitefield's Calvinistic Methodists), and in a scientific sense (as in a logical system). While acknowledging some truth in these meanings, Kuyper sees it as being far broader. He sees it in terms of a center and a circumference. For Kuyper Calvinism "embodies the Christian idea more purely and accurately than could Romanian and Lutheranism,"[9] it is a unified life-system. As such it can challenge the false life-system propounded by Modernism, a challenge that apologetics had failed to stand up to.

From its core form, from Calvinism, arose a theology which in turn gave rise to a specific church order, and then an interpretation of the moral order, as in a form for political and moral life.[10] As a comprehensive world-and-life-

---

8. Kuyper, *Lectures on Calvinism*, 11.

9. Kuyper, *Lectures on Calvinism*, 17.

10. Kuyper, *Lectures on Calvinism*, 17.

view, Calvinism is not a partial or temporary phenomenon. He then compares it with other life-systems, namely Paganism, Islamist, Romanism and Modernism. He does this by examining "three fundamental relations of all human life." These are our relationships to God, humanity, and the world. The table below provides a summary of his observations.

It must be remembered that Kuyper is writing in the nineteenth century (hence his use of the generic term "man") and

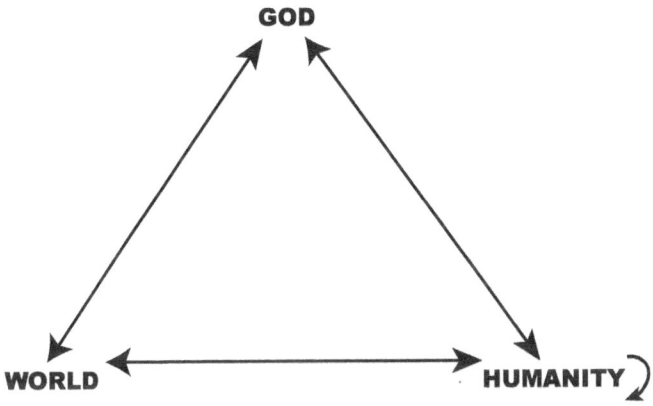

from a distinctly Reformed Calvinist position—he is taking a polemical stance to make his point of the superiority of the Calvinistic worldview. If he was writing today his observations may be slightly more nuanced.

Kuyper never fully provides a definition of a worldview, perhaps one is not fully possible, as a worldview is not a theoretical or academic construct, it is a way of life. Several others, following in the line of Kuyper, have developed Kuyper's ideas. I will briefly mention some of these in what follows.

Table 1. Summary of Kuyper's life-systems, as described in his *Lectures on Calvinism.*

Life Systems		Origins	To God	Relationships To Man/ man-man	To the world
	Paganism	Babylon, Egypt, Greece, and Rome	God in the creature	Demigod - hero worship Lower—castes, slavery.	Too high an estimate of the world loses self and stands in fear of it.
	Islamism	Israel's monism, prophet of Nazareth and Koraishites	Isolates God from the creature.	Woman slave of man	Too low an estimate of the world.
	Romanism	Joint product of Israel's priesthood, cross of Calvary and the Roman Empire.	By means of a mystic middle link—the church.	Hierarchical	Everything outside the [Catholic] church is denigrated.
	Modernism	French Revolution		Uniformity	
	Calvinism	Apprehended by Augustine Paul in Romans. Neither ecclesiastical, theological, nor sectarian conception.	Fellowship	All are creatures under God.	Divine creation— particular grace works salvation and common grace maintains the world and arrests the process of corruption We serve God in the world, developing the potencies hidden.

Kuyperian worldview discussions and definitions

In a classic exposition of worldviews, James Olthuis, writing out of the Kuyperian tradition, describes it thus: "a framework or set of fundamental beliefs through which we view the world and our calling and future in it."[11]

The Dutch philosopher, Herman Dooyeweerd sees what he terms "ground-motives" as engines of a worldview. He identifies four main ones these are similar to those that Kuyper elucidates (in brackets are Kuyper's life-systems)

- Form/matter (Paganism)
- Creation, fall, and redemption (Calvinism)
- Nature/grace (Roman Catholic)
- Freedom/Nature (Humanism)

The form/matter ground-motive is epitomized in many Greek philosophies.

Walsh and Middleton, also coming from a Kuyperian perspective use some key questions that shape every world view, which are similar to the relationships mentioned by Kuyper.[12] The questions are:

- Who am I?
- Where am I?
- What's wrong?
- What is the remedy?

---

11. James Olthuis, "On Worldviews," *Christian Scholar's Review* XIV, no. 2 (1985): 153–164. Also in *Stained Glass: Worldviews and Social Science*, ed. Paul Marshall, Sander Griffioen and Richard Mouw (University Press of America, Lanham MD, 1989), 26–40.

12. Brian J. Walsh and J. Richard Middleton, *The Transforming Vision: Shaping a Christian World View* (Downers Grove, Ill: Inter-Varsity Press, 1984).

Kuyper, as has been mentioned, was one of the first to introduce the concept of worldview to the Christian public. However, it was not until 1968 that Francis Schaeffer made the term popular.[13] Two books that popularized the term *worldview*[14] certainly among Kuyperian thinkers are *Creation Regained*[15] and *The Transforming Vision*.[16] In *Creation Regained*, Wolters defines a worldview as "the comprehensive framework of one's basic beliefs about things."[17] Both these works

---

13. Early usages of the term in Schaeffer were: *The God Who Is There* (London: Hodder & Stoughton, 1968) p. 28; 33; *He is There and He is Not Silent* (London: Hodder & Stoughton, 1972), 87. In *Art and the Bible* (Leicester: IVP Classics, 2009 [original 1973]) he has these passages:

> The third basic notion of the nature of art—the one I think is right, the one that really produces great art and the possibility of great art—is that the artist makes a work of art, and that then the body of his work shows his world-view. No one, for example, who understands Michelangelo or Leonardo can look at their work without understanding something of their respective world-views.

And:

> art forms add strength to the world-view which shows through, no matter what the world-view is or whether the world-view is true or false.

> What kind of judgment does one apply, then, to a work of art? I believe that there are four basic standards: (1) technical excellence; (2) validity; (3) intellectual content, the world-view which comes through; and (4) the integration of content and vehicle.

14. Another Christian early-adopter of the term was John Warwick Montgomery, *Shape of the Past: A Christian Response to Secular Philosophies of History* (Minneapolis, MN: Bethany Fellowship, 1976).

15. Wolters, *Creation Regained*.

16. Walsh and Middleton, *Transforming Vision*.

17. Wolters, *Creation Regained*, 2.

were influential in bringing the term into common Christian usage. Both, however, are focused on the individual. N. T. Wright—whose work has been influenced by Walsh[18]— adapted the first two worldview questions to make them more communal:

- Who are we?
- Where are we?

Wright describes a worldview thus:

> Worldviews are...the basic stuff of human existence, the lens through which the world is seen, the blueprint for how one should live in it and above all the sense of identity and place which enables human beings to be what they are. To ignore worldviews, either our own or those of the culture we are studying, would result in extraordinary shallowness.[19]

More recently Goheen and Bartholomew defined a worldview as:

> an articulation of the basic beliefs embedded in a shared grand story that are rooted in a faith commitment and that give shape and direction to the whole of our individual and corporate lives.[20]

Here emphasis is on the communal, story, and faith commitments. It is this nature of faith commitments that

---

18. See, for example, N. T. Wright, *The New Testament as the People of God* (London: SPCK 1992), xix.

19. Wright, *The New Testament as the People of God.*

20. Mike Goheen and Craig Bartholomew, *Living at the Crossroads: An Introduction to the Christian Worldview* (Grand Rapids: Baker Academic, 2008), 23.

makes the Kuyperian perspective different from other Christian approaches.

The table[21] illustrates competing worldviews with ground motives and key questions, showing illustrative, not nuanced, positions.

What a worldview is not …

Worldview is an in-vogue term that is sometimes abused or misused. No wonder Calvin College philosopher Jamie Smith suggests that "we consider a (temporary) moratorium on the notion of 'worldview'."[22] However, as has oft been said: the best solution to abuse or misuse is not disuse, but proper use.

Worldviews are not optional

Like it or not we all have a worldview. We all see the world differently, how we view the world depends upon where we stand—but we all must stand somewhere. There is no such thing as a view from nowhere.[23] Like Moliere's character from the play *Le Bourgeois gentilhomme*, Mr Jourdain, who exclaimed: "Well, what do you know about that! These forty years now I've been speaking in prose without knowing it!" We too whether we knew it or not have a worldview and operate out of a worldview. The issue is what worldview is it? A Christian or non-Christian worldview? The first step in developing a Christian worldview is to

---

21. See table in the appendix.

22. James K. A. Smith, *Desiring the Kingdom: Worship, Worldview, and Cultural Formation.* (Cultural Liturgies Volume 1) (Grand Rapids, MI: Baker Academic, 2009), 65. The irony is that Smith uses it in the subtitle of his book.

23 See, for example, Thomas Nagel, *The View from Nowhere* (Oxford: Oxford University Press, 1986).

recognize that we do indeed have a worldview and that it needs to be shaped by our Christian faith and the Scriptures.

They are not academic constructs

Worldviews operate at a pre-theoretical level. Our worldview may even be incoherent and inconsistent, but it will still mould us. Whether or not we are able to articulate our worldview is irrelevant; it will still influence how we think and live in the world: as the philosopher of science, Michael Polanyi puts it "We know more than we can tell."[24]

They are not Trojan horses for relativism or idealism

We all have a worldview—but that doesn't mean that all worldviews are valid, coherent, or true. Kuyper would contend that all worldviews apart from the Christian worldview are false.

The notion of worldview may have developed out of idealism, but that does not mean that adopting a worldview approach means accepting idealist presuppositions. To suggest so is to commit the genetic fallacy, a rejection of a view based solely on its origins.

Worldviews are ...

...shaped by faith

As we all have a worldview, so too do we all have faith.

...kardiopic

A worldview arises not from the intellect but from the heart (Greek: *kardia*). David Naugle explains it well:

---

24. Michael Polanyi, *Personal Knowledge: Towards a Post-Critical Philosophy* (London: Routledge & Kegan Paul, 1958).

It seems to me that life proceeds "kardi-optically," out of a vision of the heart. That's what I think a worldview is. More specifically, I suggest that a worldview as a "kardi-optic" is a vision of God, the universe, our world and ourselves that is rooted and grounded in the embodied human heart.[25]

...blueprints and maps of reality

A map provides a different view of the world—provided we have the right map and have it the right way up it can help us to pinpoint where we are and where we are going. Blueprints serve as models and provide guidance for design; they provide plans for action. Likewise, worldviews.

...a compass

It helps to orientate our way in the world and to understand where we are, particularly when used in conjunction with a map.

...spectacles

Those who have to wear spectacles are aware that they are needed to see things sharply and clearly. A wrong spectacle prescription can distort our perception of the world. A wrong worldview can do the same.

...a filter

Looking through a red filter shows the world in red. Items that are green, for example, will appear black—if we see the world only through a red filter green does not exist. Worldviews operate as filters. For example, someone who has a

---

25. David Naugle, "An Introduction to the Reformational Worldview," Erskine College, Staley Lectures, 2005.

physicalist worldview (i.e., the belief that everything is physical or material) will be unable to "see" God or understand the Christian faith.

Conclusion

The notion of worldviews is not without problems.[26] Many of these problems arise from the wrong use of the term. It has too often been aligned with a theoretical simplistic notion. However, what Kuyper was conveying using the term world-and-life view is that Christianity is one coherent, integrated whole. It has implications for the whole of life. As he writes in his *Honey From the Rock:* "Don't make of what must be a world-embracing religion one that is concealed and withdrawn!"[27]

---

26. See, for example, Simon P. Kennedy, *Against Worldview* (Bellingham, WA: Lexham Press, 2024.

27. Abraham Kuyper, *Honey from the Rock: Daily Devotions for the Young Kuyper* (Bellingham, WA: Lexham Press, 2018), 122.

Study Questions

1. Kuyper has been described as the theologian of the antithesis and as the theologian of common grace What grounds are there for calling Kuyper the theologian of worldview?

2. In what ways has the term worldview been hijacked?

3. Which of the images for worldview do you find most appealing? Why? Which is the least appealing?

Further Reading for Part II

Primary Sources

Kuyper, Abraham. *Lectures on Calvinism* (Grand Rapids, MI: Eerdmans, 1931).

Secondary Sources

Bishop, Steve. "Abraham Kuyper—Cultural Transformer," *Foundations* 79 (Autumn 2020): 60–76.

Mouw, Richard *He Shines in all that's Fair: Culture and Common Grace* (Grand Rapids, MI: Eerdmans, 2002).

Wagenman, Michael W. *Engaging the World with Abraham Kuyper* (Bellingham, WA: Lexham Press, 2019).

Wolters, Albert M. *Creation Regained: Biblical Basis for a Reformational Worldview* (Downers Grove: Inter Varsity Press, 1985).

PART 3

Theology

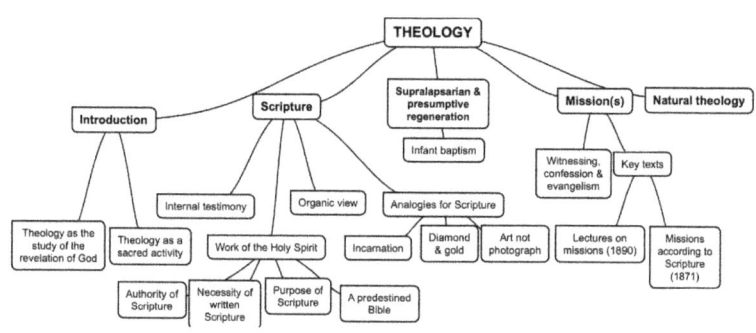

In Brief

This is a guide to the theology and works of Abraham Kuyper. It covers a range of topics, including the study of God, the authority of Scripture, and missions according to Scripture. It provides insights into Kuyper's views on these topics, as well as his unique contributions to the field of theology.

Introduction to Kuyper's Theology

IT IS SOMETIMES FORGOTTEN that Abraham Kuyper was a theologian. He was the first professor of theology at the Free University in Amsterdam and lectured in theology for over 20 years (from 1880-1901). He also wrote and published several volumes that dealt with theological topics, not least his *Principles of Sacred Theology*,[1] *The Work of the Holy Spirit*,[2] *God's Angels*[3], Particular Grace,[4] and *The Revelation of St John*.[5]

---

1. Abraham Kuyper, *Encyclopaedie der Heilige Godgeleerdheid*, 3 vols. (Amsterdam: J. A. Wormser, 1894); it was originally translated as *Encyclopedia of Sacred Theology: Its Principles*, trans. J. Hendrik De Vries (New York: Scribner, 1898); it was later republished as *Principles of Sacred Theology* (Grand Rapids: Eerdmans, 1954, 1968), translating only parts of volume 1, and all of volume 2 of the *Encyclopaedie*. Volume 3 remains untranslated. Baker republished it in 1980 and an abridged version by Jay P. Green Sr was published in 2001 by Sovereign Grace Publishers. The version used here is the 1968 edition.

2. The version used here is the paperback edition of 2001 published by AMG Publishers. The original translation by Henri De Vries was published in 1900 by Funk & Wagnalls. It was reprinted in 1941 by Eerdmans. It was a translation of the three volume *Het werk van den Heiligen Geest*, Amsterdam: J. A. Wormser, 1888 and 1889.

3. Abraham Kuyper, *God's Angels His Ministering Spirits*, trans. R. Stiensma (Vancouver, BC: Friessen Press, 2015).

4. Abraham Kuyper, *Particular Grace: A Defense of God's Sovereignty in Salvation*, trans. Marvin Kamps (Grandville, MI: Reformed Free Publishing Association, 2001).

5. This was the fourth volume of Kuyper's series "Van de Voleinding" [Of

Other works by Kuyper that have yet to be translated include the remainder of the series in *De Heraut* on "Van de Voleinding" and *E Voto*, an explanation of the Heidelberg Catechism, on which Rullman comments it "is indeed a massive edifice of monumental significance. It is the culmination of his entire theological system, in connection with the most valuable aspects that our confessions have offered us."[6] Kuyper's lectures at the VU Amsterdam were recorded by dictation by some of his students and published privately and made available to the students (from approximately 1890 to 1900). Apparently, Kuyper appointed a note-taker for each lecture series. The notes were published soon after the lecture series was completed. Students who bought the notes were not allowed to sell them on. The topics covered included God, Scripture, Creation, Providence, Sin, Covenant, Christ, the Church, the Sacraments, and the Consummation.[7]

---

the Consummation]. The first three volumes have yet to be translated. They were published posthumously. The articles were a series in *De Heraut* from 1911–1918. The published volumes (1929, 1930) were edited by Kuyper's son H. H. Kuyper.

6. J. C. Rullman, *Abraham Kuyper: een levensschets* (Kampen: Kok, 1928), 245. The original reads: "maar dat inderdaad een massief bouwwerk is van monumentale beteekenis."

7. *Locus de Deo.* College-dictaat van een der studenten [Kampen: J. H. Kok, 1910][2] (Dictaten dogmatiek van Dr. A. Kuyper, 1).
    Locus de Sacra Scriptura, Creatione, Creaturis. College-dictaat van een der studenten, met een woord vooraf van A. Kuyper, [Kampen: J. H. Kok, 1910][2] (Dictaten dogmatiek van Dr. A. Kuyper, 2).
    Locus de Providentia, Peccato, Foedere, Christo. College-dictaat van een der studenten, met een woord vooraf van A. Kuyper, [Kampen: J. H. Kok, 1910][2] (Dictaten dogmatiek van Dr. A. Kuyper, 3).
    Locus de Salute, Ecclesia, Sacramentis. College-dictaat van een der

In recent years, with the publication of The Collected Works in Public Theology (2015–2022), the emphasis has been on application rather than on Kuyper's theology. Kuyper's applications were shaped by his theology and the Scriptures. Therefore, it is fitting we examine these before looking at his approach to politics, education, the sciences, business, the family, and art and so forth.

Kuyper wrote his *Principles of Sacred Theology* to vindicate the place of theology as a science within the academy.[8] Its place had been questioned and challenged for two main reasons: "first, that the scientific character of Theology is disputed by many; and, second, that they who do not dispute this are disagreed as to what is to be understood by Theology."[9] To this end he goes to some length in outlining the "organism of science" before describing the place theology has in it.

Gordon Spykman summarizes well the Kuyperian approach to theology:[10]

---

studenten, met een woord vooraf van A. Kuyper, [Kampen: J. H. Kok) 1910][2] (Dictaten dogmatiek van Dr. A. Kuyper, 4). Locus de Magistratu, Consummatione Saeculi. College-dictaat van een der studenten, met een woord vooraf van A. Kuyper, [Kampen: J. H. Kok, 1910][2] (Dictaten dogmatiek van Dr. A. Kuyper, 5).

8. Kuyper, *Principles of Sacred Theology*, 52.

9. Kuyper, *Principles of Sacred Theology*, 45.

10. Gordon J. Spykman, *Reformational Theology: A New Paradigm for Doing Dogmatics* (Grand Rapids: Eerdmans, 1992). Others that develop this Kuyperian view of theology include John C. Vander Stelt, *Faith Life and Theology: A Reorientation* (Jordan Station: Paideia Press, 2020) and André Troost, *The Philosophy of the Science of Faith:*

...we come to recognize theology as one discipline among others. Each has its own unique object of study. Each focuses on its own peculiar aspect of reality. Yet all of them together are coherently interrelated. Within this panoply of sciences theology is no longer revered as the "queen of the sciences." Where Christ is King of all there is no need of a queen.[11]

According to Kuyper theology is a sacred activity. It is not the study of God but is the study of the revelation of God. It is one among the other sciences, but theology is not the queen of sciences. It is to be done in dependence upon God. In this sense, there is no "natural" theology. Natural theology has an important albeit limited role. It is not to be fully trusted or depended upon. There is no dualism between special and natural theology. These points will be unpacked in what follows.

1. Theology is not the study of God...

He [the theologian] cannot investigate God. There is nothing to analyze. There are no phenomena from which to draw conclusions. Only when that wondrous God will speak, can he listen. And thus the Theologian is absolutely dependent upon the pleasure of God, either to impart or not to impart knowledge of Himself.[12]

Prolegomena of Theology, trans. David Hanson (forthcoming)—although both are critical of Kuyper's semi-dualistic views.

11. Spykman, *Reformational Theology*, 102.

12. Kuyper, *Principles of Sacred Theology*, 251.

Kuyper recognizes the futility of attempting to study God. To paraphrase Calvin, how can the finite study the infinite?[13]

2. ...but is the study of the revelation of God:

Kuyper maintains that theology is "our human insight into the revealed knowledge of God."[14]

> And thus we come to this conception of Theology, viz. that it is that science which has the revealed knowledge of God as the object of its investigation, and raises it to " understanding.[15]

As theology is the study of the revelation of God this gives a problem for non-believers. If they deny the existence of God, then there can be no study of his revelation. Therefore, so many universities in Kuyper's time switched from theology to the study of religion.[16] For Kuyper *palingenesis* (regeneration) is essential if one is to study theology.

> ...the science of Theology is a task which must be accomplished, under the leading of the Holy Spirit, by regenerated humanity, and by those from among its ranks who, being partakers of palingenesis, and enriched by "enlightening," have also in their natural dis-

---

13. The phrase "*Finitum non capax infinitum*," (The finite cannot grasp the infinite) is often attributed to Calvin.

14. Kuyper, *Principles of Sacred Theology*, 293.

15. Kuyper, *Principles of Sacred Theology*, 299.

16. This is one of the key reasons why Kuyper wrote *Principles of Sacred Theology*. He wanted to defend theology as an academic discipline and to keep its place in the academy.

position those special talents which are necessary for this intellectual task.[17]

However, in his Rectorial address to the VU on "Biblical Criticism"—published in *Biblica Sacra* in 1904—he has this to say:

Theology is a science which, if it is analogous to philosophy and psychology, is distinguished from all other sciences by this fundamental point, that it does not : occupy itself with the knowledge of the creature, but of the Creator; hence of a God who, as creator, cannot be included in the range of the creaturely. The object of theology, therefore, is God.[18]

This seems to go against his argument in his 1893 *Principles of Sacred Theology* above. Why? He places theology alongside the other sciences but sees the object of theology as being God. This may reflect a a shift in his thinking.

3. Theology is to be done in dependence on God

Prayer was integral to theology for Kuyper. Theology was not merely an academic discipline, it "was not a dry abstraction, nor a cold intellectual speculation or scholastic hair-splitting, but it gripped his soul as the power of God's truth."[19] It was to be done with prayer and with the communion of the Holy Spirit.

---

17. Kuyper, *Principles of Sacred Theology*, 298.

18. Kuyper, "Biblical Criticism," 411.

19. Rullman, *Abraham Kuyper*, 243. The original reads: "Het dogma was bij hem geen dorre abstractie, geen koel verstandelijke bespiegeling of scholastieke intellectualistische haarkloverij, maar het greep zijn ziel aan als de macht der waarheid Gods."

Theology has flourished only at times when theologians have continued in prayer and, in prayer, have sought the communion of the Holy Spirit, and, on the other hand, theology loses its leaf and begins its winter sleep when ambition for learning silences prayer in the breast of theologians.[20]

Veenhof in *In Kuper's Lijn* cites Kuyper:

For "it will be of no use to a theologian on his deathbed if he knows a dizzying amount of theology, and the only question in his last breath is whether he possesses that knowledge of God of which John said, 'This is eternal life, that they may know thee, the only true God Jesus Christ, whom thou hast sent.'"[21]

4. Theology as one among the other sciences but is not the "queen of sciences"

The role of theology is often controversial, many including Kuyper's colleague and successor at the VU Amsterdam Herman Bavinck, see theology as the queen of the sciences.[22] Kuyper it appears does not. Kuyper sees it as an important sci-

---

20. Kuyper, *Principles of Sacred Theology*, 340.

21. C. Veenhof, *In Kuyper's Lijn* (Goes: Oosterbaan & Le Cointre, 1939), 58. The quote from Kuyper comes from *De Heraut* (8 March 1896), no. 190.

22. Bavinck writes: "In the circle of the sciences, theology is entitled to the place of honor, not because of the persons who pursue this science, but in virtue of the object it pursues; it is and remains–provided this expression is correctly understood–the queen of sciences." *Reformed Dogmatics Volume 1: Prolegomena* (Grand Rapids, Michigan; Baker Academic; 2003), 54.

ence, but rejects the notion that there is a hierarchy among the sciences, as he argues:

> We do not advocate, therefore, a certain subserviency of the other sciences to theology as the queen of sciences. There can never be a question of such a relation of mistress and servant, in a scientific sense, among the sciences.[23]

> All the other sciences have the data of nature and of history for their object, and Theology, in like manner, has the data of this supernatural history.[24]

Abraham Kuyper's words in the newspaper *De Heraut* of 18th June 1893 (no. 808):

> Still they tell us that Theology is Queen of the sciences… There are no underdogs in science, and there is no science that lays down the law as if it were queen. The one who reigns alone, also in science, and sets his laws down there, the one who gave his ordinances for human thought and for the conscious life, is the God of truth."[25]

5. Theology is a sacred activity

Kuyper describes theology as "Sacred." But does this imply a sacred/secular divide? What does he mean by sacred theology? He uses this phrase because it is an ancient phrase, and one he

23. Kuyper, *Principles of Sacred Theology*, 606.

24. Kuyper, *Principles of Sacred Theology*, 319.

25. Cited in D. F. M. Strauss, "Scholasticism and Reformed Scholasticism at Odds with Genuine Reformational-Christian Thinking," trans. Dr. David Hanson [it originally appeared in *Ned. Geref. Teol. Tydskrif* (*Dutch Reformed Theological Journal*), (March 1969): 97–114)], https://vcho.co.za/wp-content/uploads/2018/05/Scholasticism-and-Reformed.pdf.

does not insist on.[26] However, he uses it because in the first instance it is a means of denying secularization; it emphasizes the distinguishing character of theology it is to be done in dependence of God: "…we take no part in the secularization of Theology, but maintain that it has a sphere of its own."[27]

The terms holy and sacred were, therefore, not originally intended to give something a higher religious standing. In the second instance the term sacred as a prefix indicates "whatever stands in immediate relation to special revelation."[28] Thirdly, it indicates that theology is not governed by the fallen human mind but only as it is "animated by the Holy Ghost."[29]

In his "Biblical Criticism," he identifies some characteristics of theology, which provide a good summary of his views:

- It is a science like psychology or anthropology.
- However, it is a science unlike psychology or anthropology in that it deals with a knowledge of God rather than of of creation.
- It is a beautiful building.
- It is born from the impulsion of the Holy Spirit.
- It is God-given and is God-given for a purpose.
- Its purpose is to bear fruit to honor God.
- It can only do this because God is a self-revealing God This is primarily through the Scriptures.

This brings us to a discussion on Kuyper's view of the Scriptures.

---

26. Kuyper, *Principles of Sacred Theology*, 333–334.

27. Kuyper, *Principles of Sacred Theology*, 334.

28. Kuyper, *Principles of Sacred Theology*, 334.

29. Kuyper, *Principles of Sacred Theology*, 339.

20

Scripture, Revelation, and Inspiration

AS SCRIPTURE INFLUENCED KUYPER'S theology, politics, education, journalism, art, and the sciences, among other things, it is crucial to study his views on inspiration, revelation, and especially, his understanding of Scripture.

Most of the examinations of Kuyper's view of the Scriptures have been comparisons with others—Harris with fundamentalism and with Warfield,[1] and Gaffin Jr with Rogers and McKim.[2]

This chapter will focus primarily on Kuyper's own view of the Scriptures.[3] Kuyper continually refers to Scripture when

---

1. Harriett A. Harris, *Evangelicalism and Fundamentalism* (Oxford: Oxford University Press, 1998) and "A Diamond in the Dark," in *Religion, Pluralism, and Public Life: Abraham Kuyper's Legacy for the Twenty-First Century,* ed. L. Lugo (Grand Rapids: Eerdmans, 2000), 123–144.

2. Richard B. Gaffin Jr., *God's Word in Servant-Form: Abraham Kuyper and Herman Bavinck on Scripture* (Jackson: Reformed Academic Press, 2008).

3. Some of this draws upon my "Abraham Kuyper's view of Scripture," *Foundations* 86 (2024): 15–38.

discussing topics, so an examination of his approach is important. He continually uses phrases such as these (selected from
Honey From the Rock [4]):

> Doesn't all of Scripture show…(1.6)[5]
> According to the (Holy) Scriptures…(1.30, 1.48)
> Scripture teaches…(1.25)
> Holy Scriptures show…(1.29)
> Holy Scripture tells us…(1.29; 2.55; 2.59)
> That's why Scripture says…(1.32)
> Holy Scripture speaks…(1.55)
> Scripture itself says…(1.71)
> Scripture requires…(1.98)
> … what Scripture wants…(2.17)
> Scripture reminds us…(2. 24)
> …says Scripture…(2. 34)
> Scripture itself teaches…(2.36)
> …says the Holy Spirit in Scripture…(2.57)
> … on the basis of Scripture…(2. 84)
> Holy Scripture says…(2.88)
> Scripture itself answers…(2.93)

In the following we shall briefly examine the role of the
Holy Spirit, Kuyper's organic view of the inspiration of
the Scriptures, and the analogies Kuyper uses for Scripture, but first the notion of the self-authentication of
the Scriptures.

---

4. Abraham Kuyper, *Honey from the Rock* (Bellingham, WA: Lexham
    Press, 2018).

5. The numbers indicate volume then section.

The internal testimony of the Scriptures

In his *Work of the Holy Spirit*, Kuyper begins by examining what the Scriptures have to say about themselves and looking for any indications of inspiration. The Scriptures are self-attesting. Jesus appears to have credited the Old Testament with inspiration; he considered it to be the Word of God, agreed with Jewish beliefs of the time, and saw it as "one organic whole." As seen by his repeated use of the phrase "It is written," Jesus insisted that the Bible cannot be broken and accepted the authority of the Old Testament. This is also apparent in Mt 5:17-18—every jot and tittle. As Kuyper asserts:

> The way Jesus thought about Holy Scripture is the way you should.
>
> What Jesus confessed concerning Scripture, you should.
>
> What Jesus accepted as the sacred charter of truth, you should as well. … You have to stand rock solid in the conviction that "What Jesus says is completely true."[6]

Similarly, in his *Principles of Sacred Theology* he stresses the importance of Jesus' view of the Scriptures. We either agree with his view or see his view as being an error—to take the latter option is to reject Jesus as "the absolute guide along the way of faith."[7]

The work of the Holy Spirit and Scripture

The Scot, A. T. B. McGowan, observes: "although evangelicals have spoken about the work of the Holy Spirit in relation to

---

6. Kuyper, *Honey*, 386-388.

7. Kuyper, *Principles of Sacred Theology*, 459.

Scripture, there has been insufficient emphasis upon this theme."[8] This is not the case for Kuyper.

As mentioned, one of Kuyper's major theological works was *The Work of the Holy Spirit*. The book, as with many of Kuyper's works, appeared first in one of his newspapers, *De Heraut*, as weekly instalment and was published in Dutch in 1888. It is perhaps the first major treatise on the Holy Spirit since John Owen's (1616–1683) three volumes published in 1674, 1682, and 1693. Kuyper's book originally appeared in Dutch in three volumes. The first deals with the work of the Holy Spirit in the church. The second and third volumes dealt with the Spirit and his work in individuals. The second volume examined sin, unrighteousness, regeneration, justification, and faith; the third examined sanctification, love, and prayer.

Kuyper continually stresses the role of the Holy Spirit in relation to the Scriptures. For example, "That the Bible is the product of the Chief Artist, the Holy Spirit; that He gave it to the Church and that in the Church He uses it as His instrument, can not be over-emphasized."[9] Kuyper poses the question: "How did the Scripture originate?" His answer, "By the Holy Spirit."[10] The Holy Spirit, is for Kuyper, the "perpetual author":

> ...the Holy Spirit, who gave the Scriptures, is Himself the perpetual author (auctor perpetuus) of all appropriation of their contents by and of all application to the

---

8. A. T. B. McGowan, "The Divine Spiration of Scripture," *Scottish Bulletin of Evangelical Theology* 21, no. 1, (2007): 199-217.

9. Kuyper, *Work of the Holy Spirit*, 65.

10. Kuyper, *Work of the Holy Spirit*, 171.

individual. It is the Holy Spirit who, by illumination, enables the human consciousness to take up into itself the substance of the Scripture; in the course of ages leads our human consciousness to ever richer insights into its content; and who, while this process continues, imparts to the elect of God, as they reach the years of discretion, that personal application of the Word, which, after the Divine counsel, is both intended and indispensable for them.[11]

The role of the Holy Spirit is all-embracing, as well as the author of Scripture, he brings illumination, and rich insights to the reader. He is also responsible for the Scripture as it is "presented to the church." The content, selection, and arrangement of the Scriptures are a result of the work of the Holy Spirit.[12] The Holy Spirit is the source of inspiration both in the writing of, and in the reading of, Scripture.

> Hence inspiration is the name of that all-comprehensive operation of the Holy Spirit whereby He has bestowed on the Church a complete and infallible Scripture. We call this operation all-comprehensive, for it was organic, not mechanical.[13]

For Kuyper, the Scripture is an instrument of the Holy Spirit in his work upon the human heart and to equip a person for every good work.[14] In several places he describes the Scriptures as an instrument of the Holy Spirit.

---

11. Kuyper, *Principles of Sacred Theology*, 281.

12. Kuyper, *Work of the Holy Spirit*, 84.

13. Kuyper, *Work of the Holy Spirit*, 82-83.

14. Kuyper, *Work of the Holy Spirit*, 64.

That the Bible is the product of the Chief Artist, the Holy Spirit; that He gave it to the Church and that in the Church He uses it as His instrument, can not be over-emphasized.[15]

Without revelation the Scriptures cannot fulfil their purpose. Once Christ through the Holy Spirit opens up the Scriptures to us then they cease to be a dead letter but become life giving water:

Consequently the working of Scripture embraces not only the quickening of faith, but also the exercise of faith. Therefore instead of being a dead-letter, unspiritual, mechanically opposing the spiritual life, it is the very fountain of living water, which, being opened, springs up to eternal life.[16]

The Holy Spirit has a threefold operation, according to Kuyper:

First, a divine working giving a revelation to the apostles.

Second, a working called inspiration.

Third, a working, active to-day, creating faith in the Scripture in the heart at first unwilling to believe.[17]

The order is important: revelation comes to, for example, one of the apostles, who records it and writes it down. However, inspiration by the Holy Spirit is required to ensure it is recorded without error. Kuyper sees it as a verbal rather than mechanical inspiration. It was not a dictation; rather,

---

15. Kuyper, *Work of the Holy Spirit*, 60.

16. Kuyper, *Work of the Holy Spirit*, 59.

17. Kuyper, *Work of the Holy Spirit*, 177.

it is organic in that it is about "calling forth the words from man's consciousness."[18]

The Holy Spirit is the one who brings insight to believers as they read the Scripture. Linked to the work of the Holy Spirit in Scripture are the themes of the authority, necessity, and purpose of Scripture.

1. The authority of Scripture

The authority of the Scripture comes from the fact that it is the Holy Spirit who inspired the Scriptures. They are not merely a human product. The authority of Scripture has no say in the literary ability of the writers or on the importance of the writers; what is foremost is that they were all equally inspired by the Holy Spirit and that is why their writings are authoritative for then and for today.

> Believing in the authority of the New Testament, we must acknowledge the authority of the four evangelists to be perfectly equal. As to the contents, Matthew's gospel may surpass that of Luke, and John's may excel the gospel of Mark; but their authority is equally unquestionable. The Epistle to the Romans has higher value than that to Philemon; but their authority is the same. As to their persons, John stood above Mark, and Paul above Jude; but since we depend not upon the authority of their persons, but only upon that

---

18. Abraham Kuyper, "The Biblical Criticism of the Present Day," *Bibliotheca Sacra* LXI (1904): 409–442; 666–668. This was a rectoral address given in 1881 at the VU Amsterdam. It was later translated by Rev. J. H. De Vries for publication in *Bibliotheca Sacra*.

of the Holy Spirit, these personal differences are of no account.[19]

The authority of the Scripture means that they are accurate and true; they are reliable. This is only because of the inspiration of the Holy Spirit.

2. The necessity of written Scripture

Written Scripture was necessary to preserve truth and prevent "degeneration and falsification."[20] The apostles were under the impression of the imminent return of Christ and so had no idea that their writings would become Scriptures. They did not know what they were doing, the Holy Spirt prepared them for their work. The Scriptures were necessary, as they were God's provision for future generations. As Kuyper puts it:

> Hence two things had to be done for the Church of the future: First, the image of Christ must be received from the lips of the apostles and be committed to writing. Secondly, the things of which Jesus had said, "Ye can not bear them now, but the Holy Spirit will declare them unto you," must be recorded.[21]

3. The purpose of the Scripture

The role of the Scriptures is not to lead us to Christ, but Christ leads us to the Scriptures. He does not see the purpose of the Scriptures as an apologetic tool. The primary emphasis is on Christ not on the Scriptures.

---

19. Kuyper, *Work of the Holy Spirit*, 172.
20. Kuyper, *Work of the Holy Spirit*, 169.
21. Kuyper, *Work of the Holy Spirit*, 169.

The Scriptures are for all of life. They serve a dual purpose: "First, as an instrument of the Holy Spirit in His work upon a man's heart. Second, to qualify man perfectly and to equip him for every good work."[22] They are not a "mere paper book":

> a lifeless object, but not if we hear God speaking therein directly to the soul. Severed from the divine life, the Scripture is unprofitable, a letter that killeth. But when we realize that it radiates God's love and mercy in such form as to transform our life and address our consciousness, we see that the supernatural revelation of the life of God must precede the radiation. The revelation of God's tender mercies must precede their scintillation in the human consciousness. First, the revelation of the mystery of Godliness; then, its radiation in the Sacred Scripture, and thence into the heart of God's Church, is the natural and ordained way.[23]

4. A predestined Bible

In *Principles of Sacred Theology* Kuyper draws upon the notion of a predestined Bible, there is no chance or accident in the completion of the Scriptures:[24]

> It was not mistakenly, therefore, that a predestined Bible was spoken of in Reformed circles, by which was understood that the preconceived form of the Holy Scripture had been given already from eternity in the counsel of God. in which at the same time all events,

---

22. Kuyper, *Work of the Holy Spirit*, 64.
23. Kuyper, *Work of the Holy Spirit*, 65.
24. Kuyper, *Principles of Sacred Theology*, 475.

means and persons, by which that preconceived form would be realized in our actual life, were predestined.[25]

He recognizes the human and divine authorship of the Scripture. He describes this mode of origin as "Inspiration, theopneusty, by the Holy Spirit."[26] He rejects any rationalistic splitting of the word of God and Scripture. He affirms, "The Scripture is God's word both as a whole and in its parts."[27] This means synthetically, in its whole, and analytically, "in each of its parts."[28] The inspiration is organic rather than mechanical, by "calling forth the words from man's own consciousness."

An organic view of inspiration

Kuyper uses the term organic to describe the Scriptures, although he does not clearly define what he means by it. The term organic has a wide range of meanings. Currently, it is used in labels related to food production to denote the absence of pesticides or other artificial chemicals. It is a scientific term used to designate living plants and animals or as a term to indicate the chemistry of carbon compounds. It can also mean change that happens naturally and gradually without being forced, planned or mechanical. It can also mean a structure or community that fits together well with other parts. It is usually these last two meanings that Kuyper has in mind. Most often he uses it as the opposite of mechanical and to show a diversity within unity—"in its whole and in its parts, it is God's word."

---

25. Kuyper, *Principles of Sacred Theology*, 474.

26. Kuyper, "Biblical Criticism," 425.

27. Kuyper, "Biblical Criticism," 430.

28. Kuyper, "Biblical Criticism," 430–431.

The revelation of Scripture is "not a mosaic of pieces; rather, it constitutes an organic whole."[29]

Kuyper argues that the apostles regarded the Old Testament not as a set of literary documents but as a "codex," a complete volume. It has an organic unity it is not an anthology of writings but a whole, "organically constructed and clothed with Divine authority."[30]

As Kuyper puts it in his "Biblical Criticism": "The Scripture is God's word both as a whole and in its parts."[31] The inspiration of the Scriptures is more organic than mechanical; inspiration is not mechanical as a stenographer, but organic, impressionistic, and artistic. The Scriptures are works of art and not photographs. As he makes us aware in his *Dogmatik Dictaten*:[32]

> What Jesus said is very important. If one wished to have Jesus' words with human infallibility, they would all have to be reproduced with the exactness of a stenographer. God has, however, set aside four evangelists for the purpose of reproducing Jesus' words. God, now, works artistically; the evangelists therefore reproduce infallibly the essence of Jesus' words, but not always in the same form in which they were spoken."[33]

---

29. Kuyper, *Common Grace* 3, 185.

30. Kuyper, *Principles of Sacred Theology*, 444.

31. Kuyper, "Biblical Criticism," 430.

32. These were student notes from the dogmatic lectures that Kuyper gave at the Free University, Amsterdam.

33. A. Kuyper, *Dictaten Dogmatiek van Dr. A. Kuyper. II. Locus de Sacra Scriptura*, 92.

Thus, the role of Holy Spirit in inspiration is organic not mechanical.[34] Hence, Kuyper's main view of the inspiration of the Scriptures is organic and pneumocentric. He also uses several analogies that are linked to these two foci. These analogies include the incarnation, a portrait not a photograph, and a diamond or jewel. These analogies will be examined below.

Analogies for Scripture

For Kuyper the Scripture is a "divine jewel," "the Word and the Scripture of…God."[35] When reading it, it is not Moses or John that addresses him but "the Lord my God." He waxes lyrical about the Scriptures:

> In the midst of that sacred history I hear the Holy Spirit singing to my spiritual ear in the Psalms, which discloses the depths of my own soul; in the prophets I hear him repeat what he whispered in the soul of Israel's seers; and in which my own soul is refreshed by a perspective which is most inspiring and beautiful. Till at length, in the pages of the New Testament, God himself brings out to me the Expected One, the Desire of the fathers; shows me the place where the manger stood; points out to me the tracks of his footsteps; and on Golgotha lets me see, how the Son of his unique love, for me poor doomed one died the death of the cross. And, finally, it is the same God, the Holy Spirit, who, as it were, reads off to me what he caused to be preached by Jesus' disciples concerning the riches of that cross, and closes the record of this drama in the

---

34. Kuyper, *Work of the Holy Spirit*, 83.

35. Kuyper, "Biblical Criticism," 422

Apocalypse with the enchanting Hosanna from the heaven of heavens. Call this, if you will an almost childish faith, outgrown by your larger wisdom, but I cannot better it.[36]

1. Incarnation

Kuyper sees a parallel between the incarnation and inscripturation of the Word: "Holy Scripture clothes itself in the garment of our form of thought, and holds itself to our human reality."[37]

The human authors are seen as secondary to the Holy Spirit who is seen as the primary author. The human author is the "amanuensis of the Holy Spirit."[38] This implies an organic unity of Scripture—the Holy Spirit unifies the Scripture, through a diversity of authors.

The incarnation analogy carries with it two important aspects of the Scriptures for Kuyper. It comes in a servant form, and it is both human and divine.

Divine and human authorship

As Jesus in his incarnation was human and divine, so too are the Scriptures. They are divine in origin and of human agency.

Although the Holy Spirit spoke directly to men, human speech and language being no human inventions, yet in writing He employed human agencies. But whether He dictates directly, as in the Revelation of St. John, or governs the writing indirectly, as with historians and evangelists, the result is the same: the product

---

36. Kuyper, "Biblical Criticism," 423.

37. Kuyper, *Principles of Sacred Theology*, 478.

38. Kuyper, *Principles of Sacred Theology*, 480.

is such in form and content as the Holy Spirit designed, an infallible document for the Church of God.[39]

This role of the Holy Spirit in using human authors ensures the organic unity and authority of the Scripture. This organic view of the Scripture and inspiration also rejects the idea that the Holy Spirit dictates the words of Scripture (other than occasionally in the book of Revelation), which also means that human individuality is not stifled in the process of inspiration:

> the men employed in this work were consciously or unconsciously so controlled and directed by the Spirit, in all their thinking, selecting, sifting, choice of words, and writing, that their final product, delivered to posterity, possessed a perfect warrant of divine and absolute authority.[40]

Servant form

The Scripture also assumes the role of a servant, just as Jesus did when He came to earth. Kuyper explains how the Scripture displays this trait of a servant:

> As the Logos has not appeared in the form of glory, but in the form of a servant, joining himself to the reality of our nature...so also, for the revelation of His Logos, God the Lord accepts our consciousness, our human life as it is... The spoken limitation of our language, disturbed as it is by anomalies. As a product of writing, the Holy Scripture also bears on its forehead the mark of the form of a servant.[41]

---

39. Kuyper, *Work of the Holy Spirit*, 83–84.

40. Kuyper, *Work of the Holy Spirit*, 84.

41. Kuyper, *Principles of Sacred Theology*, 419.

2. A diamond and gold

> The Holy Scripture is like a diamond: in the dark it is like a piece of glass, but as soon as the light strikes it the water begins to sparkle, and the scintillation of life greets us. So the Word of God apart from the divine life is valueless, unworthy even of the name of Sacred Scripture. It exists only in connection with this divine life, from which it imparts life-giving thoughts to our minds. It is like the fragrance of a flower-bed that refreshes us only when the flowers and our organs of smell correspond.[42]

Here, Kuyper, in using the analogy of a diamond, shows the necessity of revelation in relation to the Scriptures. Without revelation the Scripture is dull and lifeless—as a diamond in the dark—but with the revelation of the Holy Spirit it brings life and understanding. Likewise, the Scriptures are like gold and to obtain gold there is a need for work, work to dig it out from the ground. In part, this is the purpose of biblical scholarship.

> The conceited notion that we need only to open the Scriptures in order to cite from it this or that text does not for a moment withstand serious scrutiny. This may partly suffice in letting the believer know his duty vis-à-vis the government, but it is of virtually no value for understanding the role and calling of government, or how government needs to discharge that calling down to the details in order to act in conformity with God's law.[43]

---

42. Kuyper, *Work of the Holy Spirit*, 63.

43. Kuyper, *Common Grace* 3, 187.

Biblical scholarship

Kuyper observes:

> …God's will lies hidden in the Scriptures, like gold in
> a mine, and only sustained and comprehensive study,
> by which we compare Scripture with Scripture, as well
> as a thorough working out of its meaning in our lives
> can lead to particular results.[44]

In this Kuyper endorses the importance of, and need for, biblical scholarship. There is a need to dig deep into the mine of Scripture.

At the time when Kuyper was writing on Scripture, Julius Wellhausen (1844–1918)[45] and Kuyper's fellow Dutchman, Abraham Kuenen (1828–1891), were developing their higher criticism of the Bible. The historical-critical methods were in the ascendency. At one time, as a student at Leiden Kuyper had become enamored by L. W. E. Rauwenhoff's (1828–1889) Enlightenment approach to the Scriptures. Later, particularly after his experience with the "malcontents" at Beesd, he became orthodox in in his views and critical of biblical criticism. This is most apparent in his "The Biblical Criticism of the Present Day." There he shows awareness of the dangers but also the place of biblical criticism. He warns:

> …the biblical criticism of the present day is destructive
> of the best interests of the church of the living God, for
> the reason that it revokes her theology, robs her of the

---

44. Kuyper, *Common Grace* 3, 224.

45. Wellhausen's Documentary Hypothesis of the Old Testament split the source of the Old Testament into four different sources labelled J, E, D, and P. His main works developing this were published in 1878 onwards.

Bible, and destroys her liberty in Christ. ...biblical criticism must end in the destruction of theology.[46]

He compares biblical criticism to vivisection.[47] For Kuyper the
heart of theology is dogmatics, with exegesis, church history, pastoral theology clustered around dogmatics—critical-literary
studies lie the furthest away. For this reason, biblical criticism
which at Kuyper's time dealt primarily with these critical-literary
studies is focusing on peripherals rather than what is central: "It
tears the parts of theology out of their relation, violates its character, and substitutes for it something which is no theology."[48]

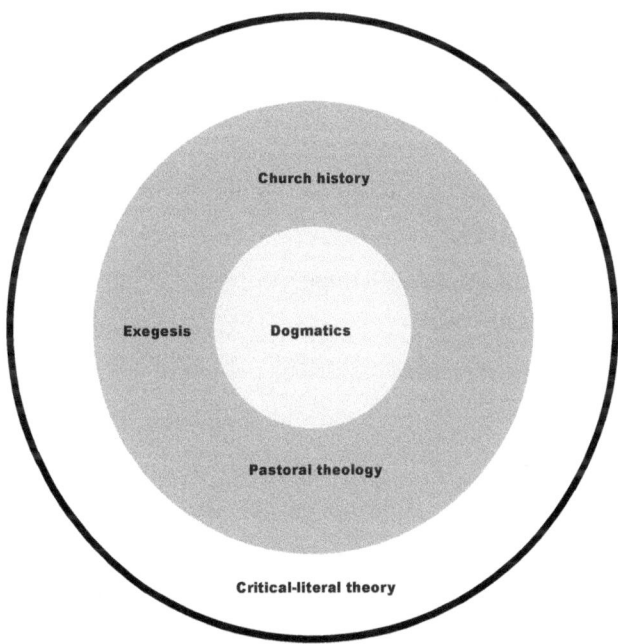

*Figure. A schematic diagram of Kuyper's view of the divisions
of theology.*

46. Kuyper, "Biblical Criticism," 410.

47. Kuyper, "Biblical Criticism," 413.

48. Kuyper, "Biblical Criticism," 410.

The work of biblical criticism is likened to a regal banquet where "all the threads of the table linens have been numbered, and every spot and scratch on the golden goblets have most carefully been recorded; while, to the mortification of the guests, the sparkling wine is wanting."[49]

The danger of biblical criticism is then that it tears theology out of its relation, and it falsifies its character.[50] It also, Kuyper argues, robs congregations of their Bible.[51] It should be stressed, however, that, as mentioned above, Kuyper was not opposed to biblical critical studies. On the contrary, he thought it could be done to the glory of God:

> Not as though critical and historical examination were prohibited. Such endeavor for the glory of God is highly commendable.[52]

Errors in the Bible?

One important question Kuyper addresses is the nature of possible errors in the Bible. Does inspiration mean that the Scriptures are error free? The ethicals, a theological school dominant in Kuyper's time, suggested that there were errors that show that "the Scripture does not pretend to be infallible."[53] Kuyper refuted this opinion in his "Biblical Criticism" address. He does so for two "decisive reasons." One, we do not have the original autographs—and so errors may have crept in

---

49. Kuyper, "Biblical Criticism," 412.
50. Kuyper, "Biblical Criticism," 415.
51. Kuyper, "Biblical Criticism," 422.
52. Kuyper, *Work of the Holy Spirit*, 69.
53. Kuyper, "Biblical Criticism," 471.

on what was without originally error; and two, more importantly, the witness of the Holy Spirit carries more authority
than human judgement:[54]

> it is the same primary author (auctor primarius) who, by
> the apostles, quotes himself, and is therefore entirely jus-
> tified in repeating his original meaning in application to
> the case for which the quotation is made, in a somewhat
> modified form, agreeably to the current translation.[55]

When the Holy Spirit freely quotes something from an earlier
Old Testament verse, he will never make a mistake, even though
the exact words may differ, as the original author he is well
within his right to express the same meaning in a different form
(Scripture is a work of art and not a photograph—see below).

In addition, in *Work of the Holy Spirit*, he wrote, "God
must condescend to our limitations. ...in order to make
Himself intelligible to man, God must clothe His thoughts
in human language and thus convey them to the human
consciousness."[56] This is in line with Calvin's view of the
Scriptures. As Dirk Jellema points out such apparent "errors" "are God's accommodation to the truth to the limited
[human] understanding."[57]

3. Art not a photograph

In his *Dictaten Dogmatik* Kuyper observes the difference between a photograph (a mechanical reproduction) and an artist's

---

54. Kuyper, "Biblical Criticism," 471.
55. Kuyper, *Principles of Sacred Theology*, 450.
56. Kuyper, *Work of the Holy Spirit*, 77.
57. Dirk W. Jellema, "God's 'Baby-Talk': Calvin and the 'Errors' in the
Bible," *The Reformed Journal* 30, no. 4 (1980): 25.

portrait, which provides an impressionistic likeness of the original, it captures hidden meanings. The artist can be seen in and through the piece of art. A photograph may capture a likeness and every hair on a sitter's head—but the artist works in a different way and the final reproduction is substantially more accurate to reality than the photograph, while not being quite as exact. As he puts it:

> Divinely infallible reproduces the essence infallibly, without retaining precisely the same forms (like a painting). Humanly infallible reproduces the form exactly (*notariëel*), but cannot guarantee the essence (like a photograph).[58]

> In the New Testament words have been quoted from the Old Testament. Human infallibility would require a literal reproduction, including even the commas and periods; it would require the kind of copying done by a court reporter or stenographer. Divine infallibility means that the Holy Spirit took over the thought of the Old Testament quotation with freedom and reproduced it in a somewhat different form. These changed quotations do not plead against but for inspiration, since God is an artist and not a photographer.[59]

Evaluation and conclusion

Kuyper's view of the Scriptures and inspiration provides a useful alternative to the static, mechanical view of inspira-

---

58. Kuyper, *Locus de Sacra Scriptura*, II, 91.

59. Kuyper, *Locus de Sacra Scriptura*, II, 91

tion that is often associated, for example, with the Princeton School of theology as epitomized by B. B. Warfield and some forms of fundamentalism.[60] Kuyper had an organic view of revelation—by this he meant that God's revelation of himself is as one whole. The Bible is not a disconnected set of anthologies[61]—it is a whole. It is one. This is an important point that is often ignored in fundamentalist proof texting.

Kuyper takes seriously the subjective without resorting to subjectivism, cultural relativism, or historicism. He takes seriously the human role in Scripture both in reading and in the writing of Scripture. However, neither nullifies that it has divine authority.

> To the person thus addressed it must seem therefore as though he had been spoken to in the ordinary way. He received the impression that he heard words of human language conveying to him divine thoughts. Hence the divine speaking is always adapted to the capacities of the person addressed. Because in condescension the Lord adapts Himself to every

---

60. Although some have overemphasized the differences between Kuyper and Warfield. They both held to a high view of inspiration. They differed on the mode and foundation of inspiration. Harris provides a good description of one of the main differences between Kuyper and Warfield: "In their respective theological battles it is safe to say that Warfield's polemic was fundamentally against subjectivism while Kuyper's was against a belief in human autonomy—although this is to impose terminology upon them." Harriett A. Harris, "A Diamond in the Dark," 127.

61. Geerhardus Van Der Leeuw, *The Bible as a Book* (St Catherines, Ont: Paideia Press, 1978).

man's consciousness, His speaking assumes the form peculiar to every man's condition. What a difference, for instance, between God's word to Cain and that to Ezekiel! [62]

A crucial point for Kuyper was that we can only know God in so far as he reveals himself to us. He distinguished between archetypa and ectypa forms of knowledge of God.[63] Theologica archetypa is the knowledge of God as he has it in all its infinite fullness; theologica ectypa is the knowledge that is communicated to humanity; it is always mediated knowledge. It is knowledge that is revealed and as humans are not infinite has to be accommodated to us—we see through a glass, darkly. As he argues: "The Scripture reveals ectypal theology mostly in facts, which must be understood; in symbols and types, which must be interpreted."[64] This archetypa/ectypa distinction can be taken as revealing the influence of the Greek form/matter ground-motive[65] or it can be seen as stressing the impor-

---

62. Kuyper, *Work of the Holy Spirit*, 77.

63. This distinction can be found in the Reformed Scholastics Franciscus Junius (1545–1602) and Francois Turretin (1623–1687) among others. See, for example, Turretin's *Institutes of Elenctic Theology* Topic 1, Second question, VI. Scotus also made a distinction between our knowledge of God (*theologia nostra*) and God's self-knowledge (*theologia in se*).

64. Kuyper, *Principles of Sacred Theology*, 568.

65. "The form–matter motive is the fundamental motive of Greek thought and culture. It originates, according to [Herman] Dooyeweerd, from a meeting of two conflicting views the pre-Homeric natural religion—corresponding to the pole of matter—and the Olympian gods' cultural

tance of the Creator/creature distinction. Unfortunately, at times for Kuyper it seems to be the former approach and illustrates a scholastic influence upon Kuyper.[66]

As we have seen Kuyper had a high view of Scripture. What marked out his uniqueness at the time was his understanding of the role of the Holy Spirit in the formation and writing of the Scriptures. His was a pneumocentric view of the Scriptures. Too little attention has been given to this issue prior to Kuyper.

His was also an organic view of inspiration and thus of the Scriptures. Scriptures are an organic whole and should be read and studied as such. He, unlike fundamentalists, understood the importance of biblical scholarship—biblical criticism was not necessarily bad and it certainly, for Kuyper, did not undermine the authority of Scripture. Scripture's authority was self-attesting and could not be undermined by naturalistic methods.

Kuyper holds to an organic, pneumocentric view of Scripture. For him Scripture is both truly human and truly divine.[67]

---

religion—corresponding to the pole of form." Steve Bishop, "Herman Dooyeweerd's Christian Philosophy," *Foundations*, 82 (Spring 2022), 66.

66. The term scholastic has often been used as a pejorative term. Unfortunately, it has a range of connotations: "Scholasticism is so much a many-sided phenomenon that, in spite of intensive research, scholars still differ considerably in their definition of the term and in the emphases that they place on individual aspects of the phenomenon" (*Britannica* art. "Scholasticism"). In one sense it is an approach or method that is based on Aristotle's logical writings—hence the Greek influences.

67. My thanks to Renato Coletto for helpful comments on a previous draft.

Supralapsarianism and presumptive regeneration

Kuyper in his "Calvinism and Confessional Revision"[68] provides his argument for presumptive regeneration. This meant that a "conversion moment or experience" was the moment of rebirth when one became aware of what was anticipated at baptism.

Bratt maintains, perhaps with some overemphasis, that the distinction between infralapsarianism and supralapsarianism[69] was the key issue that distinguished the neo-Calvinists ("supras") and the Secessionist line ("infras") of Dutch Christianity.[70] Kuyper was a supralapsarian. For Kuyper supralapsarianism was the consequence of the sovereignty of God.

The difference between the infralapsarians and the supralapsarians is the logical order in which God chooses the elect: supralapsarian before the fall and infralapsarian after the fall. The table illustrates the main difference.[71]

---

68. Abraham Kuyper, "Calvinism and Confessional Revision," *The Presbyterian and Reformed Review* 2, no. 7, (1891): 369–399.

69. The stem word "lapse" here refers to the fall.

70. James Bratt, *Dutch Calvinism in Modern America* (Grand Rapids: Eerdmans, 1984), 6–47.

71. Herman Bavinck notes that:

> neither the supralapsarian nor the infralapsarian view of predestination is capable of incorporating within its perspective the fullness and riches of the truth of Scripture and of satisfying our theological thinking. The truth inherent in supralapsarianism is that all the decrees together form a unity; that there is an ultimate goal to which all things are subordinated and serviceable; that the entrance of sin into the world was not something that took God by surprise, but in a sense willed and determined by him; that from the very beginning the creation was designed to make re-creation possible; and that even before the fall, in the creation of Adam,

Table 1. Supra- and infralapsarianism.[72]

The Supralapsarian Order	The Infralapsarian Order
1. God first decreed to glorify Himself in the salvation of some and in the damnation of other men, who at this stage existed in His mind only as possibilities. 2. Next, God created man.	1. God first decreed to create man. 2. Next, He decreed to permit the fall of man. 3. Then, He decreed to elect a certain number of the fallen and justly condemned race to eternal life and to pass the others by, consigning them to everlasting destruction for their sin. 4. Finally, He decreed to provide a way of salvation for the elect.
Advocates	
Theodore Beza, J. Piscator, A. Polanus, W. Perkins, W. Twisse, Franciscus Gomarus, J. Maccovius, G. Voetius, Witsius, A. Comrie, Herman Hoeksema, Herman Hanko, David Engelsma, Louis Berkhof(?), Geerhardus Vos, Jan Van Lonkhuyzen, Gordon Clark, and Robert Reymond	Peter Martyr Vermigli, Francis Turretin, John Owen, Matthew Henry, B. B. Warfield, W. G. T. Shedd, Charles Hodge, L. J. Hulst, Foppe M. Ten Hoor, A. A. Hoekema, R. C. Sproul, and R. Scott Clark

The position Calvin held is debated! Each "side" claiming him as their own!

Cornelius Pronk—as an infralapsarian—observes:

---

things were structured with a view to Christ.152 But the truth inherent in infralapsarianism is that the decrees, though they form a unity, are nevertheless differentiated with a view to their objects; that in these decrees one can discern not only a teleological but also a causal order; that the purpose of the creation and the fall is not exhausted by their being means to a final end; and that sin was above all and primarily a catastrophic disturbance of creation, one which of and by itself could never have been willed by God. *Reformed Dogmatics* Volume 2, (Grand Rapids: Baker, 2004), 388-389.

72. Data for the table comes in part from C. Pronk, "Supra- or Infra- : What is the Difference?" *Messenger* (29 Nov 2001).

The infralapsarian order is the one followed by all our creeds, especially the Canons of Dort and the Belgic Confession. The supralapsarian position, however, is the more logical order and helps to arrange things more systematically, but it tends to downplay the role of man as a responsible creature and moral agent.[73]

Pronk goes on to maintain:

Kuyper, being a supralapsarian with a vengeance, held views on such doctrines as the covenant of grace, justification, regeneration, and baptism, which his opponents considered unscriptural.

Supralapsarianism led Kuyper to hold to presumptive regeneration and infant baptism. In simple terms, he believed that the moment of rebirth or spiritual awakening was associated with becoming aware of the faith expected from the moment of baptism. As Wood points out, Kuyper was treading a line between a state church and a confessional church as he developed his view of baptism:

The basis for baptism was not covenant membership, which Kuyper feared would lead back to the national church but was regeneration. Regeneration, however, was presumed on the basis of covenant membership, thus to Kuyper's mind avoiding sectarianism.[74]

---

73. C. Pronk, "Supra- or Infra-".

74. John Halsey Wood, Jr, *Going Dutch in the Modern Age: Abraham Kuyper's Struggle for a Free Church in the Nineteenth-Century Netherlands* (Oxford: Oxford University Press, 2012), 135.

The issue of supra and infralapsarian was one that was one of the central concerns in the union of the *Afscheiding* and *Doleantie* groups in 1892.

Kuyper defends presumptive regeneration as meaning:

1. That children of believers are to be considered as recipients of efficacious grace, in whom the work of efficacious grace has already begun. 2. That accordingly they are to receive Baptism as being sanctified in Christ. 3. That, when dying before having attained years of discretion, they can only be regarded as saved.[75]

He also writes:

in our days Baptism is generally conceived of as being administered in hope of subsequent regeneration, whereas Calvinists have always taught that Baptism should be administered on the presumption that regeneration has preceded.[76]

In his *E. Voto* he wrote:

Therefore, as often as holy Baptism is administered in the midst of the congregation, you have to understand that at the very moment when the minister administers the water of Baptism, your Mediator and Savior from heaven, where He is exalted at the right hand of God is, a working of grace works in the soul of the child or person being baptized....[77]

---

75. Abraham Kuyper, "Calvinism and Confessional Revision," The *Presbyterian Review* 2, no. 7, (1891), 388.

76. Kuyper, "Calvinism and Confessional Revision," 388.

77. A. Kuyper, *E Voto*, II, 534.

The child being baptized was assumed to be born again unless they prove otherwise later in life. It should be noted, however, that the child was presumed to be regenerated before baptism and not by baptism.

Baptising on the basis of presumptive regeneration was not uncontroversial in the 1930s and 1940s. Schilder disagreed with Kuyper and because Kuyper's views were entrenched within the church hierarchy, Schilder's dissent was one factor that led him to be suspended.[78]

---

78. See, for example Richard Mouw, *The Challenges of Cultural Discipleship: Essays in the Line of Abraham Kuyper* (Grand Rapids: Eerdmans, 2012), 176–186.

21

Kuyper and Mission(s)

MISSION IS NOT A term that is usually associated with Kuyper. Craig Bartholomew in his *Contours of the Kuyperian Tradition* has a chapter on mission but after a brief mention of Kuyper discusses more fully the missional work of J. H. Bavinck. As Bartholomew observes, "... when it came to mission per se, Johan H. Bavinck (1895-1964), the nephew of Herman Bavinck, pioneered Kuyperian thought."[1]

Nonetheless, Kuyper did write on mission and missions, so it is worth examining his approach.[2]

---

1. Craig Bartholomew, *Contours of the Kuyperian Tradition* (Downers Grove: IVP Academic, 2017), 215. J. H. Bavinck was a professor of missiology at the VU Amsterdam. He had also been a pastor and a missionary in, what was called at the time, the Dutch Indies.

2. Two key lectures by Kuyper deal with his thoughts on mission: "Missions According to Scripture," *Calvin Theological Journal* 38 (2003), 237–247—delivered in 1871; and "Lecture on Missions," first delivered at the 1890 Mission Congress of the Dutch Reformed Churches, it was reprinted in Kuyper, *On the Church*, (Bellingham, MA: Lexham Press, 2016), 443–457.

Witnessing, confession, and evangelism

In *Pro Rege* Volume 2 he distinguishes between witnessing and confession.

> The first personal duty that you owe your King is to confess him; the second duty, which automatically follows from it, is to be a witness to him.[3]

Witnessing includes, but is more than, confession. Confession is standing up for Christ, but witnessing is an attempt to try and win others for Christ. Many, he notes, confess Christ but often fail to witness. This suggests that Kuyper asserts that for them, religion is a personal, private matter, so they think there is no need for them to witness. Each Christian, however, has a responsibility not to remain silent for his King:

> Nothing can ever excuse you of your duty to witness for your King.[4]

He also distinguishes between witnessing and evangelism. Evangelism is much narrower:

> Evangelism consists exclusively in announcing and proclaiming what Christ said and did, followed by a call to accept salvation offered in Christ.

Witnessing suggests a trial, where truth is being questioned. It has two elements: a statement and an ability to guarantee the statement's truth based on the experience of the witness and of the audience.

---

3.   Kuyper, *Pro Rege* 2 (Bellingham, MA: Lexham Press, 2018).

4.   Kuyper, "Lecture on Missions."

Address on Missions (1890)

One time that Kuyper lectured on mission was in 1890 at the Mission Conference in Amsterdam when Kuyper was 52 years old. This was when the *Afscheiding* and the *Doleantie* were in the process of reforming. As Harry Van Dyke points out, "It is remarkable that missions would receive so much interest at a time of ecclesiastical upheaval."[5] Nevertheless, Kuyper was asked to lay the groundwork for this work.

In the lecture, Kuyper outlined several theses as they relate to mission.

The first group of eight theses dealt with dogmatic propositions that focus on determining the relation between missions and the Trinity. The first eight reads:

1. All mission activity originates from the sovereignty of God; is based on the creation of human beings in the image of God; is necessitated by sin; and is grounded in the confession that the Holy Spirit proceeds from the Father and the Son.

2. All mission activity by human beings is only a shadow, representation, or instrument for the only principle (or real) mission of the Son through the Father.

3. The mission of the angels, whose name indicates that they are messengers, is the main purpose of their existence as far as we are concerned.

---

5. Harry Van Dyke, "Text Introduction," in Kuyper, *On the Church*, 441.

4. The mission of Moses and the Prophets was to be the temporary means which the Son before his Incarnation used to carry out his own mission task.

5. The Incarnation was the entry of the Son into the world in order to carry out the first phase of his mission.

6. The mission of the Evangelists and the Apostles, unlike that of the Prophets, was not representational or but rather an instrument in the hands of Christ and was different from all later mission activity as it concerned the ecumenical church in all times and places.

7. The Holy Scriptures are the lasting and continuing revelation of the mission of Christ and his charge or command to the world.

8. Throughout the ages Christ exercises his mission in the local churches through his ministers of the Word. This mission is directed to all who are baptized and thus are members of the covenant of Grace.[6]

As with most subjects, Kuyper begins with the sovereignty of God and with creation, fall, and redemption. His approach is Christological and Trinitarian. Mission is a command, not an option. We are called to mission because we are God's representatives; we are his image-bearers.

The ultimate missionary is God's Son. All mission pales into insignificance compared with his mission. The incarnation is the first stage of his mission; the church is to be the means of exercise of his mission to the world today.

---

6. Abraham Kuyper, "Address on Missions," in *On the Church*, 443–444.

Kuyper, it seems was ahead of his time: he saw the need for cultural sensitivity and contextualization in overseas missions:

> Missions among heathens and Muslims, when preaching law and gospel, should acknowledge the peculiarities of the people and their environment and leave complete freedom for confessing Christ, so that when these people are ready to form their own churches these local peculiarities and forms are preserved.[7]

Kuyper also emphasizes the need for church planting—prompting J. H. Bavinck to note "I am amazed that Kuyper already in 1890 speaks of church planting."[8]

Kuyper was also concerned that missionaries should be trained properly. He suggests that they should have a "superior education": "We have to send our best equipped people to the mission field."[9]

Kuyper sees the church as the instrument God has chosen and uses for mission, not missionary organizations. He sees the burden and the justification for missions rest with the local church. Missionaries should be the responsibility of the sending church. The aim of the missionary should be to become a pastor to those who have become Christians under his ministry; the sender church should be responsible financially until the mission church can support itself.

As Kuyper puts it, "In summary, missions deliver a command, is directed to the fallen image-bearer of God and is

---

7. Kuyper, "Address on Missions," 452 (thesis 18).

8. This was in the introduction to a Dutch version of the lecture edited by J. H. Bavinck, published in 1940.

9. Kuyper, "Address on Missions," 454.

based on the confession that the operation of the Spirit is bound to the Word."[10]

Kuyper maintains "that the Bible does not lay down specific guidelines for the conduct of missions among different peoples. Therefore, while upholding certain principles it is best to maintain as much variety as possible in terms of level, conditions, and character of the people. Variety in confession and worship is possible."

He sees the church as the instrument God has chosen and uses for mission, not missionary organizations: "The right and duty to engage in missions rest with the local church."[11] No other organization should be needed. The missionaries should be the responsibility of the sending church (thesis 26).[12]

The aim of the missionary should be to become a pastor to those who have become Christians under his ministry, and the sending church should be responsible financially until the mission church can support itself.

Missions according to Scripture (1871)

Kuyper also dealt with the topic of mission at an Introductory Speech for the Eleventh Anniversary of the Dutch Reformed Mission Society. Here he uses the text from John 20:21 "as the Father has sent me, I am sending you." Of this he states:

> This will be the word from Scripture that will sanctify the experiences of our mission and be the law of God for every mission endeavor.[13]

---

10. Kuyper, "Address on Missions," 445.

11. Kuyper, "Address on Missions," 453.

12. Kuyper, "Address on Missions," 455.

13. Kuyper, "Missions according to Scripture," 238.

He makes an important—and sobering—point, we are all missionaries:

> Every human being that lives is a missionary...missionary of Christ or missionary of the Satan.[14]

This is an important insight. The issue is what message are we giving? The urge to be a missionary comes from being created in the image of God:

> ...with our God there is an eternal counsel that is nothing else than a big mission program and that mankind is created after the image of God. After the fall into sin, mankind departed from God and went in an opposite direction; yet the driving force of a hunger for spiritual victory remained.[15]

God is a sending God, he sends his angels as missionaries, he sent the patriarchs and the prophets and his Son. Now he has sent his Spirit.

It is, however, not just Christians who engage in mission. Buddhists and Moslems often put Christian endeavors to shame:

> Ask about the courage and the dedication of the followers of Mohammed. They not only spread his teaching with the sword but have also with superior spiritual power reached into the heart of Asia and in many of her islands, in Africa, and even in Europe. Go to our colonies in the East and ask: "Who are the most dedicated missionaries?" Thousands and millions who once

---

14. Kuyper, "Missions according to Scripture," 238.
15. Kuyper, "Missions according to Scripture," 239.

were pagans have been converted to Islam. To Christendom, how few?[16]

Being a missionary is not an issue of geography:

> Generally one supposes: the missionary demands distance. This is correct if one does not mean distance in the form of space but distance in a moral and spiritual sense—a distance therefore not between space and space but between spirit and spirit.[17]

Another important observation he makes is that newspapers and magazines are "daily mission magazines."[18] This is one reason why Kuyper placed such an importance on *De Heraut* and *De Standaard*. Newspapers and the media carry a worldview, which they are very successful at portraying.

Kuyper poses three important questions, which he then goes on to answer:

- Who has the right to send?
- Who should be sent?
- What is the goal that alone gives this sending her glory and her strength?

Who has the right to send?

Kuyper asserts, that the only answer is the church, which is both invisible and visible. If missionaries want to establish churches, then they must be sent by churches, so that they stand in line with the historic church. Missionaries not only preach but are also required to administer the sacraments;

---

16. Kuyper, "Missions according to Scripture," 238.
17. Kuyper, "Missions according to Scripture," 238.
18. Kuyper, "Missions according to Scripture," 238.

this they cannot do under the auspices of a mission organisation, only under the auspices of a church. He laments that this is not always the case, sadly "the church does understand these things anymore."[19]

Who should be sent?

In short, we are all to be sent. Although not all are sent to the traditional mission field abroad as: "Every area of life is a mission field and is labored upon from different directions."[20]

What is the goal that alone gives this sending her glory and her strength?

Missions must begin and end in God. The primary purpose of missions is not the saving of souls or the conversion of the pagans, nor is it the extension of the church, rather it is for the glory of the God the Father. When this is the focus, then the others follow. The church must do nothing for its own glory, all the glory is God's. The church is the means not the goal of mission. Kuyper observes:

> Usually we hear as answer to the question, what is the purpose of missions? the conversion of the heathen, the saving of souls. All this is beautiful and good; but it is impossible that this is the final purpose that gives mission her nobility and strength. What else one may ask? The extension of the church answers another. However, the church is a means and not a goal.[21]

---

19. Kuyper, "Missions according to Scripture," 241.

20. Kuyper, "Missions according to Scripture," 238.

21. Kuyper, "Missions according to Scripture," 244.

The purpose of mission is the glory of God. He offers a salient warning:

> When the church forgets this, she moves away from the right foundation. Only when she continually keeps this goal before her eyes, will she, as means, be serious about the conversion of sinners, the saving of immortal souls and the extension of the church.[22]

---

22. Kuyper, "Missions according to Scripture," 244.

22

Natural Theology[1]

Introduction

NATURAL THEOLOGY AND NATURAL law have gained considerable notoriety in recent years. Both advocates and critics of natural theology have claimed Kuyper as one of their own. For example, J. Daryl Charles and Jordan Ballor in their introduction to Kuyper's *Common Grace* volume 3 define natural law as "the moral aspect of the penetrating arrow of general revelation"[2] They maintain that "Kuyper himself is quite clear: natural law is a manifestation of God's common grace."[3] In addition, "Kuyper frequently speaks of moral law by using the grammar of 'divine ordinance.'"[4] They also assert "Because there is such a close connection between the natural, moral law and common grace, Kuyper often uses the terms inter-changeably."[5]

---

1. Parts of this are adapted from Steve Bishop and David Kristanto, "Abraham Kuyper and Natural Theology," *Koers*, 89 (2024).
2. J. D. Charles, *Retrieving the Natural Law: A Return to Moral First Things* (Grand Rapids: Eerdmans, 2008), 130.
3. Kuyper, *Common Grace* 3, xviii
4 Kuyper, *Common Grace* 3, xviii.
5. Kuyper, *Common Grace* 3, xx.

Whereas Bruce Demarest in his overview of *General Revelation* asserts:

> although Abraham Kuyper and Karl Barth in many re-
> spects were poles apart theologically, the two theolo-
> gians converge in rejecting the ultimate utility of gen-
> eral revelation. Both insist that man's rational capacity
> to know God has been destroyed by sin both maintain
> that only through a supernatural experience is man ca-
> pable of knowledge of God in any sense.[6]

Bruce Demarest briefly examines Kuyper's approach to general revelation. He provides a diagram shown in figure 2 below.

Figure 2 (on the facing page) clearly shows that for Demar-est, Kuyper is in the line with theologians and philosophers who deny that knowledge can be mediated by general revela-tion.[7] This is a denial of natural theology.

Likewise, Michael Sudduth argues that Kuyper is among those who are critical of natural theology:

> This is particularly true of representatives of Reformed
> orthodoxy in the Dutch neo-Calvinist tradition origi-
> nating with Abraham Kuyper in the Netherlands in the
> latter part of the nineteenth century. Herman Bavinck,
> Herman Dooyeweerd, and G. H. Kersten, for example,
> provide highly negative evaluations of natural theology.[8]

---

6. Bruce Demarest, *General Revelation: Historical Views and Contemporary Issues* (Grand Rapids: Zondervan 1982), 141.

7. Demarest, *General Revelation*.

8. Michael Sudduth, *Reformed Objection to Natural Theology* (Farnham, Surrey: Ashgate, 2009), 3.

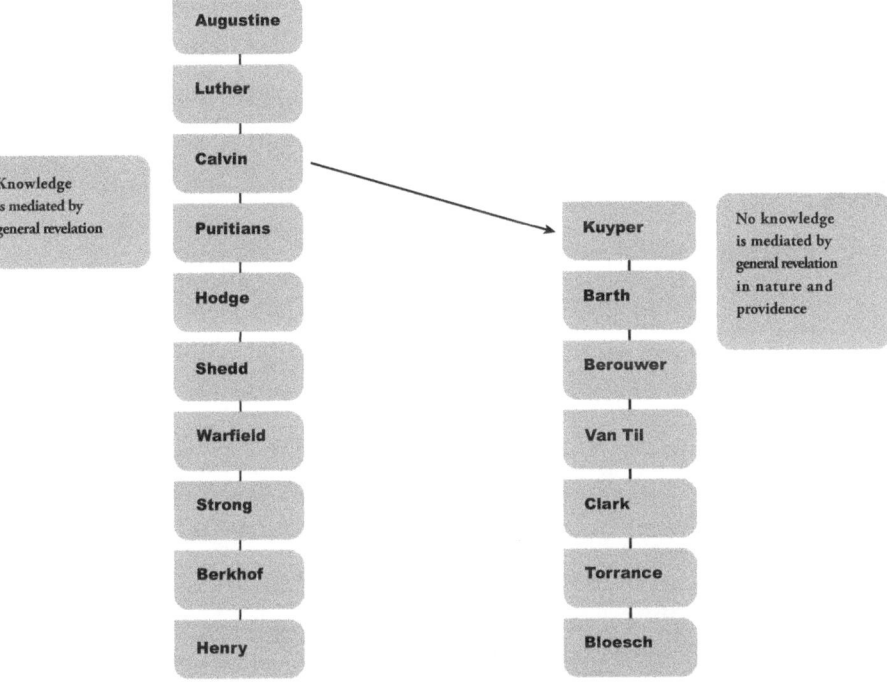

Figure 2. Two approaches to general revelation according to Demarest [9]

Alvin Plantinga remarks on the range of Reformed views to natural theology:

> A few Reformed thinkers—B. B. Warfield, for example—endorse the theistic proofs; but for the most part the Reformed attitude has ranged from tepid endorsement, through indifference, to suspicion, hostility, and outright accusations of blasphemy.[10]

---

9. Bruce A. Demarest, *General Revelation*, 244.

10. Alvin Plantinga, "The Reformed Objection to Natural Theology," *Proceedings and Addresses of the American Philosophical Association* 54 (1980): 49–63. Additionally, in "The Reformed Objection to Natural Theology," *Christian Scholar's Review* XI (1982): 187–198.

If Charles and Ballor[11] *and* Demarest[12] are both correct, then this range of views is not only in Reformed theology but also in Kuyper. To begin to understand Kuyper's position we need first to define what is meant by the seemingly elastic term "natural theology."

Defining the terms

What is the relationship between general and special revelation, common and particular grace, natural law, and natural theology? So often the terms are used loosely and interchangeably, and it has even been associated with the two kingdoms view and VanDrunen even asserts that common grace is part of natural theology.[13]

As David Novak puts it "Until quite recently, natural law thinking had been a Catholic preserve"[14] a preserve primarily associated with Thomas Aquinas. This has been changing.[15]

---

11. In *Common Grace* 3.

12. Demarest, *General Revelation*.

13. The title of David VanDrunen, *Natural Law and the Two Kingdoms: A Study in the Development of Reformed Social Thought* (Grand Rapids: Eerdmans, 2010) explicitly joins the terms "natural law" and "two kingdoms."

14. David Novak, "Does Natural Law need Theology? *First Things* https://www.firstthings.com/article/2019/11/does-natural-law-need-theology (Date of access 21 Feb 2023).

15. On the resurgence of Reformed Scholasticism see, for example, Willem J. Van Asselt, (with contributions by T. Theo J. Pleizier, Pieter L. Rouwendal, and Maarten Wisse), *Introduction to Reformed Scholasticism* (Reformation Heritage Books, 2011); Ryan McGraw, *Reformed Scholasticism: Recovering the Tools of Reformed Theology* (Edinburgh: T&T Clark, 2019); and Stephen J. Grabill, *Rediscovering the Natural Law in Reformed Theological Ethics* (Emory University Studies in Law

David Haines defines natural theology as "that part of phi-losophy which explores that which man can know about God (his existence, divine nature, etc.) from nature alone, via man's divinely bestowed faculty of reason on aided by special revela-tion from any religion, or that presupposing the truth of any religion.[16] Geerhardus Vos defines it thus: "Natural theology is a knowledge of God that takes its content and method from the world as it presents itself to us as governed by fixed laws."[17]

Michael Sudduth discerns two types of natural theology α and β.[18] He writes: "First, there is a distinction between natural theology as natural knowledge of God and natural theology as

and Religion, 2006). For the re-evaluation of the (selective) Reformed view of Aquinas see Manfred Svensson, and David VanDrunen, ed., *Aquinas Among the Protestants* (Oxford: Wiley-Blackwell, 2018).

On Kuyper's view of Aquinas see James Eglinton, "The Reception of Aquinas in Kuyper's *Encyclopaedie der heilige Godgeleerdheid*" in *The Oxford Handbook of the Reception of Aquinas*, ed., Matthew Levering and Marcus Plested (Oxford: Oxford University Press, 2021), 452–467.

16. David Haines, *Natural Theology: A Biblical and Historical Introduction and Defense* (Landry, SC: Davenant Press, 2021), 12. He also identifies some what he perceives to be objections to natural theology these include:

1. No Trinity = not the true God
2. Natural theology introduces Greek thought into Christian doctrine
3. Greek philosophy is erroneous and incoherent
4. Finding theistic proofs in the early church fathers is anachronistic.

17. Geerhardus Vos, *Natural Theology* (Grand Rapids: Reformation Heritage Books, 2022).

18. Sudduth, *Reformed Objection to Natural Theology*. Van den Brink takes issue with the title of Sudduth's book. He notes: "*The Reformed Endorsement of Natural Theology* would not only have been both a more original and provocative title but also one which would have much more truthfully captured the book's thesis," G. van den Brink, "Review

rational proofs or arguments for the existence and nature of God. ...I will designate the former natural theology α and the latter natural theology β." The β form is evident in Haines's definition above and the α in Vos's definition.

Sudduth's natural theology α appears to be a form of general revelation. Kuyper seems to have little problem with natural theology α, but would take issue with natural theology β.

Kuyper's approach

While some boundary-blurring is inevitable, some theologians have conflated natural theology and general revelation. G. C. Berkouwer, however, believes that this identification is "untenable."[19] Kuyper recognizes the difference. However, Kuyper's conception of natural theology has some ambiguity, as shown by the differing opinions of Demarest, Charles and Ballor noted above. Kuyper acknowledges both the value of natural theology and its limitations.

There has also been a tendency to separate special and natural theology. In his *Principles of Sacred Theology* he has this to say:

> It is, therefore, of the greatest importance, to see clearly, that special theology may not be considered a moment without natural theology, and that on the other hand natural theology of itself is unable to supply any pure knowledge of God. That special revelation (revelatio specialis) is not conceivable without the hypothesis

---

of Sudduth *The Reformed Objection to Natural Theology*," *Journal of Reformed Theology* 6 (2012): 309–310.

19. G. C. Berkouwer, *General Revelation* (Grand Rapids: Eerdmans, 1955), 47.

of natural theology, is simply because grace never creates one single new reality.[20]

Kuyper thus rejects separation—they are connected. Truth cannot be separated out. They are distinct but not separate. They are "allied to one another" and are thus "capable of affecting each other."[21] There is but one knowledge of God the content of which flows from "both sources, whose waters have mingled themselves."[22] He also argues, "It is on the canvas of natural knowledge of God itself that special revelation is embroidered."[23]

For Kuyper, natural theology is important because "Without natural Theology there is no *Abba, Father*, conceivable, any more than a Moloch ritual."[24] Special revelation builds upon natural theology; natural theology is the basis for special revelation:

> Natural theology is and always will be the natural pair of legs on which we must walk, while special revelation is the pair of crutches, which render help, as long as the weakened or broken legs refuse us their service.[25]

Natural theology has a limited role as it is not to be fully trusted or depended upon, so Kuyper argues. It provides no infallible information. Those who celebrate natural theology often

---

20. Kuyper, *Principles of Sacred Theology*, 373.
21. Kuyper, *Principles of Sacred Theology*, 376.
22. Kuyper, *Principles of Sacred Theology*, 377.
23. Kuyper, *Principles of Sacred Theology*, 374.
24. Kuyper, *Principles of Sacred Theology*, 301.
25. Kuyper, *Principles of Sacred Theology*, 309.

fail to consider the effects on sin on human thinking and reasoning. This is something that Kuyper stresses:

> And for this reason you cannot depend upon natural theology as it works in fallen man; and its imperfect lines and forms bring you, through the broken image, in touch with the reality of the infinite, only when an *accidens* enables you to recover this defective ideal for yourself, and natural theology receives this *accidens* only in special revelation.[26]

If by natural is meant something autonomous, then natural theology is a myth. If by natural theology is meant that which can be understood by all through reason then that is a myth too. If natural theology is the process of proving the existence of God by reason and without recourse to revelation, then natural theology is flawed.[27] Kuyper distances himself from this version of natural theology—he describes it as a "barren scheme of individual truths…which was made to stand as natural theology alongside of the supernatural."[28] This is a rejection of what Sudduth designates natural theology β.

For Kuyper, although he does not use the terms, there is a structure and direction to natural theology. There is a structure to it:

> Natural theology is with us no schema, but the knowledge of God itself, which still remains in the sinner and

---

26. Kuyper, *Principles of Sacred Theology*, 307.
27. Richard Russell, "Natural theology is it Scriptural?," *Faith and Thought* 111, no. 2, (1985): 171–174.
28. Kuyper, *Principles of Sacred Theology*, 302.

is still within his reach, entirely in harmony with the sense of Rom. i. 19 sq. and Rom. ii. 14 sq.[29]

There, as in ethics, is a normal development to it:

> With Natural Theology it is the same as it is with faith and ethics. Ethical life knows only one normal development, viz. that to holiness; but over against this positive stands the negative development along the line of sin.[30]

But...

> ...there is also a negative side. It has been clouded and darkened by sin, fortunately, mitigated by common grace. This leads to a tension, similar to that in Calvin: "It made men without excuse, and yet was not sufficient to salvation."[31]

He uses the image of a grafted tree to illustrate the distinction without separation of natural and special theology. It is worth quoting Kuyper at length:

> He who grafts, plants no new tree, but applies himself to one that exists. That tree is alive, it draws its sap from the roots, but this vital sap is wild, in consequence of which the tree can bear no fruit that is desired. And now the grafter comes, and inserts a nobler graft, and thereby brings it to pass that this vital sap of the wild tree is changed, so that the desired fruit now ripens on

---

29. Kuyper, *Principles of Sacred Theology*, 302.

30. Kuyper, *Principles of Sacred Theology*, 126.

31. John Calvin, "Commentary on Acts 14," *Calvin's Commentary on the Bible* https://www.studylight.org/commentaries/eng/cal/acts-14.html. 1840-57.

the branches. This new graft does not stand by the side of the wild tree, but is in it; and if the grafting is a success, it may equally well be said that the true graft lives by the old tree, as that the uncultivated tree is of use solely because of the new graft. And such, indeed, is the case here. The wild tree is the sinner, in whose nature works the natural principium of the knowledge of God as an inborn impelling power. If you leave this natural principium to itself, you will never have anything else than wild wood, and the fruit of knowledge does not come. But when the Lord our God introduces from without, and thus from another principium, a shoot of a true plant, even the principle of a pure knowledge into this wild tree, i.e. into this natural man, then there is not a man by the side of a man, no knowledge by the side of a knowledge, but the wild energy remains active in this human nature, i.e. incomplete knowledge; while the ingrafted new principium brings it to pass, that this impelling power is changed and produces the fruit of true knowledge. The special knowledge is, indeed, a new and proper principium, but this principium joins itself to the vital powers of our nature with its natural principium; compels this principium to let its life- sap flow through another channel; and in this way cultivates ripe fruit of knowledge from what otherwise would have produced only wood lit for fire.[32]

In his *Lectures on Calvinism*[33] Kuyper states his dislike for the term laws of nature as it suggests the laws originate from na-

---

32. Kuyper, *Principles of Sacred Theology*, 375.

33. Kuyper, *Lectures on Calvinism*, 71.

ture; they are however "imposed upon Nature." He is only prepared to accept the term provided this distinction is clear.

> What now does the Calvinist mean by his faith in the ordinances of God? Nothing less than the firmly rooted conviction that all life has first been in the *thoughts* of God, before it came to be realized in Creation. Hence all created life necessarily bears in itself a law for its existence, instituted by God Himself. There is no life outside us in Nature, without such divine ordinances,—ordinances which are called the laws of Nature—a term which we are willing to accept, provided we understand thereby, not laws originating from Nature, but laws imposed upon Nature.[34]

He designates creation as revelation. God placed within the creation ordinances or laws; it is the task of humanity to unfold the creation according to these norms. These norms "continue to this day" despite sin, but because of common grace.[35] Kuyper stresses three facts: divine ordinances exist; they are ordinances of God; and there is a way to know them.[36] They are not products of human construction, nor are they arbitrary. He argues

---

34. Kuyper, *Lectures on Calvinism*, 71.

35. This is a translation of sections from Kuyper's *Uit het Woord* III Wormser: (Amsterdam, 1879).

36. Wormser, *De Standaard* 16 October 1873, trans. Harry der Nederlander, with Gordon Spykman, extracted in James W. Skillen and Rockne M. McCarthy, ed., *Political Order and the Plural Structure of Society* (Atlanta: Scholars Press, 1991), 242. Abraham Kuyper, "The Natural Knowledge of God," trans. Harry Van Dyke. *Bavinck Review* 6 (2015): 73–112.

that the ordinances can only be known by the study of God's Word and by empirical research.

We can see this in his attitude towards art. Art, for Kuyper, has a revelatory nature:

> Art reveals ordinances of creation which neither science, nor politics, nor religious life, nor even revelation can bring to light.[37]

Art is a form of creational revelation. Art reveals to us something of the artist. So too, for Kuyper creation reveals something of the creator. It is God's handwork and "a revelation of God's attributes."[38]

Kuyper has an all-embracing view of revelation: "all creation as such belongs to the domain of revelation"[39]—it appears that there is no separation between special and general revelation.

Evaluation and conclusion

Natural theology is in many ways a loaded term. There are many varieties of natural theology—not least the α and β forms that Sudduth identifies. Others have discussed the wide range of approaches that come under natural theology.[40]

Part of the problem surrounding the topic of natural theology is its definition—if Haines's definition is adopted then Kuyper did not agree with natural theology as an option. If

---

37. Kuyper, *Lectures on Calvinism,* 163.

38. Kuyper, *Lectures on Calvinism,* 119-120.

39. Kuyper, *Principles of Sacred Theology,* 270.

40. See, for example, Alister McGrath, *Darwinism and the Divine Evolutionary Thought and Natural Theology. The 2009 Hulsean Lectures University of Cambridge* (Chichester: John Wiley, 2011), Part I.

VanDrunen is correct and that common grace and creation order are part of natural theology—then Kuyper did adopt some aspects of natural theology. The problem is that Haines' definition is too narrow and VanDrunen's is too wide. If we accept that general revelation is part of natural theology, then common grace is not a part of natural theology,[41] as common grace is not part of general revelation.

Masselink[42] defends Kuyper's (and Valentijn Hepp's (1879–1950)) view of common grace and general revelation, which he terms the "Historic Reformed faith" against the "Reconstructionist"[43] movement of Schilder, Dooyeweerd, Vollenhoven, and Van Til. Masselink helpfully identifies some misconceptions regarding general revelation—not least, common grace is not to be identified with general revelation.[44] There are a number of reasons for this difference. General revelation precedes the fall into sin, whereas common grace comes after the fall. They differ in purpose: common grace curbs sin and the effects of sin, whereas the role of general revelation is to reveal God in

---

41. Masselink maintains that the identification of general revelation with natural theology is an error that began with Scholasticism. William Masselink, *General Revelation and Common Grace*, (Grand Rapids: Eerdmans,1953), 70.

42. Masselink (1897–1973) was a student of Hepp's while he did post graduate work at the VU Amsterdam (1936–1937). He was an ordained minister in the Christian Reformed Church serving churches in Lafayette, Indiana, Holland, Michigan, Grand Rapids, Michigan, and Chicago, Illinois.

43. This should not be confused with the Reconstructionism of R. J. Rushdoony *et al.* Masselink's book was published a few years before Rushdoony's work appeared.

44. Masselink, *General Revelation*, 67–72.

his creation. Knowledge of common grace is revealed to us through the Scriptures, and not by general revelation.[45]

For Kuyper there is a distinction, but not a separation, between special and general revelation. They are in harmony and do not conflict. Special revelation points back to general revelation, which in turn in turn leads to special revelation.

Creation, fall, and redemption are key moments in the Christian story. It may be useful to explore natural theology in light of this Christian ground-motive. In creation there was no common grace all revelation was general and special—there was no distinction between special and general revelation. Humanity had an innate *sensus divinitas*, a *semen religionis*. "Knowledge of God is implanted, infused into" humanity.

> Furthermore, the natural knowledge of God exists thanks to the uninterrupted radiation of God's majesty throughout creation, hence also in man who is sensitive to this radiation and is given a sense of that majesty. That is why it is called a *sensus divinitatis*, a sense of the Divine, a *semen religionis*, a seed of the relationship that ties us to God, and a *theologia innata*, a knowledge of God that is grounded in our relation to God as creatures.[46]

The fall, however, distorted the relationship of humanity with God, with themselves, and with the rest of creation. Reason becomes clouded—there are noetic effects of sin upon human reasoning. Humans are incapable of coming to a true knowledge of God through their own reasoning. Reason may lead to

---

45. Masselink, *General Revelation*, 69.

46. Kuyper, "Natural Knowledge of God," 75.

a God of the philosophers but not to the God of the Bible. There is still "creational revelation" (for example, Psalm 19, Romans 1), but this is incapable of leading to a personal, saving knowledge of God. A knowledge of God is only possible through God's revelation of himself, "special revelation." As a result of the fall, we are unable to use reason to reach God; we cannot prove God's existence. There are no "natural" ways to God. It is not possible for human reason to arrive at a knowledge of God's existence and character on its own. Neither reason nor observation can lead us to God as Kuyper puts it:

> From the finite no conclusion can be drawn to the infinite, neither can a Divine reality be known from external or internal phenomena, unless that real God reveals Himself in my consciousness to my ego; reveals himself as God; and thereby moves and impels me to see in these finite phenomena a brightness of His glory. Formaliter, neither observation nor reasoning would ever have rendered service here as the principium of knowing.[47]

Often, those who adopt a form of natural theology downplay the noetic effects of sin. General revelation is incomplete without special revelation—it does not impart "the least knowledge of God":

> Even though for the moment we do not reckon with the darkening of sin, all that is called "natural revelation" would not impart to us the least knowledge of God, if it were not willed by God, and as such make an

---

47. Kuyper, *Principles of Sacred Theology*, 343.

intentional revelation, i.e. a disclosure in part of His Divine mystery.[48]

Kuyper also observes that the knowledge of God is suppressed but not extinguished by the fall:

> To know God is a demand of human nature. What sin corrupts is still our human nature. Amid our total depravity there is a natural knowledge of God, a knowledge that can be suppressed but never extinguished. Remnants of it, however small, are never absent. The sinner hates God, but he cannot escape Him.[49]

And "Were it not for sin, the natural knowledge of God would have led man to true knowledge of God. Hence, the absolute necessity that man be born again."[50]

Redemption—the necessity of being born again—comes only through special revelation and regeneration. This is what Kuyper termed palingenesis. With regeneration we can see the glory of the trinitarian God in his creation. In the consummation, the fulfilment of redemption, humanity will be able to know God in his creation.

Kuyper rejects the role of general revelation providing the foundations for special revelation as this results in the autonomy of reason. There is some ambiguity in Kuyper's approach. However, it seems clear that he would accept natural theology if understood as a natural knowledge of God, in the form of a *semen religionis*, but he would reject natural theology as rational proofs or arguments for the existence and nature of

---

48. Kuyper, *Principles of Sacred Theology*, 250-251.
49. Kuyper, "Natural Knowledge of God," 74.
50. Kuyper, "Natural Knowledge of God," 75.

God. As F. H. Jacobi said: "a God capable of proof would be no God at all; since this would mean that there is something higher than God from which His existence can be deduced."[51] Kuyper would agree.

The form of natural theology that Kuyper accepts is perhaps better called "creational revelation." Natural theology? No. General revelation? Yes, but better creational revelation.

---

51. Cited in James Orr, *The Christian View of God and the World*, 9th edn (New York: Charles Scribners, 1908), Lecture III, 94–95.

Study Questions

1. How would Kuyper respond to the view that theology is the queen of the sciences?
2. Does Kuyper have an ambiguous view of theology?
3. Are there scholastic influences within Kuyper's writings?
4. Why does Kuyper often use the terms organic/organism? What is (a) the meaning and (b) the origin of such terms?
5. Was Kuyper a fundamentalist?
6. What role does the Holy Spirt play in Kuyper's view of inspiration?
7. How is the Scripture authoritative for Kuyper?
8. What is Kuyper's view on the authority of Scripture and how does it differ from other theologians?
9. How does Kuyper's supralapsarianism shape his view of baptism?
10. In what ways was Kuyper's approach to mission ahead of its time?
11. In what sense are we "all missionaries"?
12. What does Kuyper mean when he uses the term "natural theology"? Can theology be natural?
13. How would Kuyper respond to the Radical Two Kingdom approach of David VanDrunen?
14. How does Kuyper compare and contrast with other theologians such as Warfield and VanDrunen with respect to Scripture, apologetics, natural theology, and reason?

Further Reading

Primary Sources

Kuyper, Abraham. *The Work of the Holy Spirit* (New York: Funk and Wagnalls, 1900).

Kuyper, Abraham. "Calvinism and Confessional Review," *The Presbyterian Quarterly* Vol. IV, No. 18 (October, 1891).

Kuyper, Abraham. *Principles of Sacred Theology*. Intro. Benjamin B. Warfield, trans. J. Hendrik De Vries (Grand Rapids, MI: Eerdmans, 1968).

Kuyper, Abraham. "The Biblical Criticism of the Present Day," *Biblica Sacra* LXI (243) (1904): 409–442; 666–668.

Secondary Sources

Bishop, Steve. "Abraham Kuyper's View of Scripture," *Foundations* 86 (2024): 15–38.

Bishop, Steve and David Kristanto. "Kuyper's View of Natural Theology," *Koers* 89 (2024) http://doi.org/10.19108/KOERS. 89.1.2547.

Bratt, James D. "The Dutch Schools," in *Reformed Theology in America: A History of Its Modern Development*, David F. Wells, ed. (Grand Rapids, Michigan: William B. Eerdmans Publishing Company, 1985).

Bratt, James D. *Dutch Calvinism in Modern America: A History of a Conservative Subculture* (Eugene, Oregon: Wipf and Stock Publishers, 2002).

Brock, Cory C. and N. Gray Sutanto, *Neo-Calvinism: A Theological Introduction* (Bellingham, WA: Lexham Press, 2023).

Dennison, William D. "Neo-Calvinism and the Roots for Transformation: An Introductory Essay," *Journal of the Evangelical Theological Society*. 42 (2) (1999): 271–291.

Mouw, Richard J. "Dutch Calvinist Philosophical Influences in North America," *Calvin Theological Journal* 24 (1) (1989): 93–120.

Spykman, Gordon. *Reformational Theology: A New Paradigm for Doing Dogmatics* (Grand Rapids: Eerdmans, 1992).

Part 4

Applications

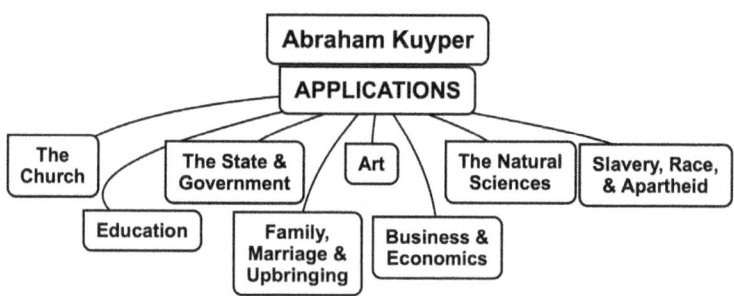

23

The Church

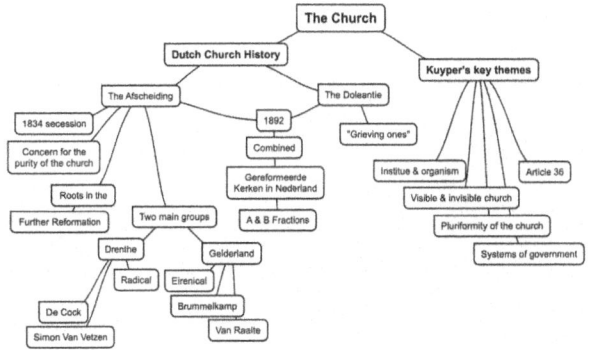

In brief

THIS CHAPTER EXAMINES THE profound theological insights of Abraham Kuyper regarding the church and its significance in the kingdom of God. Through an exploration of Kuyper's writings, his deep concern for the church's well-being and its pivotal role in shaping society is highlighted. Emphasizing the church's freedom from government interference, Kuyper's radical view of the church as both institute and organism provides a framework for understanding its diverse roles in society. The chapter also briefly examines key Dutch church movements like the *Nadere Reformatie* and the *Réveil*, showcasing their influence on Kuyper's ecclesiology. Overall, Kuyper's unwavering commitment to the church and its mission, offering valuable insights into the intersection of theology, church history, and societal engagement is emphasized.

Introduction

> ... the problem of the church is none other than the problem of Christianity itself.
>
> Abraham Kuyper in *Conservatism and Orthodoxy* (1870).

Neo-Calvinists are often accused of minimizing the importance of the church in the kingdom of God. This was certainly not the case for Abraham Kuyper, his first and last articles were on the church. As John Halsey Wood Jr. notes, the church was the bookends of Kuyper's theological writings.[1] Kuyper was a pastor in a church, led a reform of the Dutch Reformed Church and wrote his doctorate on Calvin's and à Lasco's views of the church. Kuyper always had a deep concern for the church: as he said, the "church question dominates every other issue."[2] As his biographer Rullman puts it, "Kuyper was first and foremost concerned about the church."[3] In a sense, Kuyper turned from studying church history to

---

1. J. H. Wood Jr., *Going Dutch in the Modern Age* (Oxford: Oxford University Press, 2013), 3.
2. A. Kuyper, *Rooted and Grounded* (Grand Rapids: Christian Library Press, 2013), 22.
3. J. C. Rullman, *Abraham Kuyper*, 235. The original is: "De kerk ging Kuyper het eerst en het meest ter harte."

making church history. There has been a resurgence of interest in Kuyper's ecclesiology.[4]

Dutch Church history

There is a Dutch proverb that states, "in the past lies the present, and in the present will be the future."[5] To understand Kuyper's view of the church, we must first, then, look to the past and understand the ecclesiastical context out of which Kuyper worked. To this end we will examine two important Dutch church movements, the *Afscheiding* and the *Doleantie*.

The Afscheiding and the Doleantie

In 1834 there was a secession from the Dutch state church. This has been called the *Afscheiding*, which is Dutch for separa-

---

4. Wood, *Going Dutch in the Modern Age*; H. Zwaanstra, "Abraham Kuyper's Conception of the Church," *Calvin Theological Journal* 9, no. 2 (1974): 149–81; M. E. Brinkman, "Kuyper's Concept of the Pluriformity of the Church," in *Kuyper Reconsidered: Aspects of His Life and Work*, edited by C. Kooi and J. Bruijn (Amsterdam: VU Publishers, 1999), 111–22; M. Wagenman, "Power of the Church: The Ecclesiology of Abraham Kuyper" (PhD Thesis, Bristol University, 2017); D. Strange, "Rooted and Grounded? The Legitimacy of Abraham Kuyper's Distinction between Church as Institute and Church as Organism, and Its Usefulness in Constructing an Evangelical Public Theology," *Themelios* 40, no. 3 (2015); A. Kuyper, *On the Church* (Bellingham, WA: Lexham Press, 2016); A. Bruijne, 'Colony of Heaven': Abraham Kuyper's Ecclesiology in the Twenty-First Century," *Journal of Markets & Morality* 17, no. 2 (2014): 445–90; Surya Harefa, *A Free Church in a Free State: The Possibilities of Abraham Kuyper's Ecclesiology for Japanese Evangelical Christians* (Carlisle: Langham Press, 2023).

5. Cited in G. Hoeksema, *A Watered Garden: A Brief History of the Protestant Reformed Churches in America* (Grand Rapids: Protestant Free Publishing Association, 1992), 8.

tion. There was a further separation, led by Kuyper, known as the *Doleantie* in 1886.

To understand the *Doleantie* and the role Kuyper played in it it is necessary to examine the background to the *Afscheiding*. After all, why did Kuyper not join the *Afscheiding* secession instead of founding another denomination? As we shall see, in the main, it was to do with differing theologies of the church.

The *Afscheiding* had its roots in two previous Christian movements that shaped the religious contours of the Netherlands, these were the Further Reformation and the *Réveil*. It was a reaction against the liberalising and state-dominated church. The *Nadere Reformatie*, also known as the Second or Further Reformation, took place in the Netherlands around 1600–1750. This movement resembled Puritanism in England and has been called Dutch Puritanism.[6] Key people involved in the *Nadere Reformatie* included Jean Taffin (1529–1602), Willem Teellinck (1579–1629), Gisbertus Voetius (1589–1676), Wilhelmus à Brakel (1635–1711), and Hermanus Witsius (1636–1708).[7] It promoted the notion that theology was for the heart. Much more influential in the Netherlands was the *Réveil*, which started in 1819 in Geneva, Switzerland and rapidly spread

6. Curt Daniel, *The History and Theology of Calvinism* (Darlington: Evangelical Press, 2019), 70.

7. Kuyper had a high regard for Voetius in particular, he describes him as a "goldy and learned theologian" (Kuyper, *Work of the Holy Spirit*, 300); and in Ch XXXVI of *Work of the Holy Spirit*, he discusses Brakel. On the *Nadere Reformatie* see, for example, Joel R. Beeke, Joel R. "Appendix: The Dutch Second Reformation De *Nadre Reformatie*," in *The Quest for Full Assurance* (Grand Rapids: The Banner of Truth Trust, 1999), 287–293.

around Europe. The Scot Robert Haldane had gone to Geneva and began expounding the book of Romans to some unconverted students.[8] These students included Jean-Henri Merle d'Aubigné (1794–1872), César Malan (1787–1864), François Samuel Robert Louis Gaussen (1790–1863), and the Monod brothers, Frédéric (1794–1863) and Adolphe (1802–56). They were soundly converted and spread the message across Europe. In the preface to Haldane's *Romans* Dr. Reuben Saillens (1855–1942), the influential French pastor, is cited as describing the characteristics of what he called "Haldane's Revival" as:

(1) it gave a prominent emphasis to the necessity of a personal knowledge and experience of grace;

(2) it maintained the absolute authority and Divine inspiration of the Bible;

(3) was a return to Calvinistic doctrine against Pelagianism and Arminianism. Haldane was an orthodox of the first water, but his orthodoxy was blended with love and life.[9]

Key Dutch figures of the *Réveil* were Isaäc da Costa (1798–1860), William Bilderdijk (1756–1831) and Groen Van Prinsterer.[10]

---

8. See for example, Kenneth Stewart, *Restoring the Reformation: British Evangelicalism and the Francophone 'Réveil' 1816–1849. Studies in Evangelical History and Thought* (Carlisle: Paternoster, 2006).

9. Robert Haldane, *Romans* (Edinburgh: Banner of Truth, 1958).

10. Harry Van Dyke makes the important observation, "The careers of neither Bavinck nor Kuyper—the range of their intellectual output, their reforming zeal in more than one area of life and culture—can be understood apart from Groen. He taught them to discern the problem of the spirit of modernity in its widest scope, from which viewpoint

Bilderdijk was a poet and da Costa a converted Jew. They met in each other's homes on an informal basis for Bible study, lectures in history and debates in social problems. James Bratt points out that they held to a "salvation triad:" "man's corruption, Christ's exclusive atonement and experiential conversion."[11] The emphasis was not on the reformation of the church rather it was on faith and repentance; as Van Oene notes, "the church as a whole took second place in their striving for a return to God's Word."[12]

A key person in subsequent church developments was Hendrik P. Scholte (1805–1868), who had direct links to the *Réveil* and formed a study club of his own, most of the members of the Scholte club also occasionally attended da Costa's meetings. The *Réveil* group had many sympathies with the Secession church and gave legal help. However, they disapproved of the Secession's view of the Reformed Church and were wary of the schism mentality. This may in some measure be because the *Réveil* were in the main aristocrats and they were not impressed by the tone and extremism of the Secession.[13]

The Scholte club was a loose configuration of students under the leadership of Scholte at the University of Leiden. They included:

---

they called for nothing less than a culture war across the whole spectrum of modern life." Harry Van Dyke, "Groen van Prinsterer: Godfather of Bavinck and Kuyper," *Calvin Theological Journal* 47 (2012): 72–97.

11. James D. Bratt, *Dutch Calvinism in Modern America* (Grand Rapids: Eerdmans, 1984), 11.

12. W. W. J. Van Oene, *Patrimony Profile: Our Reformed Heritage Retraced 1995–1946* (Winnipeg: Premier, 1999), 17.

13. Bratt, *Dutch Calvinism in Modern America*.

Anthony Brummelkamp (1811–1888)

Simon Van Velzen (1809–1896)

Georg Gezelle Meerburg (1806–1855)

Louis Bahler (1766–1838)

Albertus C. Van Raalte (1811–1876) was also a member but never met Scholte as Scholte had graduated before Van Raalte joined. All the members on leaving were ordained in the Dutch State church, apart from Van Raalte. Van Raalte was refused ordination because of his association with the "troublemakers." Most members of the Scholte club were instrumental in the *Afscheiding* secession.

Albertus C. Van Raalte (1811–1876)   *Hendrik P. Scholte*

This secession was seen by the *Afscheiding* supporters as not a departure from the Reformed Church but rather as preserving the Reformed Church against the reorganization imposed by the state, or more particularly by the royal decree/command of King William I. It can be seen as part of a revival that swept Europe. In addition to Scholte another of the key leaders of the *Afscheiding* was Hendrik de Cock.

H. de Cook

The secession was triggered by Hendrik de Cock (1801–1842) at Ulrum. De Cock became minister at Ulrum in 1829. Here he discovered Calvin's *Institutes* and came across Reformed believers.[14] One of them, Klaas Kuipenga, said to de Cock: "If I

---

14. J. Faber, D. Jong, and J. Mulder, *Secession and Liberation For Today. Commemorative Lectures on the Secession of 1834 and the Liberation of 1944* (London, Ont: Inter League Publication Board, 1986).

had to add one sigh to my salvation I would be lost forever." Another believer gave him a copy of the Canons of Dordt. It was symptomatic of the times that this was the first time that de Cock had come across the Canons of Dordt. All these were instrumental under the Holy Spirit to bring de Cock to a Reformed faith. His preaching was now emphasizing the gospel of grace. This resulted in many believers coming to Ulrum to hear God's Word.

They suffered much persecution from the authorities, fines and even imprisonment, but they continued to preach the gospel.

The Drenthe and Gelderland factions

There were two main parties within the *Afscheiding* secession church, the Drenthe, and the Gelderland fractions. The Drenthe were the more radical and the Gelderland the more eirenical.

The main proponents of the Drenthe group were de Cock and Simon Van Velzen. They stressed synodical and confessional authority. Like the term Drenthe, Gelderland was originally a geographical term—the main proponents were Brummelkamp and Van Raalte. These were more ecumenical than the stricter northern Calvinists.[15] They emphasized more experiential religion and more autonomy for local congregations.

Issues that caused friction and disagreement included the following:

- Hymn singing
- The clothes the ministers wore
- The free offer or well-meant offer of the gospel

---

15. R. P. Swierenga and E. J. Bruins, *Family Quarrels in the Dutch Reformed Churches in the Nineteenth Century* (Grand Rapids: Eerdmans, 1999).

315

- Infra and supralapsarian
- The state–church relationship
- The nature and number of the covenants
- Who could partake in communion
- Experimental preaching
- The nature of baptism
- Presumptive regeneration
- Church order
- Adherence to the three forms of unity (i.e., the Belgic Confession, the Canons of Dort, and the Heidelberg Catechism)

Many of these issues were interrelated and overlapped. Most of them stemmed from the nature of and the time of election. Despite the long list of disagreements, there was agreement on many things. All were concerned for Christ and his church, were Reformed, held to a high view of Scripture and to the five points of Calvinism and had concern for orthodoxy, however they interpreted it.

The secession leaders were concerned for the purity of the church and emphasized a heart religion.

During this time there was still some religious persecution with limits on religious liberty, as well as widespread poverty. Taxes and unemployment increased, and economic depression spread across Europe. These were factors that made some consider emigrating.

Prior to this time emigration was rare: in 1840, 57 Dutch went to the US and in 1841, 241.[16] The attraction of North

---

16. Marian M. Schoolland, *The Story of Van Raalte* (Grand Rapids, MI: Eerdmans, 1951), 23.

America with its freedom of worship and freedom for Christian schools proved to be compelling. Many, however, thought emigration to be unpatriotic. There was a strong loyalty to the fatherland for many Calvinists. However, going *en masse* could mean a Christian community of their own shaped by their own Calvinistic beliefs. Van Raalte and Brummelkamp thus organized a "Society for Dutch Emigration to the United States of America."

Two key secession theologians, Van Raalte and Scholte, were among those who took groups to the USA. Van Raalte and his followers settled in West Michigan and formed De Kolonie of Holland. This group eventually joined the Reformed Church in America (RCA). For Van Raalte joining the RCA meant less isolation for the community. However, this was not without problems as the RCA was found to be sending their children to state schools, were singing hymns, practised open communion, and even allowed ministers to be members of Masonic lodges. The Holland groups, and others, were not impressed. This eventually led to a split from the RCA under the leadership of Gysbert Haan (1801–1874), who had been trained by the Drenthe supporter Simon Van Vetzen. Thus, in 1857, the Holland Reformed Church was formed. This later became the True Dutch Church and eventually in the 1880s the Christian Reformed Church of North America. Van Raalte remained with the RCA—he was against lodge membership but thought it was an issue that was not worth separating over.

The Scholte group eventually settled in Pella, Iowa. The Church they formed was an independent church, in line with Scholtes's more Congregationalist ideals.

Von Raalte and Scholte were two who were most disaffect-
ed by the direction the secession churches were taking.[17] Their
emigration meant that there was more harmony among the
secession churches. This was helped with the formation of a
seminary in Kampen. The departure of Von Raalte and
Scholte meant that the secession became shaped more by
Drenthe views.

The Doleantie

Fifty years later came another secession from the state church,
this time led by Kuyper. This was known as the *Doleantie*,
which is Dutch for grieving.

For Kuyper and his followers, the *Doleantie* was a matter of the protection of orthodoxy. Not all, however, saw it
that way. One, Revd Henstra, regarded the *Doleantie* as
largely "a working out of the theories of Dr. Abraham
Kuyper in his Tract."[18]

Herman Bavinck, who later became Kuyper's successor as
professor of theology at the Free University (VU University
Amsterdam), was a key person in the remaining church.

Three years before the *Doleantie* Kuyper wrote *Tract
on the Reformation of the Churches*.[19] Kuyper writes here
as a church pastor with a heart for the right functioning
of the church. His concern is for a pure church. Kuyper

---

17. Bratt, *Dutch Calvinism in Modern America*, 7.

18. H. Bouma, *Secession, Doleantie and Union: 1834–1892* (Pella, IO:
Inheritance Publications, 1995), 214.

19. Abraham Kuyper, *Tractaat van de reformatie der kerken, aan de zonen
der Reformatie hier te lande op Luthers vierde eeuwfeest aangeboden*
(Amsterdam: Höveker & Zoon, 1884); in *On the Church*, 78–280.

argues for the severing of the church and the state. This text is a basis for a manual of Reformed Church government. It paved the way for the *Doleantie* secession from the state church.

In 1892, the *Afscheiding* and the *Doleantie* combined to form the Gereformeerde Kerken in Nederland (GKN). Not all agreed with the merger. Not least because of the lack of consultations, the secession and *Doleantie* principles were viewed by some as conflicting.[20] Many of the objections were discussed prior to the Christian Reformed Church synod in June 1892, where the proposal to unite was passed almost unanimously.[21]

Although united, there were still tensions between the two groups, so much so that the designation A and B were used to show which grouping they had previously been aligned with. Eventually, this led some to react against some of Kuyper's teachings, in particular his views on common grace and presumptive regeneration. They maintained that they were incompatible with orthodox Reformed doctrine.

In 1905 at Utrecht a session was held in an attempt to provide a compromise between the A and B factions; however, it resulted only in an uneasy truce. This truce lasted for three decades. After

---

20. C. Pronk, *A Godly Heritage: The Secession of 1834 and Its Impact on Reformed Churches in the Netherlands and North America* (Grand Rapids: Reformation Heritage Books, 2019), kindle loc.7491.

21. Three congregations took the decision to remain as the Christian Reformed Church—eventually other congregations disillusioned with the union rejoined. The church is now known as the *Christelijke Gereformeerde Kerken* in Nederland (CGKN), it is a sister church of the Free Reformed Churches of North America.

the Second World War, the disagreements resurfaced, with the result that mainly A congregations separated under the leadership of Klaas Schilder (1890–1952) and Seakle Greijdanus (18971–1948) to form what became known as the Reformed Churches in the Netherlands (Liberated) (in Dutch the Gereformeerde Kerken in Nederland (vrijgemaakt)). Rudolf Van Reest[22] commenting on the tensions within the GKN noted:

> The Kuyper of common grace was deified, while the Kuyper of the antithesis was rejected. Kuyper's ideas were unraveled, and the worst of them were canonized, for they were found useful for a Christianity that was externalizing itself and conforming to the world.[23]

A meeting was held on 11 August 1944 to discuss the way forward after Schilder was deposed. Herman Knoop (1890–1948) and Schilder addressed the group. Knoop identified several reasons for the decline—these were important and pertinent points. It is worth itemising them here. He begins by noting the influence of Kuyper.

> In the previous century Dr. A. Kuyper had called Reformed people out of their isolation, so that they began to fulfill their God-given calling in all of public

---

22. Rudolf Van Reest was the pen name of Karel Cornelis van Spronsen (1897–1979). In the introduction to the book Jacobus De Jong makes it clear that "clear that Van Reest paints a somewhat flattering picture of Schilder."

23. R. Van Reest, *Schilder's Struggle for the Unity of the Church* (Inheritance Publications, 1990).

life, in politics, education, social action, charities, sciences, arts, youth-movement, press and radio. Now what was the motivating force behind this? Was it thirst for power, a kind of Christian imperialism? No, it was the pure Calvinistic adage; the honour of God in all of life. And the Lord gave His blessing, as a reward of grace.

But how it fell prey to all kinds of dangers!

He goes on to identify seven of these dangers:

- A sense of having arrived—we are big and powerful.
- A shift in emphasis from Christ to ourselves
- A struggle for national influence at the cost of spiritual life
- There is no longer an expectation of the return of the Lord.
- The lack of persecution
- A growing materialism and secularisation
- The antithesis results in "sticking to own circle" and to the trap of self-righteousness.

These dangers may also be with us today—we need to continually check our hearts so that we do not succumb to them.

This is the context both past and present in which Kuyper formed his views of the church. I will examine some of the key texts in which Kuyper developed his view. These include *Rooted and Grounded*[24] his inaugural speech, delivered to his new congregation in 1870 Amsterdam, *Tract for the Reformation of the*

---

24. Abraham Kuyper, *Rooted and Grounded: The Church as Organism and Institution* (Grand Rapids, MI: Christian's Library Press, 2013). Also, in *On the Church*, 41–73.

Churches,[25] *Common Grace,*[26] and *Pro Rege.*[27] In these texts he discusses several key themes, such as the church as an institute and as an organism, the visible and invisible church, and the pluriformity of the church.

Key themes

Institute and organism

The distinction between the church as organism and institute was (and is) an important one and central to Kuyper's understanding of the church.[28] It was in his sermon 1840 *Rooted and Grounded* [29] that this distinction was developed. During this time Kuyper was struggling with the liberalism and modernism that had gripped the Dutch Reformed Church. It was 16 years after this work in 1886 that he would lead a secession from the National Church and form the *Doleantie.*

---

25. This was originally four lectures delivered by Kuyper to the "Circle of Brothers" in the spring of 1883. "The Circle of Brothers was a group of like-minded members of the Consistory of the Dutch Reformed Congregation of Amsterdam who advocated making subscription to the three forms of unity mandatory and who regularly consulted with one another about their lines of action in the consistory" T. Kuipers, *Abraham Kuyper: An Annotated Bibliography* (Leiden: Brill, 2011), 130. It provided a framework for the *Doleantie.* It was originally published in 1883 and translated into English in 2016.

26. A. Kuyper, *Common Grace (Volume 3): God's Gifts for a Fallen World* (Bellingham, WA: Lexham Press, 2020).

27. A. Kuyper, *Pro Rege: Living under Christ's Kingship* (Bellingham, WA: Lexham Press, 2019).

28. Some of this material in this section draws upon my discussion in Steve Bishop, "Kuyperania in Recent Years," *Koers—Bulletin for Christian Scholarship* 79(2014), Art. #2138.

29. Kuyper, *Rooted and Grounded.*

The terms "rooted" and "grounded" are taken from Ephesians 3:17. He uses these as metaphors for the church as organism and institution respectively. Both are necessary for the church to be church. As Kuyper puts it in his preface:

> Both the denial of the church's characteristic organism and the failure to maintain the church's characteristic institution betray a vacillation in the choice placed before every heart, the choice that at its deepest point exists between "election" and "humanism."[30]

For Kuyper, the church had to be free: free from money, from state control and ecclesiastical hierarchy. The church is based on God's eternal election; it is not a human creation.

He identifies three competing voices for the way forward: one emphasizes the church as organism, the other church as institution; the first so the church can flow out into society and the second to align with Rome. However, the third way forward is to see church as both institution and organism: a free church. Both rooted and grounded:

> "Rooted and grounded," says the apostle, and thereby declares with equal brevity and succinctness that twofold requirement, that double character trait of the Christian life. Rooted—that is the description of organic life; but also grounded—that is the requirement of the institution.[31]

---

30. Kuyper, *Rooted and Grounded,* xxiv.

31. Kuyper, *Rooted and Grounded,* 44.

There is growth and building; planting and organization: "From the organism the institution is born, but also through the institution the organism is fed"—both are needed; there is a symbiotic relationship.

The Reformed Church is both an organism and an institution. Its foundation is God's Word; God's eternal election is its heart and blood. The church is a response to sin. Without sin and the fall there would be no need for the church: "Leave sin out of consideration, and the church becomes inconceivable, since the world itself would then be the church."

Kuyper is opposed to the one-person ministry.[32] He places a strong emphasis on the priesthood of all believers. For the church to be truly an institution and organic the role of the institutional leaders must be to equip the church as organism to do the works of service in the marketplace, in the classroom, in business, in politics, in the laboratory....

Table 1 shows some of the images, metaphors, and illustrations that Kuyper uses to show the link between organism and institution.

Table 1. Metaphors used by Kuyper to describe the church as organism and the church as institute.[33]

Rooted (Organism)	Grounded (Institution)
Church as a body	Church as a house
Church grows	Church is built
Church is one loaf of dough that rises according to its nature	But nevertheless, kneaded by human hands

---

32. Kuyper, *Rooted and Grounded*, 29.

33. Bishop, "Kuyperania in Recent Years."

The church is a … multitude of priests, legitimated through birth	But nevertheless, kneaded by human hands
A Bride brought forth by the father	But accepting by choice
A people finally, that indeed sprouted from the living trunk Eden is planted	But nevertheless, organized with wisdom and guided with self-motivation But mankind will cultivate it
Crops grow by organic power	But human hand prepares a fertile soil, tames the wild acreage

The church is an organism because:
  she bears a unique life within herself
  and self-consciously upholds the
  independence of that life over
  against the old life
  she lives according to her own rule
  and must follow her own vital law
  what will later unfold from her buds
  is fully supplied already within
  her seed.	

	Largely neglected for a century
	Provides analysis and arrangement
	An organization is needed to regulate the mandate for everything that happens in the name of everyone
From the organism the institution is born	Feeds and expands the organism Through the institution the organism is fed

The nourishing source for the stream	
	No nurture where there is no regularity, no nursery where there is no order. But the institution is the bed that carries the current, the bank that borders its waters.

Only through the institution can the church offer us that unique life sphere .... Preserves discipline and justice, and is nevertheless flexible, tender, and supple.... |

Church as institute and organism
The church as institute. In *The Principles of Sacred Theology,*
Kuyper writes:

> The conception of the instituted Church is much nar-
> rower than the Church of Christ when taken as the
> body of Christ, for this includes in itself all the powers
> and workings that arise from re-creation. There is a
> Christian disposition and a Christian fellowship, there
> is a Christian knowledge and a Christian art, etc.,
> which indeed spring from the field of the Church and
> can flourish on this field alone, but which by no means
> therefore proceed from the instituted Church. The in-
> stituted Church finds her province bounded by her of-
> fices, and these offices are limited to the ministry of the
> Word, the Sacraments, Benevolence, and Church gov-
> ernment. These are the only offices that have been ap-
> pointed as special functions in her life. All other expres-

sions of Christian life do not work by the organ of the special offices, but by the organs of the re-created natural life: the Christian family by the believing father and mother, Christian art by the believing artist, and Christian schools by the believing magister.[34]

In his final volume of *Common Grace*, Kuyper examines the relationship between the church and the state. He is clear that here he is discussing the church as institute, not as organism. He provides a helpful outline of what he means by the church as institute. The church as an institute comprises a group of people in the same ecclesiastical association, an association that shares a confession and church order. The church as an institution has a soteriological essence, it is a group of saved people, it preaches salvation and guides the life of the saved. The church as institute is a post-fall institution. It could not exist without the fall. Without the fall there is no need for redemption and salvation.[35]

Church as organism. He writes in his *Tract* regarding the term *organism.* He notes that it should be understood correctly and has three senses.

> Moreover, the word organism must be taken in the correct sense, and this sense can be manifold. The organism of the church is complete only in the wholly mystical body of Christ. The full organism of the church includes all its parts, both those that have already grown and those that still must sprout.

---

34. Abraham Kuyper, *Principles of Sacred Theology* (Grand Rapids, MI: Eerdmans, 1968), 588.

35. Kuyper, *Common Grace* 3, Ch 14§1-2.

But if you mean a partial organic manifestation of this complete organism, insofar as the nature of the entire organism is stamped upon every cell of life, then such a church organism is present in every place where the church is unmistakably visible according to its nature as a church; and that is in every local church. Finally, we can take the word organism in a third sense, expressing the natural relationship of life that these individual organic manifestations of life have in relationship to each another. But this gives us only a relative and flexible concept, which can expand or contract, and therefore can never take the place of the organic notion of ecclesiastical unity that is already given in the local church.[36]

The relationship between church as institute and as organism

Wagenman aptly summarizes Kuyper on this point: "the organic church gives rise to the institutional church while the institutional church serves the organic church."[37] Or as Wood has it: "the institution ... [is] the tangible expression of the organism."[38]

Figure 1 is an attempt to show the relationship. The church as organism arises out and is equipped by the church as institute. Each needs the other, the relationship is, in a sense, symbiotic.

---

36. Kuyper, *Tract*, §15, 116.

37. Wagenman, *Power of the Church: The Ecclesiology of Abraham Kuyper* kindle loc. 2143.

38. Wood, *Going Dutch in the Modern Age*.

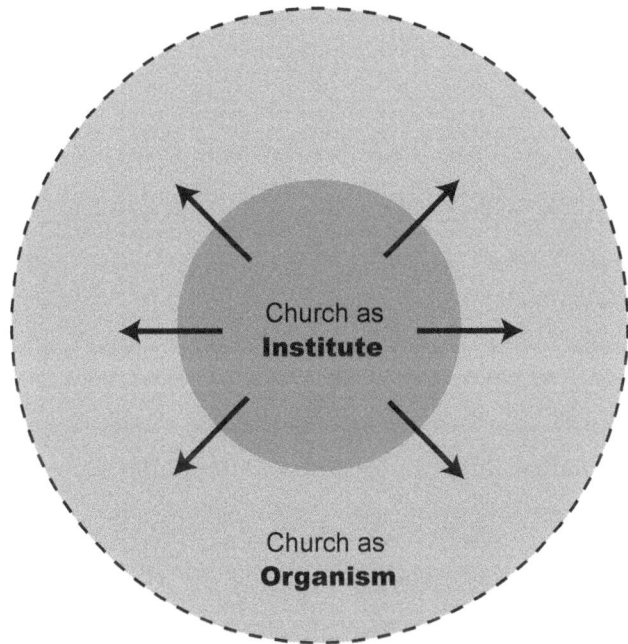

Figure 1. *The relationship between institute and organism.*

Tract for the Reformation of the Churches

The *Tract for the Reformation of the Churches* has four main parts.[39] The first dealing with general principles, the others with the formation, the deformation, and the reformation of the church. It laid the theological and biblical groundwork for the *Doleantie*.

Kuyper identifies four ways in which the church is understood on the basis of Scripture:

---

39. *The Tract for the Reformation of the Churches* was published on the date of Luther's fourth centenary. It was offered as a "sincere homage to the memory of the great man." It was an attempt, Kuyper, writes "... to honour the great Reformer by writing an essay about the reformation of the very churches whose reformational life finds its origin in Luther's courageous life."

1. The church that exists in God's counsel
2. The church as its life is hidden in Christ
3. The church as it is realized among humans on earth, and
4. The church as it will one day be in glory singing praises before the throne.[40]

These, he stresses, are four different perspectives, not four different churches.

The church in God's counsel

This is the full number of the elect. It is the church "ordained, called, justified and glorified before the face of the Triune God."[41]

The church as its life is hidden in Christ

Forgiveness and justification are eternal in God's counsel but appear in time with Christ. The church is formed through his death and resurrection. "When he died, all of the elect died with Christ. When he rose all of the elect arose with him."[42]

The church as it manifests itself on earth

Here we lose the unity of the church that it has in God's counsel and the holiness that it possesses in Christ. Here the church is in contact with the world and with "its infection with sin." It is never seen in its "pure, uncorrupted form, and it always carries unholy elements in it."[43] This is why the reformation is "an ongoing duty, because in a strict sense the [earthly] church is

---

40. Kuyper, *Tract*, §3, 88.
41. Kuyper, *Tract*, §3, 88
42. Kuyper, *Tract*, §3, 88.
43. Kuyper, *Tract*, §4, 90.

always deformed."[44] Hence, when speaking of the deformation and reformation of the church it can only apply to the church as it is manifest on earth.

The church on earth "is determined by God's Word." The administration of the sacraments affirms "their faith in that Word."

> There is, therefore, no other ministry in the visible church than the ministry of the Word, and all manifestations of the church's life flow from that one ministry.[45]

He calls the Old Testament people of God "the church in Israel."[46] Before Christ there was an organized ministry of priesthood, but not of the Word. Now there is a ministry of the Word but not of priesthood.

The organization and authority of the church

Any organization to work needs a structure to function effectively, the church is no different.

Thus, there is a threefold requirement for church formation: first, the activity of the Triune God in the communion of saints; second, an initiative by believers to join together in submission to God's Word; and third, the presence of offices to distinguish the church of God from all other societies.[47]

The church already in heaven

Here the earthly relationship gives way to a new relationship and experiences full glory rather than temporary glory. This is

---

44. Kuyper, *Tract*, §3, 90.
45. Kuyper, *Tract*, §5, 93.
46. Kuyper, *Tract*, §5, 87.
47. Kuyper, *Tract*, §13, 111.

when the church of Christ has come to full manifestation when it sits with Christ on the throne. "All preliminary manifestations" —that is, the church as it is on earth— "can only be divided and flawed."[48] They are divided by time and place.

In Tract §4 he then goes on to discuss the distinction between the invisible and visible church. Christians are part of the visible and the invisible church. This distinction, however, does not erode the essential unity of the church.

The visible and invisible church

The invisible and the visible church flow forth from a single divine idea. Both must derive from Christ.[49]

The Visible Church

The visible church appears only in parts and only locally. National churches should only arise when "mutual connections are made between these local churches." These connections, Kuyper maintains, are only temporary, loose, and flexible. The visible churches are not always one and are not holy as they "share the imperfection of all earthly life and are polluted by the power of sin, which continually undermines the well-being of the church, both internally and externally."

The Invisible Church

The invisible church is the body of Christ—that is, the organic connection of all elect, through the Holy Spirit, under Christ as their head. Therefore, if there are among the population of

---

48. Kuyper, *Tract*, §15, 114.
49. Kuyper, *Pro Rege,*123.

any city or village a certain number of living members of this body of Christ then the essence of the church *is* there.[50]

There are times Kuyper seems to be falling into the trap of dualism here, a dualism of invisible/visible church and of heavenly/earthy church. However, he mitigates this by stressing that the four aspects above are different perspectives of the same church. He also distinguishes between the essence and the actuality of a church. In its essence it has the potential to be a church; in the same way, dynamite is still dynamite even if it has not exploded, it has the potential to explode. Likewise, a church possesses the essence of a church even if it lacks the offices, provided "it carries within itself the potential to establish the office."[51]

The true marks of the church, for Kuyper, are "Word and sacrament, secured by church discipline." These take place within the local church. He sees the local church as the "primary manifestation of the church of Jesus Christ."[52] Although he rejects the view that each congregation can act as "an organic unit." He does think, however, that:

(1) that every local church possesses in itself the essence of the church; (2) that the external, juridical relationship with other churches arises only through confederation; and (3) that the organic unity consists only of the invisible church, while in this invisible church the local churches are the organic constitutive parts, and

---

50. Kuyper, *Tract*, §14, 111.
51. Kuyper, *Tract*, §14, 114.
52. Kuyper, *Tract*, §15, 115.

the classes and national church are no more than organic groups.[53]

He then poses and answers the important question (§16) can more than one church be established in the same town? His simple response is No! He does think, however, that this does not mean that a church can be subdivided into parishes provided these parishes "have as their one head, one consistory, representing the unity of the congregation." A Lutheran and a Reformed church should not ideally be existing in the same place, however, "it should sometimes be tolerated temporarily because of the imperfection of the situation." This brings us to the *pluriformity of the church*. This exists not as an ideal but as a temporary expedient. Different expressions/denominations of the church exist because some "disagree in their confession of the truth" thus they "establish churches separately."

> Therefore we must tolerate church formation alongside our church, provided it occurs on the basis of a deviating confession. And even if there is perfect agreement of confession, but due to external causes there are nevertheless two church formations in the same city or village, then in abnormal situations the one may not deny the other the right of the honorable name of church, but there must be a mutual zeal and a loving desire to unite both churches.[54]

The Pluriformity of The Church

The pluriformity or multiformity of the church was another of Kuyper's key themes. In essence this means that churches of

---

53. Kuyper, *Tract*, §15, 116.

54. Kuyper, *Tract*, §16, 118.

different confessions have a right to exist alongside one another. This, however, does not mean that there is a plurality of truth. This confusion seems to be at the heart of some objections to Kuyper's view. It does not necessarily mean that it opens the way up for ecumenism. Neither does it mean that Kuyper espouses a religious relativism.

> But we are equally conscious of the fact that we alone do not constitute the Church of Christ in the earth; that there is a conviction of truth which operates outside our circle ....[55]

The plurality stems from Kuyper's sphere sovereignty and from creation:

> The starlit heaven does not show us innumerable identical stars but endless groups of stars all different from each other. Precisely in this multiform distinction the beauty of the firmament shines. So it may not be assumed that God meant to have uniformity in his human world and that pluriformity arose as a result of sin... Moreover, the very fact that God created male and female proves conclusively that uniformity was not part of the creation plan.[56]

He discusses this multiformity in *Common Grace* volume 3 Chapter 32. He recognizes that the multiformity of the churches was not always the case. Before the Reformation in the West[57] there was only one church, the Roman Catholic Church. The

---

55. Kuyper, *Principles of Sacred Theology*, 326.

56. James D. Bratt, ed., *Abraham Kuyper: A Centennial Reader* (Grand Rapids, MI: W.B. Eerdmans, 1998), 445.

57. In the East, of course, existed the Copts and Nestorian churches.

deviances from this were called sects or schismatic. In each village there was only one church. Then came the Reformation.
All the Protestant Reformers took the position of the absolute
unity of the visible church. "Different churches alongside one
another seemed an absurdity. A church was either true or false."
However, as the Reformation developed in Lutheran and Calvinist churches the differences became more pronounced.

There was a principle of one, single church, yet in reality
there was a multiformity—this became the new form of life.
This multiformity was accepted with increasing openness.
This multiformity cannot be denied. Kuyper even goes as far
as suggesting that "it is our firm conviction that multiformity is a developmental stage to which the church of Christ
had to come...."[58]

Some, Kuyper suggests, object to this by saying it is
not a New Testament principle. He defends his position
by noting that the epistles are addressed to one church
in one city/region—to all in the same circumstances.
This was only a little more than a half-century after
Christ's ascension. The apostles did not try to ensure the
unity of all the churches by, for example, establishing a
collegium. They established no such single external organization or clerical institution to maintain unity. "It is not
the *clerical* institution but the *believers* themselves who
constitute the church."

He uses the metaphor of a plant to illustrate his point. A
plant may split into many stalks, but it was initially one. This
is so with the different manifestations of the visible church.

---

58. Kuyper, *Common Grace* 3, 268.

The objective truth remains one, but the subjective appropriation, application, and confession must differ, even as the color of light will differ depending on the glass that captures it.[59]

He goes as far as to suggest that "Opposition to the multiformity of the church arises from a false dualism."[60] The gospel is not a leaven to be put on top of the flour—it penetrates into the flour.

Systems of church government

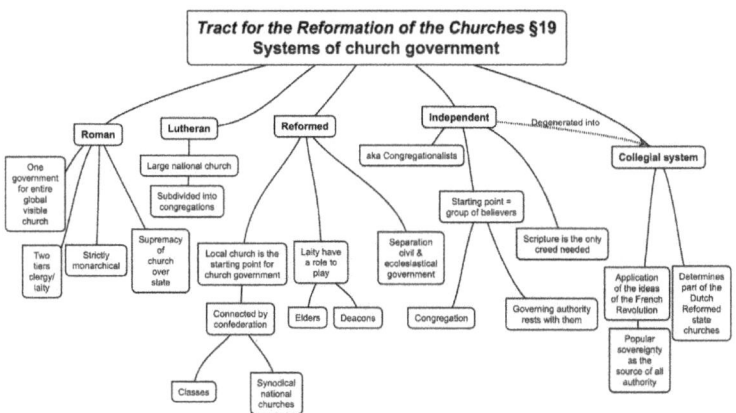

Kuyper identifies four different types of church government that have shaped the church visible. These are the Roman, Lutheran, Independent and Collegial. This concept map (above) summarizes Kuyper's views of the different systems.

For Kuyper, the Reformed position is the system which Calvin discovered was the "purest and best and required by God's Word."[61]

---

59. Kuyper, *Common Grace* 3, 271.

60. Kuyper, *Common Grace* 3, 272.

61. Kuyper, *Tract*, §19, 130.

For the Reformed view the cornerstone of the system is the local church as opposed to the Lutheran's national church or the Independent's congregation of believers or the Roman Catholic's one global visible church. The heart of the church for the Reformed is not in the means of grace but in God's sovereign election. These local churches then forge mutual relationships between local churches in classes and synods. There is also, contra the Roman Catholic view, an emphasis on the laity; there is no supremacy of the clergy as the laity is involved in the local church government as elders and deacons. There is also a separation of civil and ecclesiastical government. The Reformed also emphasize both Scripture and the confessions.

Two means of grace

Kuyper identifies two means of grace:[62] the Word and the sacraments. He holds to the view that there are two sacraments, baptism, and the breaking of bread. The purpose of the sacraments is to seal the Word and strengthen faith. The seal must be public, so he maintains that there should be no separate baptism or communion services. He suggests that the best way to administer them is "after the sermon has ended."

To receive the sacraments is a church member's duty.

> ...every church member has the duty to make use of the sacrament. Everyone is obligated to baptize his child, and likewise all believers have the obligation to

---

62. Kuyper, *Tract*, §28.

attend whenever the Lord's supper is administered. Not as if their salvation depended upon the sacrament.[63]

He advocates both infant baptism and child communion. No one who is a member of the church should be refused baptism: "The Word and the sacrament of the Lord's supper would also be appropriate for infants, if they were receptive to them."[64]

He does, however, clarify this:

> However, since this is naturally impossible, the child first acquires the right to the Word when he or she can hear, and the right to communion when he or she can confess.[65]

The means of grace "must be kept holy." This then is the role of church discipline (§30). Discipline is not through, a "fraternal admonition of love, but a moral jurisprudence exercised with authority in the name of King Jesus."[66]

He then turns to the importance of the involvement of churches in non-ecclesiastical matters (§33). These are the work of philanthropy, evangelism, and missionary work.

> A church of Christ may not be restricted to its own concerns, to living for itself. It also has a calling in terms of what lies outside of it, in three ways. First, after the household of faith is well cared for, it must extend its alms and compassionate care to those outside its gate who are in distress. Second, it must seek to win for the profession of Christ those who live in the same city or

---

63. Kuyper, *Tract*, §29, 154.
64. Kuyper, *Tract*, §29, 154.
65. Kuyper, *Tract*, §29, 154.
66. Kuyper, *Tract*, §30, 155.

village but do not share in its glorious confession. And third, it must send evangelists or missionaries to other countries and regions, to plant the church where it does not yet exist.[67]

Deformation of the churches

In Chapter 3 of his *Tract,* he looks at the Deformation of the Churches. Deformation occurs when churches lose the quality of a good foundation. However, deformation should not be interpreted as a failure to attain the ideal. He does not think that the earthly church can be perfect—he uses, for Kuyper, the pejorative term Anabaptist[68] and Donatism[69] to describe those who think that a perfect church is possible.

He identifies four different kinds of imperfect churches, but churches nonetheless, these are mission churches, occasional churches (such as those on the battlefield during wartime), churches under the cross (those suffering from persecution), and aggrieved churches (those suffering from an imposed false church government). It was this latter category that Kuyper maintained was the situation that prompted the 1886 *Doleantie.*

---

67. Kuyper, *Tract,* §33, 160.

68. For Kuyper the term Anabaptist is used as a catch-all for an escape from the world mentality.

69. The Donatists were a fourth-century North African religious group that grew out of the teaching of Tertullian and Cyprian. They held to the idea of a perfect "wrinkle-free" church, the church was the visible society of the elect only. There was no mixed church of wheat and tares.

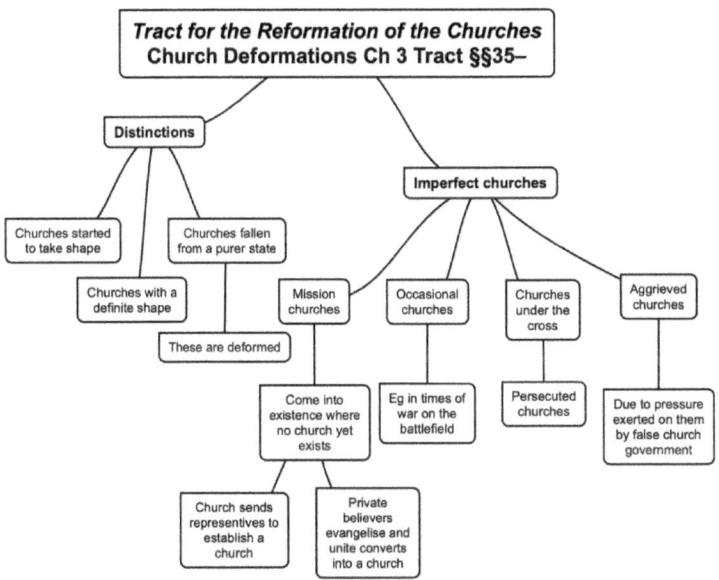

Three factors, he contends, could lie behind church deformation—the sin of individuals, the sin of the community, and the instigator of all sin, Satan. Satan has two main tools: external persecution and internal poisoning.

Deformation, he maintains, begins when faith grows cold. Piety becomes a burden and as a result they "openly fornicate with the world." Some in the church will condemn it, but not as publicly as they once did, consequently "sin and the service of the world becomes even bolder." The diseased congregation then affects the shepherds. And from the shepherds it creeps into the doctrine and worship of the churches.

The deformation trend *in general* follows this downward pattern, from the "diseased congregation to the shepherds":[70]

---

70. Kuyper, *Tract*, §39, 179.

Love grows cold

    ⟶ worldliness of members

        ⟶ worldliness of shepherds

            ⟶ corruption of doctrine and then worship

                ⟶ corruption of church government

There are, however, some exceptions, to this trend (§39). These are when little importance has been placed on good church government; the impure formation of the church with respect to its members; and when corruption has entered the church from the outside. This serves to show that the deformation of the churches does not necessarily follow a similar pattern it can have a "complicated etiology."[71]

The deformation of a church usually begins with the members. It starts with their confession rather than with their walk and life. It is important to remember that Kuyper argues:

> We must ... firmly reject any attempt to evaluate members of the church by focusing on their life. Let us retain the order that has been kept throughout the ages: confession and walk not walk and confession. Confession must be first, because it is the Christian's characteristic feature, and a person's walk can be judged only in that light.[72]

Several manifestations of degeneration are then itemized by Kuyper. These are also accompanied by deformations in conduct.

Indifference—despite agreeing with their confession, they barely know it. The consequence of this is that the difference between the church and world's behavior is indiscernible.

---

71. Kuyper, *Tract*, §39, 178.

72. Kuyper, *Tract*, §40, 178.

Externalisation—this is the opposite of indifference; confession is divorced from the heart. Confession is seen as a dry summary. This often results in Phariseeism.

Disruption of the balance—emphasis is placed on something rather than on another to the detriment of the other.

Superstition—vague and mystical elements are added to the confession. The result is what "began in the spirit ends in the flesh."

Unbelief—many proclaim a denial of the confession. This then eagerly celebrates "servitude to the world in all its glory under the shadow of the cross."

If these manifestations go unchallenged and unpunished, it leads to a deformation of the church and corruption of most of its members. This then often leads to a deformation of the office bearers. The minister can wither through a false enthusiasm or through professionalism, which can lead to an abuse of authority and onto clericalism.

The third stage is the confessional disease—this may result in "a lack of enforcement or freedom of doctrine." This then means that church discipline is lacking. Heresy and licentiousness, therefore, go unpunished.

The absolutely deformed church Kuyper labels as a "pseudo-church."[73] It is "a dead body, not yet decaying!" This is different from churches that are in a state of deformation, and from false churches "where deformation served simply to inaugurate a satanic counter-formation."[74] A false church had to

---

73. Kuyper, *Tract*, §41.

74. Kuyper, *Tract*, §50, 193.

openly deny Christ, rather than be deficient in the marks of a true church.

In Chapter 4 he then turns to the reformation of the churches.

The reformation of the churches

He begins by defining what is meant by reformation. It is in broad terms "the bringing of truth and holiness instead of error and sin," it includes "ongoing illumination" from the Holy Spirit.

In the narrow sense, using medical metaphors he delineates three aspects:

- In restoring diminished strength—this he regards as revival
- In expelling the germs that have invaded the body—this is church renewal
- A surgical operation

The type of reformation depends on the symptoms present.

In the final case where a surgical operation is needed this requires a public reformation, similar to that under Luther and Calvin. He stresses that good reformations are not the result of human activity but a work of God (§52): God is "the author of all sound reformation." If it is not a work of God, then such reformation is "profoundly sinful."[75]

He identifies spiritual revival and gradual church renewal as ways in which God reforms his church. This is the means of ridding the body of a disease. Renewal may require the restraint of evil through the exercise of church discipline, for example by rebuking, deposing unfaithful ministers, excommunicating unfaithful church members, and through the preaching of the

---

75. Kuyper, *Tract*, §52, 199.

Word. The disease cannot be allowed to run its course. "[C]hurch renewal will never be more than a vain display if the healing process does not start with rebuking sin and renewing the covenant."[76] He again stresses that church renewal must begin with the Holy Spirit.

A break with the existing church [77]

The *Afscheiding* secession of 1834, Kuyper thinks, was different from the reformation under Luther, Calvin, and Zwingli. He sees the secession of 1834 as a sprouting off from the old church. He sees two forms of a break "with that which exists." "[A] break that leads to the reformation of the old church, and a break that leads to the establishment of a new church alongside the existing church."[78]

He identifies three categories of "reformation through a break with what exists," from a lesser to a greater break:

(1) Where one nonetheless manages to salvage the existing church and its federation. The example he gives of this type is the action of the Reformed against the Remonstrants (those who adhered to Arminius's doctrine of free will).

(2) Where a new church federation is formed. The reformations of Wittenberg, Zurich, and Geneva, of Amsterdam, and Copenhagen in the sixteenth century, are examples in this category.

(3) Where one is compelled to erect a new church formation in opposition to the old. He places the secession of 1834 in this category.

---

76. Kuyper, *Tract*, §54, 207.

77. Kuyper, *Tract*, §55.

78. Kuyper, *Tract*, §55, 213.

"God himself alone is the author of 'reformation' through a break with the existing church Organization."[79] This type of reformation leaves the church federation or organization unaffected. This is the reformation of the local church.

Church reformation is not the act of a single person, Kuyper stresses. He offers this wise advice—applicable to all situations and not only to church reform:

> A Christian must do everything out of the obedience of faith, not because of prospective success. He must be guided neither by the question whether he will succeed nor the fear of ridicule, but only by the commandment of God.[80]

The type of reformation Kuyper has in mind here is "the ecclesiastical return to obedience to God and his Word, after ecclesiastical disobedience to that God and that Word."[81] This means that reformation through a break must be preceded by a spiritual awakening through conviction of guilt but also following an attempt at gradual renewal. Such a reformation must be a last resort.

This then leads Kuyper to look at what distinguishes between a true and false church. He notes that for the Reformers the necessary mark was the preaching of the Word of God, a second mark was the administration of the sacraments and the need for church discipline—these can be seen in the Belgic Confession Article 29.

---

79. Kuyper, *Tract*, §56, 216.
80. Kuyper, *Tract*, §56, 217.
81. Kuyper, *Tract*, §56, 218.

Some he observes have added the adjective pure to each of these, *pure* preaching, *pure* administration of the sacraments, and *pure* church discipline. But often this can become a means of separation—anything that does not live up to the "pure" standard is deemed as an excuse for leaving.

Kuyper identifies three directions that could be taken: the personal, the biblical and the ecclesiastical. The last was represented by Rome, and so Kuyper all but ignores it. He describes the biblical and the personal as the objective and the subjective.

The emphasis on the personal he sees in the Donatists, the Cathars,[82] the Brownists,[83] and the Labadists[84] among others. He maintains that they forgot that God's work in the soul cannot be judged externally; in this age there is a continual infiltration of sin; people may die, but the church remains.

He provides an excellent summary of his views:

Our conclusion is therefore that for a good state of the church and the well-being of the church of God—that

---

82. The Cathars, were also known as the Albigenses. They maintained that there was a god of light (spirit) and a god of darkness (matter); and they did not believe that the Son of God could be incarnate as a man.

83. The Brownists were named after Robert Browne (c. 1550s–1633), they were a group of English Dissenters, they held to a congregational form of church government.

84. The Labadists began under the French priest Jean de Labadie (1610–1674), as a separatist Christian community in three houses in Amsterdam. They argued that the true church consisted only of those who were born again, and it was not of this world, they even went as far as having their own form of dress for the women. They emphasized personal inspiration and contemplation. On Labadism see, for example, Trevor John Saxby, *The Quest for the New Jerusalem, Jean de Labadie and the Labadists, 1610–1744* (Dordrecht-Boston-Lancaster, 1987).

is, for churches in a healthy, normal state—both the pure preaching of the Word and the pure administration of the sacraments, as well as the strict exercise of discipline, are necessary and indispensable. But we also conclude that the churches of Christ, without losing their essence as a church, can be either disfigured or impure, and even, as Calvin says, partially corrupted. This disfiguring is usually seen first in the absence of discipline; this impurity, in blemishes that affect the doctrine or the administration of the sacraments; this corruption, in the rise of false doctrine alongside faithful preaching. Furthermore, where this disease and disfiguring continues, the church gradually loses its essence as a church and fades away into a spiritless association. And finally, where the toxic gases are produced in this corpse, this faded church can become a false church as soon as, under Satan's influence, it begins persecuting the truth and those who profess it.[85]

He stresses this to mitigate any desire to break with church as church, and to stress that a break is "permissible only when his church has either died or degenerated into a false church. Not for any other reason. Never any sooner." This is one of the reasons why Kuyper had reservations regarding the secession in 1837 and did not join the seceders in 1886.

Article 36
The Nederlandse Hervormed Klerk (NHK) was a national church. Most at the time favored a national established church.

---

85. Kuyper, *Tract*, §59, 252.

Kuyper did not. Kuyper in particular disagreed with Article 36 of the Belgic confession:

> And the government's task is not limited to caring for and watching over the public domain but extends also to upholding the sacred ministry, with a view to removing and destroying all idolatry and false worship of the Antichrist; to promoting the kingdom of Jesus Christ; and to furthering the preaching of the gospel everywhere; to the end that God may be honored and served by everyone, as he requires in his Word.

Kuyper's objections were several:

- It was taken over by the Reformed fathers from Romanist practices.
- It uses Constantinian language.
- The sword should not be used to kill heretics.
- It presupposes that the magistrate can judge the difference between truth and heresy.

Kuyper, however, recognized that in arguing against it he was in conflict with the Reformers including Calvin.

A change was necessary, argued Kuyper, because of the development of pluralism in society. There were now many churches with different confessions—how could democratic governments decide which was the true church? Would different successive governments change their mind over which one was the true church? This was a different age from that when Guido de Bres (1522–1567) composed the Belgic Confession. At issue, for Kuyper, was the relationship between church and state, and church and civil government.

P. J. Hoedemaker (1839–1910), who had been a colleague of Kuyper's at the Free University in Amsterdam, resigned his position as professor when Kuyper led the *Doleantie* succession from the state church. Hoedemaker remained a member of the NHK, the state church.

He agreed with Kuyper on many issues but was in conflict with him on the question of church and state. For Hoedemaker, Kuyper's approach was an advocacy of the neutrality of the state and the split between church and state. This led to his role in founding a political party separate from Kuyper's. He took issue with Kuyper over a number of points.

Hoedemaker took issue with what he considered to be Kuyper's use of pragmatic reasons over and above scriptural reasons. He also disagreed with Kuyper's view of the church. Kuyper maintained that the invisible church existed from creation, but the church as institution began at Pentecost. This was a problem for Hoedemaker.

Kuyper did not hold to a single state church institution. Hoedemaker did. For Kuyper the church was pluriform, and there were different expressions of it. Kuyper rejected a one-state, one-church position.

For Kuyper, the church arose from particular grace, the state from common grace. This meant that for Kuyper the state could not judge between heresy and truth. It went beyond the calling and vocation of government. This was not a dualism between public and private, however. The state had no right to lord it over the church.

Pro Rege

In part 2 of volume 2 of *Pro Rege* Kuyper turns to Christ's kingship within and through the church. Once again dispelling the notion that neo-Calvinism downgrades or minimizes the institutional church. He laments the fact that Christ's kingship has too often been spiritualized and "removed from the reality of the church."[86] The church, for Kuyper, is a result of grace rather than creation, of particular grace rather than common grace:

> The church is therefore alien to creation life. It has not come from it, but was added to it. It is an institution of a unique kind and order. It has entered the life of the nations as an institution with a unique origin.[87]

Christ is the one who institutes, protects, sustains, and governs the church. It was instituted as something new.[88] Throughout this section, Kuyper is eminently practical. He stresses the need for the church overseers to be personally acquainted with each member of the congregation if they are not then it is very difficult for them to admonish and warn them, the congregants could thus easily stray.

> More is called for than just preaching. Sermons can point to the pasture, but preaching does not and cannot tend to the various individual needs of each sheep in the flock. That kind of care can only be given through personal interaction.[89]

---

86. Kuyper, *Pro Rege* 2, 289.

87. Kuyper, *Pro Rege* 2, 115.

88. Kuyper, *Pro Rege* 2, 303.

89. Kuyper, *Pro Rege* 2, 248.

Kuyper often stresses the global and the local nature of the church. He sees no place for a national church.

Anyone who nationalizes the churches and gathers churches into national groups does not follow a norm deriving from the essence of the church, but one that derives from the life of the world, and can, therefore, only end up on the path of error. In addition, as he states in *Pro Rege:*

> We Reformed, however, never speak about the Calvinist Church, or about a national church, and the name "Dutch Reformed Church" (Nederlandse Hervormde Kerk) first came into use in 1816—and even then this did not happen on the basis of ecclesiastical authority, but by caesaropapism; not by virtue of a decision taken by the churches, but by the king.[90]

He goes on to identify three popular views of the church: the individualistic, the independent and the covenantal. The first is what he claims is the Anabaptist position—the members are those who have made a profession of faith out of a personal choice. In this view he maintains that the church is reduced to a club or association. In the second view, choice is not necessary, all who come are deemed members, no one is turned away and there is no restriction on baptism. The third view, the one endorsed by Kuyper, focuses on the covenant; this "model insists on the truth that the Lord's mystical body has an organic character, and that the visible church must for that reason also rest on an organic foundation."[91]

---

90. Kuyper, *Pro Rege* 2, 209.
91. Kuyper, *Pro Rege* 2, 226.

Although Kuyper's depiction of the first two positions may be something of a caricature there is much truth in it. Only the third model sits well with the Scriptures. It avoids atomism and stresses the need for discipline.

The role of the sacraments is stressed in *Pro Rege*. Typical comments from Kuyper include:

> The sacraments therefore always remain the very heart and life of the visible church, and they are what regulates the entire organization of the visible church. They require an administration according to the ordinances of the Lord, and to that end they require the appointment of a spiritual church council that is sanctified and authorized to administer the sacraments.[92]

Common Grace volume 3

One of Kuyper's main concerns in *Common Grace* volume 3 is the relationship of the state with the institutional church.

They have some elements in common. Both arise from grace, both are rooted in creation ordinances, and both are for the combatting of sin.[93] The single goal of both is the glory of the Father, Son, and Holy Spirit.[94] And the church presupposes an ordered state.[95]

There are also some marked differences that he points out. The state is the fruit of common grace, whereas the church is the result of particular grace. The church transcends nature and

---

92. Kuyper, *Pro Rege* 2, 184.
93. Kuyper, *Common Grace* 3, 139.
94. Kuyper, *Common Grace* 3, 140.
95. Kuyper, *Common Grace* 3, 141

originates with the Word and regeneration—in that sense it is miraculous, whereas the state emerges from creation.[96]

As he states in *Pro Rege*:

> In its visible form the Christian church is an institution of grace, and it would never have come had there been no fall. Sin is a precondition of the church.[97]

One important point he makes is that the organism of the church is as old as paradise and that the church was never manifested as an institution until Pentecost.[98]

He also maintains that the "government must not extend its authority over the church." As he emphatically states:

> Every infringement upon the freedom of the churches on the part of government is an abuse of authority; it is hubris and arrogance, a direct violation of what God himself has instituted as the very essence of the church.[99]

Our Worship

This book deals almost exclusively with the institutional face of the church. The book was published in 1901 but was begun in 1897. The articles were put on hold when he became Prime Minister but were resumed afterwards. He had two reasons for the book: historical and pastoral. Kuyper also appreciated good liturgy. He dealt with the architecture of church buildings and of the services. This book focuses on the church as institution. It was written later in

96. Kuyper, *Common Grace* 3, 126.

97. Kuyper, *Pro Rege* 2, 302.

98. Kuyper, *Common Grace* 3, 39, 120, 231.

99. Kuyper, *Common Grace* 3, 250.

Kuyper's life and is evidence that belies the claim that "organism was increasingly given prominence at the expense of the institute."[100]

So what?

> . . . a farmer who farms his land but neglects to say his prayers will be certainly condemned by Christians as failing in his duty. But a farmer who says his prayers, and allows weeds, bad drainage, or soil erosion to spoil his land, is failing in his primary duty as a churchman. His primary ministry in the total life of the body of Christ is to care rightly for the land entrusted to him. If he fails there, he fails in his primary Christian task.
>
> The point is succinctly put in an article in a recent number of the French Revue de l'Evangelisation. The writer, after speaking in general of the Christian conceptions of ministry and vocation, goes on: "The layman is the minister, the ambassador of Christ, in his office, his class-room, his farm. His mission is not simply to make known Jesus Christ to all those with whom he comes in contact, but still more to show how a servant of Jesus Christ understands and exercises the job of which he has charge. That is his chief job in the Church." In other words, it is on the Christian layman in his job, from Monday to Saturday, that the responsibility rests for seeing that—so far as in him lies—the will of Christ is done here on earth. That is his first task as a member of the Church.
>
> Lesslie Newbigin 1952
> The Christian Layman in the world and in the Church.

---

100. Strange, "Rooted and Grounded?"

Having examined Kuyper's ecclesiology we are left with the question, so poignantly made by Miles Davis on his *Kind of Blue* album: So What? What does a nineteenth-century statesman and theologian have to say to contemporary twenty-first Christians? I want to examine several key implications. I am perhaps being rather polemical here—perhaps too polemical—but in slaying sacred cows we often have to tread on people's toes. The first two implications I will leave undeveloped, the third I will explore in a slightly more depth.

1. The split in the Dutch church was over state–church relations and orthodoxy. How is the church to relate to the state? As Kuyper showed, the downward trend is often because our love grows cold and there is a tendency to worldliness. We need to guard against this and be aware of it if it is taking place.

2. Kuyper struggled to articulate what it means to be the church in his own context. We need to do likewise. This is particularly important today, because as I write the United Kingdom has come through a state of lockdown because of the coronavirus. Church buildings were closed and no public gathering more than three people was allowed. What does that mean for church? Can we be church without public meetings? Do telephone conversations and social media contact via Zoom or Facebook count?

3. The main insight that Kuyper provides is that the church is both an institute and an organism. Kuyper places a strong emphasis on the priesthood of all believers. For the church to be truly an institution and organism, the role of the institutional leaders

must be to equip the church as organism to do the works of service in the marketplace, in the classroom, in business, in politics, in the laboratory and so forth.

As mentioned, Kuyper used a number of metaphors to illustrate the distinction between church as an organism and church as institute. The church as an organism is a body and it grows; as an institute it is a house and is built. It is from the church organism that the institution is born. In essence the institution is the church organization with its sacraments, its ministers and so forth; the organism is the church in the world, Christians at work in society, the body of Christ, strengthened and served by the church as institute. The church as institute does not run schools, universities, coffee shops or trade unions; that is the role of the church as organism. For Kuyper, therefore, the church has to do not only with Sunday services or missions (as the institute) but as an organism it is busy reforming all facets of life and culture. He has a broad view of the calling of the church:

> The calling of the church remains irrevocable, nonetheless. The church must bring the gospel to all creatures.[101]

Some have objected to Kuyper's terminology of institute and organism. For example, Strange[102] has suggested that it might be better to use the terms "church 'gathered'" and church 'go-

---

101. Abraham Kuyper, *Particular Grace* (Reformed Free Publishing Association, 2001), 18.

102. Strange, "Rooted and Grounded?"

ing'": "Or, maybe better still: 'church gathered' and 'church dismissed' (but never dismissed!)."[103]

Whatever term is preferred the distinction is an important one. Particularly, the relationship between the two. The key question is: *How can the church as institute support the church as organism?*

Serving Christ is not all about (institutional) church-related activities. Sadly, too often the view can be implicitly put over that Christianity is a recreational activity; something we do at weekends and in our free time. As John Knapp, a founding director of Samford University's Frances Marlin Mann Center for Ethics and Leadership, remarks:

> Is faith only of value when healing is needed? Is it not essential to living our daily lives as instruments of God's healing power in the world? Church culture, like business culture, reinforces the notion that the proper place for faith is the private sphere. Despite this, many men and women in the pews are not easily persuaded that

---

103. Strange follows Bratt and Zwaanstra, in asserting that Kuyper emphasized the organism over the institute. I do not think that is the case—Strange asserts it but doesnot fully justify it. Part of the problem for Strange is that he only considered three works of Kuyper and relied on Zwaanstra for the rest of Kuyper's writings. Kuyper in his ministry moved from the church as institute, when he was a pastor, to church as organism, as a politician. His writing reflects his area of ministry rather than any desire to place church as organism over the church as institute or to separate the two. He continually stresses the relationship between the two, they are equal but different. Kuyper often emphasized "the necessary connection between organism and institution."

the God they worship on Sunday morning is uncon-
cerned with how they make their living.[104]

Watch your language

Often, the language we use can reinforce this misconception.
For example, the use of the term full-time Christian ministry:
it implies that some are not involved in Christian ministry—as
Christians we are all full-time for God! The term, "full-time
Christian ministry" applies to all Christians regardless of the
area of life in which they work. All Christians are involved in
full-time Christian ministry. There is no such thing as part-
time Christians. It would go some way to help this if we never
used the term "full-time Christian ministry" to describe only
those with a role in the church or a church-related activity.

Likewise, the term "secular" has been overused. There is no
sacred/secular divide. It's not the activity that makes it secular;
it is the attitude and approach. The term secular should not
only be used to describe work that is done outside of church.
The only thing secular is sin. The misuse of the term secular
supports the dubious sacred/secular divide, suggesting that
somethings such as institutional church activities are more
"spiritual" than others.

It is my suggestion that we place a moratorium on the term
spiritual. The biblical meaning is that being spiritual is to be
led by the Spirit. The Spirit can and does lead in the workplace.
However, common usage often, and perhaps inadvertently, implies that some activities are more spiritual than others.

---

104. J. Knapp, *How the Church Fails Businesspeople (And What Can Be Done
about It)* (Grand Rapids: Eerdmans, 2012).

Equipping the saints

Equipping the saints for ministry is not (only) about how to evangelize at work or about personal ethics in the workplace (important as these are)—it also involves finding out and incarnating God's creational purposes for all areas of creational life.

Knapp[105] and his team interviewed 230 people to see how church has helped them in their businesses. It makes for somber reading. Most found that the church was too concerned with the (so-called) private sphere of life and uninterested in the public realm. The majority found that the church had done "little or nothing to equip them for faithful living at work." The question is how can the church ministers be equipped to equip the saints?

One answer is a shift in training. This may require a change in emphasis in church ministerial training. How are church ministers to equip ministers in the workplace and in the marketplace? Benestad makes an important observation:

> Seminaries have, for the most part, not done a good job
> of preparing future priests to think about the relation
> of the Catholic faith and politics. Only a few of the
> laity would study the subject in a Catholic university or
> hear about it in a Sunday homily.[106]

This is also the case in other denominational (and non-denominational) seminaries. Church trainers need to take this seriously and examine what can be done to equip church ministers to equip others. As Lesslie Newbigin remarked:

---

105. Knapp, *How the Church Fails Businesspeople*.

106. In A. Black, ed., *Five Views on the Church and Politics* (Grand Rapids: Zondervan, 2015), 180–181.

…it must be the responsibility of the Church to equip its members for active and informed participation in the public life of society in such a way that the Christian faith shapes that participation.[107]

Sadly, most church ministers are not able to do that. This is through no fault of their own. They have not been equipped to do this. Paul in Ephesians writes that pastors and teachers are to equip the saints for works of service. Unfortunately, we have taken this to mean works of service in a Sunday service. There is nothing in Paul's writings to suggest that this is the limited scope he had in mind! On the contrary.

The understanding of a Christian worldview that can help to identify the idolatries at work in the workplace should play a key part in seminary training. Kuyperian insights such as the role of worldview, sphere sovereignty, the antithesis, and common grace, all provide useful tools for what has been termed "public theology." The Dutch philosopher Herman Dooyeweerd developed many of Kuyper's ideas into a full-blown Christian philosophy.[108] His modal aspects, a development of Kuyper's sphere sovereignty, provide an excellent tool for identify-

---

107. Lesslie Newbigin, *Truth to Tell: The Gospel as Public Truth (Osterhaven Lecture)* (Grand Rapids: Eerdmans, 1991), 8.

108. For more on Dooyeweerd's approach see, for example, Roy A Clouser, *The Myth of Religious Neutrality: An Essay on the Hidden Role of Religious Belief in Theories, Revised Edition* (University of Notre Dame Press, 2005); Jonathan Chaplin, *Herman Dooyeweerd: Christian Philosopher of State and Civil Society* (Notre Dame, Ind.: University of Notre Dame Press, 2011); Steve Bishop, "Herman Dooyeweerd's Christian Philosophy," *Foundations* 82, no. 2 (2022): 47–81; Steven R. Martins, *Towards a Christian Understanding: The Pursuit of a Christian Philosophy* (Jordan Station, ON: Cantaro Publications, 2022.

ing idolatries and for identifying reductionism; his ground-motives, an unfolding of the notion of worldview, provide a useful tool to critique prevalent paradigms and philosophies that dominate contemporary culture including those in the workplace. One only has to look at the work of Andrew Basden in Information Systems (IS) to see how an application of Dooyeweerd's approach provides an alternative to humanistic frameworks in IS.[109]

Frontier groups

Lesslie Newbigin is one person who has seen the importance of such an approach[110] He also wrote in *The Gospel in a Pluralist Society:*

> The congregation has to be a place where its members are trained, supported, and nourished in the exercise of their parts of the priestly ministry in the world. The preaching and teaching of the local church has to be such that it enables members to think out the problems that face them in their secular work in the light of their Christian faith. This is very difficult. It is divisive. One pastor, trained in the kind of theology which is traditional, is not equipped to fulfill this function. There is need for "frontier-groups," groups of Christians working in the same sectors of public life, meeting to thrash

---

109. Andrew Basden, *Foundations of Information Systems: Research and Practice, The Foundations of Information Systems: Research and Practice* (London: Routledge, 2017); Andrew Basden, *Foundations of Practice and Research: Adventures with Dooyeweerd's Philosophy* (London: Routledge, 2020).

110. Lesslie Newbigin, "The Christian Layman in the World and in the Church," *National Christian Council Review* 72 (1952): 185–89.

out the controversial issues of their business or profession in the light of their faith.[111]

Such groups may not need church minister involvement, but they would need church minister endorsement, encouragement, and support. These suggestions could go some way for the church as institute to equip the church as organism. Here are a few further tentative suggestions that may help.[112]

In church services

- Pray in the church service for those starting new jobs—not only the "overseas missionaries."
- Pray in the church service for those unemployed.
- Testimonies in church services from people in the workplace about the workplace.
- Education Sunday—pray for all those in education, preach on education, provide space testimonies from students and schoolteachers. Have a Business, a Science, a Hospitality sector...Sunday too!
- Preaching—review what topics are covered. When was the last time a sermon on work or the workplace was delivered? Use more illustrations from the work place.

Outside the church service

---

111. Lesslie Newbigin, *The Gospel in a Pluralist Society* (SPCK Publishing, 2004), 230–31.

112 Some of these have been adapted from Tom Nelson, *Work Matters: Connecting Sunday Worship to Monday Work* (Wheaton: Crossway, 2011).

- Church ministers could take a sabbatical and go and work in a different workplace for a few months to see the type of stresses and strains that the congregants are under—or at least visit congregational members in their workplace.
- Many churches have employed youth and family workers. Why not also consider having a workplace worker/chaplain?
- Stock the church library with useful books that address workplace issues. Some general books that deal with work and vocation issues, such as the following are a good starting point.

Katelyn Beaty, *A Woman's Place: A Christian Vision for Your Calling in the Office, the Home, and the World* (New York: Howard Books, 2016).

Darrell Cosden, *A Theology of Work: Work and the New Creation.* (Carlisle: Paternoster Press, 2004).

J. Daryl Charles, *Our Secular Vocation: Rethinking the Church's Calling to the Marketplace* (Brentwood, TN: B&H Publishing Group, 2023).

David W. Gill, *Workplace Discipleship 101: A Primer* (Peabody, MA: Hendrickson, 2020)

Mark Greene, *Thank God It's Monday: Ministry in the Workplace* (Bletchley: Scripture Union, 2003).

Lee Hardy, *The Fabric of This World: Inquiries into Calling, Career Choice, and the Design of the Human World.* (Grand Rapids: Eerdmans, 1990).

Matthew Kaemingk and Cory B. Willson, *Work and Worship: Reconnecting Our Labor and Liturgy* (Grand Rapids: Baker Academic, 2020).

Keller, Timothy, *Every Good Endeavour: Connecting Your Work to God's Plan for the World.* (London: Hodder & Stoughton, 2012).

Paul Marshall (ed.) *Labour of Love: Essays on Work* (Toronto: Wedge Publishing, 1980).

Paul Marshall, 'Work and Rest." *The Reformed Journal,* 38 (June 1988): 9–14.

Tom Nelson, *Work Matters: Connecting Sunday Worship to Monday Work.* (Wheaton: Crossway, 2011).

Amy Sherman, *Kingdom Calling: Vocational Stewardship for the Common Good.* (Downers Grove, IL: InterVarsity Press, 2011).

R. Paul Stevens, *The Other Six Days: Vocation, Work, and Ministry in Biblical Perspective* (Grand Rapids: Eerdmans, 1999).

R. Paul Stevens, *Work Matters: Lessons from Scripture* (Grand Rapids: Eerdmans, 2012).

Church ministers should be aware of writings from Christian perspectives that address the diverse areas of life—see for example the list of resources on www.allofliferedeemed.co.uk/subjects.

- Book reviews of the above books in the church magazine/newsletter
- Book discussion groups—discussing some of the books mentioned above.
- If frontier groups are not feasible at present, consider vocation-oriented discipleship/accountability groups or vocation-oriented prayer triplets—including those who are currently unemployed or who are working but without pay.
- Hold sessions on exploring the wide range of vocations—and look at how to discern your vocation.

Conclusion

The following are some of the key points that Kuyper develops in his ecclesiology:

- The church is a result of particular not common grace—it came about because of the fall.
- The Old Testament people of God were "the church in Israel."
- The church is temporary—there was no need for it in paradise, nor will there be need for it in the new Jerusalem.
- The church has different facets, including visible and invisible, institute and organism.
- The calling of the church is to bring the gospel to all creatures.
- The church is based on God's eternal election; it is not a human creation.
- The church as institute began at Pentecost.
- Christ's kingship over the church is absolute. The true marks of the church are Word and sacrament (baptism and breaking of bread—these are the two means of grace).
- The church on earth is determined by God's Word.
- There is a pluriformity of the church—churches of different confessions (e.g., Lutheran or Calvinistic) have a right to coexist.
- The Reformed system of church government, with its emphasis on the local church, is best.
- The church can become deformed and thus becomes a pseudo-church.
- The Reformation of the church can take place by gradual renewal and/or revival.
- The church should be free from state interference—thus the idea of a single state church is misguided.

Kuyper thus presents us with a radical view of the church. His notion of church as institute and as organism provides a framework for understanding the diverse roles of the church in society. It provides an understanding of the church and its role in shaping society. It helps to defuse a false sacred/secular divide. There is nothing secular (apart from sin) as the church as institute and organism is to pervade all of society with the message of redemption and transformation. As Kuyper famously remarked:[113]

> Oh, no single piece of our mental world is to be hermetically sealed off from the rest, and there is not a square inch[114] in the whole domain of our human exisence over which Christ, who is Sovereign over all, does not cry: "Mine!."[115]

The distinction between organism and institute also allows for organized Christian social action and the establishment of Christian institutions without it falling under the domain of the church as it did in medieval times. These Christian organizations for social action, art, business, science and so forth are part of the church as organism and not the church as institution.

It also provides the answer to the important question: "Should the church be involved in politics?" The answer is no for the institutional church, but yes for the church as organism. The church as institute does not become involved in every area

---

113. It would be remiss not to include this quote as it seems obligatory to cite it whenever Kuyper is discussed!

114. Literally "Thumb's breadth."

115. Kuyper, "Sphere Sovereignty", in Bratt *Centennial Reader*, 488.

but equips church as organism to be involved. Some of the suggestions I have made provide some examples of how institute may help organism to do that. There will be others! In this way, the institute can feed the organism.

A summary in 12 theses

1. The *Nadere Reformatie* and *Réveil* movements significantly influenced Dutch church history and theology.
2. Abraham Kuyper emphasizes the importance of the church's freedom from government interference.
3. Kuyper's writings reflect a deep concern for the church's well-being and its impact on shaping society for God's kingdom.
4. Kuyper's view on the church as both institute and organism promotes a holistic approach to Christian engagement in the world.
5. Kuyper's radical view of the church as both institute and organism shapes its role in society and rejects a sacred/secular divide.
6. The necessity of pure preaching, sacraments, and discipline for a healthy church is emphasized by Kuyper.
7. Kuyper defends the diversity within the church, rejecting the need for a single external organization for unity.
8. Kuyper identifies four church government systems and upholds the Reformed position as the purest and best.
9. The distinction between church as organism and institute enables Christian involvement in various spheres like politics.

10. Christ's sovereignty extends over all aspects of human existence, allowing for organized Christian social action outside the institutional church.
11. Kuyper's theological framework emphasizes the church's role in society and its engagement with various spheres of life.
12. Kuyper's book *Our Worship* focuses on the institutional aspect of the church, highlighting its historical and pastoral significance.

Study Questions

1. In what ways did Kuyper's historical context, particularly the Dutch church movements, shape his theological perspectives on the church?
2. Compare and contrast the organic church and the church as institute.
3. How did Kuyper's understanding of the church as both institute and organism contribute to his vision for Christian social action and cultural engagement?
4. Why did Kuyper not join the *Afscheiding* secession?
5. Does Kuyper prioritize the organic church over the institutional church?
6. For Kuyper, the calling of the church is to bring the gospel to all creatures. How can it do that?
7. Why did Kuyper think that a state church was misguided?
8. What does Kuyper understand by the pluriformity of the church?
9. Should the church be involved in politics?
10. What insights can be gained from Kuyper's writings on the church for contemporary discussions on the church's role in society?

Further Reading

Primary

Kuyper, Abraham, *On the Church* (Bellingham. WA: Lexham Press, 2019).

Kuyper, Abraham, *Rooted and Grounded* (Grand Rapids: Christian Library Press, 2013).

Secondary

Zwaanstra, H., "Abraham Kuyper's Conception of the Church," *Calvin Theological Journal* 9, no. 2 (1974): 149–81.

Wagenman, Michael, "Abraham Kuyper and the Church: from Calvin to the neo-Calvinists," in Steve Bishop and John Kok (ed.) *On Kuyper: A Collection of Readings on the Life, Work & Legacy of Abraham Kuyper* (Sioux Center: Dordt Press, 2013), 125–139.

Wagenman, Michael, "Ecclesiology," in *T&T Clark Handbook of Neo-Calvinism*, ed., N. Gray Sutanto and Cory Brock (Edinburgh: T&T Clark, 2024).

Wood, John Halsey Jr., *Going Dutch in the Modern Age* (Oxford: Oxford University Press, 2013).

24

Kuyper and Education

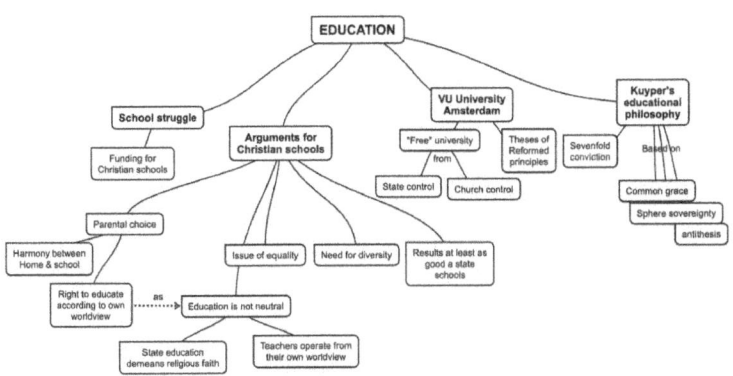

In brief

KUYPER HAD A PROFOUND impact on education through his advocacy for Christian schools and the establishment of the Free University in Amsterdam (VU Amsterdam). He believed in the freedom of Christian parents to control their children's education and fought against state interference in moral and religious teachings. His educational philosophy emphasized the role of parents, the church, and the state in shaping a child's worldview. Kuyper's sphere sovereignty approach limited the state's authority in education, leading to the formation of the

Free University based on Reformed principles. His efforts culminated in the restructuring of the Dutch school system to uphold religious liberty and provide official status to degrees awarded by Christian institutions. Kuyper's legacy continues to influence educational policies and the societal understanding of the relationship between faith, education, and governance.

Introduction

Education was an important matter for Kuyper; it was evidently close to his heart. He saw it as "the second major institution, after the church, that our King [Jesus] uses to establish his kingly dominion also in the midst of society."[1] Thus, he campaigned vigorously for Christian schools and founded a Christian university. He notes in his *Lectures on Calvinism* the role of Calvinism in education in the Netherlands, notably in the founding of the University of Leiden in 1575. Education, for Kuyper, exemplified his view of the role of the state and church, of sphere sovereignty, and of the need for institutional pluralism within society. Schools were important as they provided the means of imparting a particular worldview. However, he stressed, in keeping with his sphere sovereignty: "The school should belong, not to the church, not to the state, but to parents."[2]

Wendy Naylor, an editor of Kuyper's *On Education*, has this to say:

---

1. Kuyper, *Pro Rege* 3, 145.

2. Abraham Kuyper, *On Education (Abraham Kuyper Collected Works in Public Theology)*, ed. Wendy Naylor and Harry Dyke, trans. Harry Dyke (Bellingham, WA: Lexham Press, 2019), 198.

Abraham Kuyper accomplished much over the course of his lifetime, but perhaps his most lasting contribution to Dutch society was a radical restructuring of the Dutch school system according to the principle of religious liberty.[3]

Given the importance Kuyper placed on education it is perhaps surprising that he did not devote a lecture on it in his Stone Lectures. Harry Van Dyke one of the editors and translator of *On Education* explains why:

> Much of Kuyper's involvement with the education question required his concentrating on the financial inequality of the Dutch school system which favoured the "religionless" government schools and left alternative schools heavily underfunded, He may have felt that setting forth the intricacies of the Dutch school struggle might distract from the main purpose of the Stone Lectures, namely the portrayal of Calvinism as a full-blown match for modern humanism.
>
> It is regrettable that as a result of this more narrow focus, Kuyper's attention to the intrinsic challenges of Christian education—pedagogy, anthropology, psychology—was largely passed over. He wrote much about family life and child-rearing and seems to have assumed that a school which required the involvement of the Christian parents would automatically be a Christian school, and that if the teacher was a Christian, he would teach Christianly. For these

---

3. Wendy Naylor, "Editor's Introduction," in Abraham Kuyper, *On Education*, xi.

reasons, it was important to include the short appendix in the Education volume that dealt with a critical aspect of pedagogy.[4]

If he had added a lecture on it, what might he have included? Van Dyke surmises:

As he briefly wrote in a variety of publications and later explained in Parliament as Prime Minister, he would probably have set forth:

That no education can be religiously neutral.

That no government should support one type of school and ignore all other types.

That Christian schooling demands the involvement of at least four partners: the church (is the faith correctly presented?), the government (are pupils introduced to a proper curriculum needed for taking part in national life?), parents (does the school help them in keeping their baptismal vows of training the child in the fear of the Lord?), and teachers (are they properly trained in sound teaching methods?).[5]

Kuyper saw that the so-called neutral schools were a myth. Neutrality was a mirage. This was also the view of Kuyper's mentor Groen van Prinsterer, who had called government education "the privileged school of a specific religious sect."[6] This was one key factor that drove Kuyper's desire to see explicitly

---

4. Steve Bishop, "Interview with Harry Van Dyke," https://stevebishop. blogspot.com/2019/10/interview-with-harry-van-dyke.html.

5. Bishop, "Interview."

6. H. Van Dyke, "Government Schools or Free Schools? Abraham Kuyper Addresses a Long-Standing Controversy in the Dutch Parliament,"

Christian schools and Christian universities. Kuyper saw it was also an issue of justice:

> To be forced to send one's child to a school where it will be nurtured in a spirit that is opposed to that of its parents is an evil that may no longer be perpetuated. The rich can afford to choose private schools, but the poor cannot. They too must have the opportunity to give their children an education that is in harmony with their basic convictions.[7]

The *Schoolstrijd,* the school struggle, as it became known was the fight for parents, and not the state, to control the education of their children. It was a decades long struggle. In many ways it dated back to 1795 when Napoleonic forces took over the Dutch Republic.[8] Prior to that the Reformed Church had control over education. With the French ruling forces education came under the control of the government and liberalism and reason were seen as the tools to promote national unity. There was a form of separation of church and state, and the Reformed Church had the same status as the Roman Catholics and the Lutherans.

The 1806 School Act was passed that insisted that "All school instruction must be organized in such a way that, while learning suitable and useful skills, the rational abilities of children shall be developed, and they shall be trained in all social

---

Canadian Journal of Netherlandic Studies/Rev. Can. d'études Néerlandaises 35, no. 2 (2014): 29–45.

7. Kuyper, *On Education,* 290.

8. French dominance lasted until 1913.

and Christian virtues."[9] The aim was to remove all differences, so that a unified and religiously tolerant nation could flourish. The effect was to water down the Christian faith in schools so that it was acceptable to all.

The *Afscheiding* secession from the Dutch church in 1837 under H. de Cock and Scholte advised their members of the newly formed Christelijke Gereformeerde Kerk not to use the public schools. This was the start of the school struggle proper. Groen who was influenced by the *Réveil* but did not join the *Afscheiding* wrote a tract, "The Measures Against the Seceders Tested with Respect to Constitutional Law," supporting the position of the *Afscheiding* church members. In it he argued against forcing parents to send their children to schools that did not comport with their worldview was a violation of their God-given right. A God-given right to educate their own children in accordance with their religious beliefs.

When his arguments were met with disdain and indifference at best, he realized that more was needed to be done—constitutional reform would be necessary.

Groen's book *Unbelief and Revolution*, was published in 1847. In it he argued that the spirit of the French Revolution of 1789 lives on.[10] However, the term revolution was not only a reference to the French Revolution. It also stood for the spiritual and intellectual shift that it brought in. The

9. Cited in David A. Sikkema, *Between Isolation and Engagement: The History of the Dutch Calvinist School Movement in the Netherlands, the United States, and Canada* (Baylor University Thesis, 2010).

10. Guillaume Groen Van Prinsterer, *Unbelief and Revolution,* translated by Harry Van Dyke (Bellingham, WA: Lexham Press, 2018).

spirit of secular humanism was damaging the created order for society. Revolution was rooted in a worldview. This was another reason for the establishment and flourishing of Christian schools—to subvert this modernist and Enlightenment worldview.

The liberal J. R. Thorbecke (1798–1872) proposed a "Freedom of education" act in 1848 as part of a new political constitution. This allowed for the existence of separate religious private schools provided they met the standards of the state-controlled schools. There was, however, no state money for these schools. This meant that the poor Dutch Calvinists were unable to afford to support separate schools. Groen and others also opposed the act on the grounds that it was motivated by the ideology of the French Revolution. Groen wanted a state school system with separate schools for Calvinists, Catholics, and the Jews. The 1857 school law put paid to this as in the future only state schools would be funded and it maintained that education should be religiously neutral. Groen had to change his tactics and his approach and accepted a separatist path for Christian schools—similar to the approach of the *Afscheiding*. He became the chair of the Association of Christian National School Education (*De Vereeniging voor Christeli-jke-Nationaal Schoolonderwijs*).

It was into this situation that Kuyper came. He had been in written contact with Groen, but they first met at Utrecht in 1869 when Kuyper delivered the opening address for the Association of Christian National School Education. In Kuyper Groen recognized a worthy successor. Groen had been described as a general without an army, Kuyper could raise that army.

For Kuyper, "The school struggle is not about *organization*. It is about the *direction* of the schools."[11] In his speech, An Appeal to the Nation's Conscience, to the Association of Christian National School Education he identified "five features that constitute the demands of our movement with respect to education and which we hereby submit to the verdict of the nation's conscience."[12] He argued for the freedom of Christian parents to control the education of their children.

The school struggle was also one of the motivating factors for Kuyper's move into politics. Kuyper succeeded Groen as leader of the Anti-Revolutionary Party (ARP) and then in 1874 became a member of parliament in the Second Chamber for the Gouda district. One of his first parliamentary speeches (December 1874) included a proposal for a national educational system,[13] he concluded his speech with this:

> The Act prescribes moral education. But the state cannot teach morality because morality involves principles of anthropology and psychology of which the state is incompetent to judge. That is why Mr. Groen van Prinsterer fought tooth and nail against the education bill of 1857[14] because it would of necessity lead to the state's teaching its own brand of religion and so create a kind of state church disguised as the public school.[15]

---

11. Kuyper, *On Education*, 306.

12. Kuyper, *On Education*, 317.

13. Kuyper. *On Education*, 139ff

14. The 1857 bill was the law that began the school struggle.

15. Kuyper, *On Education*, 163.

This was several years before his sphere sovereignty speech—but here we see a sphere sovereignty approach in embryo; the state is limited in what it can legitimately do.

In 1876 Kuyper had another nervous breakdown. It was also in this year that Heemskerk's[16] higher education law was enacted—this enabled the establishment of non-state-funded universities. One of which would eventually be the Free University. On Kuyper's return from recuperation, The Society for Higher Education in Calvinist Principles was established at Utrecht in 1878, with the aim of forming the Free University.

Joannes "Jan" Kappeyne Van de Coppello's (1822–1895) Liberal government at this time proposed an Elementary Bill that meant that school buildings would need to be updated and class sizes *reduced* to 40. However, the private schools were obliged to do this without government money. His intention it seems was to "price private schools right out of the market."[17] Those involved with private schools immediately started a "People's Petition." The petition was signed by over 300 000. Kuyper presented it to King William, but despite the petition, the king felt that it was his duty to sign the bill. The result of the petition provided a groundswell for the Anti-Revolutionary Party (ARP) and provided the impetus for a coalition with the Roman Catholics.

Kuyper's *Ons Program* [Our Program[18]] was published in 1878, subtitled *A Christian Political Manifesto*, and it provided

16. J. Heemskerk Azn. (1818–1897) was the conservative leader of the cabinet (during 1874–1877 and 1883–1888).

17. Van Dyke, "Government Schools or Free Schools?" 36.

18. Abraham Kuyper, *Our Program: A Christian Political Manifesto (Abraham Kuyper Collected Works in Public Theology)*, ed. Harry Van

the manifesto for the ARP. Article 12 of the *Ons Program* was devoted to Education:

> The Anti-Revolutionary Party wants the state to relinquish all control over the direction (first principles) of education, unless an absence of resilience among the citizens makes such interference necessary. The government is not called to actually educate by her own power. We want to prevent a situation in which government schools are misused to propagandize either for or against any religion. We also want to guarantee that all citizens are granted equal rights in matters of education, regardless of their religions or educational perspective.[19]

There he identifies a "sevenfold conviction" that shapes the ARP's and Kuyper's approach to education (see below page 392).

At last Kuyper was able to table a revision of the Elementary Education Act. Its provisions were fourfold: (1) all teachers, in public or private schools, were eligible for the same civil service pensions; (2) all teachers were placed on an improved salary schedule, for which all school boards, private or public, would be reimbursed by the central government; (3) teachers must be hired on the basis of a written contract (ending some abuse in the private sector); and (4) all schools must submit a *leerplan* ("curriculum") to ensure quality of instruction.[20]

Dyke (Bellingham, WA: Lexham Press, 2015).

19. Kuyper, *Our Program*, 188. Italics in original.

20. Abraham Kuyper, *Parlementaire redevoeringen*, vol. 4 (Amsterdam: Van Holkema and Warendorf, 1908), http://www.dbnl.org/tekst/kuyp002parl04_01/index.php. (Cited in Van Dyke, "Government Schools or Free schools?")

We maintain that the first responsibility lies with the parents, not the government. ...Education is not the task of the government.[21]

Kuyper did, however, see a task for government in education: "The government has to provide public education only because private persons usually fail in this task"[22] And as he had pointed out in *Our Program:*

the government is permitted, in fact obligated, to inter- vene under three rubrics: (1) protection of the interests of the nation; (2) upholding the legal order; and (3) substituting for whoever defaults in his task.[23]

On 5 April 1905, Kuyper, as prime minister, once again ad- dressed the reputed threat to national unity. He stated with some emphasis:

National unity is absolutely not promoted by a com- mon school. Amsterdam from the beginning provid- ed separate schools for Jewish children with Jewish teachers. One would think that Jew-baiting must have been rampant in that city. There is a lot of that in Russia, in Vienna, in Berlin, but I never noticed any of it in Amsterdam.

On Education primarily contains writings that deal with the practical issues of the school struggle rather than Kuyper's edu- cational philosophy. Kuyper does draw on key emphases in his approach, most notably sphere sovereignty, notably—as point-

---

21. Kuyper, *On Education*, 289.

22. Kuyper, *On Education*, 289.

23. Kuyper, *Our Program*, 202.

ed out above—his comment that "The school should belong, not to the church, not to the state, but to parents."

One key argument that persisted was the distinction between subsidies and restitution. Kuyper argued that restitution was needed for parents who set up private schools rather than a subsidy. This was because restitution implies a refund to the private schools of the expenses that saved the state rather a handout. Or as Kuyper put it, "Why are we so opposed to subsidies? Why do we despise them with all our might? The reason is obvious. A subsidy is an arbitrary allowance given by the rich to the poor, depending on his whim and caprice."[24]

Kuyper argued, convincingly, that the private schools meant that the parents had saved the state a great deal of money because it meant the state had fewer schools to fund.

His reasons for private Christian schools that are scattered through his writings collected in the anthology *On Education* include (in no particular order).

- The harmony between home and school will be much stronger than in a state school.
- Child rearing and thus education is the role of the parents and not the state—it should be an issue of parental choice.
- It is an issue of equality:

There must be equality in the country, both for those who hold to the Christian and for those who hold to the modernist worldview.[25]

---

24. Kuyper, *On Education,* 249.
25. Kuyper, *On Education*, 186.

- Education is not neutral; state education flattens and demeans religious faith:

There is no neutral education that is not governed by a spirit of its own. And precisely that spirit of the religiously neutral school militates against every positive faith.[26]

- All teachers and educationalists operate from a set of theoretical and pre-theoretical frameworks; neutrality is thus impossible.

- The need for diversity in education to represent the different cultural and religious worldviews within the Netherlands.

State education and the arguments for it are Kuyper insists is a product of moral autonomy, and thus a rejection of the sovereignty of God, it was a deification of the state, and although he does not put in in these terms involved state indoctrination.

In addition to the school struggle, Kuyper realized the need for higher education. In *Our Program* he identifies the need for higher education to take a higher priority than primary education. Although this does not mean that primary education is of minor importance. He opines: "History shows that the flowering of universities always precedes that of primary schools."[27] Hence, his concern to develop a Christian university, a Free University.

The Free University (VU Amsterdam)
While the school struggle continued, Kuyper was also concerned with establishing a Christian University. He saw the importance of both school and higher education:

---

26. Kuyper, *On Education*, 290.
27. Kuyper, *Our Program*, 189.

For there is no time to lose if we are yet to succeed in turning the hearts of children to their fathers and to call a generation misled by false philosophy back to the word of God. The Christian primary school alone will not suffice; a free university had to be founded, for it is not just elementary education but even more so, higher education which determines the spirit that rules the mighty world of thought.[28]

Kuyper's desire, in keeping with sphere sovereignty, was for a university that was free from state, government, and church control. Van Deursen in his history of the Free University states:

In this book the founder of the Free University will occupy an important place, for no one has matched him in service to this institution. The Free University is the creation of a man who ranks among the truly towering figures in Dutch history. Kuyper's organizational abilities, his wealth of ideas and oratorical talent, his inspiring drive and discerning alertness to the demands of the age gave the *gereformeerde* world form, to start with, and then influence, and finally power. Kuyper mobilized the *gereformeerde* folk and prepared them for battle.[29]

Without Kuyper there would be "no Free University."[30] Vanden Berg comments that "the plan to establish a Calvinistic univer-

---

28. Kuyper, *On Education*, 64.
29. Arie Theodorus van Deursen, *Cornerstone of the Pillarized System: A History of the Free University* (William B Eerdmans Publishing Co, 2008), 1.
30. Van Deursen, *Cornerstone of the Pillarized System*, 2.

sity stands out prominently as the boldest and most original and most creative thought of his career."[31]

Kuyper knew that the Reformed people needed more than a theological seminary—the Free University was to be more than that. It must be an institution where the light of Christ can shine onto all subjects if Christianity was to be a leaven in society. Philip J. Hoedemaker (1839–1910) one of the first professors at the VU in his "Dedication at the Founding of the Free University in Amsterdam," describes this approach:

> A university, that is, an institution which not only provides the opportunity to cultivate the science each for itself, not only joins them or groups together, but also unites them and places them in a proper relationship to one another and the centre, through a common bond.[32]

He continues:

> With such a foundation, its goal is to save the nation from the powers of destruction which lie in ambush behind the culture, prosperity, the science of our time, to rob Jesus Christ of His honour and our people of its character and future. [33]

---

31. Frank Vanden Berg, *Abraham Kuyper: A Biography* (St Catherines, ON: Paideia Press, 1978), 103.

32. Philippus Jacobus Hoedemaker, *The Bible, Theology, and the Sciences: Addresses at the Free University 1880–1886* (Aalten: Pantocrator Press, 2022), 4.

33. Hoedemaker, *The Bible, Theology, and the Sciences,* (Alten: Pantocrator Press, 2022), 4.

At the time there were only three universities in the Netherlands, Leiden, Groningen, and Utrecht.

The Heemskerk Higher Education Act of 1876 provided the legal basis for the Free University. In 1878 Kuyper formed the Association for Higher Education on the Basis of Reformed Principles. It received royal assent in February of the following year. The way was opened for the establishment of the Free University, Amsterdam in 1880. Kuyper delivered the opening address, fittingly, the subject was sphere sovereignty. In it he uttered his famous no square inch quote.

He also stressed the need for education to be free from both church and state control—hence the free in Free University:

> A science subservient to a state, subservient to a church, subservient to a sect, cannot fulfil its divine-given calling.[34]

The Free University (now called the VU Amsterdam) began with only eight students. The professors included Kuyper, F. L. Rutgers (1836–1917), and Philip J. Hoedemaker in the theological faculty and J. Wolter (1849–1917), a classicist, D. P. D. Fabius (1851–1931), a legal scholar, and F. W. J. Dilloo (1841–1892). They were charged with the following:

1. He is to solemnly declare that the Reformed fundamental conviction is also his.
2. He is to investigate which leading ideas in the area of research assigned to him were historically derived from the Reformed principles.
3. He is to vindicate with the authority of God's word

---

34. Abraham Kuyper, *Een Geloofsstuk* (Kampen: Kok, 1912). Cited in Vanden Berg, *Abraham Kuyper*, 245.

in nature and Scripture the Reformed principles and the lines drawn from them, or else to correct them if they are at variance with that word.

4. He is to carry forward the lines from the past into the spiritual struggle of today.[35]

The eighteen theses of Reformed principles served as guidelines for the professors. These included the following:

They started by declaring that the Reformed principles are the principles of Calvinism, in which we find the most consistent worldview developed in the Reformation (thesis 1).

They continued by declaring that these principles should not be formulated in a merely negative way but should be stated positively as the governing principles of thought for all of human life (thesis 3).

Not only should the ideas of Calvin be defended, but we should try to draw logical consequences from them for our own time (thesis 5).

We know Calvinism as explained from Scripture, as explained in the confessions of the Reformed churches (thesis 11), their liturgical forms, church order and dogmatic consensus (thesis 12), and also from the polemics of the original Calvinists against the Roman Catholics, Anabaptists, Socinians, Lutherans, and Arminians (thesis 13).

A third source of knowledge is the history of the Reformed churches (thesis 14).

---

35. Kuyper, *On Education*, 92.

Still another source of knowledge is the Calvinistic scientific and aesthetic literature (thesis 15).

The study of non-theological subjects should be governed by the Calvinistic confession of creation, of the sovereign reign of God over this world, of the essence of man and the cosmos, of the fall into sin and the distortion of the original creation inside and outside of man, and of the special and common grace of God which controls the present situation (thesis 17).

The university originally used rooms in the Scottish Mission Church of Amsterdam until they were able to buy their own building in 1883: *Keizersgrafht* 162—it was first opened for use in 1885.[36]

In the meantime, the law faculty was augmented with the appointment of Alexander F. de Savornin Lohman (1837–1924). However, in 1895 Lohman was accused of not teaching according to Reformed principles—he resigned in 1896.[37] Another issue that brought Lohman and Kuyper into conflict was the issue

---

36. For a full history of the VU Amsterdam see van Deursen, *Cornerstone of the Pillarized System*.

37. On the disagreement between Kuyper and Lohman see, for example, Clifford Blake Anderson, "Neocalvinism ... Abraham Kuyper? Maybe," *Comment* (June 2006): 53–57. Anderson notes:

> De Savornin Lohman regarded Kuyper's attempt to bind the development of the Vrije Universiteit to a concrete historical worldview as a threat to the longevity of the university. Quoting Kuyper, de Savornin Lohman commented, "that 'the University endures the ages,' may be so. But 'life—and worldviews,' including those of a single people, sometimes pass quickly by or are driven out by others. As 'foundations' for an institution of such longevity they are not terribly trustworthy."

of voting rights. Lohman an aristocratic landowner did not favour the extension of voting rights Kuyper did. Consequently, Lohman and others left to form the "free anti-revolutionary" group. The group eventually became the Free Anti-Revolutionary Party in 1898. They won 9 seats in the 1901 elections.[38]

When Kuyper was PM in 1903, he introduced a Higher Education bill to give private universities the same opportunities for funding as state universities. The bill was initially defeated in the upper house, so Kuyper went to Queen Wilhelmina and asked to dissolve the upper house sparking new elections. This happened and the result was that the newly elected upper house passed the bill in 1905. This meant that the Polytechnic School in Delft was given Technical University status (now known as TU Delft). However, importantly for the VU, it meant that the degrees awarded by the VU Amsterdam were given official status.

Kuyper's educational philosophy

The cornerstone of Kuyper's educational policies was that the task of education belongs to parents and guardians.

> *The father* (or in his absence the mother, temporary caregiver, or guardian) is charged by God with the task of rearing his child so that it fears God, respects the law,

---

Johann Stellingwerff, a scholar generally quite critical of Abraham Kuyper, has even suggested—in *Dr. Abraham Kuyper en de Vrije Universiteit* (J. H. Kok, 1987)—that Kuyper's victory over de Savornin Lohmann constituted a turning-point in the history of Vrije Universiteit, making it "an entirely Kuyperian mini-university" rather than a center of free, Christian scholarly inquiry.

38. The Free Anti-Revolutionary Party merged with the Christian Historical Voters' League to form the Christian Historical Party in 1903.

develops its potential, and is prepared for its life's task, initially here below, to be continued hereafter.[39]

There are other institutions involved. These include the church, the government, and the teachers.

The father decides in what *spirit* his child will be educated. The church determines the *principle* by which that spirit can be safely preserved in the school. The government decides the *level* to which our public education shall aspire. But the manner in which the child shall be taught in that spirit, according to that principle and up to that level, is at the personal discretion of the teachers, instructors, and professors themselves.[40]

There is what Kuyper described as a "sevenfold conviction":

1. that the father is responsible for the education of his child;
2. that the church has a right to see performed what she has been promised;
3. that pedagogy must be able to make independent decisions;
4. that nurture and education are inseparable;
5. that money donated is better than money extorted;
6. that free initiatives by citizens ennobles a nation, but state meddling debases it; and
7. that a school that makes it difficult for the mind to submit to God's ordinances and so sets itself against the Christian religion must be deemed a curse and not a blessing for the nation.[41]

---

39. Kuyper, *Our Program*, §162, 199.
40. Kuyper, *Our Program*, §167, 205.
41. Kuyper, *Our Program*, 207.

Three of the scholars who have researched Kuyper's educational theory are Robert E. L. Rogers,[42] A. H. Nichols,[43] and more recently Wendy Naylor,[44] who completed a doctorate on Kuyper and education from the University of Chicago. In her dissertation, Naylor paid particular attention to the pluralism of education. Naylor was also one of the editors of Kuyper's *On Education*. In her introduction to that volume Naylor, provided the historical and cultural context of Kuyper's time and examines some mountains that Kuyper faced in attempting to reform the school system. As Naylor notes Kuyper's program involved a "multifaceted rationale"[45] for his pluralistic educational program. She examines Kuyper's argument for a pluralistic approach which consisted in freedom of conscience, the role of core beliefs, taking education out of politics, the unity of the child, sound pedagogy, parental rights, church rights, preparation for future service to society, free initiative and civil society, justice for the poor, national unity, and Dutch culture and heritage. Naylor concludes by looking at the North Amer-

---

42. R. E. L. Rogers, *The Incarnation of the Antithesis: An Introduction to the Educational Thought and Practice of Abraham Kuyper* (Pentland Press: Durham, 1992).

43. Anthony H. Nicholls, "The Educational Doctrines of Abraham Kuyper: An Evaluation," *Journal of Christian Education* 18, no.1 (1975): 26–38.

44. Wendy Naylor, "Abraham Kuyper and the Emergence of Neo-Calvinist Pluralism in the Dutch School System" (PhD Thesis., University of Chicago, 2006); Wendy Naylor, "Religious Liberty and Educational Pluralism: Abraham Kuyper's Principled Advocacy of School Choice, in *The Wiley Handbook of Christianity and Education*, ed., William Jeynes (Hoboken, NJ: Wiley-Blackwell, 2018), 325–353.

45. Kuyper, *On Education*, xiv

ican situation and sees taking place a similar scenario to that of the Dutch struggle.[46]

Rogers examines three factors, Calvinism, common grace, and sphere sovereignty, as the basis of Kuyper's educational philosophy.[47] Nichols examines five factors—in addition to Rogers, he adds the biblical doctrine of creation and the notion of the universality of faith. As Nichols comments one objection levelled at Christian schools is that they promote a "ghetto mentality" by isolating children from the world. Kuyper's emphasis on creation and common grace shows that this was not a motivation for Kuyper.[48] Education was a preparation for involvement in society. By the universality of faith, Nichols means the role of faith, as identified by Kuyper, is integral in all of life's activities—whether believer or atheist. All educational theories have their foundations in faith commitments. He finds that Kuyper's view of the antithesis is "more controversial."[49] Nichols suggests that Kuyper's "inconsistencies" have been eliminated by Cornelius Van Til. As regards sphere sovereignty while acknowledging it helps to delineate the roles of family, school, and state, he maintains it lacks biblical warrant. (In a footnote he does acknowledge that Kuyper never maintained that it did.) Nichols also asserts that there is "no Biblical doctrine of the State."

Rodgers is more sanguine regarding sphere sovereignty. However, other than discussing the roles of state, church and society Rodgers does not fully apply it to education.

---

46. Naylor, "Editor's Introduction," xi-xli.

47. Rogers, *The Incarnation of the Antithesis*, Ch 2.

48. Anthony H. Nichols, "The Educational Doctrines of Abraham Kuyper: An Evaluation," *Journal of Christian Education* (1975): 29, https://doi.org/10.1177/002196577501800103.

49. Nichols, "The Educational Doctrines of Abraham Kuyper," 31.

Sphere sovereignty for Kuyper meant that education has its own sphere. Education was to be free from the state and church. This was the intention behind the term "free" in the Free University. Education was education it was not a business—to make education a business would be to violate sphere sovereignty. Education should not be monopolized by any other of the spheres of life. Sphere sovereignty also meant ensuring that other worldviews had their own schools too. In this sense Kuyper was a pluralist.

The antithesis also has a role to play—this was in part why Kuyper wanted to establish separate institutions. It was one of the factors that spurred him on to establish Christian schools.

The controversy around Christian education

Christian education has often been controversial. It raises several questions:

- Why is there a need for Christian schools?
- What about indoctrination?
- Who are Christian schools for?
- Who will fund Christian schools?
- Is there such as thing as Christian scholarship?

These questions have been addressed by Kuyper and have been alluded to above. It is worth summarizing his responses here.

Why is there a need for Christian schools?
Education is the role of the parents and so children should be educated in accordance with their parent's worldview. Schools are not worldview neutral, and all forms of education promulgate one worldview or another.

Christian universities are essential as what is taught in universities flows to other educational institutions. Universities are needed to train teachers, pastors, engineers, economists, ... so that they can pass on a Christian perspective for all of life.

What about indoctrination?
As no school was religiously neutral, all schools implicitly or explicitly promulgate a particular worldview.

> First of all, Kuyper's own vision was never about construct-ing "pillars" in Dutch society within which the Gerefor-meerden could feel safe. Neither was the call for separate Christian organizations by Canadian Kuyperians their way of protecting their young from the negative influences of secular Canada. Rather, these actions were always meant to bring the grace of the gospel to bear on the world of educa-tion, labour, politics, the arts, etc. It was always about serv-ing the world at large by means of Christian social action.[50]

Who will fund Christian education?
The question of funding was behind the decades-long school struggle.

One key argument that persisted was the distinction be-tween subsidies and restitution. Kuyper argued that restitution was needed for parents who set up private schools rather than a subsidy. This was because restitution implies a refund to the private schools of the expenses that saved the state rather a handout. Or as Kuyper put it:

> Why are we so opposed to subsidies? Why do we de-spise them with all our might? The reason is obvious. A

---

50. Harry A. Van Belle, "Deaconhood of Believers," n.d., https://www. socialtheology.com/docs/Deaconhood_of_Believers.pdf.

subsidy is an arbitrary allowance given by the rich to the poor, depending on his whim and caprice.[51]

Is there such thing as Christian scholarship?
For many Christians the term *Christian* should not be used as an adjective. Notably among those who advocate for a (Reformed) two kingdom approach. For example, Bryan D. Estelle in his *The Primary Mission of the Church:* Writes:

> In other words, in Christian colleges and universities, the notion was planted, germinated, and grew that Christians think in fundamentally different ways than those who are not. Of course in some limited ways this is true; however, the calculus in math is the calculus and it matters not whether a person learns it at Cornell or Wheaton, as long as they learn it well, especially if they plan on being a civil engineer.
>
> So the real question that emerges from these currents in the wake of Kuyper's and Dooyeweerd's thought is: is there such a thing as "Christian" scholarship or a "Christian" approach to culture?[52]

He approvingly cites Quirinius Breen:

> But it is a mistake to think that by being a Christian, a grocer, a bricklayer, fireman, plumber, or politician is improved in the grocery business or in bricklaying, and so on. Nor is secular learning improved by it. Let nature, the world and its fullness be what they are; for God made

---

51. Kuyper, *On Education,* 249.
52. Bryan D. Estelle, *The Primary Mission of the Church: Engaging or Transforming the World.* (Fearn, Ross-shire: Christian Focus Publications, 2022).

them good, and his providence maintains them impartially, as the rain that falls on the just and the unjust unlike.[53]

Of course, being a Christian does not make one instantly better at fulfilling one's vocation. However, neither does it have no effect! Regeneration is also a regeneration of thought and thought patterns. This will influence how one goes about one's daily business as well as on one's approach to scholarship. Philosophy does have implications for calculus. Calculus is based on number—what one thinks of a number depends on one's philosophical view of number. The mathematician does not leave his faith at the classroom door! His faith will affect his ideas of number, and thus calculus, and how and why it is taught.

The civil engineer Robert Moses poses a good illustration of how civil engineering can be shaped by worldviews. According to Moses' biographer Robert A. Caro, in his book *The Power Broker*, he tells how Moses designed the bridges to the Long Island, New York beaches, with a low clearance so that it would keep out the buses from Jones Beach.[54] Those who used the buses were primarily poor blacks and Puerto Ricans—people who Robert Moses, allegedly abhorred. Worldviews affect design. Likewise with teaching methods—our view of what it is to be human affects how we teach.

Hence, the importance of *Christian* education and why Kuyper put much time and effort into establishing the VU Amsterdam and ensuring that there was a place for Christian schools.

---

53. Quirinius Breen, *Christianity and Humanism: Studies in the History of Ideas* (Grand Rapids, MI: Eerdmans, 1968).

54. Robert A. Caro, *The Power Broker: Robert Moses and the Fall of New York* (London: Bodley Head, 2019).

Kuyper's vision of education thus emphasized the necessity of a complete, Christian approach to learning that acknowledges God's sovereignty over all aspects of life.

A summary in 12 theses

1. Education is a parental responsibility, with parents entrusted to guide their children's learning.
2. The church has a right to ensure promises made regarding education are fulfilled.
3. Pedagogy should have the autonomy to make decisions independently.
4. Nurturing and education are intertwined and inseparable.
5. Voluntary donations for education are preferable to coerced funding.
6. Citizen-led initiatives elevate a nation, while state interference diminishes it.
7. Schools opposing Christian principles are detrimental rather than beneficial to society.
8. Calvinistic worldview shapes the foundation of education at the VU Amsterdam.
9. The VU Amsterdam emphasizes freedom from state and church control in education.
10. Kuyper's vision for education safeguards Jesus Christ's honor and the nation's character.
11. The Anti-Revolutionary Party gains momentum through advocacy for Christian education.
12. Kuyper's legacy establishes enduring principles for Christian education in the Netherlands.

Chronology

1575	Leiden University established
1795	Occupation of the Netherlands by Napoleon
1813	French Rule ends
1806	School law meant public schools should teach all kinds of Christian and civil virtues Church not allowed to form new schools—education becomes centralized
1823	Isaac da Costa booklet "Critique against the spirit of the century"—criticized the school law
1826–1854	*Het Réveil* (The Awakening)
1834	*Afscheiding*/secession under de Cock and Scholte Created the Christelijke Gereformeerde Kerk Advised members not to use public schools Beginning of the "school *struggle*'
1837	Groen's tract: The Measures Against the Seceders Tested With Respect to Constitutional Law
1840	Groen Van Prinsterer is elected to Parliament
1844	First parent-run Christian school is established in the Netherlands
1848	The liberal Thorbecke's "Freedom of education". The hope that common civic morality would solidify national unity
1857	Van Rappard only public schools can have funding—education should be neutral
1857	Parliament enacted the law of education and legalized the religious neutrality in primary schools, he [GvP] began the school struggle over against that decision
1860	"The Association for Christian National School Education (CNS: De Vereeniging voor *Christelijke -Nationaal Schoolonderwijs*)
1869	Kuyper addresses the Association of Christian National School Education
1870s	Groen announces Kuyper as leader of the ARP
1874	Kuyper elected to parliament, resigns pastoral ministry
1875	Discussions begin around the possibility of founding a Christian univeristy

1876	Heemskerk's higher education law enacted
1877	Kuyper returns to the Netherlands after recuperating from a nervous breakdown
1878	The Society for Higher Education in Calvinist Principles established at Utrecht, with the aim of forming the Free University
1878	Van Copello schools should fund themselves. Petition to the king
1878	*Ons* Program published—the manifesto of the ARP
1879	Kuyper organized an Anti-School law Association (Anti-Schoolwet Verbond)
1879	ARP becomes first political party with Kuyper as chairman
1880	The founding of VU Amsterdam. Kuyper delivers the first rectorial address on sphere sovereignty
1880	Kuyper professor of theology until 1901 at the VU Philip J. Hoedemaker (1839–1910) professor of theology—resigned after the Doleantie. He disagreed with Kuyper and Lohman over the separation of the church and state. He later joined the DRC, the state church
1881	Kuyper also became professor in the faculty of arts. He lectured on linguistics, literature, and aesthetics
1882	The Dutch Reformed Church decide that theological students at the Free University are not allowed to become ministers
1883	Free University purchased its first building, *Keizersgraßht* 162—it was opened in 1885
1883-1901	Kuyper lectured on Dutch language and literature
1884	The inauguration of the law faculty with A. F. de Savornin Lohman (1837–1924)
1896	Willem Hovey (1850–1915) resigns as Free University's chairman of board of governors after Lohman is dismissed
1900	Truancy act enabled—making schooling compulsory
1904	Bavinck's *Paedagogische beginselen* (Pedagogic Principles) published
1917	Enactment of Article 23 which guaranteed Christian schools equal legal status and financial support

Study Questions

1. Why did Kuyper place so much importance on education?
2. What did Kuyper mean by a "free school" and a "free university"?
3. Why did Kuyper think that neutral schools were a myth?
4. How did Abraham Kuyper's educational philosophy shape the establishment of the Free University in Amsterdam?
5. What does Kuyper mean by "Kantian deism and its doctrine of moral autonomy"?
6. Kuyper wrote: "a Christian school is not an evangelistic instrument but a training center for future warriors in God's kingdom" (*On Education*, 345). Would you agree? Justify your answer.
7. What was the school struggle?
8. What were the key principles of neo-Calvinism that influenced Kuyper's views on education?
9. Are Christian schools necessary?

Further Reading

Primary

Kuyper, Abraham "Christian Schools," in *Pro Rege: The Kingship of Christ. Volume 3: The Kingship of Christ in Its Operations.* Edited by John Kok with Nelson D. Kloosterman, Translated by Albert Gootjes. (Bellingham, WA: Lexham Press, 2019),144–151.

Kuyper, Abraham *On Education.* Edited by Wendy Naylor and Harry Van Dyke. (Bellingham, WA: Lexham Press, 2019).

Secondary

Naylor, Wendy. "School choice and religious liberty in the Netherlands: reconsidering the Dutch school struggle and the Influence of Abraham Kuyper in its resolution," in *International Handbooks of Protestant Education*, Volume 6. (Dordrecht: Springer, 2012), Part 2, ch 12, 245–274.

Rogers, R. E. L. *The Incarnation of the Antithesis: An introduction to the Educational Thought and Practice of Abraham Kuyper.* (Durham: Pentland Press, 1992)

Wolterstorff, Nicholas. 2004. "Abraham Kuyper on Christian learning," in *Educating for Shalom: Essays on Christian Higher Education.* Edited by Clarence W. Joldersma and Gloria Goris Stronks. (Grand Rapids: Eerdmans, 2004), 199–225.

Van Dyke, H. "Government Schools or Free schools? Abraham Kuyper Addresses a Long-standing Controversy in the Dutch Parliament," *Canadian Journal of Netherlandic Studies/Rev. can. d'études néerlandaises* 35 (2) (2014): 29–45.

25

Kuyper and the State
and Government

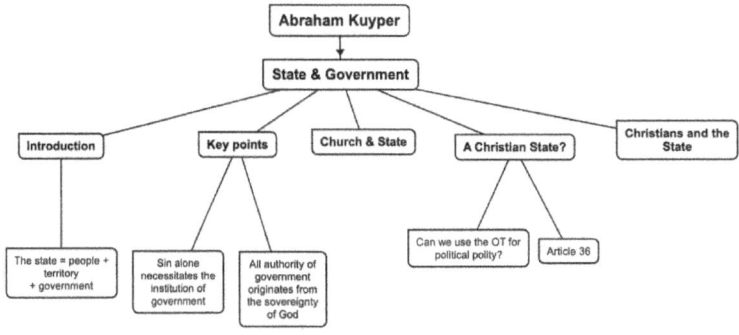

In brief

THIS CHAPTER HIGHLIGHTS ABRAHAM Kuyper's Calvinistic perspective on the state and government. Kuyper emphasizes that government is a result of sin, and that all authority originates from God. He views government as a manifestation of common grace, existing to restrain sin and maintain societal order. He advocates for a Calvinistic approach that rejects extremes like popular sovereignty and state sovereignty, emphasizing the sovereignty of God. Kuyper believes that the church and state, both products of sin, have distinct roles in combating sin. He stresses the importance of deriving principles from Scripture for governance, requiring careful study and application. Christians are encouraged to engage in politics and apply biblical principles to state matters. Kuyper's perspective underscores the temporary nature of the state and government, which will cease to exist in a sinless world. Overall, Kuyper's teachings emphasize the significance of God's sovereignty in political affairs and the duty of Christians to apply biblical principles in the realm of government.

Introduction

There is a scene in the film *Amazing Grace* where William Wilberforce (1759-1833), is considering giving up his political career for one in "religion."[1] He was visited by members of the Clapham Sect and Thomas Clarkson. Clarkson says to Wilberforce: "we understand you are wondering whether to pursue politics or religion." Hannah More responds: "we humbly suggest you can do both." That is also a Kuyperian response. We can serve God and do politics—in fact, we can serve God *in* doing politics.

Kuyper was a statesman and politician. He was the prime minster of the Netherlands from 1901–1905 and served the government in one form or another for many years. It is unsurprising that he wrote extensively on the government and the state. In *Common Grace* Volume 3, Kuyper examines the practical out workings of common grace. In this volume is his most sustained discussion of the state and the relationship between the church and the state. He also devoted one of his Stone Lectures to "Calvinism and Politics."

---

1. *Amazing Grace* (Roadside Attractions, 2006).

At times Kuyper sometimes seems to see the term state and government synonymously. The state, however, he sees as broader than the government. The state includes the territory and its citizens as well as the government—the institutions that create the rules and laws for the state. We can express this as:

The state = people + territory + government.

Kuyper writes:

> Government is a power instituted by God that, as his servant represents and maintains divine authority, whereas the state is the organized community of the whole nation....[2]

Key points

Kuyper begins his discussion of politics in his *Lectures on Calvinism* by stressing the sovereignty of God. God is sovereign; therefore, the state, society, and the church are not. The sovereignty of God is not only soteriological but cosmic:

> This dominating principle was not, soteriologically, justification by faith, but, in the widest sense cosmologically, the Sovereignty of the Triune God over the whole Cosmos, in all its spheres and kingdoms, visible and invisible.[3]

He argues that "no political scheme has ever become dominant which was not founded in a specific religious or anti-religious conception." Politics is not neutral with respect to religion. Every political theory is based on some religious conviction—hidden or otherwise. This is in part why Kuyper seeks to

---

2. Kuyper, *Common Grace* 3, 475.

3. Kuyper, *Lectures on Calvinism*, 79.

develop a distinctly Calvinistic approach to politics. This "dominating principle" for Kuyper was the sovereignty of God.

This means that there is thus a "deduced sovereignty" in the political sphere (the state). He then highlights two Calvinistic theses:

1. Sin alone necessitates the institution of government.
2. All authority of government originates from the sovereignty of God.

Stemming from these two main points are several other key points—I shall list them with a few comments below.

1. Government belongs in the realm of common grace.

As Kuyper puts it: "Government is the clearest and most tangible manifestation of common grace."[4]

The two main purposes of common grace are the restraint of sin and to account for the blessings bestowed on non-Christians and accounting for the good things they may do. We can also see these in government—government is to restrain sin and to maintain a just and equitable society. This leads to:

2. Government is instituted because of sin.

It is not a creational ordinance. In this sense it is like a plaster cast for a broken arm, or as Kuyper describes it in his *Lectures on Calvinism* as a crutch for a lame leg. Without the fall and sin there would be no need for a plaster cast or a crutch. If everyone were true believers, there would be no need for a government to be necessary. This follows from the first point above. Government is only necessary where there is sin, it is established because of sin.

---

4. Kuyper, *Common Grace* 3, 56.

Kuyper maintains that without sin and the fall there would be one worldwide state arising from the family with God as the king. However, with the fall there has arisen people nations, which become states. These then have God-appointed government. The government would not be needed if society was one of saints that knew no sin.[5]

Examples that Kuyper uses to show the need for government intervention is shop opening hours,[6] and that of workplace accidents.[7] Some factory owners took care of their employees who had accidents, while other owners did not. This meant for the former to be profitable they too could not afford to look after their employees as they had previously done: "If every year again one owner had to pay thousands of guilders for those who had suffered an accident while the others did not, the playing field would no longer have been level." Thus

> They gradually came to realize that there was only one remedy, namely, to impose on everyone the obligation to care for laborers who meet with an accident.[8]

As Kuyper goes on to observe:

> This was no doubt a rather far-reaching intervention in the free spheres of civil life, but because society had proved itself unable or unwilling, there was no other way out.[9]

This shows the need for government because of sin.

---

5. Kuyper, *Pro Rege* 3, 125.
6. Kuyper, *Pro Rege* 3, 130.
7. Kuyper, *Pro Rege* 3, 131.
8. Kuyper, *Pro Rege* 3, 131.
9. Kuyper, *Pro Rege* 3, 131.

3. God has ordained government for all nations—it may take different forms, but it is needed (again because of sin).

It has been instituted even in "pagan cultures"[10] as it is a product of common grace not particular grace.

4. Government is the servant of God

This may be the case biblically and ideally that government is the servant of God, but Kuyper recognized that it was not always the case: but what should be is not necessarily what can be.[11] However, even if they recognize it or not government officials and leaders are the servants of God. Unfortunately, many do not. We are profoundly affected by sin, and sadly we prefer darkness to light.[12]

There are also practical circumstances that often prevent those in authority exercising the servanthood of God—they may have no access to the knowledge of God, it may remain a "closed book." The ruler may not have sought out the knowledge of God.

To be God's servant requires an understanding of God's will. To understand God's will from nature, reason, Scripture, history, and so on requires extensive knowledge, but most importantly revelation. Unfortunately, the Scriptures do not present us with "ready-made answers."

> Scripture is not a book full of rules with an index that allows us immediately to find ready-made answers. We in fact can only derive *principles* from Scripture, while the *application* of those principles in specific

---

10. Kuyper, *Common Grace* 3, 57.

11. Kuyper, *Common Grace* 3, 221.

12. Kuyper, *Common Grace* 3, 160.

cases and on specific accessions requires detailed and complex study.[13]

Thus, God's servant, the government, must orient itself toward the knowledge of God's will in three respects:[14]

1. It must understand what role government must occupy.
2. It must know God's will concerning the various relationships within society that need government sanction.
3. It must also know God's will concerning the basic difference between good and evil (the moral realm).

As Kuyper puts it:

> without government, we would have fallen into horrible self-destruction; hence, God has given us political authority and structures to maintain justice, restore order, and safeguard virtue among human beings.[15]

5. Government has a limited and specific task.

As explained before one of the purposes of Kuyper's sphere sovereignty was to ensure that the different spheres do not encroach on the others. Each sphere should be sovereign in its own right. The role for government was to ensure public justice—to oil the cogs of the different spheres as it were, but not to interfere unless one sphere is challenging public justice in some way.

---

13. Kuyper, *Common Grace* 3, 224.

14. Kuyper, *Common Grace* 3, Ch24.

15. Kuyper, *Common Grace* 3, 41.

There are, therefore, boundaries that the government must respect. The supreme task of government is to demarcate the rights between the spheres of society and to guard the rights and liberties of the individuals in those spheres. Government then has a threefold right and duty:

1. Whenever different spheres clash, to compel mutual regard for the boundary-lines of each;
2. To defend individuals and the weak ones, in those spheres, against the abuse of power of the rest; and
3. To coerce all together to bear personal and financial burdens for the maintenance of the natural unity of the State. The decision cannot, however, in these cases, unilaterally rest with the magistrate. The Law here has to indicate the rights of each, and the rights of the citizens over their own purses must remain the invincible bulwark against the abuse of power on the part of the government.[16]

The state is not a center from which its tentacles are sent out to different areas of life; Kuyper makes this clear when he writes:

> The State may never become an octopus, which sti-fles the whole of life. It must occupy its own place, on its own root, among all the other trees of the forest, and thus it has to honor and maintain every form of life which grows independently in its own sacred autonomy.[17]

He also stresses this point in *Our Program*: "Every attempt by political authority to try and rule over one of those other areas

---

16. Kuyper, *Lectures on Calvinism*, 97.
17. Kuyper, *Lectures on Calvinism*, 96–97.

is therefore a violation of God's ordinances, and resistance to it is not a crime but a duty."[18]

6. The state exercises authority by the power of the sword; it is coercive
The image of the sword implies that there is a need for justice, war, and order. Justice is the "highest duty" for government:

> this sword has a threefold meaning. It is the sword of justice, to mete out corporeal punishment to the criminal. It is the sword of war to defend the honor and the rights and the interests of the State against its enemies. And it is the sword of order, to thwart at home all forcible rebellion.[19]

To be able to administer justice means that coercion is sometimes necessary. For Kuyper this also includes the death penalty. He sees the death penalty originating with Noahic covenant.[20]

7. Every government manifests some sort of religious character.
The government is not neutral. As Kuyper puts it a neutral state is an impossibility—it is a chimera.[21] However, the government should remain "neutral" towards different religious beliefs, in that the government should permit a diversity of churches, various forms of worship, and allow different religious beliefs to be held.

---

18. Kuyper, *Our Program*, §21, 21.
19. Kuyper, *Lectures on Calvinism*, 93.
20. Kuyper, *Common Grace* 3, 126.
21. Kuyper, *Common Grace* 3, 205.

8. A Calvinistic approach to government avoids the extremes
Popular sovereignty and state sovereignty are two extremes that
Calvinism protects against.

Popular sovereignty—the rule of the people arose from
the French revolution in 1789. God was replaced by humanity. The will of the people determined authority. It is an
atheistic approach. Whereas state sovereignty, Kuyper maintains, arose from German philosophical pantheism. The
state becomes the highest ideal. The actions of the government do not negate the rights of the people but must take
them into account.

Kuyper with his appeal to the sovereignty of God avoids
both of these extremes. In the same way he avoids both individualism and collectivism. Lucas Freire sums up well Kuyper's
position in regard to his rejection of secularism, individualism,
and collectivism:

> Kuyper opposed secularism and defended a form of
> limited government and a free economy that was
> grounded in Christian anthropology and Reformed
> public theology. He denounced mechanistic socialism
> as incompatible with a Christian view of the organic
> relationship between the state, the market, and the
> people. Kuyper also denounced radical individualism
> and economic anarchism, arguing that the government
> had a legitimate and God-given ordinance to pursue
> public justice.[22]

---

22. Lucas Freire, "Political Economy in Brazil," in *Reformed Public Theology:
A Global Vision for Life in the World*, ed. Mathew Kaemingk (Grand
Rapids: Bake Academic, 2021).

9. The state and government are temporary—they will disappear when there is no longer sin.

As Kuyper argues:

> Those who, *unlike us*, view the state not as a temporary expedient or as something that exists to arrest sin but as having arisen from creation, rooted in humanity's nature, and satisfying the deepest need of humanity...have ended up denying all life after death.[23]

As it was born out of the fall, in the consummation it will not be needed. God will be the sovereign, and he will rule.

The relationship between Christians and the state and government

It should be made clear that when discussing the relation between the church and state Kuyper focuses on the institutional church. Members of the institutional church are also members of the state. They live statutorily in the state and ecclesiastically in the church. The church like the state "represents a principle that demands and dominates *the whole of life*."[24]

Both the institutional church and the state are a consequence of sin. If there were no sin, there would be no need for either. Part of the purpose of each is to combat sin. Neither are they, argues Kuyper, the result of creation or a creation ordinance.

The church is also to be free from state interference: the government must "recognize the indisputable right of churches to express themselves *as churches*."[25] It must extend to all those churches that

---

23. Kuyper, *Common Grace* 3, 136—my emphasis.
24. Kuyper, *Common Grace* 3, 147.
25. Kuyper, *Common Grace* 3, 303.

confess the Apostles' Creed. Those that do not confess this creed have departed from the true understanding of the church. The table compares and contrasts the state and the *institutional* church.

Table. A comparison of church and state.[26]

	State	Institutional church
Similarities **Ch 14, 17**	Both arise from grace Neither are rooted in creation ordinances Both are for the combatting of sin Both represent a principle that demands and dominates the whole of life 17§4	
Starting point **Ch15**	Common Grace It emerges from creation	The fruit of particular grace Transcends nature Originates with Word and regeneration —it is miraculous Springs from a re-creation The church was never manifested as an institution until Pentecost
Sphere §3 **—the circle**	In the ordinary natural life	The human as a sinner The heart, soul,

---

26. Source Kuyper, *Common Grace* 3, Ch 15–16. Table from Steve Bishop, "Kuyperania 2020," *Koers—Bulletin for Christian Scholarship*, 86(1). Available at: https://doi.org/10.19108/KOERS.86.1.2504.

in which life occurs	The external features of the people e.g., the land, illnesses, dangers, income, weapons, roads, and canals, safeguarding of property, punishment It is the visible manifestations of public life	the inner person The hidden person of the heart
Means §4	External means —wood and stone to build roads; judges and magistrates; metal to form weapons; "…almost everything that is available in nature by virtue of creation to maintain its authority and to discharge its duty"	Funds for building and its duties raised by voluntary contributions rather than taxes Never coercive It's means are spiritual —God's word is its sword. Administers the sacraments
Character §5	All citizens are included—it is not voluntary We are not given a choice; we are born subjects Authority is over a certain region, and it includes all those	Has the character of voluntariness Membership is voluntary not coercive Membership is based on our convictions and will

417

	in that region Obedience and subjection	Uses spiritual urging to assert its authority Confession and faithfulness
Calling **ch 16 §1-2** **—i.e., life task**	To combat sin —but its calling is broader Ensures the continuance of the particulars and preconditions of the broken life of creation Maintains justice by formulating it, demanding it, and avenging it if violated Task falls in the present life	To combat sin —without sin it would have no calling Labors in and for a new life that was added to the broken life of creation Proclaims on God's behalf on the basis of justice of justice as formulated in God's word Task consists in perpetuating the remembrance of what God did in Christ
Ultimate Goals **ch 16 §3–4**	Lies in the present dispensation	Lies in eternity

The role of the Christian and the state

Kuyper does not advocate an individualistic approach to politics. It is not enough for Christians to have a personal conversion and to live a holy life; such an approach inadvertently leaves statecraft to unbelievers. He regards it as the duty of believers to study God's word with "an eye on matters of the state and nation."[27]

He is aware that the New Testament speaks of church and of government but little if anything on the relationship of church and government. In addition, there is nothing in the New Testament of government duty towards Christians. However, there are prescriptions for Christians in terms of how citizens of the state should behave.

Although as regards the institutionalized church-state connection there is little mention in the New Testament—at least not in a way that makes it clear how God intends for it to function. The New Testament does provide clear biblical principles, we do not yet know exactly what those principles mean or how they apply to church and state, when and where they interact with one another. Hence, Kuyper asserts, in the application of these principles the onus is on Christians to apply them:

> Scripture is not a book full of rules with an index that allows us immediately to find ready-made answers. We in fact can only derive *principles* from Scripture, while the *application* of those principles in specific cases and on specific occasions requires detailed and complex study. Discernment of relevant application is not the fruit of what one individual investigates but of what has been gradually brought to light in the course of centuries through history and scholarship.[28]

---

27. Kuyper, *Common Grace* 3, 225.

28. Kuyper, *Common Grace* 3, 224.

As there is only little insight that the New Testament offers, consequently, an appeal could be made to the Old Testament. However, Kuyper argues, such an appeal is invalid. Christian congregational life is not derived from temple ministry and a separate manifestation of the church in its own revelation and its own organization is not until Pentecost. Hence, we must reject the national institution of Israel with the institution of the Christian church.[29] The same would apply to any attempt to equate government under Israel with today's government. He suggests that "Israel's unique situation cannot serve as a model." Thus, we cannot apply the principles God gave to Israel for its polity to today. The problem in attempting to do so is that it is dependent upon cultural and temporal issues.[30] We must be able to distinguish "the permanent principles from the passing form of their application."[31] As an example he mentions the death penalty:

> a distinction must be made between the principles that underlie this Mosaic law and the specific form in which these principles were applied. From the Books of Moses, the chief point would appear to be not that someone must specifically be "stoned to death" but rather that the death penalty must be maintained.[32]

Women's rights, agrarian laws, and the relationship between church and state make it apparent that we cannot go on "parroting what was said in the past."[33]

---

29. Kuyper, *Common Grace* 3, 243–244.

30. Kuyper, *Common Grace* 3, 183–184.

31. Kuyper, *Common Grace* 3, 186.

32. Kuyper, *Common Grace* 3, 186.

33. Kuyper, *Common Grace* 3, 189.

This then raises the question is a Christian state possible, or even what is a Christian state?

A Christian state?

Kuyper poses the question: In matters of state what makes something Christian?[34] He then suggests some positions that have been proposed:

- Abolishing the army and oath taking (Anabaptists)
- When the True church is the state church.
- When government meetings begin with a prayer.
- Christian statesmen who are believers but organize the state according to mammon.

Kuyper sees these as being, at best, inadequate.

It is not enough to add the Christian adjective to a noun (state/government/law), as Kuyper explains:

> What they fail to consider is that an *adjective* (and that is what the term *Christian* is in this discussion) is always something that is *added* to a noun. The noun in this case is the state, the government, the law, or whatever other political concept we want to take, with the word *Christian* being *added* as an extra component. Hence, the state can be a state, a government can be a government, and a law can be a law *without* being Christian. The *essence* of the matter lies in being *state* or *government* or *law*, and "Christian" only expresses what quality or character that state, that government, that law manifests. Taken in this sense, the addition of the adjective *Christian* as such only sig-

---

34. Kuyper, *Common Grace* 3, 171.

nifies that that particular state or government or law
is as it must be according to the clearly revealed will
of God.[35]

Only those confessing Christ are capable of achieving a
Christian formation of the state, a Christian polity, a Christian
government.[36]

Government is God's servant, thus it should rather than
rely on its own theories, it should consider how does God
"want us to look at people and property and the various mutual relationships between them." Then government can be
labelled "Christian."[37] This cannot be done if government officials only rely on common grace. As Kuyper maintains:

> First, the light of common grace does not illuminate
> to that extent. Second, according to Romans 1, those
> who live solely under common grace have been giv-
> en over to "a debased mind" in every area related to
> the moral life. And third, the state and national life
> can be erected on a surer foundation only where the
> light of particular revelation has come to intensify the
> glow of common grace.[38]

Christianizing government is a slow and gradual process, common grace cannot do this. It requires the leavening effect of the
church. A Christian government cannot be achieved ....

> ...without belief in Holy Scripture, and no one can
> believe Holy Scripture without bowing the knee before

---

35. Kuyper, *Common Grace* 3, 172.

36. Kuyper, *Common Grace* 3, 173.

37. Kuyper, *Common Grace* 3, 173.

38. Kuyper, *Common Grace* 3, 177.

Christ. For this reason, only those confessing Christ are capable of achieving a Christian formation of the state, a Christian polity, and a Christian government.[39]

Jonathan Chaplin makes a pertinent observation:

> Kuyper's political thought begins not with *individuals* but *institutions*. This is in striking contrast to the individualistic liberalism that now dominates American—and much Canadian—political thinking. North Americans shaped by that individualism—and many North American *Christians* who have unwittingly succumbed to it—will need to work hard to make the paradigm shift Kuyper calls for.[40]

Conclusion

What is the role of the church in in politics? This question can be answered using Kuyper's distinction between the church as an organism and the church as an institute. The institution of the church, as a place of worship where the sacraments are performed, is not a vehicle for politics. However, the pastor's responsibility is to prepare the saints for deeds of service (Eph 4:12), which would include preparing them for political endeavours. As members of the organic church, as members of the body of Christ, the congregation would participate in politics as they would in any other activity that shapes society. Politics are as much an arena for Christian ministry as are church-related activities.

---

39. Kuyper, *Common Grace* 3, 173.

40. Jonathan Chaplin, "Kuyper and Politics," in *Calvinism for a Secular Age*, ed., Jessica R. Joustra and Robert J. Joustra (Downers Grove: IVP Academic, 2022), 67.

Four key theses from the basis of Kuyper's position (see table above)

- The state arises from common grace; the church from particular grace.
- Government is allowed to use force where necessary; the church arises from conviction.
- Government is national; but the church is international.
- Government is earthly, whereas the church is eternal.

These imply that the "government must not extend its authority over the church." Thus:

> Every infringement upon the freedom of the churches on the part of government is an abuse of authority; it is hubris and arrogance, a direct violation of what God himself has instituted as the very essence of the church.[41]

Government is a God-given institution, ordained because of sin. As Kuyper summarizes:

> society weakens itself by calling for and accepting the help of the state, and that, on the other hand, this too constantly manifests how the government has been ordained by God because of sin, that is, because of the sin of individuals as well as of society.[42]

For Kuyper political life was rooted in the home.[43] Kuyper's view of home and family are discussed in the next chapter.

---

41. Kuyper, *Common Grace* 3, 250.

42. Kuyper, *Pro Rege* 3, 135.

43. Abraham Kuyper, *On Charity & Justice* (The Abraham Kuyper Collected Works in Public Theology) (Bellingham, WA: Lexham Press, 2022), 267.

A summary in 12 theses

1. The state and government are temporary institutions that will cease to exist in a sinless world.

2. The church and state, both products of sin, have roles in combating sin.

3. The state should respect the autonomy of various spheres of life and not become all-encompassing.

4. The state wields coercive authority symbolized by the sword, emphasizing justice, war, and order.

5. Every government exhibits a religious character, and neutrality is deemed impossible.

6. A Kuyperian approach to government rejects extremes of popular sovereignty and state sovereignty, advocating for the sovereignty of God.

7. The church should be free from state interference and have the right to express its beliefs.

8. Christians have a duty to engage in politics and apply biblical principles to matters of the state.

9. Principles for governance are derived from Scripture, requiring careful study and application.

10. The Old Testament cannot serve as a direct model for contemporary government structures.

11. Permanent principles from Scripture must be distinguished from their historical applications.

12. Past practices, such as the death penalty, must be understood in principle rather than exact form.

Study Questions

1. Why did Kuyper leave church ministry and go into politics?
2. What are the key principles that Kuyper emphasizes in his approach to politics?
3. Should the church be involved in politics?
4. How does Kuyper avoid the extremes of individualism and collectivism?
5. In what ways could government "extend its authority over the church"? How should the church respond?
6. In what ways does Kuyper's perspective on the church-state relationship reflect his neo-Calvinistic beliefs?
7. What are Kuyper's views on the temporary nature of the state and government, and how does he envision their role in a sinless world?
8. How does Kuyper's perspective on the church's autonomy from state interference contribute to his overall political philosophy?
9. How does Kuyper's rejection of popular sovereignty and state sovereignty align with his emphasis on the sovereignty of God in political matters?

Further Reading

Primary sources

Kuyper, Abraham, "Calvinism and Politics," in *Lectures on Calvinism* (Grand Rapids, MI: Eerdmans, 1931), 41–77.

Kuyper, Abraham, "The Government," in *Pro Rege: The Kingship of Christ. Volume 3: The Kingship of Christ in Its Operations,* ed., John Kok with Nelson D. Kloosterman, Translated by Albert Gootjes. (Bellingham, WA: Lexham Press, 2019), 128–135.

Secondary Sources

Heslam, Peter, "Third Lecture: Calvinism and Politics," in *Creating a Christian Worldview: Abraham Kuyper's Lectures on Calvinism* (Grand Rapids, MI: Eerdmans, 1998), 142–166.

Chaplin, Jonathan, "Kuyper and Politics," in Joustra, Jessica R. and Joustra, Robert J. (ed.) *Calvinism for a Secular Age: A Twenty-First-Century Reading of Abraham Kuyper's Stone Lectures* (Downers Grove: IVP Academic, 2022), 64–91.

26

Family, Marrage, and Upbringing

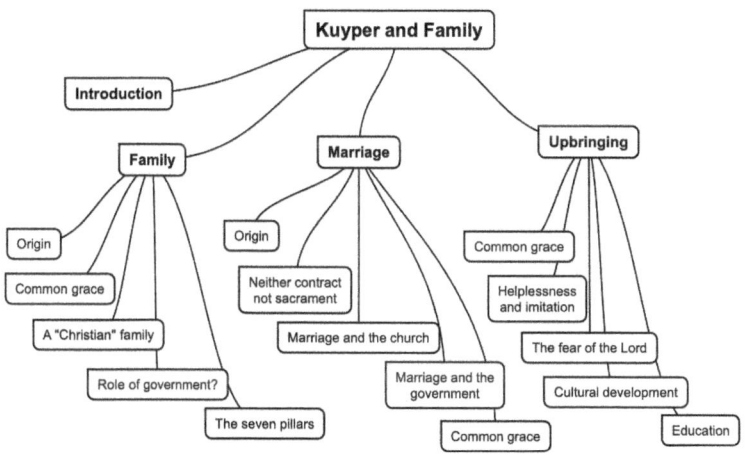

The family stems from creation. It was flawed as a result of sin and thus maintained and protected against sin by common grace.

Kuyper, *Common Grace* 3, 365.

In brief

THIS CHAPTER LOOKS AT Kuyper's perspectives on family, marriage, and upbringing, highlighting their foundational roles in society. Kuyper emphasizes that marriage is a divine institution ordained by God, distinct from mere legal arrangements. He stresses the importance of the family as a separate sphere from the government, rooted in creation and not subject to governmental control. Common grace helps mitigate the effects of sin on the family, while upbringing is seen as crucial for societal progress and development. Kuyper's view of the family reflects somewhat patriarchal norms of his time, but he also values the privacy and autonomy of the family sphere. Despite his busy schedule, Kuyper's family life is characterized by Christian values and close companionship, with a focus on joyful family gatherings and the family altar. These insights provide a comprehensive understanding of Kuyper's teachings on the significance of family, marriage, and upbringing in shaping individuals and society.

Introduction

As a family man, Kuyper knew the importance of the family: "the family takes precedence because every enrichment of personal life begins with the family and arises in part from the family," he wrote in *Pro Rege* Volume 2.[1] He regarded the family as so important that he devoted a section of volume 2 of *Pro Rege* to it. In section III, entitled Christ's Kingship and the Family, and in the practical section of *Common Grace* (Volume 3), Kuyper devotes eleven chapters to the family and four to upbringing.

---

1.   Kuyper, *Pro Rege: Living under Christ's Kingship*, 301.

In "The Family, Society, and the State,"[2] he says, "Our political, life is anchored in our homes" and maintains that "the household is the root from which the state rises." The family served as both the foundation for social order and the setting in which social order was learned. The "greatest relationships" originated in the home.[3]

In his address on sphere sovereignty, Kuyper mentioned the family as one of the spheres. It has a distinct domain. The state had no right to infringe on the family's privacy. For instance, the state should not legislate how a child should be disciplined, unless it is abuse rather than discipline.

Unfortunately, the biographies of Kuyper provide little material on Kuyper's family and his family life. Although, Vanden Berg notes:

> Kuyper's domestic life was a happy one. The spirit of Christ pervaded the home, Mrs. Kuyper was an understanding wife and devoted mother. With her husband, she trained their children well. She was a capable household manager, a warm-hearted, gracious hostess, a cultured lady who spoke the modern languages (especially English) fluently. She stood beside and with Kuyper as an inestimable blessing in his life and work. Five sons

---

2. These were originally a series of 15 articles in *De Standaard* in 1880. They were later published as *Antirevolutionair óók in uw huisgezin* [Antirevolutionary also in your household] and then included as a supplement to *Ons program*—the ARP's political manifesto. An English translation by Harry van Dyke appears in *On Charity and Justice*. Bellingham, WA: Lexham Press.

3. Abraham Kuyper, *On Charity & Justice*, 267.

and three daughters were born to the Kuypers. Of the sons, one died in 1892 at the age of nine years.

Except at luncheon and at dinner, Kuyper had few hours he could give to his family in close companionship. On festive occasions, however, he laid all else aside to spend the evening in the family circle. Dinner, especially, was the time of joyous family life, even when guests were present, as they frequently were. And in the Kuyper household, the family altar was still held in honor.

With his wife and children in the family living room, Kuyper was all life and joy. At luncheon and dinner, too. Whoever saw him at such times received the impression that he was a man not plagued by cares and difficulties. Seeing him so, one did not surmise what a tremendous load he was carrying. He bore that load not downstairs but up in his study.[4]

Vanden Berg's comment that Kuyper had "few hours he could give his family" is a sad reflection on the priority he placed on his own family, despite the high value he placed on family in his writings. It is also indicative that Kuyper lived in a different time than today—a time when the Victorian ideal that children were "seen and not heard" was commonplace. Nevertheless, despite the discontinuity between theory and practice in Kuyper, we can still appreciate his writings. Several themes shape Kuyper's view of the family and marriage: creation, common grace, and sphere sovereignty in particular.

---

4. Vanden Berg, *Abraham Kuyper*, 178–79.

Family

Origin

The origin of the family is distinct from the origin of the church and the state. For Kuyper, this is a major factor in what sets them apart. The family is rooted in the creation order, it arises out of a creation ordinance. The institutional church and the government do not. The family does not arise from common grace unlike the government and the state. However, as we shall see, common grace does have a crucial part.

This is an important point for the relationship between the family and the government. This means that family life is not subject to the government.

If the family does not result from common grace, then what is the relationship between the family and common grace?

Role of common grace

The newspapers provide ample evidence, Kuyper suggests, that sin has undermined the institution of the family and marriage. The sin of passion, for example, has wreaked havoc on the family. Compared with other institutions, it has perhaps been more severely weakened by sin. Sexually transmitted disease, rape, abuse, neglect, illegitimacy, desertion, divorce—"humans throw off their dignity and becoming like an animal"[5]—all these take their toll on the family.

It is only God's common grace that has safeguarded the family against the destruction of sin. Kuyper sees this as evident in several factors:

---

5. Cf. Kuyper, *Common Grace* 3, 344.

- the number of male and female births being "virtually identical";
- by allowing "enduring love" among couples;
- by strong maternal and paternal instincts;
- and by instilling love and respect in children for their parents.

It can also be seen in the fact that lawgivers usually take a stand in favor of marriage.[6] All these factors Kuyper attributed to the role of common grace in the family arena.

A "Christian" family

Kuyper writes for Christians, so an important question is what is meant by a Christian family? The term Christian family does not mean that good family life is only possible among Christians. As an example, he gives the Jewish family who "could give many a Christian family a good lesson in family virtue"[7] and "Jewish domestic life is often found in such an ideal form that it can put us to shame."[8] Likewise, among the peoples of Asia.

> The state of affairs cannot be otherwise, since family life spontaneously and quite naturally springs from the fundamental characterisations of human nature. Man did not conjure it up or invent it; God himself laid its foundation in creation.[9]

The family is therefore not a fruit of Christianity—although the Christian family may display it in its highest expression; it

---

6. Sadly, this is not always the case today.
7. Kuyper, *Common Grace* 3, 354.
8. Kuyper, *Common Grace* 3, 354.
9. Kuyper, *Common Grace* 3, 372.

is the result not of redemption but of creation. Its flourishing is due to common grace:

> We belong to a tribe of people that was richly endowed with common grace, and it is owing to common grace that the family would have continued to flourish among us even without the gospel.[10]

By a Christian family, Kuyper understands it "to refer to a family that exists and behaves in accordance with a higher understanding of family that has been introduced in Christian lands, became indigenous, and still has validity through custom and law."[11] It encompasses the three foundational moral relationships: between husband and wife; between parents and children; and between siblings.

Kuyper provides two characteristics of the Christian family. It can be Christian to the extent that the Christian ethic works out the fundamental traits of family; and second, it has become a miniature expression of the church.

> The family can be a "house church" only when the head of the household confesses Christ as Lord and King, and maintains the service of Christ in his family. And precisely this illustrates how the twofold notion of the Christian family differs according to the distinction between common grace and particular grace.[12]

Although the family belongs to the realm of common grace, a Christian family is in the realm of particular grace.

---

10. Kuyper, *Common Grace* 3, 356.

11. Kuyper, *Common Grace* 3, 3642

12. Kuyper, *Common Grace* 3, 363.

Generally, does Christianity lead to a higher understanding of the relationship between members of the family? History and experience seem to Kuyper suggest that it does.

However, family life is still entirely a creation ordinance; redemption is not a factor at all. It is sin alone that has threatened to corrupt the moral relationships of family life. Conversion and sanctification can provide greater insight and clearer light. "But" he stresses, "this truth does not decide the matter," as sadly some Christians "do not take the raising of their children seriously."[13]

A Christian family is not only about good relationships between the husband and wife and children, but also the head of the family is also a Christian and is responsible for the "place of religion in his house."[14] From 1 Cor 11:3, Kuyper maintains that the head of the house is the husband. However, it may fall to the wife if the husband is absent or has left the family, by desertion or death, for example.

For a family to have the adjective "Christian" it means that it should be constituted and ordered as God requires it to be. As Kuyper puts it:

> For a family to be Christian, three things must be present in it through the Spirit of Christ and the result of his work. The first is the restoration of what sin and misery have corrupted. The second is the elevation of original family life to its ideal. And thirdly, in order that this blessing might not be passing but fix its roots in the family and seek to be nourished there, the family

---

13. Kuyper, *Common Grace* 3, 361.
14. Kuyper, *Common Grace* 3, 370.

must sanctify its communion by establishing a family altar before which the entire family (that is, parents, children, and servants) kneel so as to give to God the honor and worship he is due for what he in his grace has given the family and to ask him to bless its life. Only in this way can Christ exercise his dominion as our King over the family as well.[15]

Family and the role of government

As mentioned above, family life is not subject to the government. Not least because the family is rooted in the creation and government—according to Kuyper—is a post-fall institution. They are distinct spheres. This means that the form and the design of the family are not subject to the whim or insights of a government. The government "can and must do nothing except codify, recognize and take into account the independent rights of the family."[16] This also means that the head of every family "has the right and duty to resist the government when and where the government misperceives or threatens this independent character of the family."[17] These are important points and are consistent with Kuyper's sphere sovereignty. It also means that if the family is negligent in the discharge of its duty, then the government has a legitimate right to intervene.[18]

Government issues entirely from common grace, the family does not. Sin weakened and ultimately destroyed the patriarchal family structures; it was established and is maintained by

15. Kuyper, *Pro Rege* 2, 317.

16. Kuyper, *Common Grace* 3, 341.

17. Kuyper, *Common Grace* 3, 341.

18 Kuyper, *Common Grace* 3, 341.

shared grace. The government is "not merely an extension of paternal government."[19]

Seven pillars of the family

Kuyper identifies seven pillars on which the "entire edification of the family rests."[20] These provide a good summary of Kuyper's view of the family; he notes that these are foundations laid by God in creation:

- first, by splitting humanity into two genders;
- second, by ordaining that humans reproduce other humans;
- third, by ordaining the utter helplessness of the infant;
- fourth, by ordaining the necessity of having a human "home";
- fifth, by permitting the difficulty of acquiring our "dailybread";
- sixth, by the human need to join together for reasons of safety and legal certainty; and,
- seventh, by the natural love for one another that he created in man and wife, parents and children, brothers, and sisters.[21]

Marriage

Marriage is not a human invention but instituted by God. It is he who created us in two genders, who made the man different from the woman and the woman different from the man, and who ordained that the child would come from the union of man and woman.[22]

---

19. Kuyper, *Common Grace* 3, 365.
20. Kuyper, *Common Grace* 3, 355.
21. Kuyper, *Common Grace* 3, 355–356.
22. Kuyper, *Common Grace* 3, 404–405

"The family derives from marriage,"[23] observes Kuyper. In his writings on marriage Kuyper examines several facets. These include the following: the origin of marriage; the nature of marriage; the relationship of marriage to the church and to the state and to government; and he maintains that it is neither a sacrament nor a contact. I shall discuss these in the following.

The origins of marriage: common grace
Christian marriage may imply that marriage is seen from an ecclesiastical perspective and thus stems from particular grace. Kuyper would beg to differ. According to him, marriage belongs to common grace because it is a natural element of life. Marriage is a regular occurrence among people of all faiths; thus, it must fall within the category of common grace. Marriage was instituted before the fall. God created one man and one woman and designated them for one another.

A "better understanding of the origin and history of marriage"[24] is necessary, according to Kuyper. He identifies two conflicting perspectives regarding the family's origin. In the Christian view human society began perfect but was deformed by the fall yet preserved by common grace. The opposing viewpoint holds that humans evolved through evolution, rising from animal status to a higher status and transitioning from polyandry to monogamy. In this view, Christian marriage is not seen as the highest form of marriage.

A Christian marriage is not something that belongs to particular grace and, therefore, to church life in the narrow sense. God instituted marriage before Adam's fall. God created one

---

23. Kuyper, *Common Grace* 3, 378.
24. Kuyper, Common Grace 3, Ch46.

man and one woman and designated them for one another. Woman was created from man—"bone of my bone, flesh of my flesh." The marriage ideal is summarized in the phrase: "Leave, cleave and become one flesh." Marriage would have existed even if sin had not come. Consequently, we cannot state that Christian marriage is the only genuine and true marriage, and that marriage only arose from the Christian religion. It does not belong to the domain of the church argues Kuyper.

Neither a contract nor a sacrament

Both the assumption that marriage is a contract and the belief that it is a sacrament are objected to by Kuyper. The notion that marriage is a sacrament he thinks it is only a partial truth. If it were a sacrament, it would "conceptualize marriage as being a work of particular grace."[25] As he sees marriage as part of the creation order and thus not arising from particular grace, thus, it cannot be a sacrament. For the Reformers a sacrament relates directly to the atonement in the blood of Christ and, therefore, is needed of all believers. As marriage is for all, but not all get married, it cannot, therefore, be a sacrament.

He also disagrees with the idea of marriage as a contract, as this can easily descend into "free love" thinking. As "...the marriage relationship is a shadow and expression of the relationship between Christ and his church," it is thus not merely a social bond established by human will. It is more profound "a divine union, a divine resolving of two into one ...."[26]

---

25. Kuyper, *Common Grace* 3, 342.
26. Kuyper, *Common Grace* 3, 413.

Marriage, the church, and government

Christian marriage has a general and specific term. In general terms, it complies with the laws and customs of "Christian Europe." As regards specific terms it exists only for devout Christians, and only then if they live according to God's laws and norms.

As marriage derives from creation, it touches on the church. For Christians in particular marriage is planned and then solemnized in the institutional church. Preparations end in solemnisation. Only after that does the marriage begin to function.

Unfortunately, Kuyper thinks that the church has not done justice to marriage. The marriage ceremony should be more than invoking the prayer of the congregation. The marriage service has too often become detached from the Sunday service and has become a weekday event with only family and friends and not the church congregation in attendance. It has become a "private ceremony" that remained connected with the church only to the extent that it took place in the church building and was conducted by the church's administration, often with a collection for the poor of the church.

In the Old Testament Kuyper writes, "there was no trace of an official part of government in establishing marriage, which was left entirely to the family." This need not necessarily be the case today. However, the government cannot bring forth something that existed before it! Government is the result of common grace; marriage is from creation. The government cannot establish marriage as such.

Kuyper does see a limited role for the government in marriage which is in keeping with sphere sovereignty. However, this has meant that marriage becomes reduced to "an official contract and all that remains is the association between two members of the civil community." Government increasingly views church life as a private matter. "… it no longer acknowledges that marriage is a matter to be established in the name of God." Therefore, that in the eyes of many marriage is only thought of in terms of "the actions of the official at the county clerk's office." The role of the family and the church have been squeezed out, "marriage becomes a private arrangement." Marriage means far more to Kuyper than this.

Upbringing

Kuyper spends several chapters in his *Common Grace* volume 3 discussing the upbringing of children. This indicates the importance he places on it and its important function for the family. He prefers the term "upbringing" to training as he points out that we train horses and dogs but not children. We do not "train" children as we do dogs! "We are brought up to be children but educated (or trained) to be a gardener, engineer, lawyer …."[27] Upbringing is "to transmit from the present generation to the next the capital of human development that already has been gained," thus, the role of upbringing is clearly part of the family. It is a duty of all parents. Upbringing, Kuyper maintains, is part of civil life and thus "falls under common grace." However, the raising of children in the fear of the Lord goes beyond common grace. Upbringing is a task imposed on parents by God and they are responsible to God for it.

The role of common grace in upbringing can be seen in God's provision of food, clothing, and parental instinct. Chil-

---

27. Kuyper, *Common Grace* 3, 460.

dren are born helpless and have physical and spiritual needs—these are to be met in the family.

Upbringing is also part of cultural development. It is a uniquely human activity. "A child who grows up without any human contact cannot build a house, weave a tapestry, or forge iron."[28] The innate ability of animals is instinctual rather than the result of upbringing. Humans are not stagnant! Compare the construction of a swallow's nest or the bees' honeycomb with human dwellings. In the animal world there is stagnation—which brings repetition of what was. In humanity in general there is not stagnation: "rather there is always change and alteration. Taken as a whole, there is development, a moving forward, a progression."[29] This is the fruit of upbringing, and without common grace "there would have been no civilization, no development, no progress."[30]

As part of upbringing, Kuyper includes education. Kuyper discusses the school in the broadest sense. It includes what today we call apprenticeships. Naturally, the school question—as we saw in chapter 24—looms large in Kuyper's mind. He stresses that it is important that the parents are able to choose a school that is in line with their own worldview, their approach to life.[31] Parents thus have a duty and a right to entrust their child only to a school that continues on the foundation laid at home.

---

28. Kuyper, *Common Grace* 3, 448.

29. Kuyper, *Common Grace* 3, 448.

30. Kuyper, *Common Grace* 3, 450.

31. Kuyper, *Common Grace* 3, 458.

Upbringing involves intentionality; therefore, it is important that parents and teachers in the context of a child's schooling "see themselves as instruments in the service of God and fulfill their holy task."[32]

Conclusion

While having its roots in creation, the fall has affected the family, and it is in need of redemption. Common grace helps the family lessen the effects of sin.

Kuyper was unavoidably a product of his time. His view of the family is rather patriarchal and assumes separate responsibilities for the husband and wife, with the wife as a homemaker and the husband as the breadwinner. Such a strategy can seem out of date given the social changes that have occurred since Kuyper wrote, especially in cases where both parents may be forced to work for financial reasons to pay the rent or mortgage on a family home.

Although Kuyper stresses the origin of the family with creation, he attributes the hierarchical nature of the family to the fall. There is no basis for a family hierarchy pre-fall. Both family and marriage are grounded in creation and are preserved by common grace. These two factors distinguish the family from the institutions of the church and the government. It implies that neither the church nor the government should meddle in family affairs—doing so oversteps the role of the church, government, and family and would be a violation of Kuyper's sphere sovereignty. In the family, common grace plays a crucial role in maintaining and fostering well-being.

The family has a significant role in cultural development because it is a child's primary way of upbringing. The task of

---

32. Kuyper, *Common Grace* 3,450.

passing down the capital of human growth from one generation to the next, which is implicit in rearing, primarily falls on
the parents and, by extension, the family.

A summary in 12 theses

1. Marriage is a divine institution ordained by God,
   not a human invention.
2. The church plays a significant role in solemnizing
   marriages for Christians.
3. The government has a limited role in marriage due to
   sphere sovereignty.
4. Family life is rooted in creation and not subject to
   government interference.
5. The family is a distinct sphere separate from the
   government.
6. Common grace helps mitigate the effects of sin on
   the family.
7. Upbringing, including education, is crucial for societal
   progress and development.
8. The family structure has been affected by sin and
   requires redemption.
9. Kuyper's view of the family is somewhat patriarchal,
   reflecting the norms of his time.
10. The state should respect the privacy and autonomy of
    the family sphere.
11. Kuyper's family life was characterized by Christian
    values and close companionship.
12. Kuyper emphasizes the importance of the family altar
    and joyful family gatherings.

Study Questions

1. How would you define a Christian family?
2. Kuyper maintained that the structure of the state relies on five relationships. What are those five relationships?
3. How does Kuyper view the origin and signficance of the family compared with other societal institutions?
4. Would you agree with Kuyper's patriarchal view of the family? Why?
5. What did Kuyper mean when he wrote "Our political, life is rooted in our homes"? Do you agree?
6. "It simply cannot be argued at all that the Christian ideal of family life has been only realized among the converted." What do you think Kuyper means by this?
7. Why did Kuyper think that the family, not the individual, is the basis for social order?
8. How does Kuyper address the impact of sin on the institution of the family and the role of common grace in preserving it?
9. Why was Kuyper in favor of household voting rather than individual voting?
10. In *Our Program*, Kuyper poses the following questions: Does the responsibility for good order in the family rest with the head of the family or with the head of the state? Does your calling as a father to keep order in your family extend only to the things that the state leaves unordered? Or, inversely, does government have a right to intervene in your family only if you scandalously neglect your calling with respect to your family? In the matter of ruling your household, do you

complement the state, or does the state complement you?

(a) How would Kuyper answer them? And (b) how would
you answer them?

Further Reading

Primary sources

Kuyper, Abraham. *Common Grace* Volume 3 (Bellingham,
WA: Lexham Press, 2020), Chapters 41–56.

Kuyper, Abraham "The Family, Society, and the State," in On
Charity and Justice (Bellingham, WA: Lexham Press, 2022).

Secondary sources

Bavinck, Herman. *The Christian Family* (Translated by Nelson
Kloosterman) (Grand Rapids: Christian's Library Press,
2012).

Hebden Taylor, E. L. *The Reformational Understanding of
Marriage* (Nutley, NJ: Craig Press, 1970).

Olthius, James. *Keeping our Troth.* Staying in Love through
the Five Stages of Marriage (San Francisco: Harper, 1986)

Olthius, James. *I Pledge You My Troth: A Christian View of
Marriage, Family, Friendship* (San Francisco: Harper, 1989)

Storkey, Alan. *Marriage and Its Modern Crisis* (London:
Hodder & Stoughton, 1996)

Van Leeuwen, Mary Stewart "Abraham Kuyper and the Cult
of True Womanhood: An Analysis of De Eerepositie der
Vrouw" in *On Kuyper: A Collection of Readings on the Life,
Work & Legacy of Abraham Kuyper* ed., Steve Bishop and
John Kok (Sioux Center: Dordt Press, 2013), 423–442.

27

Kuyper and Art[1]

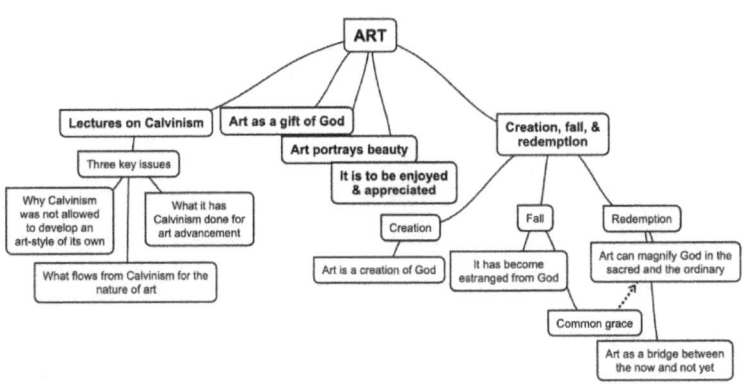

In brief

THIS CHAPTER EXAMINES THE relationship between neo-Calvinism and art, challenging the perception that Calvinists devalue artistic expression. It highlights Kuyper's defense of art against common misconceptions and his promotion of a "Calvinistic aesthetics." Kuyper emphasizes the importance of art as a gift from God, accessible to all, and a bridge between the present and future kingdom. His writings show the value of beauty and cre-

---

1. Some of this draws upon my "Abraham Kuyper's Nascent Views on Art," *Journal for Christian Scholarship*, 55 (3) (2019): 107–29.

ativity, advocating for a holistic view of life that includes the enjoyment and appreciation of art. Kuyper's legacy continues to inspire discussions on the intersection of religion and artistic expression.

Introduction

The cultural stereotype of Calvinists as boring, dull, killjoys may have gone some way to explain why some have suggested that Calvinists devalued art.[2] It may seem surprising that Kuyper discussed art in his *Lectures on Calvinism*. He was no artist, nor do we have any record of him collecting art. It might have at the time appeared to be a strange choice of topic. The notion that the arts appeared to be denigrated by Calvinism was one of the reasons that Kuyper had to defend art against this commonly held view.

In many cases art is considered as a flourish to Christianity; or to borrow a phrase from Kuyper, art is frequently viewed as looking at the lace on a garment. This was not Kuyper's interpretation of art. Instead of seeing art as a supplement to Christianity, he sees religion as having a fundamental function in it. Kuyper's goal was, according to Peter Heslam, to foster the formation of a consciously and unapologetically "Calvinistic aesthetics."[3]

Kuyper wrote about art in several places, but most extensively in *Pro Rege*. Chapter 5 of *Lectures in Calvinism, Wisdom and Wonder* and his rectorial address to the VU in 1888 enti-

---

2. The Protestant Reformers who opposed to the veneration of religious icons and images in churches during the Reformation. Iconoclasm was a movement that sought to remove or destroy religious artwork and symbols in churches. This may well be another reason for the perception of Calvinists as being indifferent to art.

3. Peter Heslam, *Creating a Christian Worldview: Abraham Kuyper's Lectures on Calvinism* (Grand Rapids, MI: Eerdmans, 1998), 213.

tled "Calvinism and art" *Het Calvinisme en de Kunst*, are the other main places that Kuyper discusses art. I will begin by looking at lecture five of his Stone Lectures.

Lectures on Calvinism

Kuyper begins by saying that art is one of God's richest gifts,[4] it is beautiful and sublime and that an artistic instinct is a universal phenomenon. So, why then did Calvinists seemingly have a poor regard for the arts? He thus begins the lecture as an apologist for Calvin and Calvinists and their attitude to the arts. He defends Calvinism on three fronts by examining:

1. Why Calvinism was not allowed to develop an art-style of its own
2. What flows from its principle for the nature of art; and
3. What it has actually done for its advancement.[5]

Why did Calvinism not develop an art style? Kuyper draws on G. W. F. Hegel and Eduard Von Hartmann (1842–1906) in particular. They argued that higher forms of religion were able to develop independently of art, as art was unable to express the essence of religion. Kuyper had argued that the highest form of religion was Calvinism. Such an approach was supported by Kuyper's sphere sovereignty: religion and art should be free from interference from each other.

Calvinism thus had advanced the arts, not by building cathedrals, palaces, or amphitheatres; but rather it released art

---

4. This is also the title of a book on Christianity and art by John Wilson, *One of the Richest Gifts* (Edinburgh: Handsel Press, 1981). Wilson wrote from a Kuyperian perspective.
5. Kuyper, *Lectures on Calvinism*, 145.

from religion's custody. Previously, art and music could only flourish as far as it could serve the church.

> Protestantism in general, but Calvinism more consistently, bridled the tutelage of the church, so also was music emancipated by it, and the way opened up to its so splendid modern development.[6]

With common grace it meant that the arts were not limited to the regenerate. Kuyper shows that art is a creation of God and not of Satan.

> If the Sovereignty of God is and remains, for Calvinism, its unchangeable point of departure, then art cannot originate from the Evil One; for Satan is destitute of every creative power. All he can do is to abuse the good gifts of God.[7]

This concept alone should be enough to show the importance of the arts for Christians. The arts also have a significant role: "Art reveals ordinances of creation which neither science, nor politics, nor religious life, nor even revelation can bring to light."[8]

Pro Rege

Series VII in volume three of *Pro Rege* deals with "The kingship of Christ and art." Here, Kuyper looks at art in its "entirety." He stresses that art is not merely a human fabrication but is a "function of the human mind that God himself placed in our lives." It "cannot be anything but a gift of God." In *The Work of the Holy Spirit*—echoing a theme in

---

6. Kuyper, *Lectures on Calvinism*, 168.

7. Kuyper, *Lectures on Calvinism*, 155.

8. Kuyper, *Lectures on Calvinism*, 163.

his Stone lectures—he states emphatically: "Art is not man's [sic] invention, but God's creation."[9]

In this final section of the three-volume *Pro Rege* he develops the notion that: Art is a gift of God that shows itself in an ability, which portrays beauty and is to be enjoyed by all.[10]

Below I will examine this in more detail this view.

Art is a gift of God that shows itself in an ability, which portrays beauty and is to be enjoyed by all

Kuyper begins by discussing art in terms of the fine arts—these include painting, sculpture, poetry, music and (to a lesser degree) architecture. Where architecture and, to some extent, music are concerned, they have an ideal but also a practical goal—a place to live or worship, for example.

He is concerned, however, that that there is no separation between the high ideal and primarily practical, and there should be no condescension. Both may reveal God's power and majesty.

Art is a gift

He stresses that art is a gift, however, it is one that can be "wasted, abused, and spoiled."[11]

It is egalitarian in that it is distributed among all different social classes and statuses. It is being able to do something God equips you to do. It is a talent in that sense, but that does not

---

9.   Abraham Kuyper, *The Work of the Holy Spirit* (Chattanooga, TN: AMG Publishers, 2001), 40.

10.   This is not a direct quote from Kuyper, but a summary of his view.

11.   Kuyper, *Pro Rege* 3, 384.

mean it requires no practice, as he puts it "Practice presupposes the presence of talent."[12]

It is a gift of God

Art exists only because of the grace of God, not because humans conceived or invented it.

For Kuyper, God is the Master Designer and Builder (Heb 11:10). Humans are created in the image of God—if God is the Master Artist then it follows we have an "inclination for art and the gift to enjoy it"[13]

However, there is a distance between what God and people can do, but between the divine and the derived art, they have a common root.

All human art is only an echo, imitation, and reflection of the divine art that expresses itself in all creation.[14]

As it is a gift of God it means that artists should not, then, seek their own glory: "Art is ... unthinkable without the ordination of God."[15]

---

12. Kuyper, *Pro Rege* 3, 384. Lambert Zuidervaart, in his discussion of Hans Rookmaaker (1922–1977), Calvin Seerveld (b. 1930), and Nicholas Wolterstorf (b. 1932), all of which were influenced by Kuyper, observes that: "All three scholars share an anti-elitism that resists both the deification of artistic genius and the denegration of daily life." Lambert Zuidervaart, "A Tradition Transfigured: Art And Culture In Reformation Aesthetics," *Faith and Philosophy: Journal of the Society of Christian Philosophers* 21, no. 3 (2004): 387. This anti-elitism was true also of Kuyper.

13. Kuyper, *Pro Rege* 3, 338.

14. Kuyper, *Pro Rege* 3, 388–389.

15. Kuyper, *Pro Rege* 3, 388.

It is an indispensable part of a full and rich life. It is not that art had a demonic character as some Christians suppose. We do need, however, to distinguish between the legitimate and sinful use of art. Many still adopt a negative attitude towards art because they confuse the sinful misuse of art with true art. Art exists only by the grace of God and by virtue of his ordinances. Art is not something subsidiary, which we could do without. Life would be impoverished without this gift.

It is an ability
He offers a note of caution, "people err when they start from the notion of beauty. The point of departure must rather be sought in the much more general notion of ability ... . All art is an ability, a capacity, to do something that someone else cannot."[16]

This ability is God given: "Anyone who is not born a Rembrandt or Bach will never become one."[17] The goal of artistic ability is to glorify a God and to magnify his name. To do that it portrays beauty.

It portrays beauty
Kuyper notes that beauty has become a word used less and less. Nice, charming, lovely, and attractive are used in place of beauty. Whereas the Scriptures tend to use beauty and glorious. Beauty tends to be used for "the most excellent here on earth" and glorious for the things of God and the new heaven and new earth.

---

16. Kuyper, *Pro Rege* 3, 393.
17. Kuyper, *Pro Rege* 3, 393–394.

As we are created in God's image, we have the capacity to delight in the beauty of the divine. Art finds its purpose in giving delight in the beautiful; this characterizes its higher origin.

Beauty is elusive. Harmony, rhythm, symmetry, proportion, unity in multiplicity, liveliness and vibrancy all play a part. It must also engage our interest, it will captivate us, a work of art must give the impression of completion of being finished, "it must not leave a void." These are important, but do not define beauty. The human dimension is also a factor in the perception of beauty. The desire for beauty comes from what God has created in us.

Without the entrance of sin into creation, he identifies three things:

> (1) The beauty of paradise would have shone in unbroken radiance, albeit as a beauty of a lower order. (2) In paradise the human race would have had the capacity to enjoy the beauty of paradise, albeit while thirsting for a greater beauty. And (3) this perfection of beauty would not have been in paradise, but with God, and the human race would have passed into that world of perfect beauty without first dying.[18]

Beauty is not static—as the human race develops there is a greater and greater thirst for beauty for higher enjoyment.

He distances himself from Plato's flawed view of beauty, which led to a "distaste for earthly beauty and an aversion to art." Sadly, this platonic view crept into the church. So that a similar aversion to art was seen in the Puritans. However, not for the same reasons, they emphasized the written over the pic-

---

18. Kuyper, *Pro Rege* 3, 418.

torial. As the Puritan Daniel Featley (1578–1645), in his "An Advertisement to the Christian Reader" wrote:

> Why delve they continually in humane arts and secular sciences, full of dregs and drosse? Why do they not rather dig into the mines of the gold of Ophyr [Scripture] where every line is a vein of truth, every page leafe gold?

Beauty was not unaffected by the fall—we shall examine this in more detail later.

It is to be enjoyed.

We can enjoy art; indeed, we are created to do so. God too enjoys and delights in his creation.

> It is important for a proper view on art to note how Scripture depicts God delighting.[19]

There is a playfulness in beauty that is to be enjoyed. Kuyper was no killjoy Calvinist!

All are able to appreciate it

Art is not the provenance of the wealthy—it is and should be open to all irrespective of position, status, and rank. Kuyper had an egalitarian view of art. This follows from art being a gift of God:

> … this gift shows itself to be bound neither to social position nor to rank, it would be merciless to make the enjoyment of art accessible only to those who came from the upper levels of society.[20]

---

19. Kuyper, *Pro Rege* 3, 409.
20. Kuyper, *Pro Rege* 3, 388.

It is part of a full and rich life: "Human life would ... shrink and be impoverished, if art were cut off from it."[21]

Kuyper has a full-orbed view and art; it is a creation of God and so should be a legitimate area for Christians to work in and enjoy. Although it is a creation that does not mean it has not been affected by the fall. It is to creation, fall, and redemption I now turn.

Art with respect to creation, fall, and redemption

> Scripture offers us an even more profound account. It tells us of a paradise that once radiated in all its beauty but then was lost, and of a curse that came over humankind and nature through and because of sin.[22]

Creation

As Kuyper has reiterated, art is a creation of God. Even without the fall there would have been art:

> There would have been art if the human race had stood firm in the face of Satan's first temptation.[23]

Art is a creation; this reveals the importance art should have in a fully developed Christian worldview. It is important to see though that it has been tainted in some ways by the fall.

Fall

> All art worthy of that name comes from God. It is a gift of God not only for the artist, but in the artist also for

---

21. Kuyper, *Pro Rege* 3, 386–387.

22. Kuyper, *Pro Rege* 3, 420.

23. Kuyper, *Pro Rege* 3, 433.

our entire generation. But praising the Lord's name in art is—even more now than in the past—entirely alien to most. The art world shuts itself up within itself, and therefore becomes estranged from God. Yet even this may never tempt us to reject art as such. As a phenoenon in human life it remains a gift of God's grace—just like we do not appreciate the nightingale's song because the nightingale is singing to God, but because whoever knows God also knows that he alone gave the nightingale its wonderful song.[24]

Beauty and art have been affected by the fall. Art became estranged from God, "it became detached from the support that piety could offer, it then became at "even greater risk of being poisoned by sin." This may happen in several possible ways:

An idolising of art—it becomes the object of veneration.

A fuelling of an artist's pride—the artist may be tempted to self-glorification and seek to gratify the audience rather than glorify God.

It becomes independent with respect to morality and the sacred—it attempts to free itself from the laws and ordinances of God.

The result is that art becomes "vulgar and depraved" in search of greater material profit. Thus,

For that reason, art can lend itself equally well to the satanic and demonic as it does to the lofty, divine, and sacred.[25]

---

24. Kuyper, *Pro Rege* 3, 423.
25. Kuyper, *Pro Rege* 3, 430.

Redemption

Kuyper goes on to: "investigate whether art itself and as such lies within the dominion of the king of God's kingdom—that is, whether there is something in the origin of art that is directly related to Christ, and whether its historical course is, therefore, governed by him or not."[26] For Christians, and especially Christian artists, this is a crucial question.

To answer this question Kuyper seeks to look at what art would have been without sin and to see how it has developed in the sinful world. As he rightly asserts:

> If Christ's kingship is all-encompassing, then that obviously must include the field of art; the aberrations in that field notwithstanding.[27]

He sees the role of Christ, not as some add-on to art, including him to give him glory, but rather as an integral part. Christ existed before eternity, before beauty he was. It is through him that beauty can be revealed. To deal with art apart from a Christ is to "tear the tree from its roots." His view of art is Christological, thus:

> For this reason every Christian is all the more duty bound, wherever the heathen world has robbed beauty for itself and its idols, to restore Christ through quiet worship to the honor he deserves, above all for the world of art and beauty.[28]

He places much store by the fact that, at least as far as Kuyper is concerned, that it was in Christian countries, or at least those touched by the gospel, that

---

26. Kuyper, *Pro Rege* 3, 443.

27. Kuyper, *Pro Rege* 3, 441.

28. Kuyper, *Pro Rege* 3, 439.

music [and other art forms] first reached its acme,
and why it never reached under paganism or Islam
the enormous heights encountered in Christian
countries.[29]

This does not mean, however, that beauty and art cannot be
opened up by unbelievers. Unfortunately, this point is left un-
derdeveloped in Kuyper.

Finally, Kuyper identifies three spheres for art: the sacred,
normal human life, and that of evil and unclean. According to
Kuyper, beauty can be found in the first two spheres. Art can
magnify God in both the sacred and in ordinary human life.

Kuyper in his *Lectures* sums up the creation, fall, and redemption aspects of art:

> But if you confess that the world once was beautiful, but
> by the curse has become undone, and by a final catastro-
> phe is to pass to its full state of glory, excelling even the
> beautiful of paradise, then art has the mystical task of
> reminding us in its productions of the beautiful that was
> lost and of anticipating its perfect coming luster.[30]

Common grace was an important theme for Kuyper. Therefore, it is not surprising that his articles on common grace in
De Heraut included chapters in art. It is to these I will briefly
examine in the next section.

Wisdom and Wonder

Wisdom and Wonder was first published in Dutch in 1905 as a
supplement to *De gemeene gratie*. These chapters had been acci-

---

29. Kuyper, *Pro Rege* 3, 447.

30. Kuyper, *Lectures on Calvinism*, 155.

dentally left out by the publisher of the three volumes that comprised Kuyper's newspaper series on common grace from *De Heraut* and so were published separately. In it, Kuyper develops his ideas of science and art.

Inevitably, there are echoes of what has been discussed in his *Lectures* and in *Pro Rege*. What is additional is a fuller unfolding of his view of art and the *eschaton*. Art is seen as a bridge between the now and the not yet of the kingdom. It foreshadows the new Jerusalem and provides "prophetic glimmerings." Art provides a form of homesickness for beauty.

The book is in two parts: Part 1 on science and Part 2 on art. The original title of the book was *De gemeene gratie in wetenschap en kunst* [Common grace in science and art}. The difference with which science and art are treated is marked. In the science chapters there is much emphasis on two kinds of knowledge, two kinds of people—the antithesis; but this is largely missing from the section on art.

The emphasis on the consummated kingdom in the discussion on art is another important emphasis of Kuyper. Beauty has been affected by the fall, but common grace has preserved us from a complete loss of beauty. In the kingdom of glory there will be a higher degree of beauty; it will be restored and more. Art foreshadows and provides us with prophetic glimmerings of the New Jerusalem. It provides a form of bridge between the now and the not yet of the kingdom.

In particular, the book is about the role of common grace. It has a number of important aspects that Kuyper in *Wisdom & Wonder* elucidates. In particular in relation to art, it preserves us from a complete loss of beauty, and it assures the independence of art.

Evaluation

When Kuyper discusses the physical sciences there is an emphasis on both common grace and the antithesis and on two kinds of people, two kinds of knowledge. In his writings on art, common grace is to the fore, but the antithesis is largely missing. He sees to almost fall into a dualistic split of sacred and non-sacred art. Although he does show how art is tainted by the fall, he does not fully develop the difference between Christian and non-Christian art.

Beauty has been affected by the fall, but common grace has preserved us from a complete loss of beauty. In the kingdom of glory there will be a higher degree of beauty, which will be restored and more. Art foreshadows and provides us with prophetic glimmerings of the New Jerusalem. It provides a form of bridge between the now and the not yet of the kingdom. Perhaps Kuyper is placing too much on the artists, is this a task artists can fulfil? And what about non-Christian artists are they able to do this? I wonder if beauty is being asked too much by Kuyper—it carries more than it can bear.

This is echoed by Begbie:

First, few will deny that some kind of beauty is a desirable feature in a piece of art, and it may indeed be possible to give this conviction strong theological backing. But I am less than convinced that the presence of, or aspiration towards beauty is a necessary condition for something to qualify as "art," and even less convinced that the arts are to be distinguished from other cultural activities and products by their investment in beauty. Can we really do justice to the sheer range and variety of the arts in this way? If we allow discussions to be magnetized too quickly around questions of beauty, have we not foreclosed too much too early?[31]

In his 1998 dissertation on Kuyper's *Lectures on Calvinism* Heslam states Kuyper's ideas on art have been virtually neglected.[32] The intervening years have seen little to improve that situation. Heslam[33] and Henderson[34] are the only noticeable exceptions. This is despite the renewed interest in Christianity and art.[35]

---

31. J. Begbie, *Voicing Creation's Praise: Towards a Theology of the Arts* (Edinburgh: T&T Clark, 1991).

32. Heslam, *Creating a Christian Worldview: Abraham Kuyper's Lectures on Calvinism.*

33. Peter S. Heslam, "A Theology of the Arts: Kuyper's Ideas on Art and Religion," in Steve Bishop and John Kok (ed.) *On Kuyper: A Collection of Readings on the Life, Work & Legacy of Abraham Kuyper.* Sioux Center: Dordt Press, 2013, 351–364.

34. R. Henderson, "Rumors of Glory: Abraham Kuyper's Neo-Calvinist Theory of Art," *Pro Rege* 45, no. 4 (2017): 1–9.

35. See, for example, P. J. Ryken, *Art for God's Sake, A Call to Recover the Arts* (Phillipsburg: Presbyterian and Reformed, 2006); J. A. Anderson and W. A. Dryness, *Modern Art and the Life of a Culture: The Religious Impulses of Modernism* (Downers Grove: InterVarsity Press, 2016); H. Brand and A. Chaplin, *Art & Soul: Signposts for Christians in the Arts*, 2nd edn (Carlisle: Piquant, 2001); D. A. Siedell, *God in the Gallery: A Christian Embrace of Modern Art* (Baker Academic, 2008); D. A. Siedell, *Who's Afraid of Modern Art?: Essays on Modern Art and Theology in Conversation* (Eugene OR: Cascade, 2015); D. Thistlewaite, *The Art of God and the Religions of Art* (Carlisle: Solway/Paternoster, 1998); Nicholas Wolterstorff, *Art Rethought: The Social Practices of Art* (Cambridge: Cambridge University Press, 2015); Lambert Zuidervaart, *Artistic Truth: Aesthetics, Discourse, and Imaginative Disclosure*

Research has been forthcoming on Calvinism and art—
Hardman Moore shows that although to some extent Calvin
was an iconoclast it was done in a way that emphasizes the
written over the visual, the written Scriptures over depictions
of biblical scenes.[36] Joby as also reassessed Calvin's view of the
arts; he observes:

> Although many believe John Calvin had a negative
> attitude towards the arts, particularly visual art,
> my contention is that we find within his writings
> and the development of the Reformed tradition a
> more positive attitude to the arts than has hitherto
> been recognized.[37]

And suggests that Calvin's

> epistemology, eschatology, understanding of music
> and ontology of church all provide us with the oppor-
> tunity to argue more strongly in favour of visual art.[38]

Kuyper's linking of art and beauty has also come under criticism,
particularly by Calvin Seerveld. Seerveld maintains that this reflects a merger of a platonic view with Christianity in Kuyper.
These criticisms were also picked up by Jeremy Begbie.[39]

(Cambridge: Cambridge University Press, 2004); Lambert Zuidervaart, *Art, Education, and Cultural Renewal: Essays in Reformational Philosophy* (Montreal: McGill-Queen's University Press, 2017).

36. S. Hardman More, "Calvinism and the Arts," *Theology in Scotland* 16, no. 2 (2019): 75–92.

37. C. R. Joby, "Calvinism and the Arts: A Re-Assessment." Durham Theses, Durham University," 2005, http://etheses.dur.ac.uk/2873/.

38. Joby, "Calvinism and the Arts," v-vi.

39. J. Begbie, *Voicing Creation's Praise*.

More recently, artist Makoto Fujimura, who admits to being influenced by Kuyper,[40] has argued for a re-emphasis on beauty. He asserts:

> Beauty is the quality connected with those things that are in themselves appealing and desirable. Beautiful things are a delight to the senses, a pleasure to the mind, and a refreshment for the spirit. Beauty invites us in, capturing our attention and making us want to linger. Beautiful things are worth our scrutiny, rewarding to contemplate, deserving of pursuit. They inspire—or even demand—a response, whether sharing them in community or acting to extend their beauty into other spheres.[41]

There has been a resurgence in the notion of beauty,[42] and there may be something in this. However, care is needed to avoid a platonic view of beauty.

Kuyper's aim was according to Heslam to develop a Calvinistic aesthetic. He did not fully succeed in this. However, what he did do was to lay the groundwork for such an approach and show that such an approach was feasible and necessary. It was Dooyeweerd who was able to build upon Kuyper's ideas:

> Everyone who has even the slightest acquaintance with the theory of law-spheres of the *Philosophy of the Cosmonomic Idea* will have to concede that in the scientific

---

40. Makoto Fujimura, "Breathing Eden's Air," *Books & Culture,* 2012.

41. Makoto Fujimura, *Culture Care: Reconnecting with Beauty for Our Common Life* (Downers Grove, IL: InterVarsity Press, 2017), 50.

42. For example, J. King, *The Beauty of the Lord: Theology as Aesthetics* (*Studies in Historical and Systematic Theology*) (Bellingham, WA: Lexham Press, 2018).

investigation of the structure of reality it is nothing but thinking through and elaborating this religious under-standing of law found in the thought of Kuyper.

...Can it be said that the *Philosophy of the Cosmo-nomic Idea,* while elaborating this religious basic con-ception of Kuyper and radically cuts off lines of thought foreign to Calvinism, is guilty of undermining Kuyper's work? Much rather, the opposite is the case. Proceeding in this way indeed does justice to the restorer of Calvin-ism in the highest sense of the term.[43]

Seerveld, despite the reservations mentioned above, writes out of a Kuyperian spirit and draws on the categories of the Dutch Christian philosopher D. H. Th. Vollenhoven. Vol-lenhoven likewise was influenced by Kuyper.[44] Vollenhoven was Herman Dooyeweerd's brother-in-law. Kuyper via Dooyeweerd was an influence on Hans Rookmaaker, who likewise influenced Francis Schaeffer. Flawed though Kuyper's view may have been they were certainly influential, and in identifying its weaknesses, these others were able to develop a more fully Christian approach to art and aesthetics. We all stand on the shoulders of giants, and in this case, the giant was Kuyper.

---

43. H. Dooyeweerd, "Kuyper's Philosophy of Science," in *On Kuyper: A Collection of Readings on the Life, Work & Legacy of Abraham Kuyper,* ed. S. Bishop and J.H. Kok (Sioux Center, IA: Dordt College Press, 2013), 169, 178.

44. Jeremy G. A. Ive, "The Contribution and Philosophical Development of the Reformational Philosopher, Dirk H. Th. Vollenhoven," *Philosophia Reformata* 80, no. 2 (2015): 159–77.

A summary in 12 theses

1. Kuyper rejects the stereotype of Calvinists as art-devaluing killjoys and instead advocates for the enjoyment and appreciation of art as a gift from God.

2. Kuyper emphasizes that art is not limited to the elite but should be accessible to all, regardless of social status.

3. Scripture depicts God as delighting in His creation, reflecting the importance of enjoying beauty and art.

4. Kuyper identifies three spheres for art: the sacred, normal human life, and that of evil and unclean, finding beauty in the first two spheres.

5. Art serves as a bridge between the present and the future kingdom, providing glimpses of the new Jerusalem.

6. Kuyper's aim was to develop a Calvinistic aesthetic, laying the groundwork for future scholars like Dooyeweerd to build upon.

7. Despite some criticisms, Kuyper's ideas on art have influenced subsequent thinkers like Rookmaaker and Seerveld.

8. Kuyper's writings highlight the importance of art in reflecting the beauty that was lost and anticipating its future restoration.

9. Art is seen as a form of homesickness for beauty, connecting the present world with the future glory.

10. Kuyper's view on art challenges the misconception that Calvinists disregard artistic expression, emphasizing the value of beauty and creativity.

11. Through his writings, Kuyper promotes a holistic view of life that includes the enjoyment and appreciation of art as part of a rich and fulfilling existence.

12. Kuyper's legacy in defending art against misconceptions and promoting a Calvinistic aesthetics continues to inspire discussions on the relationship between religion and artistic expression.

Study Questions

1. Why did Kuyper see the need to justify a Christian approach to art?
2. How does Kuyper challenge the stereotype that Calvinists devalue art?
3. What did Kuyper mean by some approaches to Christian art is "examining the lace on a garment"?
4. Is art a gift from God as Kuyper maintains?
5. What is the significance of Kuyper's emphasis on art as a gift of God in the context of Calvinistic beliefs?
6. Kuyper's view of beauty shows platonic influences. Discuss.
7. Art foreshadows and provides us with prophetic glimmerings of the New Jerusalem. What does Kuyper mean by this?
8. Will we see art by non-Christian artists on the new earth?
9. What impact has Kuyper's defense of art had on subsequent discussions on the relationship between religion and the arts?

Further Reading

Primary sources

Kuyper, Abraham. "Calvinism and Art" in *Lectures on Calvinism* (Grand Rapids, MI: Eerdmans. 1931)

Kuyper, Abraham. *Wisdom & Wonder: Common Grace in Science in Art* (Grand Rapids, MI: Christian's Library Press, 2011)

Secondary sources

Bishop, Steve. "Abraham Kuyper's Nascent Views on Art," *Journal for Christian Scholarship*, 55 (3) (2019): 107–29.

Dengerink Chaplin, Adrienne "Kuyper and Art," in Joustra, Jessica R. and Joustra, Robert J. (ed.) *Calvinism for a Secular Age: A Twenty-First-Century Reading of Abraham Kuyper's Stone Lectures.* (Downers Grove: IVP Academic, 2022), 106–124.

Henderson, Roger D. and Marleen Hengelaar-Rookmaaker, ed., *The Artistic Sphere: The Arts in Neo-Calvinist Perspective* (Downers Grove: IVP Academic, 2024).

Henderson, Roger, "Rumors of Glory: Abraham Kuyper's Neo-Calvinist Theory of Art," *Pro Rege* 45 (4) (2017): 1–9.

Heslam, Peter, "A Theology of the Arts: Kuyper's Ideas on Art and Religion," in Steve Bishop and John Kok (ed.) *On Kuyper: A Collection of Readings on the Life, Work & Legacy of Abraham Kuyper* (Sioux Center: Dordt Press, 2013), 351–364.

28

Business & Economics

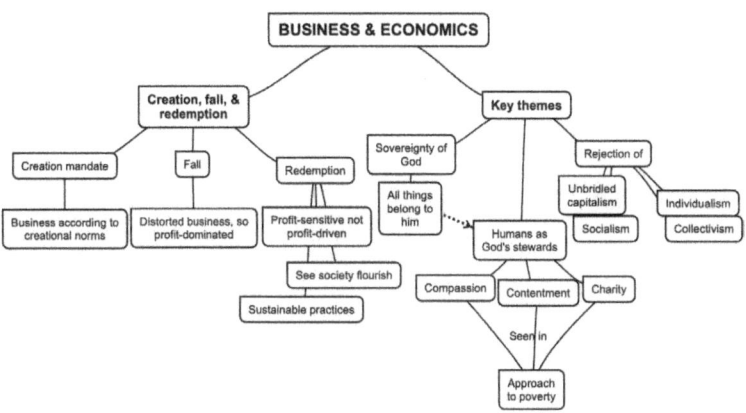

In brief

THE INTERTWINING REALMS OF business, economics, and Christian principles are examined in this chapter, focusing on the teachings of Kuyper. Key themes highlighted include compassion, contentment, and charity in economic activities. Kuyper, often referred to as an "amateur economist," extensively referenced various economic works in his writings. The Eighth Commandment is explored in relation to wealth distribution, ownership rights, and property, emphasizing the importance of using possessions for the good of others. The concept of stewardship is central, with the belief that God is the ultimate owner of all things, and humans are stewards of His possessions. This chapter also addresses the relationship between private property rights, Biblical principles, and economic systems like capitalism and socialism. Kuyper underscores the significance of aligning business practices with Christian values, promoting justice, stewardship, and care for others in economic endeavors.

Introduction

"Business is the business of business" proclaimed Milton Friedman. So, what does business and economics have to do with Christianity? Everything if Kuyper's no square inch claim is correct. However, Peter Heslam laments the lack of resources and writings on Kuyper and business—it would be remiss then, not to include a chapter on it here!

Has Kuyper overlooked business and economics in his writing? He could be excused for doing so as no one can cover the entirety of creation in their writings. Kuyper was a pastor and politician; he was not a businessman or an economist—so it is hardly surprising that he did not address the issue directly. However, he did offer insights on the matter.

For Kuyper, the business of business is to do business according to the creation ordinances, under the sovereignty of God. The problem with business is that it prioritizes profits and success (often solely measured in monetary terms). Kuyper would disagree. Profits and success do not come from good business practices but ultimately from God. The motivation for business comes from the creation mandate, unfortunately, the fall distorted business such that profit at all costs often becomes a measure of success. Christians should be involved in transforming and renewing business so that it is profit-sensitive but not profit-dominated; business can serve rather than despoil society.[1] Business should enable society to flourish and be able to provide meaningful work.[2]

Three key themes dominate Kuyper's view on business and economics: compassion, contentment, and charity. These themes will be explored below.

Kuyper was aware of economics even though there was then no academic discipline at the time known as "economics." Joost Hengstmengel describes Kuyper as "The amateur economist."[3] Hengstemengel has compiled a list of over 40 works on economics that Kuyper referred to in his writings ranging from to Georg Adler to Caroll D. Wright.[4] As George Harinck observes: "Though Kuyper hardly ever talked about economy in

---

1. The chocolatier businessman George Cadbury provides a good example of this approach to business. See for example, Mark Roques, "Cadbury and Dooyeweerd: A Response to Henk Jochemsen, & Johan Hegeman. Connecting Christian Faith and Professional Practice in a Pluralist Society," in *Bridging the Gap: Connecting Christian Faith and Professional Practice in a Pluralistic Society*, ed., B. de Muynck, J. Hegeman, and P. Vos (Sioux Center, IO: Dordt Press, 2009); and Mark Roques and Steve Bishop, "Stewardship Epistemology," *Findings* 2 (2021): 30–48.

2. See, for example, Jeff Van Duzer, *Why Business Matters to God (And What Still Needs to Be Fixed)* (Downers Grove, Illinois: IVP Academic, 2010).

3. Joost W. Hengstmengel, "The Amateur Economist," *Abraham Kuyper and Economic Journal of Economics, Theology and Religion* 1, no. 2 (2021): 137–58.

4. Hengstmengel, "The Amateur Economist."

the strict sense of the word, he certainly influenced Dutch economy and economic thinking."[5]

The recent anthology volume of Kuyper's writings *On Business & Economics* attests to this. It includes articles on pensions, labor unions, and government subsidies among other topics. The volume begins with three articles Kuyper wrote on the Heidelberg Catechism. Several biblical texts have been used to justify either capitalism or communism. Kuyper examines several of these in his commentary on the Heidelberg Catechism.[6] In doing so, one important theological point shapes his approach:

> Absolute right of ownership ... only be conceived of in God. He who created everything does with everything as he pleases. He alone has total control over all that exists.[7]

Kuyper continually reiterates this theme, for example:

---

5. George Harinck, "Dinner Speech at Second Kuyper Consultation on Theology and Economic Life: Exploring Hidden Links," in *Princeton Theological Seminary*, 2003.

6. The editors of *On Business and Economics* have the following to say regarding the Heidelberg Catechism:

    The Heidelberg Catechism is a manual for basic instruction in Christian doctrine. Published in 1563, the catechism consists of 129 questions and answers and quickly proved useful for faith formation of children and adults alike. Divided into 52 parts, each "Lord's Day" enables the entirety of the teachings of the catechism to be covered in weekly sermons throughout the year.

7. Abraham Kuyper, *On Business & Economics: Abraham Kuyper Collected Works in Public Theology*, ed. Peter S. Heslam (Bellingham, WA: Lexham Press, 2021), 48.

God's Holy Word has been misused for so long that with the increasing seriousness of the times we should reflect seriously on how we can make room for the conviction that absolute ownership of all natural goods cannot belong to anyone but the Lord our God.[8]

If God is indeed the sole and absolute owner of all things [and he is!], it follows immediately that nobody, however unparalleled he may be in his riches, can claim an absolute right of ownership over even a single thing on earth.[9]

In God's name he has to bear witness that there can be no question of absolute ownership except in the case of God himself, and that all our possessions are only held on loan from him. We manage our possessions only as a form of stewardship.[10]

This is linked to the notion that humans are God's stewards:

In God's name he has to bear witness that there can be no question of absolute ownership except in the case of God himself, and that all our possessions are only held on loan from him. We manage our possessions only as a form of stewardship.[11]

What Scripture says about the owner as steward points us in the one and only safe direction, and Christ's church abandons her calling if she does not

---

8. Kuyper, *On Business and Economics*, 44.

9. Kuyper, *On Business and Economics*, 48.

10. Kuyper, *On Business and Economics*, 55.

11. Kuyper, *On Business and Economics*, 217.

constantly and ceaselessly preach and imprint on humankind the sacred truth that the Lord God is the only lawful owner, and that no person ever is or can be anything but a steward over a part of that which belongs to God alone.[12]

Once the realization that "God is owner and we—great or small—are stewards" penetrates us once and for all, the absurd notion that we can do with our property as we like can arise in no sound mind.[13]

Every good on earth is bound to four relationships: (1) it is related to itself, because it is handled in accordance with the nature God has established in it; (2) it is related to God, who created and maintains it, and who is its absolute Sovereign; (3) it is related to its temporal stewards whom God has appointed over it; and (4) it is related to our fellow creatures, that is, to our neighbors, to all stakeholders, to our community, our society and even our country as a whole. The situation concerning earthly possessions is only as it should be when justice is done to those four relationships.[14]

Give us this day our daily bread
In his commentary on Lord's Day 50 of the Heidelberg Catechism, which addresses the phrase "Give us this day our daily bread," Kuyper is clear that "any spiritualization

---

12. Kuyper, *On Business and Economics*, 44.

13. Kuyper, *On Business and Economics*, 54.

14. Kuyper, *On Business and Economics*, 60–61.

of this petition is misplaced and improper."[15] He notes that the order of prayer for first physical and then spiritual needs is important—even though the ratio of physical to spiritual is 1:5 in this prayer: "Nor should we lose sight of the fact that the petition for our physical needs comes first in this triad. That corresponds perfectly to our human condition. You must first live before you can live for God." (10). This praying does not negate the need to also work for our daily bread.

The Eighth Commandment: "You shall not steal" (Ex 20:13)
The Lord's Day 42 of the Heidelberg Catechism poses the question: "What does God forbid in the Eighth Commandment?" and "But what does God require of you in this Commandment?" The Eighth Commandment, "you shall not steal," has often been used to justify the right to own property, capitalism, and the injustice of a tax system. A few quotes are sufficient to illustrate this approach.

E. Calvin Beisner states, "The Eighth Commandment says, 'You shall not steal.' This presupposes that people have a right to private property and to use it as they please so long as they don't harm others' property, health, or life."[16]

According to Andrew Sandlin: "The Bible expressly defends the notion of private property and requires the civil magistrate to protect it (Ex. 20:15; 22:1)." He goes on to assert:

---

15. Kuyper, *On Business and Economics,* 10.

16. E. Calvin Beisner, 'Is Capitalism Bad for the Environment? The Eighth Commandment Offers a Clue," 2017, https://cornwallalliance. org/2017/12/is-capitalism-bad-for-the-environment-the-eighth-commandment-offers-a-clue/.

The idea of "Christian" socialism, in any case, is wrong on two counts. First, it violates the Eighth Commandment. Second, it vests the state with authority that the Bible never gives it (Rom. 13). Free market economics, or what in some quarters is known as classical liberalism, is actually a recovery of the Biblical view of property and wealth.[17]

And Doug Wilson suggests that:

The Bible requires some form of capitalist society in the basic commandment, "Thou shalt not steal." This command presupposes the institution of private ownership—private property as a divine institution—and sets up a fundamental protection against assaults on the right to own property.[18]

There are some elements of truth in each of these statements, however, as Kuyper suggests "it is most incorrect the way many people have appealed to the Eighth Commandment in order to defend today's distribution of wealth as well as current rights of ownership and property."[19]

He continues:

A simple reading of the Heidelberg Catechism's explanation of the eighth commandment would have sufficed for this purpose. It states that this commandment

17. Andrew Sandlin, "In Praise of the Market 'Christian,' Socialism Versus Christian Capitalism," *Chalcedon Report* (April, 1998), no. 393.

18. Doug Wilson, "Football Players or Pirates" (Blog Post) *Blog & Mablog*, 2010, https://dougwils.com/books-and-culture/s22-money-love-desire/football-players-or-pirates.html.

19 Kuyper, *On Business and Economics,* 39.

is transgressed (1) by all who have in their posses-
sion something that was obtained by a scheme, by
deception, by usury, and so forth; (2) by all who
are greedy or who squander what they have; and
finally (3) by all who do not use their possessions
in order to promote their neighbor's utmost good
and to help the poor.[20]

This commandment is not to be used as an endorsement of
unbridled capitalism. Kuyper travels a third way. He stresses
that strong objections should be made to any assertion that the
Eighth Commandment forbids collective ownership. He maintains that it neither expresses nor hints at this:

If a person considers (in light of or even on the basis of)
the eighth commandment that a society where property is largely communal is forbidden by God, he or she
is entirely mistaken.[21]

Matthew 20:14–15: the parable of the landowner

As the Eighth Commandment has been used to justify capitalism,
the parable of the landowner has been used to justify some form of
socialism.[22] Even though the workers did different amounts of
work, they all took home the same pay packet. It has also been
used to justify that "every owner can do with his possessions as
he pleases."[23] It is this issue that Kuyper addresses.

---

20. Kuyper, *On Business and Economics,* 40.

21. Kuyper, *On Business and Economics,* 42.

22. Chuck McKnight, "Jesus was a Socialist," 2019, https://www.patheos.
com/blogs/hippieheretic/2019/03/jesus-was-a-socialist.html#laborers-in-vineyard.

23. Kuyper, *On Business and Economics,* .

In discussing this passage, Kuyper points out three things. First, the words are not Jesus' they are the vineyard owners. The landowner has free reign over his belongings "for the purpose of doing good."[24] The landowner then questions the motivation of the original workers; as Kuyper has it, in the words of the landowner, "You challenge my right to do good with what is mine, and this stems from the fact that I am good while you are envious."

Thus, Kuyper sums up this passage:

> Accordingly, every appeal to these words of Jesus as if he places an official stamp of approval on the absolute concept of private ownership will have to be abandoned. Furthermore, the owners of today who are so ready to appeal to the landowner in this parable for confirming their absolute rights would perhaps be of more benefit to themselves and to society if they asked themselves whether they are using their freedom to do good with their money as liberally as did the owner of this vineyard.[25]

This and other passages show, Kuyper maintains, that we need to consider that "all that is yours as the property of your Father in heaven."

Kuyper then turns to Matthew 26:11 and Jesus' remark that "You will always have the poor with you."

Matthew 26:11: You will always have the poor with you

This passage has been used to justify the notion that we will always have the rich and the poor and that it is, therefore, useless to try to alleviate poverty.

---

24. Kuyper, *On Business and Economics*, 43—emphasis in the original.
25. Kuyper, *On Business and Economics*, 44.

Kuyper uses an extreme example to show the invalidity of this type of argument:

> Had Jesus said, "You will to the very end of time always have people who commit suicide," would people conclude that we should make no effort to combat suicide? If that were indeed the case it would be as if there were no difference between saying how things will always be, given human nature and its implications, and saying how things must be by instituting a rule or promulgating an ordinance.[26]

Kuyper contends that this verse is a prophecy. He goes on, mocking those who adopt the approach of doing nothing for the poor, accepting it as the way things should be:

> He who knows the hearts of humankind and knows what consequences sin would continue to bring along with it to the very end said to Judas: "You always have the poor with you." If, in contrast, it were indeed a rule for how things ought to be, we suggest that today's fortunate owners trade places for a year by making rich those who are now poor and to take upon themselves the role of a poor person for an entire year. Would that not likewise be a way to fulfill the ordinance that they assume these words of Jesus contain?[27]

Thus, by hyperbole and what philosophers term a *reductio ad absurdum*,[28] Kuyper shows the nonsense of such an approach. These passages all serve to underline one key thing:

---

26. Kuyper, *On Business and Economics*, 46.

27. Kuyper, *On Business and Economics*, 46.

28. As The Big Bang Theory's Sheldon Cooper states, a *reductio ad absurdum* is "the logical fallacy of extending someone's argument to ridiculous proportions ... ."

Absolute right of ownership can for that reason only be conceived of in God. He who created everything does with everything as he pleases. He alone has total control over all that exists.[29]

Response to poverty

For Kuyper poverty was one of the most pressing social and economic problems of the time. It was a time marked by growing urbanization, and the poor were struggling to survive. "What should we, as confessors of Christ, do about the social needs of our time?" is the question Kuyper put forward in his opening address at the first Christian Social Congress in the Netherlands in November 1891.

He maintains that there is a relationship between Christianity and the social problem. However, that there is a relationship is not enough, it "must take on form and shape."

He begins by examining the contrast between art and nature. By art he means the way that humans act on nature, not to destroy it but rather to unfold the power within nature. This he sees as an ordinance of God: to preserve and cultivate.

Two problems, however, exist: error and sin. Error is seen in ignorance of the role of humanity in creation and sin is seen in in the greed and lust for power over creation. This has led to inequalities, the strong are able to bend customs and laws to their own ends so that profit is their own and the weak suffer loss. This was not because the strong were more evil than the weak, but rather humans are not regarded as being created in the image of God.

Should the Christian faith take no stand against such an evil state of affairs, asked Kuyper. He then looks at Jesus as be-

---

29   Kuyper, *On Business and Economics,* 48.

ing more than a social reformer. Jesus never preached revolution; we are to obey the governmental authorities set over us. Jesus knew the answer to the roots of sin and error was truth against error and to break the power of sin. Jesus knew poverty, he was born in a stable and had no place to lay his head; he had compassion for those who were poor and oppressed. His message to seek first the kingdom was a message both to the rich and the poor.

Jesus also organized. He established his church to influence society. This was to be done Kuyper proposed in three ways:

1. A ministry of the Word—the word comforts the poor and the oppressed and brings compassion for the poor.
2. A ministry of charity—no one was to have need.
3. Instituting the equality of brotherhood—rich and poor were to share in the Lord's table as equals.

Unfortunately, as the centuries went on, the salt lost its savor and the conversion of Constantine led to church wedding itself to the power of the world.

For Kuyper the French Revolution was a dark point in history. The French Revolution threw out the sovereignty of God and replaced it with human sovereignty, with individual free will. The underlying root principle of the French Revolution is "neither God, nor master": humanity freed from God and his order. From this comes two principles: all there is only an individual and his free choices; the other is to sit on your own throne and create a new order. The latter Kuyper sees as social democracy.

> Social democracy wants to erect a social structure (by means of universal suffrage) on the foundation of the sovereignty of the people, and thus on individual will.[30]

---

30. Kuyper, *On Business and Economics*, 60.

As mentioned above the Kuyperian response is to be shaped by three themes: compassion, contentment, and charity. Like the Good Samaritan, we should be moved by divine sympathy and compassion. In addition, if we have food and clothing, then we should be content with that. Charity does not mean only the giving of money, it also requires time, energy, and resources.

Kuyper considers several issues or problems related to the social question and poverty.

1. The problem of a wrong emphasis

As Kuyper observes, "The first article of any social program that will bring salvation … must remain: 'I believe in God the Father Almighty, Maker of Heaven and Earth.'" By this he does not mean to imply a social program brings salvation—his is no social gospel. Rather he is stressing that the focus is on God. He goes on to clarify: "… whoever says I believe in God thereby acknowledges God's ordering of nature and an ordinance of God above conscience."

In any program God is at the center and that means the emphasis is to be on God's authority and lordship.

As he writes later:

Legislation by itself will not cure our sick society unless at the same time drops of the medicine enter the hearts of rich and poor. Sin is such a terrible power that it makes a mockery of your dikes and dams. Regardless of your legal system, time and again sin will inundate the terrain of human life with the waters of desire and self-interest.[31]

---

31. Kuyper, *On Business and Economics,* 224.

Eternal life is to be placed at the foreground: "Only he who reckons with an eternal life knows the real price of this earthly life."[32]

2. State and society

Kuyper's notion of sphere sovereignty means that the state and society each have their own sphere. This implies that the social democrats are wrong by allowing the state to be absorbed by society. Likewise, the socialists are wrong in permitting society to be absorbed by the state. The social problem can only be begun to be resolved if we honour both the state and society; the state clears the way for a free society.[33]

This brings us to another issue: what is the nature of society? Is society an aggregate of individuals (individualism) or an organic body (collectivism)?

3. Individualism or collectivism?

Individualism is not an option for Christians, Kuyper maintains, as Christians have been joined in a single covenant with God. Kuyper was critical of the French Revolution's individualism, the undermining of the organic relationship, and its destruction of the spiritual and moral foundations of society.[34] Kuyper saw that individualism and collectivism came from the same root. As Heslam points out:

---

32. Kuyper, *On Business and Economics,* 73.

33. Abraham Kuyper, *The Problem of Poverty,* ed. James W Skillen (Sioux Center, IA: Dordt College Press, 2011).

34. See, for example, the discussion in Peter S. Heslam "Prophet of a Third Way: The Shape of Kuyper's Socio-Political Vision. *Journal of Markets & Morality* 5, no.1, (2002): 11–33.

It must also have been with prophetic intuition that he [Kuyper] stressed the tendency for individualism to produce collectivist forms of government, and that these forms ultimately undermine the rights of the individuals and groups they set out to protect.[35]

4. Property

Absolute property belongs to God. All our property is thus on loan from him. There was no community of goods in Israel or in the early church. Neither is there the right to dispose of property as if we were God. There are the needs of others to consider.

It is so profoundly false that God's Word lets us hear only calls for the salvation of our souls. No, God's Word gives us fixed ordinances—even for our national existence and our common social life. It marks out clearly visible lines. We are unfaithful to God's Word if we fail to take notice if this fact and, for convenience sake, impiously permit our theory and practice to be determined by prevailing opinion or current law.[36]

5. State aid

Finally, a brief word about state aid is discussed. God instituted the basic rule for the duty of government. Government exists to administer and uphold God's justice.[37] In this sense Kuyper was no political libertarian. However, the government is not to take over other spheres of life, "the state should withdraw its hands from them."[38]

---

35. Peter S Heslam, "Prophet of a Third Way," 23.

36. Kuyper, *On Business and Economics,* 68.

37. Kuyper, *On Business and Economics,* 223.

38. Kuyper, *On Business and Economics,* 223.

State aid for the poor may be necessary at times, "it was not precluded from Israel's laws,"[39] observes Kuyper. It should however be kept to a minimum otherwise it might "weaken the working classes." The best and most enduring solution he suggests is "found only in powerful private initiative."[40]

The social question rests, Kuyper maintains, on recognizing that the poor are of our own flesh and blood.

> the holy art of "giving for Jesus' sake" [see 2 Cor 4:11] should become much more developed among us Christians. All poverty relief by the state, never forget, always leaves a blot on the honor of your Savior.[41]

Individual giving, charity, has an important part to play. Governments are not to be relied on to solve all the social problems. Kuyper concludes his address by noting that the social question is not only a national issue, but also has an international character.

Kuyper's line

A number of those in Kuyper's line have dealt with business issues. One in particular is Maarten Verkerk. Verkerk worked for several years as a manager in Eindhoven in a small factory that produced image intensifiers before becoming a professor in Reformational philosophy at Maastricht University and the Technical University of Eindhoven until his retirement in 2019. His second PhD was entitled Trust and Power on the

---

39. Kuyper, *On Business and Economics*, 223.

40. Kuyper, *On Business and Economics*, 223.

41. Kuyper, *On Business and Economics*, 228.

Shop Floor,[42] which examined the dynamics between management and shopfloor workers and examined responsible behavior in industrial organizations and did so from a Kuyperian perspective. He is also the co-author of *Ecclesiastes for Managers*.[43]

Others while they may not mention Kuyper explicitly use a Kuyperian framework e.g., Denise Daniels. She explores a "theology of business" using the "biblical worldview" of creation, fall, and redemption. She concludes:

> Creation establishes the vocation of business as good. Fall convinces us that the problem goes deeper than regulatory oversight or even personal morality (although both of these are important). The fundamental mission of business and the organization of self-supporting, free enterprise companies are all acceptable—but the underlying structure of those companies and their assumed models of people and the distribution of rights and responsibilities is profoundly broken. Redemption calls us to participate with God in transforming business. [44]

Harry Antonides (1931–2022) was involved in the formation of the Christian Labour Association of Canada and a

---

42. Maarten J. Verkerk, "Trust and Power on the Shop Floor," in *An Ethnographical, Ethical, and Philosophical Study on Responsible Behaviour in Industrial Organizations* (Delft: Eubron Academic Publishers, 2004).

43 Maarten J. Verkerk and Jan Hoogland, *Ecclesiastes for Managers: Worldly Wisdom for Managers and Professionals* (Sioux Center: Dordt Press, 2018).

44 Densie Daniels, "Toward a Theology of Business," in *Finding Meaning in Business: Theology, Ethics, and Vocation*, ed. B. O. Okonkwo (New York: Palgrave Macmillan, 2012), 59–75.

founder member of the Work Research Foundation (now known as Cardus)– and has written on collective bargaining[45] and multinationals[46] among other topics.

Peter Heslam has also been doing much work on transforming business—he is the director of "Faith in Business." As well as his doctoral thesis on Kuyper (Creating a Christian Worldview) he edited Kuyper's *On Business & Economics* and written on capitalism and globalization.[47] For Heslam, business is a means of providing wealth and bringing relief from poverty. For him business is not boardrooms, accountants, business plans; it is not the rich getting richer: "What lifts the poor is the creation of wealth and the empowerment and the dignity and the self-reliance that comes from that."

There have also been critics of Kuyper's approach too.[48] One vocal critic was Fredrick Nymeyer (1897–1981). Nymeyer was associated with the Vienna or Austrian school of economics and the approach of Ludwig Von Mises (1881–1973).[49]

Fredrick Nymeyer (1897–1981), in his magazine *Progressive Christian*—takes issue with Kuyper and his sphere

---

45 Harry Antonides, *Renewal in the Workplace: A Critical Look at Collective Bargaining* (London, Ont: CLAC, 1982).

46. Harry Antonides, *Multinationals and the Peaceable Kingdom* (Toronto/ Vancouver: Clarke, Irwin & Company, 1978).

47. Peter S. Heslam, *Globalization: Unravelling the New Capitalism* (London: SPCK, 2003); *Transforming Capitalism: Entrepreneurship and the Renewal of Thrift* (Cambridge: Grove, 2010).

48 See also the discussion in Paul Oslington "The Kuyperian Dream of Reconstructing Economics on Christian Foundations," *Faith & Economics* 75 (Spring 2020): 7–36.

49. Others associated with the Austrian school were Carl Menger, Eugen von Bohm-Bawerk, and Friedrich Hayek.

sovereignty.[50] *Progressive Christian* was produced as the magazine of the Progressive Calvinism League. One of the key themes of the League was to promote a "genuine free market economy; we are against the coercion of markets or of society generally (except to restrain the evils prohibited in the Second table of the Law)." The league promoted von Mises' Austrian economics, libertarianism, and individualism. They are opposed to Kuyper's neo-Calvinism, which according to Nymeyer:

> neo-Calvinism (in our opinion) is not in any such capitalistic tradition; to the contrary, it is in the interventionist tradition which by its nature develops coerced and not free markets. (Interventionism eventually leads to socialism.)[51]

He also takes issue with Kuyper's anti-individualism:

> Abraham Kuyper and his numerous American followers condemn and detest Individualism. This exposes PROGRESSIVE CALVINISM to criticism and contempt, because its publishers are avowed Individualists and are unqualifiedly in favor of Individualism.[52]

Nymeyer goes on, setting up a false choice:

> The opposite of Individualism is Collectivism. Those are the two basic philosophies for the structure of society.[53]

He concludes:

---

50. F. Nymeyer, "A Great Netherlander on Sphere Sovereignty," *Progressive Calvinism* 2, no. 2 (1956): 51–55.

51. F. Nymeyer, "Abraham Kuyper's Unscriptural and Unsound Ideas on Tariff Production," *Progressive Calvinism* 2, no. 1 (1956): 12.

52. F. Nymeyer, "Prevalence Of Interventionism Among Some Modern Calvinists," *Progressive Calvinism* 3, no. 6 (1957): 168–80.

53. Nymeyer, "Prevalence Of Interventionism," 168.

In summary, Collectivism under the flag of brotherly love is always violent and oppressive; and Individualism under the banner of humility is always meek
and lowly.

Interventionism is in principle a stage on the
road to Collectivism. The principle underlying it is
Collectivist; Interventionism when full-grown is
always Collectivism.

However, Kuyper is neither an individualist nor a collectivist.[54]
As Heslam points out:

Kuyper maintained that neither enlightenment individualism nor the collectivism of state socialism offered
viable solutions to the endemic poverty associated with
the industrial revolution.[55]

Nymeyer was discussing a strawman, a position that Kuyper
never held.

Conclusion
Kuyper described himself as "just a dilettante economist," nevertheless as Hengstmengel points out he was the source of inspiration for Calvinist economics as developed by economists
such as Bob Goudzwaard,[56] Alan Storkey, Tony Cramp, Ad-

---

54. Freire, "Political Economy in Brazil."

55. "On Entrepreneurship, Poverty and Insights from Abraham Kuyper
and John Wesley: An Interview between Peter Heslam and Joseph E.
Gorra," published by the Evangelical Philosophical Society, 2012.
Online: https://www.epsociety.org/userfiles/Interview%20
with%2Peter%20Heslam%204

56. Bruce Wearne, *Cultivating Care within a Vulnerable Economy an
Annotated Bibliography of the English Writings of Bob Goudzwaard*

olfo Garcia de la Sienra, Joost W. Hengstmengel, and Kent Van Til[57] among others. Although it seems that Kuyper had a "love-hate relationship" with the new science of economics: "On the one hand, he could not help but see economics as a legitimate and essential field of research. On the other, he was critical of the methodology and conclusions of mainstream classical economics."[58]

A summary in 12 theses

1. Absolute ownership of all natural goods belongs solely to God, making humans stewards of His possessions.
2. No individual, regardless of wealth, can claim absolute ownership over anything on earth.
3. The sacred truth is that God is the only lawful owner, and humans are stewards of His possessions.
4. The Eighth Commandment prohibits schemes, deception, greed, and neglect of using possessions for the good of others.
5. The Eighth Commandment does not endorse unbridled

1967–2007, (Bristol: All of Life Redeemed, 2008) https://alloflife redeemed.co.uk/bob-goudzwaard.

57. A. B. Cramp, *Notes Towards a Christian Critique of Secular Economic Theory* (Toronto: Institute for Christian Studies, 1975); Alan Storkey, *Transforming Economics* (London: SPCK, Third Way Books, 1986); Bob Goudzwaard, *Capitalism and Progress: A Diagnosis of Western Society*(Grand Rapids: Eerdmans, 1979); Kent A Van Til, *Less Than Two Dollars a Day: A Christian View of Poverty and the Free Market* (Grand Rapids, MI: Eerdmans, 2007); Hengstmengel, "The Amateur Economist"; Adolpho Garcia de la Sienra, *A Structuralist Theory of Economics* (London: Routledge, 2019).

58. Hengstmengel, "The Amateur Economist."

capitalism but emphasizes promoting the utmost good for neighbors and helping the poor.

6. The parable of the landowner challenges interpretations that justify capitalism or socialism.

7. Kuyper's view on business and economics emphasizes compassion, contentment, and charity.

8. The Bible defends private property rights and requires protection of property by civil authorities.

9. Capitalism aligns with the Biblical view of property and wealth protection against theft.

10. Every earthly good is related to itself, God, stewards, and fellow creatures, requiring justice in these relationships.

11. The prayer for daily bread highlights the importance of physical needs.

12. The Eighth Commandment prohibits stealing and emphasizes the responsibility to work for sustenance while also caring for others.

Study Questions

1. Why does Hengstmengel describe Kuyper as "The amateur economist"?
2. Why have Christians been slow to develop a Christian view of business?
3. What implications for business and economics does Kuyper draw out from the sovereignty of God?
4. How does Kuyper's perspective on business differ from conventional profit-driven approaches?
5. How would Kuyper respond to those who espouse a free-market approach to economics?
6. In what ways does the concept of stewardship play a role in Kuyper's teachings on business and economics?
7. How does Kuyper's interpretation of the Eighth Commandment challenge traditional economic ideologies?
8. How does Kuyper navigate the tension between individual ownership rights and communal responsibilities in economic matters?
9. How does Kuyper think Christians should respond to poverty?
10. What creational norms should shape business and economics?
11. What might a Kuyperian economics look like?
12. In what ways can Kuyper's teachings on business and economics be applied in contemporary society to promote ethical business conduct and societal well-being?

Further Reading

Primary Sources

Kuyper, Abraham. *The Problem of Poverty* (Sioux Center, IO: Dordt Press, 2011).

Kuyper, Abraham. *On Business & Economics* Heslam, Peter S. (ed.) (Bellingham, WA: Lexham Press, 2021).

Secondary Sources

Goudzwaard, Bob. "Economics, Christianity and the Crisis: Kuyper's Heritage and Relevance Today," *Philosophia Reformata* 78, no. 2, (2013): 95–101.

Hengstmengel, Joost W. "The Amateur Economist: Abraham Kuyper and Economics," Journal *of Economics, Theology and Religion*, 1, no. 2 (2021): 137–158.

Heslam, Peter S. 2015. "The Spirit of Enterprise: Abraham Kuyper and Common Grace in Business," *Journal of Markets & Morality*, 18 (1): 7–20.

29

The Natural Sciences[1]

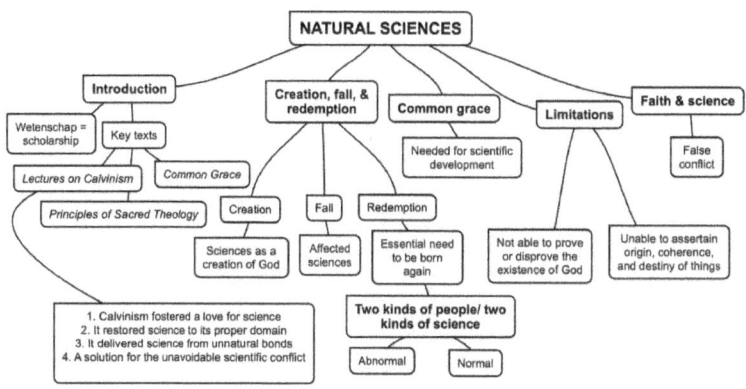

In brief

IN HIS EXPLORATION OF the relationship between Calvinism and science, Abraham Kuyper emphasized the significant role of Calvinism in fostering a love for science and restoring its proper domain. He argued that Calvinism rejected dualism between the spiritual and physical realms, allowing for a holistic

---

1. Some of this chapter draws upon Steve Bishop, "Abraham Kuyper's View of the Natural Sciences," *Koers—Bulletin for Christian Scholarship* 86, no. 1 (June 2021): 2497, https://doi.org/10.19108/KO ERS.86.1.2497.

view of creation and the cosmos. Kuyper highlighted the importance of common grace in recognizing the value of temporal and cosmic aspects of life, restoring the worth of creation as God's handiwork. He acknowledged the limitations of science in determining absolute truth and emphasized the need for humility in the pursuit of knowledge. Kuyper's discussions on the antithesis and palingenesis aimed to distinguish between normal and abnormal conditions in the cosmos, rather than a conflict between faith and science. Kuyper's views show the interconnectedness of faith, worldviews, and scientific activity, suggesting that these factors impact all scientific endeavors, from mathematics to the human sciences.

Introduction

Kuyper, a polymath, was not a scientist in the contemporary sense, but he did write about science. This is not surprising because science played a crucial role in culture during Kuyper's time, and it was emerging as an all-encompassing worldview, especially with the rise of evolutionism. Darwin's *On the Origin of Species* (1859) had not long been published and Ernst Haeckel (1834–1919) and Herbert Spencer (1820–1903), among others were applying Darwin's ideas to society, a project that became known as Social Darwinism.

Kuyper was well-versed in scientific theories and seemed to stay updated with scientific advancements and the history of science. He was, for instance, aware of the conflicts within science regarding homeopaths and allopaths, Darwinists and anti-Darwinists, among others.[2]

---

2. Kuyper, *Lectures on Calvinism*, 131.

500

There are three major sources for Kuyper's approach to the natural sciences. One of his Stone Lectures, *Lectures on Calvinism*, was on science; several chapters in his *Common Grace* volume 3 dealt with it;[3] and in his *Principles of Sacred Theology*, he develops his view of theology as a science and in doing so discusses in some detail in the section on "The organism of science."

Several scholars have reviewed and evaluated Kuyper's view of science.[4] Ratzsch is correct that Kuyper nowhere gives "a formal, detailed philosophy of science" although "there are bits

---

3. This has been published separately as Abraham Kuyper, *Wisdom & Wonder: Common Grace in Science and Art* (Grand Rapids: Christian Library Press, 2011).

4. These include: D. Ratzsch, "Kuyper's Philosophy of Science," in *On Kuyper: A Collection of Readings on the Life, Work & Legacy of Abraham Kuyper*, ed. S. Bishop and J. H. Kok (Sioux Center, IA: Dordt College Press, 2013); H. Dooyeweerd, "Kuyper's Philosophy of Science," in *On Kuyper*, ed. S. Bishop and J.H. Kok (Sioux Center, IA: Dordt College Press, 2013), 153–178; J. Klapwijk, "Abraham Kuyper on Science, Theology and the University," in *On Kuyper*, ed. S. Bishop and J.H. Kok (Sioux Center, IA: Dordt College Press, 2013); Rene Van Woudenberg, "Abraham Kuyper on Faith and Science," in *Abraham Kuyper on Faith and Science*, ed., Cornelis van der Kooi and J. de Bruijn (Amsterdam: VU University, 1999), 147–57; C. B. Anderson, "A Canopy of Grace: Common and Particular Grace in Abraham Kuyper's Philosophy of Science," *The Princeton Seminary Bulletin* 24, no. 1 (2003): 122–40; N. J. Grönum and F. J. Rensburg, "Abraham Kuyper's Christian Science and Empirical Science—Different yet Similar: An Investigation into Epistemological Structures," *Die Skriflig* 48, no. 1 (2014): 8; Jordan J. Ballor, "Abraham Kuyper on Science and Religion: An Introduction to His Texts and Contexts," Faraday Institute, 24 September 2020, https://www.faraday.cam.ac.uk/resources/multimedia/abraham-kuyper-on-science-and-religion-an-introduction-to-his-texts-and-contexts/.

and hints in many different places."[5] There is also an added complication as Klapwijk observes: "Kuyper's concepts are far from always consistent, even with respect to science, theology, and the university."[6]

The term "science" has different meanings in Britain and North America compared with many European countries.[7] In Europe, it encompasses not only the physical and natural sciences but also the human sciences such as sociology, law, linguistics, and philosophy. It is in this way that Kuyper understands science. In his discussion regarding science the term science could often be replaced by the term scholarship—the term is that broad. Although many of the examples he uses are from the natural sciences.

Unlike his contemporary B. B. Warfield Kuyper did not hold to the view that science was simply an objective, unified and a cumulative enterprise. Neither was Kuyper captivated nor enchanted by Enlightenment science.[8] He saw the sciences as a God-given cultural activity that is to be done in depen-

---

5. Ratzsch gives one of the most comprehensive overviews of Kuyper's philosophy of science in the list mentioned—he, however, focuses primarily on *Principles of Sacred Theology* and "Evolution"; little discussion is given to Kuyper's *Common Grace*.

6. J. Klapwijk, "Antithesis and Common Grace," 223.

7. In *Principles of Sacred Theology* Kuyper notes that "In England … science, in its absolute sense, is more and more the exclusive name for the natural science; while the honorary title of 'scientific' is withheld from psychological investigations," *Principles of Sacred Theology*, 91. The term Kuyper uses and is usually translated as science is *wetenschap*.

8. P. Heslam, "Architects of Evangelical Intellectual Thought: Abraham Kuyper and Benjamin Warfield," *Themelios* 24, no. 2 (1999): 11.

dence on God and his Holy Spirit. It is not an autonomous activity; it is not a body of knowledge independent of God.

Observation is the basis of science—what we measure, weigh and count, according to Kuyper, provide a kind of certainty. However, although science is based on observation, observation is not science. Observing microbes under a microscope is no more an act of science as observing a cow in a pasture.[9] In a telling passage Kuyper rejects a full-blown empiricism:[10]

> All human intercourse is founded on this fact, as is also all observation, and consequently all scientific knowledge, which is built up on observation; and this fact falls away at once if faith does not work in you to make your ego believe in your senses.
>
> This is so true, that the most exact science properly begins its scientific task in the higher sense only when observation is finished. To observe bacteria or microbes is by itself as little an act of science as the perception of horses and cows pasturing in the meadow. The only difference between the two is, that horses and cows in the meadow are perceptible with the naked eye, and bacteria and microbes can be observed only with the reinforced eye.[11]

Thus, for Kuyper, science begins when observation has finished.[12] In brief Kuyper's approach could be summarized accordingly: science is by design a unique creature of God, it

---

9. Kuyper, *Principles of Sacred Theology*, 134.

10. Empiricism is the view that all knowledge comes from sensory experience.

11. Kuyper, *Principles of Sacred Theology*, 134.

12. Kuyper, *Principles of Sacred Theology*, 134.

flourishes with society, it grows and develops. It is part of creation, so even if there was no fall, we would still have science. The fall, however, has affected science. Science should be independent of both church and state, and science must be allowed to flourish unhampered by both. Science, for Kuyper, involves thinking God's thoughts after him. There is an antithesis at work in science as there are two kinds of science and two kinds of people: *normalists* and *abnormalists*—what makes the difference is a "spiritual rebirth" or *palingenesis*. Common grace is important for science without it the post-fall decline of science would be absolute.

In what follows I shall expand on this; first by using the framework of creation, fall, and redemption.

Creation, fall, and redemption

Science for Kuyper is fundamentally rooted in the creation and is a creature of God. It roots are in creation not in the fall. However, the fall did impact both science and human scientific activity. The effects of the fall on science, in part, were mitigated by common grace.

Creation
Science is by divine design, a unique creature of God. Science is part of creation. Seen this way, however, science is then also "an invention of God, which he called into being as his creation."[13] It is Kuyper writes—echoing the synodical report written by Herman Bavinck—a "'unique creature of God' with its own principle of life."[14]

---

13. Kuyper, *Common Grace* 3, 531.

14. Kuyper, *Common Grace* 3, 523.

If there was no fall we would still have science. Science, unlike the state or the institutional church, belongs to the realm of creation, not the realm of redemption (particular grace). As Kuyper puts it: "Without sin there would be no state, and apart from sin there would have been no Christian church, but there would have been science."[15]

However, as we shall see the fall has had an effect of science.

Science flourishes within society. Science as a creature of God is to "develop in freedom."[16] This flourishing Kuyper maintains occurs in stages: an emergence until adult hood is reached and then a full-grown stage where it becomes self-sufficient. In the first stage the support of the government and the church was needed—now it has become more mature and should be independent of both the church and the state and should no longer be submissive to either; but neither should it seek to dominate them.

Science should now have an independent character. This is consistent with his view of sphere sovereignty. Science has an independent character, and it has "a calling independent of the state and the church."[17]

The growth and development of science Kuyper attributes to common grace. Despite the fall, science is able to prove fruitful and aid progress. This rather rosy view of science, however, this may in part be coloured by the cultural assumptions of his time.

---

15. Kuyper, *Common Grace* 3, 524.

16. Kuyper, *Common Grace* 3, 523.

17. Kuyper, *Common Grace* 3, 524.

Science is a communal activity. For science to grow and develop, it needs collaboration—science is not an individual activity.

> Science in this exalted sense originates only through the cooperation of many people. It advances only gradually in the generations that come on the scene, and thus only gradually acquires that stability and that rich content that guarantee it an independent existence, and begins to appear only in this more general form as an influence in life.[18]

Science is thinking God's thoughts after him. Everything expresses God in some way and for Kuyper that includes science. This notion rests on three truths:

1. Clarity of God's thoughts existed before creation.
2. God has revealed his thoughts in creation.
3. God created in humans the capacity to grasp, reflect and arrange these thoughts in a totality expressed in creation.

In this way, we obtain knowledge when these three truths that fit together. First, the full and rich clarity of God's thoughts existed in God from eternity. Second, in the creation God has revealed, embedded, and embodied a rich fullness of his thoughts. Third, God created in human beings, as his image-bearers, the capacity to understand, to grasp, to reflect, and to arrange within a totality these thoughts expressed in the creation. The essence of human science rests on these three realities. Some aspects of this are problematic in that they betray a scholastic tendency within Kuyper—see below.

---

18. Kuyper, *Common Grace* 3, 530.

Science is part of a unified coherent organic whole. This is in keeping with Kuyper's declaration that "not one part of our world of thought can be hermetically separated for the other parts." It is all God's creation, and it all belongs to him. Natural sciences are part of the whole of the sciences—theology included. The role of philosophy, argues Kuyper, is "to construct the human knowledge, which has been brought to light by all the other sciences, into one architectonic whole, to show how the building arises from one basis."[19]

However, then came the fall.

Fall

The fall has profound consequences, altering the entire cosmic order. The creation is no longer what it was created to be. The world is now abnormal. Those who reject the fall see the world as being normal. This distinction between normal and abnormal, as we have seen, is an important one for Kuyper.

Without the fall and sin: "The cosmos would have been before us as an open book." However, that is not now the case. For those who maintain that sin has had no effect on the creation, it is "natural … to represent science as an absolute power…." The result is either to limit science to the "exact sciences," or to "interpret it as a philosophic system after whose standards reality must be distorted."[20] However, the fall and sin have also changed the nature of the world but also of science:

> Sin is what lures and tempts people to place science outside of a relationship with God, thereby stealing science from God, and ultimately turning science against

19. Kuyper, *Principles of Sacred Theology*, 614.

20. Kuyper, *Principles of Sacred Theology*, 91.

God. The flower of true science possesses its root in the fear of the Lord, grows forth from the fear of the Lord, and finds in that fear of the Lord its principle, its motive, its starting point. If through sin a person is cut off from this root that proceeds from the fear of the Lord, the inevitable result must be that such a person will present as science something that is a facade without any essence. [21]

It also affects our understanding:

The distinction between the true science and the false science lies not in the arena where people perform their investigations, but in the manner with which they investigate, and in the principle from which people begin to investigate. Sin has not only corrupted our moral life, but has also darkened our understanding.[22]

However, even a broken mirror can assist in seeing things:

Therefore, we can postulate that the mirror of our consciousness became cracked by sin, and the reflection of the world on that cracked surface would provide us with a knowledge of the world that is not altogether incorrect.[23]

Sin has an effect not only on science but also on the scientist.

The disorganization which is the result of sin consists not merely in the break in the natural life-harmony be-

---

21. Kuyper, *Wisdom & Wonder*, 51.
22. Kuyper, *Wisdom & Wonder*, 52.
23. Kuyper, *Wisdom & Wonder*, 63.

tween us and the cosmos but also in a break in the life-harmony in our own selves.[24]

Scientists like us all are subject to self-delusion and self-deception,[25] as Kuyper puts it: "Ignorance wrought by sin is the most difficult obstacle in the way of all true science."[26]

Consciously or unconsciously, self-interest affects moral differences. We all see things from a certain perspective, "Everybody preaches for his own parish."[27] Roman Catholics view the Reformation very differently from Protestants. A Dutch historian will view the naval battles with the English very differently from an English historian. This "darkening of our understanding" caused by sin,[28] however, "Does not mean that we have lost the capacity of thinking logically, for as far as the impulse of its law of life is concerned, the logica has *not* been impaired by sin."[29]

The higher and lower sciences—an increasing subjectivity. Kuyper recognized some differences between what he termed the lower sciences and the higher sciences. For Kuyper the lower sciences were the subjects such as mathematics, physics, chemistry, and biology; the higher sciences were psychology, sociology, law and so on. The lower sciences such as mathematics and the physical sciences are less subject to subjectivity. The-

---

24. Kuyper, *Principles of Sacred Theology*, 112.

25. Kuyper, *Principles of Sacred Theology*, 107.

26. Kuyper, *Principles of Sacred Theology*, 114.

27. Kuyper, *Principles of Sacred Theology*, 110.

28. Kuyper, *Principles of Sacred Theology*, 110.

29. Kuyper, *Principles of Sacred Theology*, 110.

higher sciences are more so. There is an increasing subjectivity, this is he sees is a consequence of the fall.

Redemption

Science can also become a tool of common redemption—obviously it is not a means of salvation. (Although some may have seen it that way.) Common grace working with science may redeem some aspects of the fall and sin.

> In the ordination of God's common grace, science is also one of the most powerful means for combating sin together with the error and misery flowing from sin. Science practiced in the Lord's name functions as an antidote to the poison of sin, but not as if science would ever possess the power to effect the transition of any person's soul from death unto life. The instrument that God has ordained for that kind of transition is faith, and this saving faith can arise only from the re-creation of a person's soul, namely, from regeneration, which God himself imparts within the secrecy of the soul without us and without any instrument. For that reason, science does not belong to particular grace, nor can it belong there, but occupies its own place in that glorious work of common grace that restrains sin, error, and misery in their manifestations.[30]

Some areas in which science may provide a common redemption include, according to Kuyper, the treatment of diseases, the fostering of social order, an improvement in the standard of living, and managing natural forces such as hurricanes, earthquakes, and volcanic activity.

---

30. Kuyper, *Common Grace* 3, 520.

Regeneration—being born again—is essential for scientists. It enables a believer to see things differently from the nonbeliever. Being able to see in full colour we see the world differently to someone who is colour blind or can only see in black and white. This is the basis for Kuyper's two kinds of people, two kinds of science distinction.

Two kinds of people/two kinds of science

In *Principles of Scared Theology* chapter III, the "Twofold development of science" §49 entitled "Two kinds of people," and "Two kinds of science." There Kuyper boldly states: "'regeneration' breaks humanity in two."[31] In essence what Kuyper is describing is that regeneration makes a difference to the way we see the world and the way in which science is performed:

> What we mean is, that both parts of humanity, that which has been wrought upon by palingenesis and that which lacks it, feel the impulse to investigate the object, and, by doing this in a scientific way, to obtain a scientific systemization of that which exists.[32]

There is an antithesis between these two kinds of people, between those who have experienced regeneration and those who have not, i.e., the "spiritual" person and the "natural" person.

> To the extent that results are governed by factual observation, obtained by weighing and measuring and counting, all scientific researchers are equal. As soon as people move above this lower kind of science, however, to higher forms of science, at that point the

---

31. Kuyper, *Principles of Sacred Theology*, 152.
32. Kuyper, *Principles of Sacred Theology*, 155.

personal subject makes a contribution, in terms of which the difference between the "natural" man and the "spiritual" man comes into play. This phenomenon is definitely not restricted to the science of theology, but is present in every spiritual science, including the philosophical framework for the natural sciences.[33]

It is clear that with its antithesis between a "natural" man and a "spiritual" man, Scripture is not merely referring to a person who does and another who does not take Holy Scripture into account. Its pronouncement goes much deeper by positing the distinction between having and not having received the Spirit of God.[34]

In *Lectures on Calvinism*, he distinguishes between abnormalists and normalists. Again, this difference arises from the regeneration of the scientist. This is the activity of the inward work of the Holy Spirit through particular grace. Such regeneration means that the light of special revelation can now be seen in and through common grace. However, he sees no split between Christian and non-Christian science at the lower levels (there is only one logic), yet this split becomes apparent at the higher levels. But then he sees the antithesis working at all levels.

If regeneration, palingenesis, made no difference then this "leads to the rejection of the Christian religion."[35] Regeneration by the Holy Spirit means that the Christian sees things

---

33. Kuyper, *Wisdom & Wonder*, 80.

34. Kuyper, *Wisdom & Wonder*, 80.

35. Kuyper, *Principles of Sacred Theology*, 154.

from a different perspective and is "impelled by different impulses."[36] This inevitably affects the sciences. As Kuyper puts it:

> But we emphatically assert that these two kinds of peo-
> ple devote their time and their strength to the erection
> of two different structures, each of which purposes to be
> a complete building of science. If, however, one of these
> two is asked, whether the building, on which he labors,
> will truly provide us what we need in the scientific
> realm, he will of course claim for himself the high and
> noble name of science, and withhold it from the other.[37]

Common grace

Without common grace the decline of the sciences post-fall
would be absolute. Common grace provides an explanation
for scientific and cultural developments by non-Christians.
It also provides a rationale for the involvement of Christians in so-called "secular realms." How else can we explain
the works of Socrates, Plato, and Aristotle? What it does
not do is provide a basis for the Christianisation of culture
and society.

It also counteracts the repercussions of the fall.

> Apart from common grace, the decline of science
> would have become absolute without that illumination
> by the Holy Spirit. Left to itself, sin progresses from
> bad to worse. Sin makes you slide down a slope on
> which no one can remain standing. Anyone who ig-
> nores common grace can come to no other conclusion

---

36. Kuyper, *Principles of Sacred Theology*, 154.
37. Kuyper, *Principles of Sacred Theology*, 156.

than that all science done outside the arena of the holy lives off appearance and delusion, and necessarily results in misleading anyone listening to its voice. Yet the outcome shows that this is not the case.[38]

We can explain this only by saying that although sin does indeed spread its corruption, nevertheless common grace has intervened in order to temper and restrain this operation of sin.[39]

Has sin resulted in our inability any longer to think logically? Has sin induced in us an inability to perceive what exists and occurs around us? Does sin place a blindfold over our eyes so that we no longer see or observe? Absolutely not.[40]

The effect of sin is to move the focus on the microscope, whereas, common grace, in part, re-adjusts it.

If I focus the microscope for a student and he changes the lens or the adjustment so that he sees nothing, the blame for not being able to see is his, not mine. This is exactly what we did when we fell into sin. Having no right to complain, we should rather be grateful that it pleased God to help us in this helpless situation by re-adjusting the microscope through common grace so that we can at least see something, even if not with the former clarity.[41]

---

38. Kuyper, *Wisdom & Wonder*, 52.

39. Kuyper, *Wisdom & Wonder*, 53.

40. Kuyper, *Wisdom & Wonder*, 54.

41. Kuyper, *Wisdom & Wonder*, 74.

The limitations of science

Kuyper was well aware of the limits of science. It is unable, for example to prove or disprove the existence of God: "Every effort to prove the existence of God by so-called evidences must fail and has failed."[42]

All scientists search for truth—"to champion the truth."[43] Despite the differences and conflict between scientists—each would claim the other is wrong. Science, Kuyper claims, is unable to "settle this dispute." He goes further:

> To believe that an absolute science in the above-given sense can ever decide the question between truth and falsehood is nothing but a criminal self-deception.[44]

To the extent that science clings to the visible and the observable, it cannot even entertain the question of the origin, coherence, and destiny of things.[45]

In addition to his work on common grace, and the *Principles of Sacred Theology*, Kuyper devotes the fourth of his 1889 Stone *Lectures on Calvinism* on science.

Lectures on Calvinism

In his lectures he makes four key points. Each point is an apologetic for the role of Calvinism in the sciences.[46]

1. Calvinism fostered a love for science.
2. It restored science to its proper domain.

42. Kuyper, *Principles of Sacred Theology*, 112.

43. Kuyper, *Principles of Sacred Theology*, 17.

44. Kuyper, *Principles of Sacred Theology*, 118.

45. Kuyper, *Wisdom & Wonder*, 71.

46. Kuyper, *Lectures on Calvinism*, 110.

3. It delivered science from unnatural bonds

4. A solution for the unavoidable scientific conflict.

Within Calvinism, Kuyper writes, there is "an impulse, an inclination, an incentive, to scientific investigation."[47] Calvinism has fostered science. He looks to history to back this up. He focuses on the events that led up to the establishment of the University of Leiden, a university of the sciences—a place where science flourished. It was the Dutch that invented the telescope, the microscope, and the thermometer. Instruments that were crucial for empirical science. Although, he denies that "mere empiricism in itself is the perfect science."[48]

> Predestination also provides a strong motive for science. This recognizes that the cosmos is a creation rather than an accident; it is a "building erected in a severely consistent style."[49]

If it were not:

> There is no interconnection, no development, no continuity: a chronicle but no history.[50]

And there could be no science.

In Calvinism we find "one Supreme will in God, the cause of all existing things, subjecting them to fixed ordinances and directing them towards a pre-established plan."[51] Without this there could be no science: "God's decrees are the foundations

---

47. Kuyper, *Lectures on Calvinism*, 110.

48. Kuyper, *Lectures on Calvinism*, 112.

49. Kuyper, *Lectures on Calvinism*, 114

50. Kuyper, *Lectures on Calvinism*, 114.

51. Kuyper, *Lectures on Calvinism*, 115.

of the natural laws."[52] Faith in unity, stability, and order is foundational to science:

> Without a deep conviction of this unity, this stability and this order, science is unable to go beyond mere conjectures, and only when there is faith in the organic interconnection of the Universe, will there be also a possibility for science to ascend from the empirical investigation of the special phenomena to the general, and from the general to the law which rules over it, and from that law to the principle, which is dominant over all.[53]

His second point was that "Calvinism restored to science its domain." What does he mean by this?

It was common grace that "threw open to science the vast field of the cosmos ...." He notes that Christianity is soteriological—in that it is concerned with personal salvation. However, that is not the whole story. Sadly, the "*cosmological* significance was lost out of sight." The result was a neglection of "the world of God's creation."[54] It resulted in a dualism of heaven/ earth of soul/body and so forth. This dualism Kuyper argues "is by no means countenanced by the Holy Scriptures."[55] It is this dualism that was undermined by Calvinism. Science could be a legitimate area for Christian ministry.

> In keeping with this, the final outcome of the future, foreshadowed in the H. Scriptures, is not the merely spiritual existence of saved souls, but the restoration of

---

52. Kuyper, *Lectures on Calvinism*, 115.

53. Kuyper, *Lectures on Calvinism*, 115–116.

54. Kuyper, *Lectures on Calvinism*, 118.

55. Kuyper, *Lectures on Calvinism*, 118.

the entire cosmos, when God will be all in all under the renewed heaven on the renewed earth.[56]

The contempt for and of the world is rejected by Calvinism, "the temporal and cosmically things" are no longer undervalued:

> Cosmically life has regained its worth not at the expense of things eternal, but by virtue of its capacity as God's handiwork and as a revelation of God's attributes.[57]

Having established the role of Calvinism in restoring the position of science he goes on to discuss the role of common grace.

Given the totality of sin, how does the unregenerate excel in many things? The answer for Kuyper is common grace. Common grace has "arrested sin in its course in order to prevent the total annihilation of [God's] handiwork."[58] Common grace does not "kill the core of sin, nor does it save unto eternal life, but it arrests the complete effectuation of sin...."[59]

Calvinism makes the scientific enterprise permissible and does not limit Christians to theology. Common grace is the means whereby the unregenerate can make scientific developments. Common grace removes the "interdict, under which secular life has been bound ..." Thus, the domain of science is a legitimate domain for Christians to engage in.

Third, Kuyper shows that Calvinism has advanced the "indispensable liberty" of science. Liberty, of course, does not mean there are no restrictions. As Kuyper states "a fish lying on

---

56. Kuyper, *Lectures on Calvinism*, 119.

57. Kuyper, *Lectures on Calvinism*, 120.

58. Kuyper, *Lectures on Calvinism*, 123.

59. Kuyper, *Lectures on Calvinism*, 123–124.

dry land is perfectly free, *viz.* to die and perish..."[60] For many years there were only two dominant powers: the church and the state. The Calvinistic Reformation, Kuyper maintained, freed the universities from church control and thus gave science a freedom it did not previously have.

His final point was that Calvinism was able to find a solution to the so-called conflict between science and faith. Kuyper maintained that "every science in a certain degree starts from faith." In *Lectures on Calvinism* he notes the conflicts between scientists and scientific theories, be it between Darwinists and anti-Darwinists, between formalists and realists, and between van Humbolt, Jacob Grimm, and Max Muller in linguistics. The main conflict he sees is between "those who hold to a confession of the Triune God and His Word, and those who seek the solution of the world-problem in Deism, Pantheism and Naturalism."[61] The conflict is thus not between faith and science, as Kuyper puts it: "Such a conflict does not exist." Rather faith is integral to science:

> Every science in a certain degree starts *from faith,* and, on the contrary, faith, which does not lead to science, is mistaken faith or superstition, but real, genuine faith it is not.[62]

He goes on to list several areas where faith is evident in the scientific enterprise. These include:

- Fath in self-consciousness.
- In the accurate working of our senses.

---

60. Kuyper, *Lectures on Calvinism*, 126.

61. Kuyper, *Lectures on Calvinism*, 131.

62. Kuyper, *Lectures on Calvinism*, 131.

- In the correctness of the laws of thought.
- In something hidden behind the special phenomena.
- In the principles from which we proceed.

These, he notes, "are indispensable axioms, needed in a productive scientific investigation, do not come to us by proof, but are established in our judgment by our inner conception and given with our self-consciousness."[63] The conflict is not then between faith and science, "but between the assertion that the cosmos, as it exists today, is either in a *normal* or *abnormal* condition."[64] This distinction—and Kuyper is keen on making distinctions—is an important one. It is rooted in the notion of the antithesis and in what he terms palingenesis.

The difference is between those who have been regenerated by the Holy Spirit and those who are not. For Kuyper, regeneration makes a difference. This is why there are two kinds of people. We all start from a faith position—the Christian faith makes a difference to how the world is seen. The world as it is not normal but abnormal, it has been affected by the fall. The way things are is not normal, it has not always been this way. The Christian faith will affect how we see reality, and how we interpret data, even if it may not make a change in the way we measure or weigh things.

All scientists may make the same observations, the same reading on a scale or thermometer, and because of common grace may come to the same conclusions. However, science starts not from observations but from faith.[65]

---

63. Kuyper, *Lectures on Calvinism*, 131.

64. Kuyper, *Lectures on Calvinism*, 132.

65. Kuyper, *Lectures on Calvinism*, 131.

Evaluation

Strengths of Kuyper's position

There are many strengths in Kuyper's position. He provides a basis for Christian involvement in the sciences. He ably shows how Calvinism enabled the flourishing of science and that it was not inimical to it. He thus shows that science and the engagement of science could be a Christian ministry.

He took seriously the sovereignty of God over the sciences, the effect of sin on the creation, he affirmed the creator/creation distinction, he saw the need for a distinctively Christian approach to the sciences not least because our starting points affect our view of things.

He identified the role of faith in science—unfortunately, this is not fully developed—and identified the supposed conflict between science and faith as being fallacious as every science presupposes faith. The conflict between science and faith Klapwijk describes as a pseudo-conflict.[66] The conflict model has dominated the relationship between science and religion for decades. It is one of many models proposed for the way science and religion may relate.[67] Kuyper saw the error of the conflict view of science and religion—he realized and advocated the view that both science and religion rested on faith and were derived from worldviews.

As such, Kuyper's views predate the insights of Michael Polanyi who also came to see the role of the personal and faith within science. Herman Dooyeweerd also took seriously the role of faith commitments within the scientific enterprise. It

66. Klapwijk, "Abraham Kuyper on Science, Theology and the University."
67. See, for example, Steve Bishop, "A Typology of Science and Religion," *Evangelical Quarterly* 72, no. 1 (2000): 35–56.

was then Dooyeweerd following in Kuyper's line, who developed Kuyper's insights into a Christian philosophy.

Kuyper also saw the limits of the sciences—it was an important but not all-important role in unlocking knowledge and wisdom. He rejected strict empiricism and saw that faith, not observation was the starting point for science.

In addition to rejecting strict empiricism, Kuyper also rejected Kantian idealism. Knowledge was more than rational thought. The revelation of God and his creation is also important—this in part justifies the two kinds of people and two kinds of science he advocated. The Christian faith does make a difference.

Common grace provided a biblical framework in which to appreciate and appropriate the developments of science made by non-Christians. It also provided a basis for Christian involvement in the sciences. The antithesis, however, revealed that Christians and non-Christians have different starting points and thus the need for a distinctly Christian approach to science.

Weaknesses of Kuyper's position

Common grace and the antithesis provided a basis in which to provide an understanding of Christian and non-Christian approaches to science. Common grace without the antithesis would diminish the effect of *palingenesis*. The antithesis without common grace could result in Christian isolation or separatism. Both common grace and the antithesis are essential to a Christian approach to the natural sciences. However, the relationship between the two was left ambiguous and undeveloped in Kuyper.[68]

---

68. S. U. Zuidema, "Common Grace and Christian Action in Abraham Kuyper," in *On Kuyper*, ed. S. Bishop and J. Kok (Sioux Center, IO:

There are some areas in which Kuyper was unable to escape dualistic and scholastic traits. I will focus on two below.

Thinking God's thoughts. Dooyeweerd identified two streams within Kuyper's thought—a Reformational and a scholastic stream.[69] We see Kuyper's scholastic strand in his notion of "thinking God's thoughts after him." For Kuyper, "divine thinking is embedded in all of creation,"[70] he develops this point:

> God's thoughts constitute the core of the essence of things, and it was the divine intention to prescribe for created things their manner of existence, their form, their principle of life, their destiny, and their progress.[71]

This reflects a logos doctrine and has neo-platonic overtones (see for example, the discussion in Klapwijk, Dooyeweerd,[72] and Anderson[73]). Kuyper poses an important question:

Dordt Press, 2013); T. McConnel, "Common Grace or the Antithesis? Towards a Consistent Understanding of Kuyper's 'Sphere Sovereignty'," in *On Kuyper*, ed. S. Bishop and J. H. Kok (Sioux Center, IO: Dordt Press, 2013).

69. Dooyeweerd, "Kuyper's Philosophy of Science."

70. Kuyper, *Common Grace* 23, 527.

71. Kuyper, *Common Grace* 23. 527.

72. Dooyeweerd asserts: "The scholastic line mainly expresses itself in the view of soul and body, the theory of the logos and in the idea-realism, while the modern influence manifests itself in the various subdivisions of Kuyper's philosophy of science which bears the stamp of critical realism" ("Kuyper's Philosophy of Science", 155).

73. Klapwijk, "Abraham Kuyper on Science, Theology and the University;" Dooyeweerd, "Kuyper's Philosophy of Science;" Anderson, "A canopy of grace: Common and Particular Grace in Abraham Kuyper's Philosophy of Science."

The only question is whether we human beings are gift-
ed with a capacity to reflect that thinking of God.[74]

And there lies the rub. Kuper thinks that humans as a micro-
cosm of the cosmos can—I would maintain that we can only
know what God has chosen to reveal. We cannot know God's
thoughts only what he accommodates to us.[75] This also reflects
a semi-mysticism that is implicit within Kuyper.[76]

> In this way, then, we perceive three truths that are related:
> first, *the full and rich clarity of God's thoughts existed in God
> from eternity;* second, in the creation God has revealed, em-
> bedded, and embodied a rich fullness of his thoughts; and,
> third, God created in human beings, as his image-bearers,
> the capacity to comprehend, reflect upon, and construe as
> a unity these thoughts expressed in creation. Indeed, the
> very essence of human science rests on these three realities.[77]

It is this first point that reflects Kuyper's scholasticism (italics
my emphasis). Such a position also fails to consider the noetic
effects of the fall—something that elsewhere Kuyper advocates.

Higher and lower sciences. If Kuyper had developed his view
of the role of faith in science, he may have concluded that faith
and worldviews impact on all of scientific activity rather than
having an increasing effect as one moves from the mathe-

74. Kuyper, *Common Grace* 3, 527.

75. Roy A. Clouser, *The Myth of Religious Neutrality*, 219–233.

76. See, for example, John C. Vander Stelt, "Kuyper's Semi-mystical
Conception," *Philosophia Reformata* 38 (1) (1973): 178–190; B. J. van
Der Walt, "Semi-mistieke Spiritualiteit by Johannes Calvyn en by
Abraham Kuyper," *Journal for Christian Scholarship = Tydskrif vir
Christelike Wetenskap,* 51(3) (2015): 99–124.

77. Kuyper, *Common Grace* 3, 528.

matical sciences (lower sciences) to the human sciences (higher sciences). This can be seen from the work of Dooyeweerd—see figure 2.[78] Mathematical statements such as 2 x 2 = 4 have meaning only within a mathematical framework (such as formalism, logicism, nominalism and so forth) each of which depends on responses to a philosophical view of reality, with the answers to questions such as the origin, coherence and totality of all which are answered in terms of ground motives.[79]

Mathematics as the typical lower science is thus not immune to faith beliefs.[80] The question of what a number is has

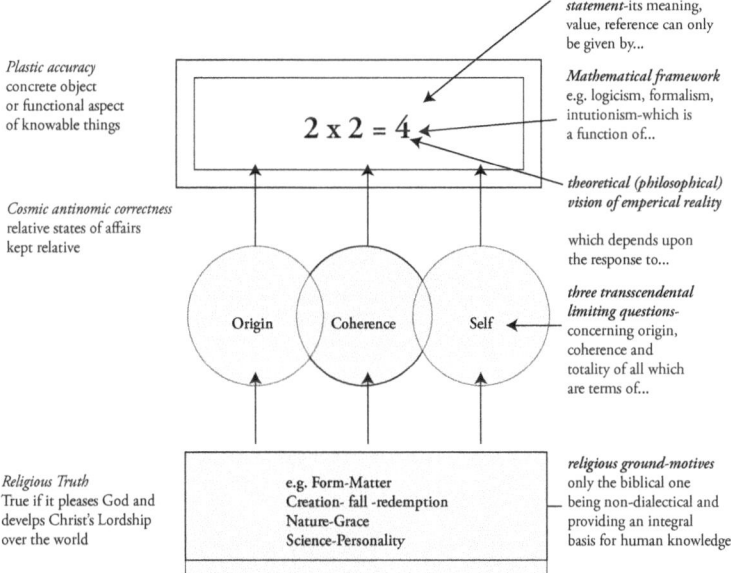

Figure 2. Source Russell, *Christian Philosophy Diagrams*, figure 22.

78. R. A. Russell, *Christian Philosophy Diagrams* (Bristol: All of Life Redeemed, 2020), https://www.allofliferedeemed.co.uk/russell.htm.

79. Herman Dooyeweerd, *New Critique of Theoretical Thought* (Presbyterian & Reformed Pub Co, 1953), 47.

80. Clouser, *The Myth of Religious Neutrality*; Steve Bishop, "Beliefs Shape Mathematics," *Spectrum* 28, no. 2 (1996): 131–41; Steve Bishop,

different responses depending on the worldview or ground-motive of the respondent.

Conclusion

Although Kuyper's approach to the natural sciences shows elements of scholasticism, he does provide a solid foundation for a distinctively Christian approach to the natural sciences. One that does justice to sphere sovereignty and to the antithesis and common grace, even though their relationship is left ambiguous by Kuyper. His creational view of science avoids the extremes of idealism and empiricism. In line with his sphere sovereignty the sciences should be independent of both church and state; the sciences must be allowed to flourish unhampered by both.

A summary in 12 theses

1. Kuyper believed that Calvinism played a crucial role in restoring the domain of science by emphasizing the significance of the cosmos and God's creation. Science is a unique creature of God.
2. Calvinism rejected dualism between the spiritual and physical realms, allowing science to be a legitimate area for Christian ministry.
3. Kuyper highlighted the importance of common grace in recognizing the value of temporal and cosmic aspects of life, restoring the worth of creation as God's handiwork. Without it the post-fall decline of the sciences would be absolute.

"Mathematics and the Myth of Neutrality," *Christian School Education* 5, no. 4 (2001): 19–21.

4. Kuyper acknowledged the limitations of science in determining absolute truth. He emphasized the need for humility in the pursuit of knowledge.
5. The sciences are part of creation, so even if there were no fall, we would still have the sciences. The fall, however, affected, the sciences.
6. There is an antithesis at work in the sciences as there are two kinds of people: normalists and abnormalists—what makes the difference is a "spiritual rebirth" or palingenesis. This results in two kinds of science.
7. Kuyper's discussions on the antithesis and palingenesis highlighted the distinction between normal and abnormal conditions in the cosmos, rather than a conflict between faith and science.
8. Kuyper's emphasis on the image-bearing capacity of humans to understand God's thoughts in creation underpins the essence of human science.
9. The rejection of contempt for the world by Calvinism allowed for a holistic view of the future restoration of the cosmos under God's reign.
10. Kuyper's semi-mystical perspective reflected in his belief that humans have the capacity to comprehend and reflect upon God's thoughts revealed in creation.
11. Kuyper's recognition of the interconnectedness of various scientific disciplines aimed to present a unified understanding of the cosmos.
12. Kuyper's exploration of the relationship between faith, worldviews, and scientific activity suggests that these factors impact all scientific endeavors.

Study Questions

1. Kuyper uses the Dutch term *wetenschap* to describe science. What does he mean by this term?
2. What are meant by the terms *abnormalist* and *normalist* in regard to science?
3. How has the fall affected the sciences?
4. How does palingenesis affect the sciences and the scientist?
5. Kuyper maintained that "every science in a certain degree starts from faith." What did he mean by this?
6. Are we able to think God's thoughts after him?
7. Is there a scholastic strand in Kuyper's view of the sciences? Any neo-platonic overtones?

Further Reading

Primary sources

Kuyper, Abraham. "Calvinism and Science," in *Lectures on Calvinism*. (Grand Rapids, MI: Eerdmans, 1931)

Kuyper, Abraham. *Wisdom & Wonder: Common Grace in Science in Art* (Grand Rapids, MI: Christian's Library Press, 2011)

Secondary sources

Ratzsch, D. "Kuyper's philosophy of science," in Steve Bishop and John Kok (ed.) *On Kuyper: A Collection of Readings on the Life, Work & Legacy of Abraham Kuyper* (Sioux Center: Dordt Press, 2013)

30

Slavery, Race, and Apartheid

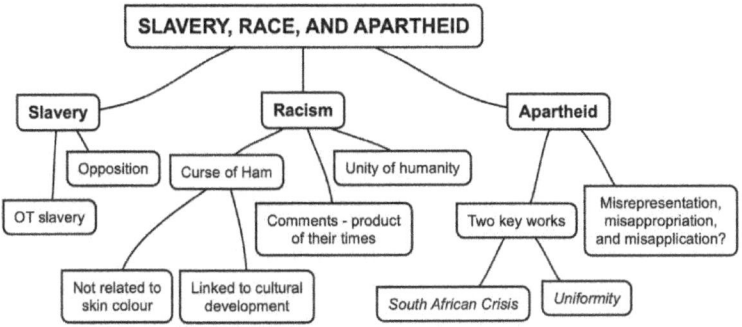

In brief

THIS CHAPTER DISCUSSES THE interpretation of biblical texts and the views of Kuyper in relation to race, slavery, and apartheid. It addresses the misinterpretation of biblical passages to justify slavery and segregation, particularly the misrepresentation of the curse of Ham as a basis for African slavery. It also examines Kuyper's views on race, slavery, and cultural chauvinism, highlighting his opposition to slavery and his belief in the diversity of nations and races. It further explores Kuyper's "Uniformity: The Curse of Modern Life," which has been linked to the so-called "apartheid Bible," and discusses how Kuyper's ideas were misapplied to support apartheid. The conclusion emphasizes that while Kuyper's views on race may have been common in his time, he would not have supported apartheid, and his work was misused to justify it.

Introduction

Some of Kuyper's views have raised significant concerns and criticisms, particularly in the areas of slavery and race. This chapter will focus on these aspects, examining whether Kuyper's theological ideas may have contributed to the theological underpinnings of South African apartheid. Let us start with the issue of slavery.

Slavery

Slavery has historically posed moral dilemmas for Christians. Notably, prominent figures such as George Whitfield and Jonathan Edwards, both influential theologians, not only owned slaves but also supported the institution of slavery. As historian Hugh Thomas pointed out, during their time, many Calvinists seemed to accept slavery without question, often attributing it to what they referred to as the "curse of Ham."[1]

The "curse of Ham" is derived from a passage in Genesis 9:20–27. According to this narrative, Ham observed the drunken Noah's nakedness, while his brothers, Shem, and Japeth, covered their father discreetly. In response, Canaan, Ham's son, was singled out to be a slave to Shem and Japeth. Regrettably, these verses were used during the slave trade as an explanation for black skin and to justify

---

1. Hugh Thomas, *Documents From Old Testament Times* (London: Nelson, 1958), 162.

slavery, they have also been utilized to justify white supremacy. As David Whitford observes: "Though Ham is
not cursed and race is never mentioned in the text, it is
this section of Genesis 9 that became one of the most per-
sistent ideological and theological defenses for African
slavery and segregation."[2]

Such an interpretation, to put it mildly, is ludicrous! Ham's
misdemeanour had nothing to do with skin colour. Ham had
four children Cush, Egypt, Put, and Canaan, yet only Canaan
was cursed—Ham was not!

The Scriptures appear to support some form of slavery.
However, Israelite slavery was of a different form from that of
the ancient Near East. The issue of slavery provides a poignant
example of how our world-and-life view influences our interpretation of Scripture. In the nineteenth century there was a
lively debate among Christians about the ethics of slavery: "to
argue against slavery in 1850 was to argue the inspiration and
inerrancy of the authorative word of God."[3] It is immediately
apparent that those who strongly opposed the abolition of slavery were those who stood to benefit directly from it. The Quak-
er John Woolman claimed that:

---

2.   David M. Whitford, *The Curse of Ham in the Early Modern Era: The
      Bible and the Justifications for Slavery* (London: Routledge, 2017). See
      also David Goldberg, *The Curse of Ham: Race and Slavery in Early
      Judaism, Christianity, and Islam* (Princeton: Princeton University Press,
      2005); Stephen R. Haynes, *Noah's Curse: The Biblical Justification of
      American Slavery* (Oxford: Oxford University Press, 2002).

3.   Willard M Swartley, *Slavery, Sabbath, War and Women: Case Issues in
      Biblical Interpretation (Conrad Grebel Lecture)* (Harrisonburg, Va:
      Herald Press, 1987), 199.

The love of ease and gain are the motives in general of keeping slaves, and men are wont to take hold of weak arguments to support a cause which is unreasonable.[4]

In using the Scripture for self-justification, they failed to let themselves be confronted by the text and let the Scriptures affect their prior assumptions. If the Scriptures are to have more than a paper authority, we should approach them with the full knowledge that we have our presuppositions and be willing for the Scriptures to challenge them. This much we can learn from the nineteenth-century slave owners.

In the Near East, slaves were the property of another;[5] they were essential to the economic order and had no rights. They were treated as merchandise[6] and even had a redeemable cash value (30 shekels).[7] The Code of Hammurabi, discovered in 1902 at Susa on an eight-foot-high black stele, was the law code of Hammurabi the king of Babylon (c. 1792–50 BC); it recognized three classes of people: *awleum*, the normal free citizens; *muskenum*, members of a social group that was free but dependent upon the crown; and *slaves*. The code of Hammuurabi contains a death penalty for negligence in the settlement of a slave (§ 7); the death penalty for anyone who conceals a slave (§ 19); and (§ 17) a reward for the capture and return of a runaway slave.

---

4. Cited in Swartley, *Slavery, Sabbath, War and Women*, 55.

5. J. P. M. van der Ploog, "Slavery in the Old Testament," *Vestus Testament Suppl.* 22 (1972): 85.

6. Hans Jochem Boecker, *Law and the Administration of Justice in Old Testament and Ancient East* (London: SPCK,1980), 77.

7. E. W. Heaton, *Everyday Life in Old Testament Times* (London: Batsford, 1961), 148.

Israel's law was in marked contrast to this; they had all but abolished slavery. (This may have been because of Israel's long history as a nation of slaves, which gave them empathy with other slaves.) Hebrews were to be released in the seventh year (Ex 21:2; Deut 15:12); they were not to be released empty handed (Deut 15:13); slaves could choose to remain with their masters (Deut 15:16)—the fact that some took up this option shows that slavery was preferable for some to freedom. The Law also offered protection from physical abuse (Ex 21:26–7), athough perhaps the most radical provision in the Law was the law of asylum (Deut 23:15ff) (cf Code of Hammurabi §19,17). This law almost gave the slaves a right to run away, though it presumes that runaways will be the exception.[8]

Despite evangelical heroes such as Warfield and Edwards supporting and even advocating slavery Christians today would be vociferous against slavery. It was Christians who were at the forefront of the movement for the abolition of slavery. It is unsurprising then that Kuyper's mentor Groen van Prinsterer sided with those who were anti-slavery. As Kuiper observes: Groen was "zealous for the abolition of slavery in the Dutch colonies."[9]

Likewise, Kuyper opposed slavery, he wrote in "The Social Question":

---

8. Christopher J. H. Wright, *Living as the People of God: Relevance of Old Testament Ethics* (Leicester: IVP, 1984), 182.

9. D. Th Kuiper, "Groen and Kuyper on the Racial Issue," in *Kuyper Reconsidered*, ed. J de Bruijn and C van der Kooi (Amsterdam: VU Uitgeverij), 73.

Initially, Christians felt they could not join the nascent labor movement. They certainly believed that mutual aid and charity were needed, but they were slow to realize that at stake were fundamental rights and that the social question was an issue concerning justice. Did Scripture, they asked, not condone even slavery as a normal phenomenon? Not even the apostle Paul dared question the right of a slave owner (though he softened it by speaking of brotherly love). And in ancient Israel, was the owning of slaves not legitimate (though they might go free after seven years)?

Granted, in the sin-ridden evolution of the human race, slavery was an inevitable phase which no doubt had benefits. The short epistle of James does not even mention slavery, but what we do read there is very instructive: "Behold, the wages of the laborers who mowed your fields, which you kept back by fraud, are crying out against you, and the cries of the harvesters have reached the ears of the Lord of hosts" (Jas 5:4).

Two facts must be recognized. First, the relation between servant and master varies from age to age and culture to culture, and no uniform response will do; what once was condoned is now an abomination. And second, each phase has its own evils, today including evils that can be exorcized only through godliness and love of neighbor. The present state of social relations has juridical, economic, religious, and ethical dimensions. We must work to change a variety of social relations and strive for a more just economic order. Society

SLAVERY, RACE, AND APARTHEID

needs constantly to undergo the operation of moral and religious forces.[10]

In *Our Program* he writes:

If slavery is a sin against the eighth commandment [Ex 20:15] when applied to single persons, as all will agree, how much more sinful is enslaving whole groups of people, not as a means of defense or reprisal, but purely for the sake of profit.[11]

Racism

If Kuyper and Groen opposed slavery does this also mean they opposed racism? It is clear that Groen did oppose racism: "An examination of the evidence concerning Groen's position on racial issues leaves no doubt about where he stood. With the exception of a shading early in his career, he uniformly condemned on fundamental grounds what we now call racism"[12] But what about Kuyper?

There is no doubt that Kuyper made racist comments. However, as P. J. Strauss observes—specifically related to the use of Kuyper in support of the apartheid movement—but equally applicable to the discussion on racism. He notes that commentators have neglected:

- The historical context in which Kuyper wrote and worked.
- Apparent internal inconsistencies within his writings

---

10. Kuyper, *On Business & Economics*, 323.

11. Kuyper, *Our Program*, 301.

12. Kuiper, 73.

- Kuyper's own application to the racial question.[13]

This is not to suggest that racism is to be supported. It is wrong, and it is a sin.

There does appears to be some ambiguity in Kuyper's approach. In *Lectures on Calvinism*:

> Calvinism condemns not merely all open slavery and systems of caste, but also all covert slavery of woman and of the poor; it is opposed to all hierarchy among men; it tolerates no aristocracy save such as is able, either in person or in family, by the grace of God, to exhibit superiority of character or talent, and to show that it does not claim this superiority for self-aggrandizement or ambitious pride, but for the sake of spending it in the service of God.[14]

Here, Kuyper stresses any hierarchy among humanity—all are created in the image of God and are, therefore, valuable. Likewise in his book of meditations, *Draw Near to God* he observes:

> According to the teaching of Scripture, sin is not an evil that cleaves to a few individuals, but a poison that has infected the whole human race. The creation of man was not individual either, for we are created a race. All mankind, therefore, through all ages and among all nations form one whole. We are not a great number of

---

13. P. J. Strauss, "Abraham Kuyper and Pro-Apartheid Theologians in South Africa: The Former Misused by the Latter?," in *Kuyper Reconsidered: Aspects of His Life and Word*, ed. Cornelius van der Kooi (Amsterdam: VU Uitgeverij, 1999), 225–226.

14. Kuyper, *Lectures on Calvinism*, 27.

people, who only afterwards by laws and other means are counted as one whole, but we are a human race from which individuals spring, and to which they belong as twigs and leaves to a tree.[15]

Here he acknowledges the unity of humanity.

The classification of humanity into three races, according to the three sons of Noah, ostensibly does not agree, at least not with the necessary accuracy, with the variety of races that are actually found on earth.[16]

Kuyper seems to hold to some form of the "curse of Ham." In his *Lectures on Calvinism* he writes:

From the highlands of Asia our human race came down in groups, and these in turn have been divided into races and nations; and in entire conformity to the prophetic blessing of Noah the children of Shem and of Japheth have been the sole bearers of the development of the race. No impulse for any higher life has ever gone forth from the third group. With the two other groups a twofold phenomenon presents itself. There are tribal nations which have *isolated* themselves and others which have *intermingled.* Thus on the one hand there are groups which have dominated exclusively their own inherent forces, and on the other hand groups which by commingling have crossed their traits with those of other

---

15. Kuyper, *Draw Near Unto God*, §LXXXIV

16　Kuyper, *Common Grace* 1, 357.

tribes, and thus have attained a higher perfection. It is noteworthy that the process of human development steadily proceeds with those groups whose historic characteristic is not isolation but the commingling of blood.[17]

However, he does not connect the "curse" to race or skin color—rather he links it to cultural development, or lack of it. The children of Ham have "no impulse for higher life." This he attributes not to race but to the process of intermingling and comingling of blood. Isolation does not promote cultural development. It is evident that Kuyper does not have skin color in mind, as he goes on:

On the whole the Mongolian race has held itself apart, and in its isolation has bestowed no benefits upon our race at large. Behind the Himalayas a similar life secluded itself, and hence failed to impart any permanent impulse to the outside world. Even in Europe we find that with the Scandinavians and Slavs there was hardly any intermingling of blood, and, consequently having failed to develop a richer type, they have taken little part in the general development of human life.[18]

The native Scandinavians are largely white skinned and in the thirteenth century, Mongolians were regarded as "white."[19]

---

17 Kuyper, *Lectures on Calvinism*, 35.

18. Kuyper, *Lectures on Calvinism*, 25.

19. Michael Keevak, *Becoming Yellow: A Short History of Racial Thinking* (Princeton: Princeton University Press, 2011).

Kuyper's views were certainly a product of his time. And like the views of the time Kuyper was wrong. His views display cultural imperialism and superiority as was common with most at that time.[20]

Kuyper: the father of South African apartheid?

Kuyper was initially disinterested in South Africa. However, his interest increased from 1880 onwards. As VU historian Gerrit Schutte notes:

> Kuyper thus placed himself firmly behind the Transvaalers, and quickly became one of the leaders of the pro-Boer movement in the Netherlands. He became co-founder and an influential committee member of the *Nederlands Zuid-Afrikaanse Vereniging* (NZAV, Dutch-South-African Society), which was founded on 11 May 1881.[21]

---

20. Compare the research of Nina G. Jabolonki, she writes:

    Early investigations of skin color and human diversity focused on understanding the central polarity between "white" Europeans and nonwhite others, with most attention devoted to explaining the origin and meaning of the blackness of Africans. Consistently negative associations with black and darkness influenced philosophers David Hume and Immanuel Kant to consider Africans as less than fully human and lacking in personal agency. Hume and Kant's views on skin color, the integrity of separate races, and the lower status of Africans provided support to diverse political, economic, and religious constituencies in Europe and the Americas interested in maintaining the transatlantic slave trade and upholding chattel slavery. "Skin Colour and Race," *American Journal of Physical Anthropology* G175 (2021): 437–447.

21. G. J. Schutte, "Abraham Kuyper and his South African Brethren," *Rozenberg Quarterly* accessed 18 October 2023, https://rozenbergquarterly.

Kuyper never visited South Africa. He had hoped to do so, but in June 1881, he was denied a leave of absence by the governors of the VU:

> The chairman wishes to inform the rector [Kuyper] that an absence of at least four months, as such a journey would require, would be detrimental to the welfare of the university in its present state.[22]

Apartheid in Afrikaans means "apartness." It was a legal framework that supported segregation against South Africans who were non-white. The all-white National Party government in South Africa implemented the country's pre-existing laws of racial segregation after taking office in 1948. The majority of South Africans who are not white were required to live separately from white people and had to use separate public facilities throughout the country's apartheid era. There was little interaction between the two groups.

Obviously, Kuyper never saw the implementation of the racism-inspired apartheid. However, numerous academics have claimed that Kuyper was influential in the development of apartheid theology. Typical is the comment of Elizabeth Corrado:

> The work of the Dutch theologian Abraham Kuyper was also highly influential in the development of an apartheid theology despite his support for the separation of the church and state.[23]

---

com/abraham-kuyper-and-his-south-african-brethren/.
22. Cited in Schutte "Abraham Kuyper and His South African Brethren."
23. Elizabeth Corrado, "The Godliness of Apartheid Planning," *South Africa History Online*, n.d., https://www.sahistory.org.za/archive/

Likewise, Patrick Baskwell notes:

> While "Verzuiling" in the Netherlands was the result in society of Kuyper's theological concept of "sphere sovereignty," in a South African context "sphere sovereignty" provided for a significant variant: Apartheid. Viewed from another perspective, it could be said that Kuyper's idea of "sphere sovereignty" gave cohesion and structure to the prevailing romantic nationalism not previously considered, ultimately producing South Africa's system of Apartheid.[24]

There is no denying that several neo-Calvinists have employed Kuyperian themes such as creation ordinances and sphere sovereignty in support of apartheid.[25] Including H. G. Stoker (1899–1993) and J. D. du Toit (Totius) (1877–1953).[26] And Ernst Conradie notes that he was "quite familiar with the way in which apartheid theologians employed the "neo-Calvinism" of Kuyper and others to legitimize apartheid theologically."[27]

---

godliness-apartheid-planning-elizabeth-corrado-university-illinois-5-october-2013.

24. Patrick Baskwell, "Kuyper and Apartheid: A Revisiting," *HTS Teologiese Studies/Theological Studies* (2006), https://doi.org/10.4102/hts.v62i4.401.

25. E. M. Conradie makes an interesting observation—he claims that anti-apartheid theologians such as Keet and Maraias followed Bavinck, while pro-apartheid theologians "followed Kuyper more closely." *Creation and Salvation* (Leiden: Brill, 2011), 16.

26. Totius's father the Revd S.J du Toit was influenced by Kuyper and met him in 1880 and subsequently corresponded with him. Toitus was the first South African to complete his PhD at the VU, Amsterdam.

27. Conradie, *Creation and Salvation*, 19.

To deal with such claims would take a monograph. But what I want to do here is to examine two key pertinent works of Kuyper to see if there is any justification for these claims. The two works are *The South-African Crisis*[28] and "Uniformity, the Curse of Modern Life,"[29] both of which have been used in support of an apartheid theology.

The South-African Crisis

The *South-African Crisis* was written in 1900 during the British-Boer War (1899–1902). Kuyper sided with the Boers. It was the British Imperialism,[30] their misuse of power, and their involvement in South Africa that turned Kuyper from an Anglophile to an Anglophobe. There had always been strong links between the Afrikaans and the Dutch. There was a strong Kuyperian influence among the Calvinism of the Afrikaans. The Boer War was as Adonis puts it: "the culumination of the struggle between Afikaner nationalism and British imperialism."[31]

The South-African Crisis is best understood as an apologetic for the Boers against the aggression and imperialism of

---

28 Abraham Kuyper, *The South-African Crisis*, trans. A. E. Fletcher (London: Stop the War Committee, 1900).

29. Abraham Kuyper, "Uniformity: The Curse of Modern Life," in *Abraham Kuyper: A Centennial Reader, edited by* James D. Bratt (Grand Rapids, Michigan: Eerdmans, 1998).

30. J. C. Adonis, "The Role of Abraham Kuyper in South Africa: A Critical Historical Evaluation," in *Kuyper Reconsidered. VU Studies on Protestant History 3*, ed. C. van der Kooi and J. de Bruin (Amsterdam: VU University Press, 1999) notes that the war was a struggle between British imperialism and Afrikaner nationalism, 260.

31. J. C. Adonis "The Role of Abraham Kuyper in South Africa," 260.

the British. Kuyper defends the Boers as being agents of civilisation. He thus suggests that the "blacks" are inferior
and in need of the civilisation that comes from the gospel.
As mentioned above, Kuyper had never visited South Africa,
so he did not write from first-hand experience. It seems he
was overemphasising the contemporary cultural stereotypes
to be an advocate for the Boers against the British. There is
no suggestion, however, that he thought the "blacks" were
biologically inferior, rather only culturally inferior. In this
Kuyper was, sadly, accommodating to the white, Eurocentric, cultural imperialism of the time. This was not so much
racism as cultural chauvinism.

Uniformity, the Curse of Modern Life

It was Kuyper's pamphlet "Uniformity, the Curse of Modern
Life" (1869),[32] which it has been claimed, served as the basis
for the "apartheid Bible."[33]

In it, Kuyper expounds the problem of (false) uniformity,
he describes it as "a dubious feature—I dare say, the *curse*—of
modern life." He begins with the reasons he sees it as a curse
and then goes on to discuss how Christians can fight it, particularly in regard to church and state.

His opening thesis seems to undermine his argument:
"unity is the goal of all the ways of God." What Kuyper is

---

32. Kuyper, "Uniformity: The Curse of Modern Life."

33. A. J. Loubser comments: "In 1869, Kuyper published a brief, thirty-
four-page pamphlet, Uniformity, The Curse of Modern Life. The manner
in which Kuyper treated the Bible in this pamphlet can be seen as the
true source of the 'apartheid bible.'" ("Apartheid Theology: A Contextual
Theology Gone Wrong?" *Journal of Church and State* 38 (1996):
321–337.)

proposing is a unity without uniformity; uniformity is a counterfeit of unity:

> In God's plan vital unity develops by internal strength precisely from the diversity of nations and races; but sin, by a reckless levelling and the elimination of diversity, seeks a false, deceptive unity, the uniformity of death.

Kuyper uses several examples of "spurious unity"; these include, architecture, age difference (children are no longer children), masculine and feminine, which become a "neutral hybrid of the two," fashion and language. He also sees this as heading towards the death of nationalism and patriotism. This levelling, he sees as being counter to the ordinances of God. This unity he sees as the oneness of one body, every member has a part and is of equal importance. It is this that the architects of apartheid seem to have overlooked in Kuyper. As Kuyper stresses: "The wall of *separation* has been demolished by Christ, the lines of *distinction* have not been abolished" (emphasis in the original). The former is as important as the latter—apartheid stressed the latter and ignored the former. Apartheid is a misrepresentation of what Kuyper intended. It is difficult to see how a right reading of Kuyper's vision could result in the separation and discrimination that characterized apartheid.

Misrepresentation, misappropriation, and misapplication
Kuyper's sphere sovereignty maintains that the only sovereign is God. He has established laws or norms for other areas of society such as the family, the church and so on. Within their own sphere, these areas are thus sovereign under God's laws and norms for that aspect of life. No one

institution should dominate or dictate to another, and there is no hierarchy of institutions.

Sphere sovereignty led to the pillarization of society in the Netherlands. The pillarization there was according to worldview, not skin color. In the South African context "sphere sovereignty" was used to endorse and provide a theological basis for apartheid. This, however, was a misrepresentation of Kuyper's view. As Schutte observes:

> In naming the various organic spheres, he skips the nation and jumps straight from societies in villages and cities to the state. The state meant far more to Kuyper than the nation—but then as a necessary evil, a makeshift measure. The state was "*a surgical dressing* made necessary by sin," Kuyper postulated ... His principle of sphere sovereignty implied a fundamental attack on state power. In opposition to the state, he placed not the nation, but the freedom of the various sectors of the population. Central to his thought was the "*re-Christening*" of Dutch society. Yet not the nation, but the church (the church as an organism, so the Christian organizations), i.e., the Christian sector of the population, was to bring healing.[34]

Kuyper never considered folk or nation as one of the spheres—this was a clear misinterpretation and misapplication of Kuyper's approach. Not that this misappropriation was done deliberately. However, it was probably more a case of confirmation bias, that is, the tendency to prefer information that supports previously held beliefs. Kuyper was read and interpreted in ways that con-

---

34 Schutte, "Abraham Kuyper and his South African Brethren."

firm pre-existing ideas and prejudices regarding separation; those aspects that contradicted the view were ignored or suppressed.

Kuyper made clear in his *Lectures on Calvinism*: "The state may never become an octopus which stifles the whole of life." Apartheid was a government-imposition implemented, at times, at gun point. In doing so, the government acted like an octopus, overreaching its God-given vocation, and calling. In *Ons program* Kuyper writes:

> sovereign authority flows out from God Almighty *to all parts of his creation*—to air and soil, to plant and animal, to a person's body and a person's soul, and in that soul to one's thinking, feeling, and will; and further, to society in all its organic spheres of scholarship and business; and finally, to families, to rural and urban communities, and to the sphere that encompasses all these spheres and has to safeguard them all: to the state.
>
> Thus political authority operates alongside many other authorities that are equally absolute and sacred in the natural and spiritual world, in society and family. Every attempt by political authority to try and rule over one of those other areas is therefore a violation of God's ordinances, and resistance to it is not a crime but a duty.[35]

In apartheid it is one sphere the political that is ruling over another area of life, that of race.

Also, in his *Lectures on Calvinism* Kuyper held that the commingling of blood is necessary for the development of the human race. This in itself is evidence that apartheid was blatantly a distortion of Kuyper's view.

---

35. Kuyper, *Our Program*, 21.

Conclusion

Kuyperian themes were utilized in support of apartheid; however, Kuyper's formulation of sphere sovereignty was certainly misapplied by South African Calvinists in an attempt to support it. The key here is that Kuyperian themes were *misapplied*. Kuyper held views, common in his day, regarding race, that we would deem racist today, but he would not have supported apartheid and would have been disturbed if not appalled that his work was used to justify it.

The Bible has been used to endorse capitalism; it has also been used to endorse Marxism; does that mean that the Bible is the father of both Marxism and capitalism? It would be nonsense to suggest so; likewise, it is ridiculous to claim that Kuyper is the father of apartheid.

Kuyper's views have used it to support lenient and supportive approaches to immigration and those of other faiths. [36] And one key anti-apartheid campaigner, Allan Boesak (b. 1946), one of the primary authors of the Belhar Confession, drew upon Kuyper and remarked:

> We believe passionately with Abraham Kuyper that there is not a single inch of life that does not fall under the lordship of Christ.... Here the reformed tradition comes so close to the African idea of the wholeness of life that these two should combine to renew the thrust that was brought to Christian life by the followers of Calvin.[37]

---

36. Matthew Kaemingk, *Christian Hospitality and Muslim Immigration in an Age of Fear* (Grand Raids: Eerdmans, 2018).

37. Alan Boesak, *Black and Reformed: Apartheid, Liberation and the Calvinist Tradition* (Johannesburg: Skotaville, 1984), 87.

Let Kuyper have the last word, this from his *Lectures on Calvinism*, shows how far he was from the ethos of apartheid:

If Calvinism places our entire human life immediately before God, then it follows that all men or women, rich or poor, weak or strong, dull or talented, as creatures of God, and as lost sinners, have no claim whatsoever to lord over one another, and that we stand as equals before God, and consequently equal as man to man. Hence we cannot recognize any distinction among men... Hence Calvinism condemns not merely all open slavery and systems of caste, but also all covert slavery of woman and of the poor; it is opposed to all hierarchy among men ... So Calvinism was bound to find its utterance in the democratic interpretation of life; to proclaim the liberty of nations; and not to rest until both politically and socially every man, simply because he is man, should be recognized, respected and dealt with as a creature created after the Divine likeness.[38]

A summary in 12 theses

1. Calvinism, as articulated by Kuyper, condemns all forms of slavery and hierarchy among humanity.
2. Kuyper emphasizes the unity of humanity, rejecting the classification of races based on the sons of Noah.
3. Kuyper's pamphlet "Uniformity, the Curse of Modern Life" critiques false uniformity and advocates for unity without uniformity.
4. Kuyper's opposition to slavery extends to the enslavement

---

38. Kuyper, *Lectures on Calvinism*, 52–53.

of entire groups for profit, emphasizing the sinfulness of such actions.

5. While Groen and Kuyper opposed slavery, Kuyper's stance on racism appears ambiguous, with historical context and internal inconsistencies playing a role.

6. Kuyper's writings highlight the need for social justice and a more just economic order, acknowledging the evolving nature of social relations.

7. Slavery in the Near East was characterized by the lack of rights for slaves, who were treated as property with redeemable cash value.

8. The Code of Hammurabi recognized three classes of people, including slaves, with severe penalties for negligence and concealment.

9. Kuyper's theological perspective rejects the idea of humans lording over one another, emphasizing equality before God and condemning all forms of slavery.

10. Kuyper's democratic interpretation of life advocates for the liberty of nations and the equal treatment of all individuals.

11. Kuyper's theological views stand in stark contrast to the ethos of apartheid, emphasizing respect for all individuals as creatures created in the Divine likeness.

12. Kuyper's teachings emphasize the importance of recognizing the inherent value of every individual and promoting equality in all aspects of life.

Study Questions

1. Was Kuyper a racist? Justify your answer.
2. To what extent was Kuyper responsible for South African apartheid?
3. Is Kuyper's writing interwoven with colonialism?
4. To what extent is the claim that Kuyper was a man of his time justification for some of his Eurocentric views?
5. In what ways did Kuyper's rejection of false uniformity and emphasis on unity without uniformity resonate with his broader theological framework?
6. What historical and cultural factors shaped Kuyper's views on slavery, race, and apartheid, and how did he address these influences in his theological works?
7. How did Kuyper's theological ideas contribute to the misapplication of his views in support of apartheid?
8. What was the significance of the "curse of Ham" in the context of slavery and race, and how was it used to justify certain ideologies?
9. What implications do Kuyper's theological perspectives on slavery, race, and apartheid have for modern discussions on social justice, equality, and human rights?

Further Reading

Primary sources

Kuyper, Abraham. *The South-African Crisis*, translated by A.E. Fletcher (London: Stop the War Committee, 1900).

Kuyper, Abraham. "Uniformity: The Curse of Modern Life," in James D. Bratt, (ed.) *Abraham Kuyper: A Centennial Reader* (Grand Rapids, MI: Eerdmans, 1998)

Kuyper, Abraham. *Address to the members of the Anti-Slavery Society and the Aborigines Protection Society* (London: Harrison and Sons, 1883)

Secondary sources

Bacote, Vincent. "Kuyper and Race," in Joustra, Jessica R. and Joustra, Robert J. (ed.) *Calvinism for a Secular Age: A Twenty-First-Century Reading of Abraham Kuyper's Stone Lectures.* (Downers Grove: IVP Academic, 2022)

Harinck, George. "Abraham Kuyper, South Africa, and Apartheid," in Steve Bishop and John Kok (ed.) *On Kuyper: A Collection of Readings on the Life, Work & Legacy of Abraham Kuyper* (Sioux Center: Dordt Press, 2013), 419–422.

PART 5

Kuyper's Legacy

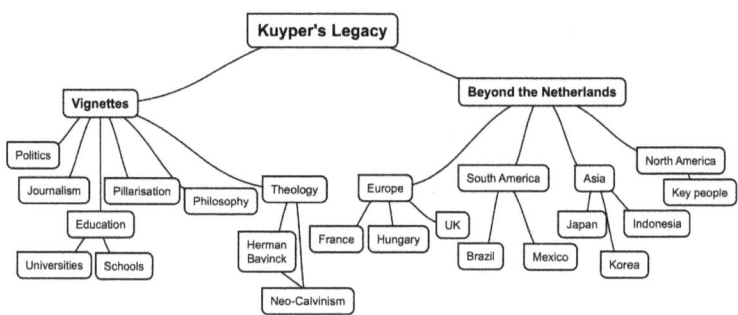

31

Vignettes and Beyond the Netherlands

In brief

ABRAHAM KUYPER'S LEGACY IS vast and impactful across multiple domains of Christian life, including politics, journalism, education, philosophy, and theology. He founded the Anti-Revolutionary Party (ARP) in politics, leaving a lasting mark on Dutch political landscape. His influence extended to journalism through *De Standaard*, later becoming *Trouw*, and his contributions to education, notably founding the Free University of Amsterdam (VU Amsterdam).

In philosophy, Kuyper's ideas laid the groundwork for a distinctively Christian perspective, influencing figures like Herman Dooyeweerd. While controversies surrounded Kuyper's teachings on common grace and political alliances, his visionary leadership, commitment to Christian values, and intellectual rigor left an indelible mark on Dutch society.

Beyond the Netherlands, Kuyper's influence reached global proportions, particularly in North and South America, South Africa, and Southeast Asia, where scholars and institutions continue to engage with his ideas. Kuyper's enduring legacy is his significant contributions to Christian thought and societal transformation.

Introduction

The legacy of Abraham Kuyper is profound and far-reaching, leaving an lasting mark on various facets of Christian life, including politics, journalism, education, and philosophy. It is no wonder that on April 22, 1897, Charles Boissevain (1842–1927), an influential journalist, editor, and owner of the leading Dutch newspaper Amsterdam *Algemeen Handelsblad*, called Abraham Kuyper: "een tegenstander, die tien hoofden en honderd armen bezit" (an opponent with ten heads and a hundred arms).

In the following, I will look at the legacy of some of the topics the ten-headed man engaged in and then briefly look at the influence of Kuyper in other countries. I start by examining vignettes that illustrate the development of Kuyper's initiative.

Politics

Kuyper, following Groen's initiative, founded the Christian political party, the Anti-Revolutionary Party (ARP). Hendrikus Colijn (1896–1944) took up Kuyper's mantle in becoming the leader of the ARP and editor of *De Standaard*. He was the prime minister of the Netherlands (1925, and 1933 to 1939).

In 1977, the ARP merged with the Catholic People's Party (KVP) and the Christian Historical Union (CHU) to form the Christian Democratic Appeal (CDA). Jan Peter

Balkende (1956–)[1] a member of the CDA, was the Dutch prime minister from 2002 to 2010. In 2010, at the unveiling of a statue of Kuyper in Massilus, he stated:

> In case any of you should still doubt this: I am a Kuyperian in heart and soul. That is due to my upbringing, my education and the path of my career. But I am especially a Kuyperian from conviction.[2]

In the Afterword to Kuyper's *On Business and Economics*, he writes:

> As a successor to Abraham Kuyper as prime minister of the Netherlands, I feel deeply indebted to him. I was a student and then a professor at the VU University Amsterdam he founded. I led the Christian Democratic Appeal, a party formed from a merger involving the Antirevolutionary Party, which Kuyper also founded. I was honored, in addition, to receive the prestigious Kuyper Prize at

---

1. He obtained his doctorate in law in 1992 from the VU University, Amsterdam. His Dutch thesis was on "Government regulations and social organizations." In 2022, he was appointed Minister of State. He was awarded the Abraham Kuyper Prize from Princeton in 2004. His acceptance speech highlighted the relevance of Kuyper's ideas for today. He mentioned in particular sphere sovereignty, the freedom of education and religion, and emphasized the importance of applying Kuyper's values, responsibility, and social engagement to create conditions for a better future. "Solid Values for a Better Future," *Princeton Seminary* Bulletin (2004): 143–152.

2. J. P. Balkenende, "Speech by Prime Minister J. P. Balkenende on the Occasion of the Unveiling of the Statue of Abraham Kuyper in the Town of Maassluis on 5 November, 2008," cited by Jan H. Boer "Translator–Editor Preface," *Mystery of Islam*. Online: https://ccel.org/ccel/kuyper/islam/islam. Also, Balkenende, "Solid Values for a Better Future."

Princeton in 2004. More importantly, I've been inspired throughout my adult life by his vision of Christianity offering a worldview that engages with every area of life.[3]

Many Dutch Christian Kuyperians served as CDA candidates and members of parliament (including Bob Goudzwaard and Egbert Schuurman).

Journalism

Hendrikus Colijn, as mentioned above, took over as editor of *De Standaard* in 1920. It ceased publication during the Second World War and later became *Trouw*. During the Second World War, the editors took a "neutral" position towards the German occupation, which was viewed as accommodation by some. This coupled with the shortage of paper led to its cessation of publication in December 1944—it had become a weekly. Its successor is *Trouw*, which is still published, and was opposed to the German occupation.

Education

The VU and Christian Universities

The history of the Free University is well told by van Deursen.[4] From its beginnings with six professors and eight students in rented rooms has now almost 3 000 staff and 1600 support staff with approximately 24 000 students. It is now called the Vrije Universiteit Amsterdam (VU Amsterdam).

---

3.   Balkenende "Afterword," in Abraham Kuyper, *On Business & Economics: Abraham Kuyper Collected Works in Public Theology*, ed. Peter S. Heslam (Bellingham, WA: Lexham Press, 2021).

4   Arie Theodorus van Deursen, *Cornerstone of the Pillarized System: A History of the Free University* (William B Eerdmans Publishing Co, 2008).

Van Deursen has rightly said, that without Kuyper there would be "no Free University."[5] Professors at the VU Amsterdam have included Herman Bavinck, Valentijn Hepp, G. C. Berkouwer, G. Ch. Aalders, F. W. Grosheide, Herman Dooyeweerd, D. H. Th. Vollenhoven, Reijer Hooykaas, Jacob Klapwijk, and Jan Lever, among others.

The VU University is now a thriving university. Although it has lost much of its Kuyperian ethos there are still professors there who have Kuyperian sympathies.

There are also several North American universities that work out of a broadly Kuyperian tradition. These include:

Calvin University[6]

Dordt University[7]

ICS, Toronto[8]

Redeemer University College, Canada[9]

---

5. Van Deursen, *Cornerstone of the Pillarized System*, 2.

6. Harry Boonstra, *Our School: Calvin College and the Christian Reformed Church* (Grand Rapids, MI: Eerdmans, 2001).

7. B. J. Haan, *A Zeal for Christian Education: The Memoirs of B. J. Haan* (Sioux Center: Dordt College Press, 1992).

8. Robert E. VanderVennen, *A University for the People: A History of the Institute for Christian Studies* (Sioux Center: Dordt College Press, 2008). Their website has this: "We describe our approach to scholarship as 'reformational.' This means several things. First, we work as conscious heirs to the stream in the Reformed intellectual tradition that goes by this name (also described as Kuyperian or neo-Calvinist)." https://www.icscanada.edu/about/our-story. Date of access 11 February 2024.

9. A history of Redeemer is to be found in Henry R. De Boer, *Stepping Forward in Faith: Redeemer University College 1974-1994* (Belville, Ont: Guardian, 2001).

And one college has even named itself after Kuyper.[10]

Christian schools

In addition to founding the VU Amsterdam, Kuyper did much for Christian schooling. The Christian School movement in North America was, certainly initially, developed on Kuyperian lines, as Dutch immigrants to North America brought with them a Kuyperian influence. See, for example, John E. Hull's *Education for Hope*.[11] Hull helpfully identifies "five formative features" of a neo-Calvinist approach to education at the end of the nineteenth-century. These were:

- Envisioning the Christian school as a dissident social institution in that it needs to "expose and defeat modernity"
- The school is to be a transforming social institution
- The need for curricular-pedagogical reform
- The school is to be parent-controlled not state-owned
- The school stands in the rich theological-philosophical tradition of Augustine, Calvin, and Kuyper:

  This heritage defines a Christian perspective in terms of the grand themes of Scripture: the creation-fall-redemption-restoration meta-narrative, the covenant relationship between God and His people, the Kingdom of God on earth, and the lordship of Jesus Christ.[12]

---

10. Kuyper College was founded in 1939 as Reformed Bible Institute (RBI).

11. John E. Hull, *Education for Hope: A Course Correction.* (Friesen Press, 2023). Also: Harro Van Brummelen, *Telling the Next Generation: Educational Development in North American Calvinist Christian Schools* (Langham, MD: University Press of America, 1986).

12. Hull, *Education for Hope.*

Pillarisation

Kuyper's concept of sphere sovereignty, manifested in the pillarization of society, shaped Dutch political and cultural life for decades after his death. As Harry Van Dyke astutely observes:

> This hallmark of "accommodation politics"—more accurately named "institutionalized worldview pluralism"—is one of the enduring legacies of the culture in which Abraham Kuyper played such a dominant role.[13]

Philosophy

South African philosopher Anna Conradie remarks: "The first sign of the emergence of such a 'radically unique system of philosophy' is to be found in the thought of Abraham Kuyper the founder of neo-Calvinistic philosophy."[14] Similarly Veenhof writes:

> One can speak of a Calvinist philosophy — it is possible to draw the philosophy of the idea of law more sharply from the historical point of view. After all, there is a figure whose connection is even closer, whose influence has been even deeper.

The figure is Dr. Abraham Kuyper.

> Without him, a philosophy of the idea of law would never have arisen. It is from him that she derives her

---

13. Harry Van Dyke, *The Legacy of Abraham Kuyper* (Aalten: Wordbridge, 2024), 85.

14. A. L. Conradie, *The Neo-Calvinistic Concept of Philosophy: A Study in the Problem of Philosophic Communication* (Natal: University Press, 1960).

most authentic characteristics. Any unbiased observer must recognize that immediately.[15]

This is perhaps overstating the case; however, Kuyper's sphere sovereignty, his view of faith/religion, worldview, the antithesis, and the heart, were key foundations in the development of a Reformational philosophy by Herman Dooyeweerd and D. H. Th. Vollenhoven.[16] Dooyeweerd explicitly stated his debt to Kuyper in a TV interview: While at work at the "Kuyper Institute,"[17] he read one of Kuyper's meditations on Pente-

ANTIREVOLUTIONAIRE
STAATKUNDE

ORGAAN VAN DE
Dr ABRAHAM KUYPERSTICHTING
TER BEVORDERING VAN DE STUDIE
DER ANTIREVOLUTIONAIRE BEGINSELEN

ONDER REDACTIE VAN
Prof. Mr A. ANEMA · Dr E. J. BEUMER · H. COLIJN
Mr H. A. DAMBRINK · Dr H. DOOYEWEERD
Mr V. H. RUTGERS · J. SCHOUTEN · Dr J. SEVERIJN

EERSTE JAARGANG
OCT. 1924—DEC. 1925

UITGAVE VAN J. H. KOK TE KAMPEN

---

15. C. Veenhof, *Kuyper's lijn: enkele opmerkingen over den invloed van Dr. A. Kuyper op de "wijsbegeerte der wetsidee"* (Goes: Ossterbaan & Le Cointre, 1939), 19.

16. On Vollenhoven, see Steve Bishop, "Why We Should Read Vollenhoven Today," *Ethics in Conversation* (November 2023) 27, no. 5, Online: https://kirbylaingcentre.co.uk/wp-content/uploads/2023/11/EiC-Steve-Bishop-27.5-November-2023.pdf

17. The Abraham Kuyperstichting [Kuyper Institute] was formed after Kuyper's death by the leaders of the ARP in 1922 as an institute for "research, information, and propaganda." Its aim was the spread of Kuyper's political views. The Institute was originally based in Kuyper's former home in the Hague. The journal *Antirevolutionaire Staatkunde Orgaan Van De Dr Abraham Kuyperstichting Ter Bevordering Van De Studie Der Antirevolutionaire Beginselen* was published by the Institute. Dr. C. Beekenkamp "The Dr. Kuyper Institute," *The Calvin Forum* 3, no. 5, (Dec 1937): 107-109.

cost, and Dooyeweerd "discovered" a new Kuyper. In a 1973 interview, Dooyeweerd comments:

> I was working in Kuyper's old office, sitting at his enormous old desk, I noticed a stack of little booklets. I picked the first one that came to hand, which was Kuyper's meditations about Pentecost.[18] I would never have picked up such booklets to read earlier in my life, but I thought to myself that I should take a look at what he made of such meditations. I started to read and four hours later I was still there! I was so moved by what Kuyper had to say in these meditations that I realized that this was a completely different Kuyper from the one I knew from his theological works. In theology he is scholastic but not at all in these meditations.[19]

Dooyeweerd was struck by Kuyper's account of the role of the heart as the religious center of human existence:

> what really gripped me was that Kuyper had rediscovered the Biblical truth that the centre of our human existence lies in our heart, something that had been completely lost in scholasticism.[20]

Kuyper's mainly social vision was developed into an (ontological) account of the whole of reality with the philosophical rigor

---

18. This was Kuyper's *Op den Pinksterdag (met Hemelvaart)* (Kampen: Kok, 1923).
19. H. Dooyeweerd, "IKOR Television Interview," 1973. 16 May 1973, Media Room, Vrije Universiteit". (Translated by J. Van Meggelen, 2004.)
20. Dooyeweerd, "IKOR "Television Interview."

Kuyper was unable to give it. [21] Veenhof even suggests that it is perfectly justified to call the philosophy of the law idea by the name "Kuyperian philosophy".[22]

Dooyeweerd acknowledges Kuyper's "great and continuing influence."[23] For Dooyeweerd, Kuyper's greatest contribution was "to set the principle of sovereignty in its own sphere against the state absolutism that was dominant" in his time.[24] It was this notion of sphere sovereignty that Dooyeweerd developed along philosophical lines. He argues:

the way in which Kuyper worked it out was not theoretically or philosophically thought through.[25]

In his "Christian Philosophy: An Exploration," he once more pays tribute to Kuyper and emphasizes:

---

21. J. G. A. Ive, "A Critically Comparative Kuyperian Analysis and a Trinitarian 'Perichoretic' Reconstruction of the Reformational Philosophies of Dirk H. Th. Vollenhoven, and Herman Dooyweerd" (PhD Thesis., London, King's College London, 2012).

22. Veenhof, *Kuyper's Lijn* §VII.

23. Herman Dooyeweerd, "The Last Interview of Dooyeweerd," in *Acht Civilisten in Burger*, ed. J. M. Dunné et al., trans. J. Glenn Friesen (Zwolle: W. E. J. Tjeenk Willink, 2013), 38–67. Although Dooyeweerd does acknowledge some departures from Kuyper's more scholastic traits: Herman Dooyeweerd, "Kuyper's Philosophy of Science," in *On Kuyper: A Collection of Readings on the Life, Work & Legacy of Abraham Kuyper*, ed. S. Bishop and J.H. Kok (Sioux Center, IA: Dordt College Press, 2013), 153–178.

24. Dooyeweerd, "The last interview," 49.

25. Herman Dooyeweerd, "Interview of Herman Dooyeweerd by Magnus Verbrugge dated September 23, 1974," trans. J. G. Friesen, 2007.

Kuyper penetrated beyond the theological and philosophical issues of the day to the deepest and absolutely central spiritual forces that set human life and thought in motion.[26]

And in his *Reformation and Scholasticism*, he remarks:

The rise of a philosophy that is re-formed from within by the Christian religion is a phenomenon of very recent date. It is directly related to the Calvinist revival that occurred under the inspiring leadership of Dr. Abraham Kuyper in the latter part of the nineteenth century. This spiritual movement had to become conscious of its own life-embracing character before it could press on to the fields of philosophy and science in general. It first had to develop into a real worldview. This worldview, having been born of a new Christian attitude toward engaging life, would draw its unique impulse and its spiritual power exclusively from its own Scriptural Christian ground-motive.[27]

Theology

Matthew Kaemingk's edited volume on *Reformed Public Theology*[28] is another illustration of the continuing legacy of Kuyper.[29] This

---

26. Herman Dooyeweerd, *Christian Philosophy and the Meaning of History* (Lewiston: E. Mellen Press, 1996).

27. Herman Dooyeweerd, *Reformation and Scholasticism in Philosophy* Vol II (Grand Rapids, MI: Paideia Press, 2013), 1.

28. *Reformed Public Theology: A Global Vision for Life in the Word* (Grand Rapids: Eerdmans, 2021).

29. Some of this draws upon my review in "Kuyperania 2021and 2023: An overview of English-language works on Kuyper," *Koers* 90(1)(2025). https://doi.org/10.19108/KOERS.90.1.2606

book is split into four parts: Public Culture, Public Markets, Public Justice, and Public Aesthetics—and Kuyper and his works make an appearance in all parts. By my reckoning, we have 75 mentions of common grace, and 21 for sphere sovereignty. Calvin has 424 mentions, 205 for Kuyper, and 139 for Bavinck. These mentions far outweigh those of other Reformed scholars, for example:

Jonathan Edwards 5
John Owen 15
H. Bullinger and H. Zwingli 0
Theodore Beza 1
Johannes Althusius 14
Groen van Prinsterer 5
John Knox 3

Although not a book on Kuyper as such, his insights dominate this book. These include:

- His positive view of doctors and medicine. His elevation but not deification of modern medicine
- A corrective to the triumphalism of Indonesia's attraction to the Seven Mountains Theory
- His "Public fight for the political and economic rights of the *kleine luyden*", his opposition to "collectivism and individualism", "political overreach and overregulation of markets"
- His view that "economic and political justice require something the states and markets cannot provide: spiritual life and vitality"
- His sphere sovereignty provides a basis for a just and public order
- A "more communal and institutional approach to

politics and human flourishing"

- His views are applicable to American suburbs and architecture
- His connection between sin and systems and evil and social structures.

This illustrates that Kuyper is as relevant today as he was in the early twentieth century.

Systematic theologian Michael Allen observes that Kuyperian "neo-Calvinism has shaped the Reformed theological world like no other movement in the late nineteenth and twentieth centuries."[30] Many theologians and philosophers have taken and developed Kuyper's ideas and concepts.

James Skillen is typical of many when he writes:

As a student with a deep desire to live as a sincere Christian, I struggled agonizing with [a] sacred/secular dualism until I read Kuyper's American "Lectures in Calvinism" (1898). Then I began to understand that all of life is religion. Then I began to see that God's sovereignty over the world concerns the very character of the creation order and the shape of contemporary human society. Kuyper's illumination of the conflict between different religions and his interpretation of Calvinism as "way of life" immediately began to help me understand the world around me as well as help me resolve

---

30. Even though Allen takes issues with what he perceives as the "eschatologcal naturalism" of the later Kuyperians. Michael Allen, *Grounded in Heaven* (Grand Rapids: Eerdmans, 2018), 23.

some of my own personal struggles caused by the false sacred/secular dualism.[31]

Bavinck scholars Brock and Sutanto have written a theological introduction to Kuyper and Herman Bavinck.[32] They show that neo-Calvinist theological insights are still insightful and have much to say to the academy today.

Herman Bavinck

There has been a renewed interest in both Abraham Kuyper and Herman Bavinck. Kuyper significantly influenced Bavinck, with Bavinck even having a poster of Kuyper in his room during his student days. Together, their names are almost like a brand, representing neo-Calvinism.[33] However, some caricatured distinctions have been made between them, J. H. Landwehr, had this to say of the two:

> Bavinck was an Aristotelian, Kuyper had a Platonic spirit. Bavinck was the man of clear concept, Kuyper the man of the fecund idea. Bavinck worked with the historically given; Kuyper proceeded speculatively by way of intuition. Bavinck's was primarily an inductive mind; Kuyper's primarily deductive.[34]

---

31. James Skillen, "Kuyper was on Time and Ahead of his Time: An Essay on Religion as a Way of Life and Societal Differentiation," *Reformed Ecumenical Council's Theological Forum: "Abraham Kuyper: his international influence"* 16(2) (June 1988): 15.

32. Cory C. Brock and N. Gray Sutanto, *Neo-Calvinism: A Theological Introduction* (Bellingham, WA: Lexham Press, 2023).

33. George Harinck, "Herman Bavinck and Geerhardus Vos," *Calvin Theological Journal* 45, no. 1 (April 2010): 18–31.

34. Cited in Henry Zylstra, "Preface," in Herman Bavinck, *Our Reasonable Faith: A Survey of Christian Doctrine*, trans. Henry Zylstra (Grand Rapids:

Similarly, A. B. W. M. Kok writes:

> There are similarities and differences between the two. Kuyper was a militant figure; Bavinck was more irenic in nature. Rather than avoiding conflict, Kuyper would provoke it, while Bavinck would only attack after every attempt to avoid it had failed. Kuyper was feisty in his approach and had the gift of leadership. Bavinck was not suited for politics, but, rather, fit better in the study, the pulpit, the conference or congress. Kuyper was more original and had a more sparkling spirit; Bavinck was broader and more erudite.[35]

For a long time, Bavinck was overshadowed by Kuyper and often labeled as Kuyper's henchman.[36] Henry Dosker even compared them to Luther and Melanchthon.[37] While they shared common ground in their studies at the University of Leiden and their advocacy of concepts like the antithesis and common grace, differences also emerged. Kuyper was a supralapsarian thinker, while Bavinck was not. Kuyper tend-

---

Baker1956), 5. (Presumably from J. H. Landwher, *In Memorian: Prof. Dr. H. Bavinck* (Kampen: Kok, 1921)).

35. A. B. W. M. Kok, *Herman Bavinck: Profile of a Reformational Pioneer*, trans. Jan Boer (Vancouver: Social Theology.com)—original: Amsterdam: S. J. P. Bakker, 1945.

36. James Hutton MacKay called him "Kuyper's loyal and leaned henchman." *Religious Thought in Holland During the Nineteenth Century* (London: Hodder & Stoughton, 1911), x.

37. Herman Bavinck, *Essays on Religion, Science, and Society*, ed. John Bolt, trans. Harry Boonstra and Gerrit Sheeres (Grand Rapids, MI: Baker Academic, 2008).

ed to think broadly, while Bavinck delved into details, and their distance grew towards the end of their lives.

Bavinck has often been seen as a mere reflection of Kuyper due to their friendship, Kuyper's dominant presence, and the superficial similarity of their thoughts. Critics have lamented that this identification of their ideas continues without much scrutiny.

Bavinck's disillusionment with certain aspects of neo-Calvinism towards the end of his life reflected a concern about worldliness, superficiality, and pride within the movement. He observed a growing one-sidedness among proponents of Calvinism, where the church's confession became confined, and the realm of "common grace" took precedence. In his view, a balance was needed to ensure that Calvinism did not stray from its core focus.[38]

Recent scholarship has increasingly recognized Kuyper and Bavinck as distinct figures rather than a unified neo-Calvinist entity.[39] This acknowledgment has led to a more nuanced understanding of their theological differences, emphasizing their individual contributions to neo-Calvinism. Some even consider Herman Bavinck a "greater theologian" than Abraham Kuyper.[40]

Beyond the Netherlands

In many ways the contemporary impact of Kuyper has been greater outside the Netherlands than inside it. Kuyper's impact

38. Herman Bavinck, "Belijdenis of beginselen," *De Bazuin* 49, no. 51 (1901).

39. See, for example, Brock and Sutanto, *Neo-Calvinism* (Bellingham, WA: Lexham Press).

40. I. John Hesselink, *On Being Reformed: Distinctive Characteristics and Common Misunderstandings* (Ann Arbor, MI: Servant Books, 1983), 110.

extends globally, notably in North and South America, South Africa, and Indonesia.

North America: Kuyper's influence in North America began with Dutch immigrants, fostering educational and political institutions, and notably through figures like H. Evan Runner and his Groen Club at Calvin College. Different philosophical strands birthed in North America, including Reformed epistemology, and Reconstructionism/Theonomy, to various degrees have been influenced by Kuyper.

South America: In Mexico, scholars like John Paul Haines Roberts and Adolfo García de la Sienra Guajardo have promoted Kuyperian ideas, while Brazil has seen the rise of neo-Calvinism through figures like Thiago Machado Silva and Guilherme de Carvalho.

South Africa: Despite mixed reception due to apartheid associations, Kuyperian ideas flourished in higher education institutions like Potchefstroom (now North West University) with individuals such as J. A. L. Taljaard, B. Duvenage, H. G. Stoker, B. J. Van der Walt, J. J. Venter, Elaine Botha, Renato Coletto, and Michael Heyns, and the University of the Free State (Danie Strauss and Albert Weidman). South African journals such as *Koers* and *Journal for Christian Scholarship* have large Kuyperian influences.

East and Southeast Asia: The Asia Kuyper Institute (https://www.asiakuyper.org/) and scholars such as Surya Harefa, Junggi Kim, and David Kristanto in countries like Japan, Korea, and Indonesia are exploring Kuyper's relevance in Asian contexts. Also in Korea is John Choi (http://alloflife-redeemed.co.uk/john-choi/).

Europe: Overlooked figures like Auguste Lecerf,[41] Pierre Marcel, and Jenö Sebestyén[42] in France and Hungary have furthered Kuyperian ideas. Lecerf and Sebestyén were involved with the International Calvinistic Congresses between the wars. Marcel, Jan Dengerink, and Jacob T. Hoogstra[43] were involved with the formation of International Association for Reformational Faith and Action (IARFA). IARFA was founded to unite individuals of a Reformed confession, it facilitated discussions on integrating Christianity into various spheres of life, and produced the journal *International Reformed Bulletin*. Also, key member of IARFA were Bernie Zylstra (ICS, Toronto), Paul Schrotenboer, and latterly David Hanson. Hanson was also instrumental with his wife Ruth in setting up the West Yorkshire School of Christian Studies (WYSOCS), in Leeds, England. WYSOCS is now the Thinking Faith Network.

Also in the UK were Influential figures like E. L. Hebden Taylor, John Peck, and Richard Russell, Alan and Elaine Storkey, Jonathan Chaplin, Andrew Basden, and Jeremy Ive, who

---

41. On Lecerf, see, for example, Steve Bishop, "Auguste Lecerf: The Most Influential French Neocalvinist of the Twentieth Century," *Neocalviniana* (2024) Online:

42. On Sebestyen, see Steve Bishop "Jenő Sebestyén—The Hungarian Kuyper," *Findings* 6 (2024): 30–36.

43. Jacob Tunis Hoogstra had organised the first American Calvinistic Conference in the States. and was involved with the US's Calvinistic Action Committee, founded in 1945. The American Calvinistic Fellowship became a regional chapter of IARFA. Hoogstra was also closely involved with the American Christian University Association, 1943-1946, and the Association for Reformed Scientific Studies, 1962-1970.

have promoted Kuyperian thought, contributing to its intellectual and spiritual development.

Evaluation

Abraham Kuyper, an opponent with ten heads and a hundred arms, he did more in one lifetime than others could have done in ten.

There can no doubt Kuyper was a great man, who did great things. But at what cost?

Several times he succumbed to nervous breakdowns, which could be attributed to overwork. There seems to be no doubt that he was a workaholic. No doubt his family life and his children suffered because of it, as his daughter mentioned.

There are several areas controversial aspects of Kuyper's life and work; this highlights the complexities and debates surrounding his legacy as a prominent figure in Dutch history. Some of the most controversial aspects of Abraham Kuyper's life and work include:

Common Grace and Presumptive Regeneration: Kuyper's teachings on common grace and presumptive regeneration were controversial within orthodox Reformed circles, leading to disagreements and debates over theological doctrines.

Political Alliances: Kuyper's decision to seek a political coalition with Roman Catholics, despite being a Calvinist, raised eyebrows and sparked criticism among some of his contemporaries.

World War I Alignment: Kuyper's support for the Germans during World War I was seen as controversial, especially considering his Calvinist background and the historical context of the war.

Church Attendance: Kuyper's choice to stop attending church in order to focus on writing his meditations was a controversial decision that raised questions about his priorities and commitment to traditional religious practices.

Legacy and Dissent: While Kuyper left a lasting legacy in Dutch society, there were dissenters who criticized his ideas and actions, prompting discussions about the extent of his influence and the validity of his teachings.

However, Abraham Kuyper possessed several strengths that contributed to his influential legacy and showed his significant role as a leader, thinker, and advocate for Christian principles in every area of life:

Visionary Leadership: Kuyper was known for his visionary leadership in various fields, including politics, education, and theology. His ability to articulate a comprehensive worldview and implement reforms demonstrated his forward-thinking approach.

Multifaceted Contributions: As a theologian, journalist, politician, and educator, Kuyper made multifaceted contributions to Dutch society. His diverse skills and interests allowed him to have a significant impact on various aspects of culture and governance.

Commitment to Christian Values: Kuyper's unwavering commitment to Christian values and principles, as evidenced by his founding of the Free University of Amsterdam and advocacy for a free church and school, showcased his dedication to promoting Christian ideals in all spheres of life.

Intellectual Rigor: With over 200 books and over 2000 meditations, and innumerable newspaper articles to his name, Kuyper demonstrated intellectual rigor and depth in his writings. His works on theology, journalism, politics, education, and culture reflected a profound understanding of complex issues and a willingness to engage with diverse topics from a Christian perspective. Tjitze Kuiper's annotated bibliography of Kuyper's works runs to over 700 pages, listing all the works Kuyper has written from 1857. This is testimony enough to Kuyper's legacy.

Legacy and Influence: Kuyper's enduring legacy and continued influence on Dutch society underscore the strength of his ideas and the lasting impact of his contributions. His emphasis on Calvinism as a comprehensive worldview continues to shape discussions in theology and politics.

Summary

Abraham Kuyper, a towering figure in Dutch history, was not one to suffer fools gladly. He staunchly defended his beliefs.

Despite his strong convictions and influence, Kuyper was not universally admired. Cartoonist Albert Hahn frequently depicted him in a negative light, portraying him as "Abraham the Terrible", symbolizing his multifaceted and often controversial personality.

Descriptions of Kuyper vary widely. Some saw him as aggressive and intransigent,[44] while others hailed him as a visionary and a born strategist. He fought passionately for free-

---

44. Kasteel, his Roman Catholic biographer, describes him as "Aggressive, and intransigent, democratic but also dictatorial and aristocratic." Cited in Louis Praamsma *Let Christ Be King* (Jordan Station, Ont: Paideia Press, 1985), 171.

dom, advocating for a free church, university, school, political party, and labor movement, free from interference.

Kuyperian themes, profoundly influenced Reformed thought and life. He emphasized the sovereignty of God over all aspects of life, the importance of separate Christian institutions, and the necessity for Christians to engage actively in society and develop a Christian perspective on issues.

His worldview, rooted in Calvinism, emphasized the positive influence of Christianity on culture and the imperative to transform it. However, despite his significant impact, some questioned the extent of his success. While Kuyper left an indelible mark on Dutch civilization, his absence led to a decline in the Anti-Revolutionary party's dynamism, perhaps signaling that his charisma and leadership were irreplaceable. Dirk Jellema poses the question: "How successful was Kuyper?" He answers it thus:

> There can be little doubt that he "placed a stamp on the civilization of the Netherlands it was never to lose," and most of his program was carried out by the Coalition he did so much to inspire. But as one goes through the history of the Antirevolutionary party after 1920, one is struck by an increasing tendency to be satisfied with the status quo. In a sense, the party was perhaps ruined by success; once a party's program has been carried out, what more can it do?
>
> Perhaps the loss of Kuyper also had something to do with it. Kuyper was a powerful figure, a charismatic

leader, a Napoleonic character, a man about whom legends clustered, "Abraham the Terrible."[45]

Conclusion

Abraham Kuyper's legacy is profound and far-reaching, spanning various aspects of Christian life and thought. His visionary leadership, unwavering commitment to Christian values, and intellectual rigor left an indelible mark on Dutch society and beyond. Despite controversies and criticisms surrounding some of his teachings and actions, Kuyper's enduring influence persists, evidenced by the continued exploration and application of his ideas in contemporary discussions on politics, education, philosophy, and theology.

Kuyper's collaboration with figures like Herman Bavinck showcased the depth and breadth of neo-Calvinist thought, contributing to a rich theological tradition that continues to shape Reformed theology worldwide. Moreover, his impact extended beyond the Netherlands, reaching regions like North and South America, South Africa, and Southeast Asia, where scholars and institutions engage with his ideas to address contemporary challenges and opportunities.

While questions remain about the extent of Kuyper's success and the ongoing relevance of his teachings, there is no denying the enduring significance of his legacy. As scholars, theologians, and practitioners continue to grapple with his ideas, Abraham Kuyper remains a towering figure in Christian history, whose multifaceted contributions continue to inspire and influence generations to come.

---

45. Dirk Jellema, "Abraham Kuyper's Attack on Liberalism," *The Review of Politics* (1957): 484-485)

Study Questions

1. What are the most important contributions that Kuyper made?
2. How was one person able to do so much?
3. Why was Kuyper not universally admired?
4. How did Kuyper's ideas on sphere sovereignty and common grace impact his political and theological views?
5. How did Kuyper and Herman Bavinck contribute to the development of neo-Calvinist thought?
6. How did Kuyper's legacy shape Dutch society and culture, both during his lifetime and in the years following his death?
7. What are some of the criticisms and debates surrounding Abraham Kuyper's legacy, and how have scholars and theologians addressed these concerns?
8. In what ways do Kuyper's ideas remain relevant in contemporary discussions on politics, education, philosophy, and theology?

Further Reading

Harinck, George. "Transition and Translation: The International Kuyper Research," in *Weltgestaltender Calvinismus: Studien zur Rezeption Abraham Kuypers* [World-shaping Calvinism: Studies on the reception of Abraham Kuyper] Edited by Martin Laube and Hans-Georg Ulrichs (Göttingen: Vandenhoeck & Ruprecht, 2021), 16-39.

Van Dyke, Harry. *Kuyper's Legacy* (Aalten: Wordbridge, 2024).

Ground-motives*	Form/Matter Worldviews	Nature/Grace Worldview	
	Gnosticism	*Thomism*	*Critical theor*
Key figures/ writings	Valentinus (100–160 AD)	Thomas Aquinas (1225–1274) *Summa Theologica* (1485)	Max Horkhei▪ (1895–1973) Theodor W. Adorno (1903–1969) *The Dialectic ▫ Enlightenment▪*
Where are we now?	A world that is part spiritual and part physical—each struggling for dominance The world has been created flawed	In a world created out of God—in a uni- (not multi) verse, as God is one. We are created out of the mind of God.	In a world characterized ▪ oppressive po▪ structures.

Freedom/Nature Worldview			Creation, Fall, and Redemption
ersonality Ideal		Science ideal	
Anthroposophy	*Deep ecology*	*Positivism/ Empiricism*	*Reformational*
udolf Steiner (861–1925) *heosophy* (1922)	Arne Naess (1912–2009) *Ecology, community and lifestyle* (1989)	Auguste Comte (1798–1857) A. J. Ayer *Language, Truth and Logic* (1936)	Abraham Kuyper *Lectures on Calvinism* Herman Dooyeweerd (1894–1977) *New Critique of Theoretical Thought* (1953)
Ve are in a mysterious universe, vith which ve have essential onnection	The greens would see the earth as a single self-regulating organism; the term Gaia, first coined by Jim Lovelock, is often used to describe this concept.	In a self-existent universe There is no world beyond the ordinary world of science and common sense	In a creation, created by a loving, holy God—a purposeful, lawful creation. A good although fallen creation

What is God like?	There are two gods a false creator god (demiurge) and the true god (pleroma); they are fighting for supremacy.	Theistic. Logical and rational—his existence can be proved using the 5 ways	There is no God. A human invention to maintain the power structure
Who are we?	We are strangers living in a flawed world. We are part material (made by the demiurge) and part spiritual (a fragment of the true divine essence: a "divine spark"). We are largely	We are souls trapped in a body	We are many selves—we are either members of a dominant or a marginalize group (be it rac gender, sexual orientation, ...

		In a world of resources that can be understood by science and controlled by technology and economics	
Pantheistic in general	Pantheistic	There is no God(s)	Theism—a trinity
Threefold as body, soul, and spirit Fourfold as four bodies: physical, ethereal, astral and ego We are the same stuff as the earth and the universe; there are essential connections between all three	humans are not the center of the universe—indeed , as we shall see below, anthropocentrici-ty (the view that the universe exists for man) is named as one of the causes of the problems that the earth faces.	We are autonomous individuals.	We are the image bearers of God To subdue and rule the creation as stewards of God. To develop and unfold God's good creation To play our part in God's developing story

	ignorant of this divine spark within us.

There are two classes of human: the pneumatics and the hyletics. The The pneumatics are ready for liberation; the hylectics recognize only the physical reality and they mistake the demiurge for the one true god. | | |
| **What is wrong?** | Metaphysical alienation: the world is flawed because it was created in a flawed manner; the fault is the creator's. It is the product of a lesser god who was unable to create a world of permanence. Humans need to be freed from | We are in a fallen and wicked world. | The misuse of power and power structures The oppression of others Capitalism |

One problem is that we gloss over the mystery; the advances in science have not been matched by a corresponding advance in spirituality.	For the greens the source of contemporary alienation is that we have become estranged from nature. Man (and not just in the generic sense) has become too central, dominating nature, and disturbing the	We are not rational or **scientific enough** in our dealings with each other and the world Metaphysics and irrational speculation—especially theology and philosophy	We are wilful rebels against the God who made us, addicted followers of an arch rebel

What is the remedy?	Deep within humans is a divine spark that connects us with the true god, who is hidden from creation. Our only hope is to acquire the information we need to perfect ourselves and evolve out of our current physical state. Jesus descended from the spiritual realm to make available the knowedge (gnosis)	To escape from the world to enjoy the delight of heaven. Spiritual disciplines will help us to crucify the body and help us experience the eternal bliss.	To either get ri of power or obtain power tc liberate others. Redemption comes from liberation. Be awoken, woke The need for activism to get ri of capitalism

586

		natural order: he is upsetting Gaia's balance. This anthropocentricity results in too much growth, both in population and in economic terms, hence the earth's resources are rapidly depleting.	
There needs to be a refining of the scientific method to overcome its materialism and an increasing self-knowledge. The human spirit needs a full unfolding. The purpose of education is thus the full unfolding of the human spirit.	Most greens would agree that what is needed is a total change in the structure of society. Growth needs to be drastically cut. Sustainable development, i.e., one that can be sustained without using up the earth's resources, and the need to get back into harmony with nature by having a reverence and	Science and rational thought as seen through experiment and observation. The verification principle as a means of irradiating metaphysics and for establishing what is true.	Redemption and restoration through Jesus Christ

necessary for
self-perfection.

| **Where are we going?** | Our bodies and souls are part of this corrupt, flawed creation; redemption is only for the spirit. Death releases us from the prison of the material body. If there has not been a substantial work of gnosis by the soul than the divine spark will be hurled back and embodied into the physical world again. | Ultimately to an entirely non-earthly, spiritual existence |

	and respect for the earth and its ecosystem, are for the greens their means of salvation.		
Reincarnation	Towards disaster if we don't do something about it	Nowhere This life all there is and death the end	To a renewed heaven and earth

Ground-motives*	Form/Matter Worldviews	Nature/Grace Worldview	
	Platonism	*Aristotelianism*	*Pietistic evangelicalis*
Key figures/ writings	Plato	Aristotle (384–322BC)	
Where are they now?	In a visible world comprising matter which is temporal and changing and in an invisible world of forms that are eternal and unchanging	In a world of forms and matter.	In a fallen creation dominated by Satan

Freedom/Nature Worldview			Creation, Fall, and Redemption
ersonality Ideal		Science ideal	
Vietzsche nd nihilism	*Pragmatism*	*Darwinism*	*Theonomy/ Reconstructionism*
Iietzsche	William James James Dewey	Richard Dawkins	R. J. Rushdoony (1916–2001) - *The Institutes of Biblical Law* (1973)
1 an irrational orld, that cares othing for umanity and 1eir values	A world that causes experience In a world where only individuals exis	In a world characterized by chance	We are on Earth, which is a God-given place for humans to pursue dominion. .

Who are we?	The measure of all things. Humanity in their thinking can grasp the true nature of things. The soul is the rational part of a human The highest creation as we can partake of that which is divine in the universe.	A mixture of form and matter Reason is the highest part of human nature; itis what makes us unique. Humanity is essentially good and capable.	Sinful fallen creatures
What is worng?	Matter	Ignorance	Worldly areas encroach on spirituality Too much emphasis on head religion.

eople who are ed by instincts.	Darwinian view of humanity.	We are a trousered ape—the product of chance and survival instincts.	We are dominion men created and designed to subdue and rule on the Earth under God's authority. We are special creations of God not evolved creatures.
Reason, Christianity	Metaphysical idealism	Nothing	The human desire to 'be as gods, knowing good and evil" (Gen. 3:5), to be independent and autonomous. We fail to keep the biblical laws. The question and issue of authority is key—we have given authority over to the state. The state usurps authority from the family and the church. Men

What is the remedy?	We have in us what is necessary to rise above matter.	Human reason can help us to reach true and certain knowledge—it can help us attain union with the divine.	Escape worldly desires—take our cross Prayer evangelism. Focus on heart religion. Emphasis on self-discipline, inner experience. Emphasis on personal religious experience.

			do not take up their roles of headship within the family and church.
To accept our own instincts Self-preservation and self-promotion The will to power Let the powerful win.	Increase of human control over nature The importance of practical knowledge.	Survival of the fittest—the fittest will survive.	There is a need to go back to the Bible which speaks to every area of life and to the biblical laws. The remedy doesn't come through legislation or politics (by which is meant civil government), but with a biblical social order beginning with the family (and male headship). Each of the God-ordained institutions of family, church and state are to function, without encroaching on each other, under the authority of God. This requires a minimal state

| Where are we going? | Reincarnation the transmigration if the soul. | Human thought may survive death and be absorbed into the one eternal mind. | To heaven |

			and limited government.
Who cares?		Nowhere	Christians through the church should continue to expand and build the kingdom of God and then Jesus will return.

---

* Worldview Questions and Ground-motives

These responses are oversimplified and not nuanced—the aim is not to provide detailed answers to each of the questions merely suggestive, illustrative, and indicative of the different positions.

Source for the figures

My thanks to Myrthe Bleeker, Curator Archives, Special Collections, University Library, Vrije Universiteit Amsterdam for help in tracing some of the images.

Part I

Page 4. Saint Abraham cartoon by Albert Hahn.

Source: BG C13/88 (print), The Dutch labour movement until 1918, International Institute of Social History, Amsterdam (public domain)

Page 18. Kuyper as a student in 1862.

Source: https://commons.wikimedia.org/wiki/File:Abraham_Kuyper_1862.jpg (public domain)

Page 31. Pietronella Baltus, (1830–1914).

Source: illustration from Biographical Dictionary Gelderland (BWG)

Page 33 at top. The church building in Beesd.

Source: J. C. Rullman, Abraham Kuyper Een Levensschets (Kampen: Kok, 1928).

Page 33 at bottom. The parsonage in Beesd.

Source: J. C. Rullman, *Abraham Kuyper Een Levensschets* (Kampen: Kok, 1928).

Page 37. The Domkerk, Utrecht.

Source: J. C. Rullman, *Abraham Kuyper Een Levensschets* (Kampen: Kok, 1928).

Page 42. Guillaume Groen van Prinsterer (1801–1876)

Source: https://commons.wikimedia.org/wiki/File:GGvP.gif (public domain)

Page 46. Cover of Groen van Prinsterer's *Archives ou Correspondance Inedite de la Maison d'Orange-Nassau.*

Source: https://www.dbnl.org/tekst/groe009arch05_01/index.php

Page 101. Abraham Kuyper in 1905.

Source: https://commons.wikimedia.org/wiki/File:Abraham_Kuyper_1905_(1).jpg (Public Domain)

Page 107. Albert Hahn's "Abraham de Geweldige" cartoon.

Source: https://commons.wikimedia.org/wiki/File:De_Ware_Jacob_3e_jaargang_nr._16_16_januari_1904_Tekening_van_Albert_Hahn.jpg (public domain)

Page 116. Kuyper's seventieth birthday photograph.

Source: VU University Amsterdam, HDC | Protestant Heritage, Portrait family Kuyper, 1907. Used with permission.

Page 118. Herman Huber Kuyper (1864–1945).

Source: https://en.wikipedia.org/wiki/H._H._Kuyper#/media/File:HHKuyper.jpg (public domain)

Page 119. Documents concerning the death of H. H. Kuyper, 1945, inv.nr. 450 // Herman Huber Kuyper, 1574-1945.

Archief van Abraham Kuyper, Vrije Universiteit Amsterdam.

Source: https://sources.neocalvinism.org/archive/?id_item=2151

Page 122. The three sisters.

Source: VU University Amsterdam, HDC | Protestant Heritage, Picture with C.M.E. Kuyper, J.H. Kuyper and

H.S.S. Kuyper, ca. 1890, C. J. L. Vermeulen, The Hague. Used with permission.

Figure 123. Henriëtte S. S. Kuyper (1870–1933).
Source: VU University Amsterdam, HDC | Protestant Heritage, Portrait H.S.S. (Henriëtte) Kuyper, 1902. Used with permission.

Page 129. H. S. S. and J. H. Kuyper as members of the Dutch Ambulance in Budapest (1916).
Spaarnestad Collection, photographer unknown https:// geheugen.delpher.nl/nl/geheugen/view?coll=ngvn&identifier=SFA03:SFA022804900.

Page 129. Obituary and clipping about the death of C. M .E. Kuyper, 1955, inv.nr. 471 // Catharina Maria Eunice Kuyper, 1944-1955. Archief van Abraham Kuyper, Vrije Universiteit Amsterdam.
Source: https://sources.neocalvinism.org/archive/?id_item=2193

Page 131. C. M. E. Kuyper (1944–1955).
Source: https://www.geheugenvandevu.nl/application/ files/8416/0024/6387/Kuyper_CME_eerbetoon_A1933.pdf

Page 132. C. M. E. Kuyper and the sculptor László Hűvös (1873–1972) in 1936 while designing a bust of Kuyper. Photo © Maarten J. Aalders. Used with permission.
Source: https://mjaalders.nl/wp-content/uploads/2021/06/ eerbetoon.pdf

Page 132. Unsigned portrait of C. M. E. 'Katalin' Kuyper, by Oszkár Glatz (1872–1958), painted ca. 1926. Photo © Maarten J. Aalders. Used with permission.
Source: https://mjaalders.nl/wp-content/uploads/2021/06/ eerbetoon.pdf

Page 133. Abraham Kuyper Jr. (1872–1941).

Source: Jan de Bruijn, *Abraham Kuyper—leven en wek in beeld (Amsterdam: Passage, 1987), 239.*

Page 135. Guillaume Kuyper (1878-1941).
Picture © F.J. Malgo.

Source: Jan de Bruijn, *Abraham Kuyper—leven en wek in beeld* (Amsterdam: Passage, 1987), 230.

Part 2

Page 147. Louis Raemaekers's cartoon criticizes Kuyper's use of the antithesis as a form of dominance or suppression over opponent.

Source: *Dr. A. Kuvper in De Caricaltuur* (Amsterdam: van Holkema & Warendorf, 1909).

Page 313. Albertus C. Van Raalte (1811–1876).

Source: https://en.wikipedia.org/wiki/Albertus_van_Raalte#/media/File:Albertus_Christiaan_van_Raalte_(1811-1876).jpg

Page 313. Hendrik P. Scholte (1805–1868).

Source: https://commons.wikimedia.org/wiki/File:Portret_van_de_predikant_Hendrik_Peter_Scholte,_RP-P-1900-A-22056.jpg

Page 314. Hendrik de Cock (1801–1842).

Source: https://en.wikipedia.org/wiki/Hendrik_de_Cock#/media/File:Hendrik_de_Cock.jpg (Public domain)

Page 525.

Source: Richard A. Russell *Christian Philosophy Diagrams* (Bristol: All of life Redeemed, 2020), #22.

Page 526.

Cover of the *Anti-Revolutionaire Staatkunde journal.*

Appendices

Concept Maps

Some concept maps of Abraham Kuyper's writings are available here: https://alloflliferedeemed.co.uk/kuyper-primer-concept-maps/

These include:

Lectures on Calvinism. Grand Rapids: Eerdmans, 1899.

Rooted and Grounded Grand Rapids: Christian's Library Press, 2013.

The Problem of Poverty. Grand Rapids: Baker, 1991.

Wisdom & Wonder: Common Grace in Science & Art. Grand Rapids: Christian's Library Press, 2011.

"Maranatha," in *Abraham Kuyper: A Centennial Reader*. Edited by James D. Bratt. Grand Rapids: Eerdmans, 1998.

Doctoral Theses on Kuyper

Updates to this list can be found here:
http://allofliferedeemed.co.uk/kuyper-theses/

In chronological order

Young, William. 1943 "The development of a Protestant philosophy in Dutch Calvinist thought since the time of Abraham Kuyper." Union Theological.

Van Heukelom, Raymond R. 1952/53. "Abraham Kuyper's View of the Function of the Church in the World." PhD diss., Northern Baptist.

Rooy, Sidney H. 1956. "Kuyper vs. Warfield: An Historical Approach to the Nature of Apologetics." PhD diss., Union Theological Seminary.

Douma, Jochem. 1966. *Common Grace in Kuyper, Schilder, and Calvin: Exposition, Comparison, and Evaluation.* Lucerna: Crts Publications, 2017.

Westra, John. 1972. "Confessional Political Parties in the Netherlands, 1813–1949." PhD diss., University of Michigan.

Casey, Ramon J. 1988. "Abraham Kuyper's Political Worldview." PhD diss., Regent University, Virginia.

Campbell-Jack, Walter Campbell. 1992. "Grace without Christ? The Doctrine of Common Grace in Dutch-American Neo-Calvinism." PhD diss., University of Edinburgh.

Heslam, Peter S. 1993. "Abraham Kuyper's Lectures on Calvinism: An Historical Study." PhD diss., Oxford University. Published as *Creating a Christian Worldview*, Paternoster, 1998.

Kobes, Wayne A. 1993. "Sphere Sovereignty and the University: Theological Foundations of Abraham Kuyper's View of the University and Its Role in Society." PhD diss., Florida State University.

Langley, McKendree R. 1995. "Emancipation and Apologetics: The Formation of Abraham Kuyper's Anti-Revolutionary Party in the Netherlands, 1872–1880." PhD diss., Westminster Theological Seminary.

Duk, Kwang. 1999. "Ecclesiology and Social Ethics: A Comparative Study of the Social and Ethical Role of the Church in the Views of Abraham Kuyper and Stanley Hauerwas." PhD diss., Kampen.

Bacote, Vincent. 2002. "The Role of the Holy Spirit in Creation and History with Special Reference to Abraham Kuyper." PhD diss., Drew University.

Naylor, Wendy Fish. 2006. Abraham Kuyper and the emergence of neo-calvinist pluralism in the Dutch school struggle." PhD diss., University of Chicago

Wood, John Halsey, Jr. 2010. "Going Dutch in the Modern Age: Abraham Kuyper's Struggle for a Free Church in the Nineteenth-Century Netherlands." PhD diss., Oxford University Press, 2013.

Porter, Jacob. 2011. "Abraham Kuyper's Sphere Sovereignty: Theological Comparisons and Application to Poverty." PhD diss., Southern Baptist Theological Seminary.

Kaemingk, Matthew. 2013. "Mecca and Amsterdam: Christian Ethics between Islam and Liberalism." PhD diss., Vrije Universiteit and Fuller Seminary. Published as *Christian Hospitality and Muslim Immigration in an Age of Fear*, Eerdmans, 2018.

Himes, Brant Micah. 2015. "For a Better Worldliness: The Theological Discipleship of Abraham Kuyper and Dietrich Bonhoeffer." PhD diss., Fuller Theological Seminary, Center for Advanced Theological Study.

Chiu, Agnes S. 2016. "Common Grace and Common Good For China: An Exposition of Abraham Kuyper and Leo XIII on Labor Struggles in Twenty-First Century China." PhD diss., Fuller Theological Seminary.

Park, Jae-Eun. 2016. "Driven By God: Active Justification and Definitive Sanctification in the Soteriology of Bavinck, Comrie, Witsius, and Kuyper."

Liou, Jeff M. 2017. "Much in Every Way: Employing the Concept of Race in Theological Anthropology and Christian Practice." PhD diss., [University Name].

Wagenman, M.R. 2017. "The Power of The Church: The Ecclesiology of Abraham Kuyper." PhD diss., Bristol University and Trinity College. Published by Pickwick Publications, 2020.

Dagley, Logan. 2018. "The Missional Church as an Institution and Organism: How Abraham Kuyper's Ecclesiological Distinction Clarifies the Church's Mission in Relation to Selected Contemporary Missiological Challenges." PhD diss., Southeastern Baptist Theological Seminary.

Harefa, Surya Hadianto. 2020. "A Free Church in a Free State: The Possibilities of Abraham Kuyper's Ecclesiology-for Japanese Evangelical Christians." PhD diss., Kampen.

Prideaux, Louise. 2020. "Approaching the Complex, Cultural Other: Towards a Renewal of Christian Cultural Engagement in the Reformed Tradition." PhD diss., University of Exeter.

Un, Steven A. 2020. "Theology of the Public Sphere: An Interpretation of the Philosophy of Hannah Arendt and Jürgen Habermas from the Perspective of the Theology of Abraham Kuyper with Implications for Public Theology and the Indonesian Context." PhD diss., VU Amsterdam.

Greeson, Dennis. 2021. "Common Grace, Providence, and the Saeculum: Abraham Kuyper's Theology of Culture Revisited." PhD diss., Southeastern Baptist Theological Seminary.

Jones, Timothy. 2024. "Saving Common Grace: Kuyper and Present Possibilities for Public Theology in the UK." PhD diss., King's College London.

Some non-English dissertations

Ridderbos, Simon Jan. 1947. *De Theologische Cultuurbeschouwing van Abraham Kuyper.* Kampen.

Dengerink, Jan Dirk. 1948. *Critisch-historisch Onderzoek naar de Sociologische Ontwikkeling van het Beginsel der 'Soevereiniteit in Eigen Kring'.* Kampen.

De Ru, Cornelis. 1953. *De Strijd over het Hoger Onderwijs tijdens het Ministerie-Kuyper.* Kampen.

Velema, Willem H. 1957. *De Leer van de Heilige Geest bij Abraham Kuyper.* 's-Gravenhage.

ABOUT THE CÁNTARO INSTITUTE

Inheriting, Informing, Inspiring

Cántaro Institute is a reformed evangelical organization committed to advancing the Christian worldview for the reformation and renewal of the church and culture.

We believe that as the Christian church returns to the fount of the Scriptures as its ultimate authority for all knowledge and life, and wisely applies God's truth to every aspect of life, its missiological activity will result not only in the renewal of the human person but also in the reformation of culture—an inevitable outcome when the true scope and nature of the gospel are made known and applied.

www.ingramcontent.com/pod-product-compliance
Lightning Source LLC
Chambersburg PA
CBHW051128120626
46547CB00012B/712